# Strategy
## *for Business*

# Strategy for Business: A Reader

This book – *Strategy for Business: A Reader* – is one of a series of three readers which constitute the main teaching texts of the Open University course Business Behaviour in a Changing World (B300). The other titles are *Decision Making for Business: A Reader*, edited by Graeme Salaman and *Policy Issues for Business: A Reader*, edited by Vivek Suneja.

This course is one of three core courses which are compulsory elements in the Open University's BA in Business Studies. In addition to the compulsory courses, students who intend to gain this degree also study courses which include topics such as Economics, Organizational Change, Design and Innovation, Quantitative Methods.

Business Behaviour in a Changing World (B300) is innovative in terms of the breadth of material studied. The course covers decision-making, strategy and policy from a variety of different theoretical stances supplemented by a range of empirical findings. In this way B300 provides a synthesis of each of the fields while at the same time considering the important linkages between them.

As with all Open University courses, students are not only supplied with teaching texts; they also receive comprehensive guidance on how to study and work through these texts. In the case of B300, this guidance is contained in three Study Guides which are supplied to students separately. These guides explain the choice of readings, identify key points and guide the students' work and understanding. A core feature of the guides is an explicit focus on the identification, development, deployment and testing of a series of business graduate skills. These include study skills, cognitive skills of analysis and assessment, IT and numeracy.

Each student is allocated a local tutor and is encouraged to participate in a strategically integrated set of tutorials which are held during the course.

Details of this and other Open University courses can be obtained from the Course Reservations Centre, PO Box 724, The Open University, Milton Keynes MK7 6ZS, United Kingdom. Tel.: +44 (0)1908 653231, e-mail: ces-gen@open.ac.uk. Alternatively, you may visit the Open University website at http://www.open.ac.uk where you can learn more about the wide range of courses and packs offered at all levels by the Open University.

For information about the purchase of Open University course components, contact Open University Worldwide Ltd, The Berrill Building, Walton Hall, Milton Keynes MK7 6AA, United Kingdom. Tel.: +44 (0)1908 858785; fax: +44 (0)1908 858787; e-mail: ouwenq@open.ac.uk; website: http://www.ouw.co.uk.

# Strategy
## *for Business*

**A READER**

E D I T E D   B Y   M A R I A N A   M A Z Z U C A T O

**SAGE Publications**
London · Thousand Oaks · New Delhi
**www.sagepub.co.uk**

**in association with**

The Open
University

**www.open.ac.uk**

SAGE Publications Ltd
6 Bonhill Street
London EC2A 4PU

SAGE Publications Inc
2455 Teller Road
Thousand Oaks, California 91320

SAGE Publications India Pvt Ltd
32, M-Block Market
Greater Kailash – I
New Delhi 110 048

**British Library Cataloguing in Publication data**

A catalogue record for this book is available from the British Library

ISBN 0–7619–7412–1
ISBN 0–7619–7413–x (pbk)

**Library of Congress control number available**

Typeset by Keystroke, Jacaranda Lodge, Wolverhampton
Printed in Great Britain by The Alden Press, Oxford

The importance and influence of business in the modern world has been widely recognized. For us as citizens, consumers, employees, managers, voters and so on, understanding how firms and indeed all forms of organization work, is therefore of direct relevance. The way that businesses conduct themselves affects us all. As a consequence it is vital for us to understand how they make decisions, for example to invest in some products or services rather than others. The variety of factors that are taken into account, the way in which conclusions are reached, all help us get to grips, with these sorts of issues. This involves developing an understanding of how decisions in organizations are made. We also should understand the strategies that businesses pursue, the development of their core competencies as well as how organizations innovate. Finally, the range of policy issues from regulation of competition to environment and the developing world provide a rich contextual seam within which strategies and decisions are made in a world where the norm is change.

This book is one in a series of three readers which bring together classic and seminal materials, many of them summaries and reviews, which are designed to achieve the teaching objectives of the Open University course Business Behaviour in a Changing World (B300) – a core course in the Open University's BA in Business Studies. The volumes are organized in an innovative way around three important themes: decision-making, strategy and policy. The volumes have been designed to supply a selection of articles, theoretical and empirical, in each of these areas. They are supported by study guides so that together they allow the identification, development, deployment and practice of a range of skills required by the Business Studies courses in general. Therefore while they constitute the core teaching resources of this Open University course, the volumes would also make admirable selections for any course concerned with these areas. They are not intended to be cutting edge or fashionable. They are designed as a resource for anyone seeking an understanding of the changing nature of organizations and of the world of business.

Each of these volumes has been edited by members of the course team. But in a very real sense they are collective products of the course team as a whole. That is why all the members of the course team deserve recognition and acknowledgement for their contribution to the course and to these collections.

# CONTENTS

# ACKNOWLEDGEMENTS

Chapter 1: *Harvard Business Review* for an extract from 'What is Strategy' by Michael E. Porter, Nov/Dec 1996. Copyright © 1996 by the Harvard Business School Publishing Corporation. All rights reserved.

Chapter 2: International Thomson Business Press for an extract from *What Is Strategy and Does It Matter?* (2nd edn) by Richard Whittington © Richard Whittington, 2001.

Chapter 3: John Wiley & Sons Limited for 'Of Strategies, Deliberate and Emergent' by Henry Mintzberg and J. Waters © *Strategic Management Journal*, 1985.

Chapter 4: Blackwell Publishers for an extract from *Contemporary Strategy Analysis* by Robert M. Grant © Robert M. Grant, 1998.

Chapter 5: Blackwell Publishers for an extract from *Contemporary Strategy Analysis* by Robert M. Grant © Robert M. Grant, 1998.

Chapter 6: International Thomson Business Press (excluding North America) for an extract from *Rejuvenating the Mature Business* (2nd edn) by Charles Baden-Fuller and John Stopford © Charles Baden-Fuller and John Stopford, 1999. Harvard Business School Press (North America) for an extract from *Rejuvenating the Mature Business: The Competitive Challenge* by Charles Baden-Fuller and John Stopford. Boston, MA 1994, pp. 23–40. Copyright © 1994 by the Harvard Business School Publishing Corporation. All rights reserved.

Chapter 7: Oxford University Press for an extract from *The Theory of the Growth of the Firm* by Edith Penrose © Edith Penrose Estate, 1959.

Chapter 8: Academy of Management for 'Looking Inside for Competitive Advantage' by J. Barney © *Academy of Management Executive*, 1995.

Chapter 9: John Wiley & Sons Limited for 'Dynamic Capabilities and Strategic Management' by David Teece, G. Pisano and A. Shuen © *Strategic Management Journal*, 1997.

Chapter 10: *Harvard Business Review* for an extract from 'Limits of the Learning Curve' by William J. Abernathy and Kenneth Wayne, Sept/Oct 1974. Copyright © 1974 by the Harvard Business School Publishing Corporation. All rights reserved.

Chapter 11: *Administrative Science Quarterly* for 'Architectural Innovation: The Reconfiguration of Existing Product Technologies and the Failure of Established Firms' by Rebecca M. Henderson and Kim B. Clark, Vol 35, No 1 © *Administrative Science Quarterly*, March 1990.

Chapter 12: Massachusetts Institute of Technology for 'Strategic Innovation in Established Companies' by Costantinos Markides, *MIT Sloan Management Review*, Spring 1998. Copyright © 1998 by Massachusetts Institute of Technology. All rights reserved.

Chapter 13: *Journal of Economic Literature* for 'The Dynamics of Industrial Capitalism: Perspectives on Alfred Chandler's Scale and Scope' by David Teece © *Journal of Economic Literature*, 1993.

Chapter 14: *Administrative Science Quarterly* for 'Absorptive Capacity: A New Perspective on Learning and Innovation' by Wesley M. Cohen and Daniel A. Levinthal, vol 35, no 1 © *Administrative Science Quarterly*, March 1990.

Chapter 15: commissioned by the Open University Business School for the course *Managing Knowledge* (B823). © The Open University 1999.

Chapter 16: John Wiley & Sons Limited for 'Global Strategy: An Organising Framework' by Sumantra Ghoshal © *Strategic Management Journal*, 1987.

Chapter 17: *Harvard Business Review* for 'Increasing Returns and the New World of Business' by W. Brian Arthur, July/August 1996. Copyright © 1996 by the Harvard Business School Publishing Corporation. All rights reserved.

Chapter 18: Prentice Hall for an extract from *Financial Times Handbook of Management* by Stuart Crainer and Des Dearlove © George S. Yip, 2001.

# INTRODUCTION

## Different views of strategy

Strategy is about organizational *change*.[1] An action is strategic when it allows a firm to become better than its competitors, and when this 'competitive advantage' can be *sustained*. This means that not all decisions are strategic: some decisions are, for example, simply dedicated to maintaining the status quo. Others might increase a firm's competitiveness but in a way that is not sustainable in the future. The readings will introduce you to the lively, often heated debate amongst strategy researchers regarding 'what' strategy is and 'how' it comes about.

In answering the question 'What is strategy?', some theorists focus more on the role of strategy in allowing a firm to 'position' itself in an industry, hence to make choices regarding 'what game to play'. Others focus more on the role of strategy in determining how well a given game is played. Strategy is about both: choosing new games to play and playing existing games better.

One of the biggest disagreements amongst strategy researchers concerns the *process* by which strategies emerge (see readings in Section 1). Some describe strategy as a rational and deliberate process (the Design school), while others describe it as an evolutionary process which emerges from experimentation and trial and error (the Evolutionary and Processual schools). Some place more emphasis on external factors, like the structure of the industry to which the firm belongs (e.g. the Industrial Organization approach), while others place more emphasis on factors internal to the organization, like the way production is organized (e.g. the Resource-Based approach). Furthermore, some describe a relatively *static* relationship between strategy and the environment where firms respond to external conditions (the Structure–Conduct–Performance approach), while others describe a *dynamic* picture of competition, where firms not only are influenced by the environment, but also actively seek to change it (e.g. the Schumpetarian approach). This feedback relationship between firm strategy and the environment is the focus of industry 'lifecycle' studies which look at the sources and effects of changes in industry structure.

## Internal versus external factors

Today the study of strategic management pays much more attention to intra-organizational dynamics than it did in the past 20 or so years. Strategy is seen as primarily determined no longer by market conditions external to the firm but by organization-specific factors, for example the way that information flows inside an organization and how new knowledge is created.

The 'competitive forces' approach to strategy, developed by Michael Porter in the 1980s (see readings in Section 2), is an example of the view of strategy that places primary importance on external conditions faced by the firm. In this view, strategy is about the firm creating for itself a 'market position' whereby it can defend itself from competitive forces and/or influence them in a way that places it at an advantage *vis-à-vis* its competitors and suppliers. Porter focuses on the effect of five industry-level forces impacting on strategy and performance: entry barriers, threat of substitution, bargaining power of buyers, bargaining power of suppliers and rivalry among industry incumbents. This framework is connected to the 'structure–conduct–performance' approach to industrial organization, where the structure of an industry (e.g. how easy it is for new firms to enter) determines firm conduct/strategy (e.g. innovation strategies) and hence firm performance (e.g. profits).

A different way of thinking about strategy is to give primary role to intra-organizational factors. This view is best exemplified by the 'resource-based theory of the firm', which has its roots in the work of Edith Penrose. Penrose suggested viewing the firm as a 'pool of resources'. Resources include not just tangible resources (like buildings, machinery and research labs) but also intangible ones embodied in skills and in the interactions between people and systems. Intangible resources are *unique* to each firm and, when a firm finds itself with different uses for its excess resources, it will often choose those combinations that are tied most closely with its previous activities. The fact that the firm's prior experience and history matter means that firm growth is often path-dependent: where the firm goes tomorrow depends on *how* it got to where it is today (its future path depends on its previous path). The main point is that value is created not only by the quantity of physical capital, land and labour that the firm owns but also, and especially, how it combines its different resources (i.e. how the different resources interact). Modern strategy theorists, inspired by Penrose, have called this ability to combine resources in an innovative and efficient way the firm's 'capabilities' or 'competencies'. Unique capabilities refer to the productive activities that the firm is very good at. Core competencies refer to those broad capabilities that are essential to the firm's performance and that allow it to enter different product markets. Competencies are unique, and hence hard to imitate, because they are the results of particular combinations and interactions between different resources. Since different firms have different capabilities, their implementation of strategies will differ.

The focus on intra-organizational dynamics is supported by empirical studies which have shown that inter-firm differences in rates of return are primarily due to firm-specific factors. For example, Rumelt (1991) found that 46.4 per cent of a business unit's profitability can be accounted for by business-specific factors (i.e. choice of strategy) and only 8.3 per cent by general factors related to the industry to which it belongs. The reading by Baden-Fuller and Stopford in Chapter 6 will also support this by providing case study evidence of firms succeeding in industries which are considered no longer profitable (or 'attractive'). However, the fact that intra-organizational factors are very important does not mean that industry-specific factors, like industry structure, do not matter! In fact one of the most innovative areas of strategy analysis has to do with how firm strategy changes over the industry life-cycle and how strategy and structure co-evolve (Klepper, 1997). These studies have focused especially on the changing role of firm-led technological change: the structure of an industry will constrain the amount and type of firm innovation at any one moment in time, yet industry structure will itself evolve depending on the characteristics of the innovation activity. One of the biggest challenges in strategy analysis is to find an innovative framework through which firm-level and industry-level factors can both be analysed.

## Inter-firm differences

Theories of strategy embody specific explanations for why firms within and between industries differ in their performance. For example, the market positioning framework views differences between firms as resulting from the different characteristics of the markets they operate in. 'Imperfect competition' is often blamed for not allowing all firms to achieve the same level of efficiency and hence performance. Examples of market imperfections are barriers to entry which prevent new firms from competing with incumbents, or information asymmetries that allow only some firms access to special information/knowledge. It is assumed that such differences will disappear in the 'long run' when 'perfect competition' is restored. Instead, in the 'resource based approach' firm differences arise not from imperfect markets but from firms actively seeking to differentiate themselves via their unique competencies and capabilities. These differences will persist even in the long run since by definition competencies and capabilities are difficult to imitate and strategy is about renewing core competencies.

Since capabilities are developed over time in a cumulative and complex manner, firm differences are accentuated by the dynamics of increasing returns and path dependency: those firms able to develop unique capabilities today are more likely to develop them tomorrow. In fact empirical studies on technological change have found firm innovation to often (not always) be characterized by persistence: successful innovators today are likely to innovate in the future. This is because the ability to innovate depends on prior innovation, prior related knowledge and diversity of background – what Cohen and Levinthal in Chapter 14 call 'absorptive capacity'. This 'rich gets richer' dynamic can lead to concentrated markets until the industry undergoes a fundamental product change (or 'architectural innovation' as studied in Chapter 11). And yet, sometimes, it is new players who are not burdened by tradition and existing rules that are the best innovators. They are more prone to 'think differently' and to thus challenge the status quo. The readings in Sections 4 and 5 will examine under which conditions it is the incumbents or new comers that are more likely to lead the innovation process. The readings in Section

6 explore how the path-dependent nature of the development of capabilities is even stronger in knowledge-based sectors, such as information technology.

## Competition

The fact that, in the resource-based perspective, differences between firms are due not to 'market imperfections' but to the competitive process by which firms actively try to differentiate themselves, means that what is also at stake in strategy theory is the underlying view of competition. The resource-based perspective is more compatible with a Schumpeterian view of competition where firms are viewed as actively competing against each other for technological superiority. Schumpeter (1934) called this process 'creative destruction', i.e. the process by which firms *create* new products, processes and markets *destroys* the advantage of firms that built their success with previous, now obsolete, technologies. Technological change thus often leads to turbulence in market shares of firms, especially when new firms enter an industry through the introduction of a radical innovation. The readings in Section 4 study different reasons why large incumbent firms are often not the best innovators.

A relatively new branch of economics called 'evolutionary economics' has concentrated its efforts in using Schumpeter's work on technological change to develop a new theory of competition where the focus is on the co-evolution of mechanisms that create differences between firms and mechanisms of competitive selection that winnow firms via those differences (Nelson and Winter, 1982). Competition is described here as a disequilibrium process whereby firm-specific technological change and processes of increasing returns shape both the internal organization of the firm and market outcomes. Nelson (1991) connects the point about inter-firm differences to competition in this way:

> I want to put forth the argument that it is organizational differences, especially differences in abilities to generate and gain from innovation, rather than differences in command over particular technologies, that are the source of durable, not easily imitable, differences among firms. Particular technologies are much easier to understand, and imitate, than broader firm dynamic capabilities . . . Competition can be seen as not merely about incentives and pressures to keep prices in line with minimal feasible costs . . . but, much more important, about exploring new potentially better ways of doing things.

## Content of volume

The readings in this volume were chosen for their ability to together tell a 'dynamic' story about strategy: a story which explores the feedback relationship between firm strategy and the environment. The older pieces are classics in the field of strategy and continue to provide the theoretical background for more recent innovative pieces. The issues addressed by these newer pieces lie at the centre of strategy analysis today.

Section 1 introduces the study of strategic management by diving into a particular definition of strategy and then stepping back and looking at various theoretical perspectives on the processes that determine strategy, each of which embodies specific assumptions on human nature and on the interaction between individual action and the environment. Section 2 introduces a fundamental distinction in strategy analysis: the focus on external industry characteristics versus the focus on the internal organizational dynamics. As reviewed briefly earlier in this introduction, the former looks at the role of industry structure in determining firm strategy and performance, while the latter looks at the role of resources and capabilities developed *inside* the firm. Section 3 focuses on how the *internal* organization of the firm affects strategy and performance. It builds on Penrose's notion of the firm as a 'pool of resources' to study the origin of firm-specific capabilities and competencies. Section 4 focuses on a particular type of organizational capability: the capability to innovate. The readings illustrate how technological innovation depends on firm-specific characteristics like firm size (are small firms or large firms better innovators?) and the internal organization of the firm. Section 5 continues the discussion by considering the ways in which organizations can be structured to stimulate individual and organizational learning and the management of new knowledge. Section 6 considers the implication of recent changes in the world economy for strategic behaviour. The changes considered are the rise of information technology and the increasingly global nature of competition, both of which are considered to be part of the 'new economy'.

## Note

1    Although the word 'firm' (or business) is used here and in most of the readings, the unit of analysis in strategy theory is the organization. We use the two words interchangeably.

## References

Klepper, S. (1997) 'Industry life-cycles', *Industrial and Corporate Change*, 6 (1): 145–81.

Nelson, R. (1991) 'Why do firms differ, and how does it matter?', *Strategic Management Journal*, 12: 61–74.

Nelson, R.R. and Winter, S.G. (1982) *An Evolutionary Theory of Economic Change*. Cambridge, MA: Harvard University Press.

Rumelt, R. (1991) 'How much does industry matter?', *Strategic Management Journal*, 12: 167–85.

Schumpeter, J. (1934) *The Theory of Economic Development*. Cambridge, MA: Harvard University Press.

# Different Views of Strategy

The readings in this first section introduce business strategy in two ways. The first is by diving into a *particular* definition of strategy, allowing the reader to get a sense of what the big issues are through some provocative statements by one of the most well known strategy theorists. The second way is by stepping back and considering different approaches to the study of strategy and the assumptions that underlie them. The reading by Porter fulfils the first task while the readings by Whittington and by Mintzberg and Waters fulfil the second task.

Porter claims that strategic decisions are ones that are aimed at differentiating an organization from its competitors in a way that is sustainable in the future. This is different from decisions based on *operational effectiveness* which are aimed simply at doing existing activities better. The reading serves as a good starting point by providing a 'working definition' of strategy which will undergo many changes as the readings progress. For example, the reading by Abernathy and Wayne in Chapter 10 will indirectly challenge Porter's distinction by allowing for the possibility that even decisions based on operational effectiveness, such as learning curve strategies, may be strategic under certain types of conditions, for example when technology changes slowly. What types of decisions are strategic depends on the context and that context changes over time, for example over the 'industry life-cycle'. Thus, strategy is both about doing new things as well as doing existing things better.

The reading by Whittington steps back and compares how different theories of strategy answer the questions '*What* is strategy?' and '*How* do strategies come about?'. He exposes the different assumptions underlying the different theories regarding human nature and the relationship between individual action and the environment. His description allows deeper insight into the difference between the 'Design' school of strategy, which holds that strategy can be planned, and the 'Emergent' (or Processual) view of strategy, which holds that strategy is not the result of rational calculation but of experimentation and trial and error. The reading by Mintzberg and Waters provides an excellent example of the Processual view.

## M. E. Porter: 'What is Strategy?'

This reading appeared in the *Harvard Business Review* in 1996. Porter claims that not all business decisions are strategic. Decisions can only be defined as strategic if they involve consciously doing something 'differently' from competitors and if that difference results in a sustainable advantage. To be sustainable it must be difficult to imitate. Activities which simply increase productivity by making existing methods more efficient ('operational efficiency') are not strategic since they can be easily copied by others. Although a firm must engage in both types of activities, it is strategic activities that will allow it to develop a sustainable superior performance. One of the factors that renders strategies hard to imitate, hence unique, is that they are the result of a complex interaction between different activities, which is not reducible to the sum of the individual activities. It is this synergy between activities that produces value, not the activities in themselves. Porter provides various examples of companies that he thinks have behaved strategically and others which have not. He claims that Japanese firms are losing their competitiveness owing to their focus mainly on operational efficiency.

## R. Whittington: 'Theories of Strategy'

This piece comes from a chapter in Whittington's book *What Is Strategy — and Does It Matter?* (2000). Whittington introduces us to four different perspectives on strategy: the classical perspective, the evolutionary perspective, the processual perspective and the systemic perspective. The *classical* perspective assumes that the manager has near to complete control over how to allocate the internal and external resources of the firm, and can thus manipulate the internal organization of the firm to better suit these objectives. In this view, strategic behaviour is guided by rationality, opportunism and self-interest. The *evolutionary* perspective places emphasis on behavioural differences between firms (e.g. some firms base their decisions on rational calculations, others simply on imitation) and on the market selection mechanisms that allow some firms to grow and survive and others to fail. This view causes the image of the heroic entrepreneur, central to the classical perspective, to fall apart: it is not one manager but the mix between the forces of market selection, random events, and processes of positive feedback that determine performance. The *processual* perspective holds that economic outcomes *emerge* from the interactions between individuals and between individuals and their environment. The result of this interaction is unpredictable because actions are often *unintended*. Humans are not perfectly rational but 'bounded' in their rationality. This, along with the fact that interaction between individuals is guided not only by self-interest but also by collective bargaining and compromise, causes economic dynamics to be fuzzy and unpredictable. The *systemic* perspective argues that each of the above approaches is characterized by a narrow view of the world: a Western, often Anglo-Saxon, view. The 'rationality' of a particular strategy depends on its specific historical, social and cultural context. Strategic behaviour is 'embedded' in a network of social relations that includes cultural norms, class and educational background, religion and so on. Hence what is labelled as 'irrational' behaviour in one context may be perfectly rational in another.

## H. Mintzberg and J. A. Waters: 'Of Strategies, Deliberate and Emergent'

This reading appeared in the *Strategic Management Journal* in 1985. Mintzberg and Waters explore the process by which strategies form within organizations. They compare intended strategies (strategies that come from a planning process) with realized strategies (what the organization actually did). They provide a framework to study the difference between these two concepts through a continuum where at one end lies the completely planned strategy and at the other end lies the completely emergent strategy. In the planned strategy, intentions are very clear and directly translated into actions. In emergent strategies, decisions emerge from bargaining, chance and positive feedback. An example is the strategy based on consensus. In the middle of these two extremes lie what the authors call the entrepreneurial, ideological and umbrella strategies. Instead of saying that any one type of strategy is better than the other, the authors claim that what is best depends on the nature of the organization.

# CHAPTER 1

# *What is Strategy?*

MICHAEL E. PORTER*

## Operational effectiveness is not strategy

For almost two decades, managers have been learning to play by a new set of rules. Companies must be flexible to respond rapidly to competitive and market changes. They must benchmark continuously to achieve best practice. They must outsource aggressively to gain efficiencies. And they must nurture a few core competencies in the race to stay ahead of rivals.

Positioning – once the heart of strategy – is rejected as too static for today's dynamic markets and changing technologies. According to the new dogma, rivals can quickly copy any market position, and competitive advantage is, at best, temporary.

But those beliefs are dangerous half-truths, and they are leading more and more companies down the path of mutually destructive competition. True, some barriers to competition are falling as regulation eases and markets become global. True, companies have properly invested energy in becoming leaner and more nimble. In many industries, however, what some call *hypercompetition* is a self-inflicted wound, not the inevitable outcome of a changing paradigm of competition.

The root of the problem is the failure to distinguish between operational effectiveness and strategy. The quest for productivity, quality, and speed has spawned a remarkable number of management tools and techniques: total quality management benchmarking, time-based competition, outsourcing, partnering, reengineering, change management. Although the resulting operational improvements have often been dramatic, many companies have been frustrated by their inability to translate those gains into sustainable profitability. And bit by bit, almost imperceptibly, management tools have taken the place of strategy. As managers push to improve on all fronts, they move farther away from viable competitive positions.

* *Harvard Business Review* for an extract from 'What is Strategy' by Michael E. Porter, Nov/Dec 1996. Copyright © 1996 by the Harvard Business School Publishing Corporation. All rights reserved.

## *Operational effectiveness: necessary but not sufficient*

Operational effectiveness and strategy are both essential to superior performance, which, after all, is the primary goal of any enterprise. But they work in very different ways.

A company can outperform rivals only if it can establish a difference that it can preserve. It must deliver greater value to customers or create comparable value at a lower cost, or do both. The arithmetic of superior profitability then follows: delivering greater value allows a company to charge higher average unit prices; greater efficiency results in lower average unit costs.

Ultimately, all differences between companies in cost or price derive from the hundreds of activities required to create, produce, sell, and deliver their products or services, such as calling on customers, assembling final products, and training employees. Cost is generated by performing activities, and cost advantage arises from performing particular activities more efficiently than competitors. Similarly, differentiation arises from both the choice of activities and how they are performed. Activities, then, are the basic units of competitive advantage. Overall advantage or disadvantage results from all a company's activities, not only a few.[1]

Operational effectiveness (OE) means performing similar activities *better* than rivals perform them. Operational effectiveness includes but is not limited to efficiency. It refers to any number of practices that allow a company to better utilize its inputs by, for example, reducing defects in products or developing better products faster. In contrast, strategic positioning means performing *different* activities from rivals' or performing similar activities in *different ways*.

Differences in operational effectiveness among companies are pervasive. Some companies are able to get more out of their inputs than others because they eliminate wasted effort, employ more advanced technology, motivate employees better, or have greater insight into managing particular activities or sets of activities. Such differences in operational effectiveness are an important source of differences in profitability among competitors because they directly affect relative cost positions and levels of differentiation.

Differences in operational effectiveness were at the heart of the Japanese challenge to Western companies in the 1980s. The Japanese were so far ahead of rivals in operational effectiveness that they could offer lower cost and superior quality at the same time. It is worth dwelling on this point, because so much recent thinking about competition depends on it.

[. . .]

For at least the past decade, managers have been preoccupied with improving operational effectiveness. Through programs such as TQM, time-based competition, and benchmarking, they have changed how they perform activities in order to eliminate inefficiencies, improve customer satisfaction, and achieve best practice.

[. . .]

Constant improvement in operational effectiveness is necessary to achieve superior profitability. However, it is not usually sufficient. Few companies have competed successfully on the basis of operational effectiveness over an extended period, and staying ahead of rivals gets harder every day. The most obvious reason for that is the rapid diffusion of best practices. Competitors can quickly imitate management techniques, new technologies, input improvements, and superior ways of meeting customers' needs. The most generic solutions – those that can be used in multiple settings – diffuse the fastest. Witness the proliferation of OE techniques accelerated by support from consultants.

OE competition shifts the productivity frontier outward, effectively raising the bar for everyone. But although such competition produces absolute improvement in operational effectiveness, it leads to relative improvement for no one. Consider the $5 billion-plus US commercial-printing industry. The major players – R.R. Donnelley & Sons Company, Quebecor, World Color Press, and Big Flower Press – are competing head to head, serving all types of customers, offering the same array of printing technologies (gravure and web offset), investing heavily in the same new equipment, running their presses faster, and reducing crew sizes. But the resulting major productivity gains are being captured by customers and equipment suppliers, not retained in superior profitability. Even industry-leader Donnelley's profit margin, consistently higher than 7% in the 1980s, fell to less than 4.6% in 1995. This pattern is playing itself out in industry after industry. Even the Japanese, pioneers of the new competition, suffer from persistently low profits (Box 1.1).

## Box 1.1
## Japanese companies rarely have strategies

The Japanese triggered a global revolution in operational effectiveness in the 1970s and 1980s, pioneering practices such as total quality management and continuous improvement. As a result, Japanese manufacturers enjoyed substantial cost and quality advantages for many years.

But Japanese companies rarely developed distinct strategic positions of the kind discussed in this article. Those that did – Sony, Canon, and Sega, for example – were the exception rather than the rule. Most Japanese companies imitate and emulate one another. All rivals offer most if not all product varieties, features, and services; they employ all channels and match one anothers' plant configurations.

The dangers of Japanese-style competition are now becoming easier to recognize. In the 1980s, with rivals operating far from the productivity frontier, it seemed possible to win on both cost and quality indefinitely. Japanese companies were all able to grow in an expanding domestic economy and by penetrating global markets. They appeared unstoppable. But as the gap in operational effectiveness narrows, Japanese companies are increasingly caught in a trap of their own making. If they are to escape the mutually destructive battles now ravaging their performance, Japanese companies will have to learn strategy.

To do so, they may have to overcome strong cultural barriers. Japan is notoriously consensus oriented, and companies have a strong tendency to mediate differences among individuals rather than accentuate them. Strategy, on the other hand, requires hard choices. The Japanese also have a deeply ingrained service tradition that predisposes them to go to great lengths to satisfy any need a customer expresses. Companies that compete in that way end up blurring their distinct positioning, becoming all things to all customers.

This discussion of Japan is drawn from the author's research with Hirotaka Takeuchi, with help from Mariko Sakakibara.

The second reason that improved operational effectiveness is insufficient – competitive convergence – is more subtle and insidious. The more benchmarking companies do, the more they look alike. The more that rivals outsource activities to efficient third parties, often the same ones, the more generic those activities become. As rivals imitate one another's improvements in quality, cycle times, or supplier partnerships, strategies converge and competition becomes a series of races down identical paths that no one can win. Competition based on operational effectiveness alone is mutually destructive, leading to wars of attrition that can be arrested only by limiting competition.

The recent wave of industry consolidation through mergers makes sense in the context of GE competition. Driven by performance pressures but lacking strategic vision, company after company has had no better idea than to buy up its rivals. The competitors left standing are often those that outlasted others, not companies with real advantage.

After a decade of impressive gains in operational effectiveness, many companies are facing diminishing returns. Continuous improvement has been etched on managers' brains. But its tools unwittingly draw companies toward imitation and homogeneity. Gradually, managers have let operational effectiveness supplant strategy. The result is zero-sum competition, static or declining prices, and pressures on costs that compromise companies' ability to invest in the business for the long term.

## Strategy rests on unique activities

Competitive strategy is about being different. It means deliberately choosing a different set of activities to deliver a unique mix of value.

Southwest Airlines Company, for example, offers short-haul, low-cost, point-to-point service between midsize cities and secondary airports in large cities.

Southwest avoids large airports and does not fly great distances. Its customers include business travelers, families, and students. Southwest's frequent departures and low fares attract price-sensitive customers who otherwise would travel by bus or car, and convenience-oriented travelers who would choose a full-service airline on other routes.

Most managers describe strategic positioning in terms of their customers: 'Southwest Airlines serves price- and convenience-sensitive travelers,' for example. But the essence of strategy is in the activities – choosing to perform activities differently or to perform different activities than rivals. Otherwise, a strategy is nothing more than a marketing slogan that will not withstand competition.

A full-service airline is configured to get passengers from almost any point A to any point B. To reach a large number of destinations and serve passengers with connecting flights, full-service airlines employ a hub-and-spoke system centered on major airports. To attract passengers who desire more comfort, they offer first-class or business-class service. To accommodate passengers who must change planes, they coordinate schedules and check and transfer baggage. Because some passengers will be traveling for many hours, full-service airlines serve meals.

Southwest, in contrast, tailors all its activities to deliver low-cost, convenient service on its particular type of route. Through fast turnarounds at the gate of only 15 minutes, Southwest is able to keep planes flying longer hours than rivals and provide frequent departures with fewer aircraft. Southwest does not offer meals, assigned seats, interline baggage checking, or premium classes of service. Automated ticketing at the gate encourages customers to bypass travel agents, allowing Southwest to avoid their commissions. A standardized fleet of 737 aircraft boosts the efficiency of maintenance.

Southwest has staked out a unique and valuable strategic position based on a tailored set of activities. On the routes served by Southwest, a full-service airline could never be as convenient or as low cost.

IKEA, the global furniture retailer based in Sweden, also has a clear strategic positioning. IKEA targets young furniture buyers who want style at low cost. What turns this marketing concept into a strategic positioning is the tailored set of activities that make it work. Like Southwest, IKEA has chosen to perform activities differently from its rivals.

Consider the typical furniture store. Showrooms display samples of the merchandise. One area might contain 25 sofas; another will display five dining tables. But those items represent only a fraction of the choices available to customers. Dozens of books displaying fabric swatches or wood samples or alternate styles offer customers thousands of product varieties to choose from. Salespeople often escort customers through the store, answering questions and helping them navigate this maze of choices. Once a customer makes a selection, the order is relayed to a third-party manufacturer. With luck, the furniture will be delivered to the customer's home within six to eight weeks. This is a value chain that maximizes customization and service but does so at high cost.

In contrast, IKEA serves customers who are happy to trade off service for cost. Instead of having a sales associate trail customers around the store, IKEA uses a self-service model based on clear, in-store displays. Rather than rely solely on third-party manufacturers, IKEA designs its own low-cost, modular, ready-to-assemble furniture to fit its positioning. In huge stores, IKEA displays every product it sells in room-like settings, so customers don't need a decorator to help them imagine how to put the pieces together. Adjacent to the furnished showrooms is a warehouse section with the products in boxes on pallets. Customers are expected to do their own pickup and delivery, and IKEA will even sell you a roof rack for your car that you can return for a refund on your next visit.

Although much of its low-cost position comes from having customers 'do it themselves', IKEA offers a number of extra services that its competitors do not. In-store child care is one. Extended hours are another. Those services are uniquely aligned with the needs of its customers, who are young, not wealthy, likely to have children (but no nanny), and, because they work for a living, have a need to shop at odd hours.

## The origins of strategic positions

Strategic positions emerge from three distinct sources, which are not mutually exclusive and often overlap. First, positioning can be based on producing a subset of an industry's products or services. I call this *variety-based positioning* because it is based on the choice of product or service varieties rather than customer segments. Variety-based positioning makes economic sense when a company can best produce particular products or services using distinctive sets of activities.

Jiffy Lube International, for instance, specializes in automotive lubricants and does not offer other car repair or maintenance services. Its value chain produces faster service at a lower cost than broader line repair shops, a combination so attractive that many customers subdivide their purchases, buying oil changes from the focused competitor, Jiffy Lube, and going to rivals for other services.

The Vanguard Group, a leader in the mutual fund industry, is another example of variety-based positioning. Vanguard provides an array of common stock, bond, and money market funds that offer predictable performance and rock-bottom expenses. The company's investment approach deliberately sacrifices the possibility of extraordinary performance in any one year for good relative performance in every year. Vanguard is known, for example, for its index funds. It avoids making bets on interest rates and steers clear of narrow stock groups. Fund managers keep trading levels low, which holds expenses down; in addition, the company discourages customers from rapid buying and selling because doing so drives up costs and can force a fund manager to trade in order to deploy new capital and raise cash for redemptions. Vanguard also takes a consistent low-cost approach to managing distribution, customer service, and marketing. Many investors include one or more Vanguard funds in their portfolio, while buying aggressively managed or specialized funds from competitors.

The people who use Vanguard or Jiffy Lube are responding to a superior value chain for a particular type of service. A variety-based positioning can serve a wide array of customers, but for most it will meet only a subset of their needs.

A second basis for positioning is that of serving most or all the needs of a particular group of customers. I call this *needs-based positioning*, which comes closer to traditional thinking about targeting a segment of customers. It arises when there are groups of customers with differing needs, and when a tailored set of activities can serve those needs best. Some groups of customers are more price sensitive than others, demand different product features, and need varying amounts of information, support, and services. IKEA's customers are a good example of such a group. IKEA seeks to meet all the home furnishing needs of its target customers, not just a subset of them.

A variant of needs-based positioning arises when the same customer has different needs on different occasions or for different types of transactions. The same person, for example, may have different needs when traveling on business than when traveling for pleasure with the family. Buyers of cans – beverage companies, for example – will likely have different needs from their primary supplier than from their secondary source.

It is intuitive for most managers to conceive of their business in terms of the customers' needs they are meeting. But a critical element of needs-based positioning is not at all intuitive and is often overlooked. Differences in needs will not translate into meaningful positions unless the best set of activities to satisfy them *also* differs. If that were not the case, every competitor could meet those same needs, and there would be nothing unique or valuable about the positioning.

In private banking, for example, Bessemer Trust Company targets families with a minimum of $5 million in investable assets who want capital preservation combined with wealth accumulation. By assigning one sophisticated account officer for every 14 families, Bessemer has configured its activities for personalized service. Meetings, for example, are more likely to be held at a client's ranch or yacht than in the office. Bessemer offers a wide array of customized services, including investment management and estate administration, oversight of oil and gas investments, and accounting for racehorses and aircraft. Loans, a staple of most private banks, are rarely needed by Bessemer's clients and make up a tiny fraction of its client balances and income. Despite the most generous compensation of account officers and the highest personnel cost as a percentage of operating expenses, Bessemer's differentiation with its target families produces a return on equity estimated to be the highest of any private banking competitor.

Citibank's private bank, on the other hand, serves clients with minimum assets of about $250,000 who, in contrast to Bessemer's clients, want convenient access to loans – from jumbo mortgages to deal financing. Citibank's account managers are primarily lenders. When clients need other services, their account manager refers them to other Citibank specialists, each of whom handles prepackaged products. Citibank's system is less customized than Bessemer's and allows it to have a lower manager-to-client ratio of 1:125. Biannual office meetings are offered only for the largest clients. Both Bessemer and Citibank have tailored their activities to meet the needs of a different group of private banking customers. The same value chain cannot profitably meet the needs of both groups.

The third basis for positioning is that of segmenting customers who are accessible in different ways. Although their needs are similar to those of other customers, the best configuration of activities to reach them is different. I call this *access-based positioning*. Access can be a function of customer geography or customer scale – or of anything that requires a different set of activities to reach customers in the best way.

Segmenting by access is less common and less well understood than the other two bases. Carmike Cinemas, for example, operates movie theaters exclusively in cities and towns with populations under 200,000. How does Carmike make money in markets that are not only small but also won't support big-city ticket prices? It does so through a set of activities that result in a lean cost structure. Carmike's small-town customers can be served through standardized, low-cost theater complexes requiring fewer screens and less sophisticated projection technology than big-city theaters. The company's proprietary information system and management process eliminate the need for local administrative staff beyond a single theater manager. Carmike also reaps advantages from centralized purchasing, lower rent and payroll costs (because of its locations), and rock-bottom corporate overhead of 2% (the industry average is 5%). Operating in small communities also allows Carmike to practice a highly personal form of marketing in which the theater manager knows patrons and promotes attendance through personal contacts. By being the dominant if not the only theater in its markets – the main competition is often the high school football team – Carmike is also able to get its pick of films and negotiate better terms with distributors.

Rural versus urban-based customers are one example of access driving differences in activities. Serving small rather than large customers or densely rather than sparsely situated customers are other examples in which the best way to configure marketing, order processing, logistics, and after-sale service activities to meet the similar needs of distinct groups will often differ.

Positioning is not only about carving out a niche. A position emerging from any of the sources can be broad or narrow. A focused competitor, such as IKEA, targets the special needs of a subset of customers and designs its activities accordingly. Focused competitors thrive on groups of customers who are overserved (and hence overpriced) by more broadly targeted competitors, or underserved (and hence underpriced). A broadly targeted competitor – for example, Vanguard or Delta Air Lines – serves a wide array of customers, performing a set of activities designed to meet their common needs. It ignores or meets only partially the more idiosyncratic needs of particular customer groups.

Whatever the basis – variety, needs, access, or some combination of the three – positioning requires a tailored set of activities because it is always a function of differences on the supply side; that is, of differences in activities. However, positioning is not always a function of differences on the demand, or customer, side.

Variety and access positionings, in particular, do not rely on any customer differences. In practice, however, variety or access differences often accompany needs differences. The tastes – that is, the needs – of Carmike's small-town customers, for instance, run more toward comedies, Westerns, action films, and family entertainment. Carmike does not run any films rated NC-17.

Having defined positioning, we can now begin to answer the question, 'What is strategy?' Strategy is the creation of a unique and valuable position, involving a different set of activities. If there were only one ideal position, there would be no need for strategy. Companies would face a simple imperative – win the race to discover and preempt it. The essence of strategic positioning is to choose activities that are different from rivals'. If the same set of activities were best to produce all varieties, meet all needs, and access all customers, companies could easily shift among them and operational effectiveness would determine performance.

## A sustainable strategic position requires trade-offs

Choosing a unique position, however, is not enough to guarantee a sustainable advantage. A valuable position will attract imitation by incumbents, who are likely to copy it in one of two ways.

First, a competitor can reposition itself to match the superior performer. J.C. Penney, for instance, has been repositioning itself from a Sears clone to a more upscale, fashion-oriented, soft-goods retailer. A second and far more common type of imitation is straddling. The straddler seeks to match the benefits of a successful position while maintaining its existing position. It grafts new features, services, or technologies onto the activities it already performs.

For those who argue that competitors can copy any market position, the airline industry is a perfect test case. It would seem that nearly any competitor could imitate any other airline's activities. Any airline can buy the same planes, lease the gates, and match the menus and ticketing and baggage handling services offered by other airlines.

Continental Airlines saw how well Southwest was doing and decided to straddle. While maintaining its position as a full-service airline, Continental also set out to match Southwest on a number of point-to-point routes. The airline dubbed the new service Continental Lite. It eliminated meals and first-class service, increased departure frequency, lowered fares, and shortened turnaround time at the gate. Because Continental remained a full-service airline on other routes, it continued to use travel agents and its mixed fleet of planes and to provide baggage checking and seat assignments.

But a strategic position is not sustainable unless there are trade-offs with other positions. Trade-offs occur when activities are incompatible. Simply put, a trade-off means that more of one thing necessitates less of another. An airline can choose to serve meals – adding cost and slowing turnaround time at the gate – or it can choose not to, but it cannot do both without bearing major inefficiencies.

Trade-offs create the need for choice and protect against repositioners and straddlers. Consider Neutrogena soap. Neutrogena Corporation's variety-based positioning is built on a 'kind to the skin', residue-free formulated for pH balance. With a large detail force calling on dermatologists, Neutrogena's marketing strategy looks more like a drug company's than a soap maker's. It advertises in medical journals, sends direct mail to doctors, attends medical conferences, and performs research at its own Skincare Institute. To reinforce its positioning, Neutrogena originally focused its distribution on drugstores and avoided price promotions. Neutrogena uses a slow, more expensive manufacturing process to mold its fragile soap.

In choosing this position, Neutrogena said no to the deodorants and skin softeners that many customers desire in their soap. It gave up the large-volume potential of selling through supermarkets and using price promotions. It sacrificed manufacturing efficiencies to achieve the soap's desired attributes. In its original positioning, Neutrogena made a whole raft of trade-offs like those, trade-offs that protected the company from imitators.

Trade-offs arise for three reasons. The first is inconsistencies in image or reputation. A company known for delivering one kind of value may lack credibility and confuse customers – or even undermine its reputation – if it delivers another kind of value or attempts to deliver two inconsistent things at the same time. For example, Ivory soap, with its position as a basic, inexpensive everyday soap, would have a hard time reshaping its image to match Neutrogena's premium 'medical' reputation. Efforts to create a new image typically cost tens or even hundreds of millions of dollars in a major industry – a powerful barrier to imitation.

Second, and more important, trade-offs arise from activities themselves. Different positions (with their tailored activities) require different product configurations, different equipment, different employee behavior, different skills, and different management systems. Many trade-offs reflect inflexibilities in machinery, people, or systems. The more IKEA has configured its activities to lower costs by having its customers do their own assembly and delivery, the less able it is to satisfy customers who require higher levels of service.

However, trade-offs can be even more basic. In general, value is destroyed if an activity is overdesigned or underdesigned for its use. For example, even if a given salesperson were capable of providing a high level of assistance to one customer and none to another, the salesperson's talent (and some of his or her cost) would be wasted on the second customer. Moreover, productivity can improve when variation of an activity is limited. By providing a high level of assistance all the time, the salesperson and the entire sales activity can often achieve efficiencies of learning and scale.

Finally, trade-offs arise from limits on internal coordination and control. By clearly choosing to compete in one way and not another, senior management makes organizational priorities clear. Companies that try to be all things to all customers, in contrast, risk confusion in the trenches as employees attempt to make day-to-day operating decisions without a clear framework.

Positioning trade-offs are pervasive in competition and essential to strategy. They create the need for choice and purposefully limit what a company offers. They deter straddling or repositioning, because competitors that engage in those approaches undermine their strategies and degrade the value of their existing activities.

Trade-offs ultimately grounded Continental Lite. The airline lost hundreds of millions of dollars, and the CEO lost his job. Its planes were delayed leaving congested hub cities or slowed at the gate by baggage transfers. Late flights and cancellations generated a thousand complaints a day. Continental Lite could not afford to compete on price and still pay standard travel-agent commissions, but neither could it do without agents for its full-service business. The airline compromised by cutting commissions for all Continental flights across the board. Similarly, it could not afford to offer the same frequent-flier benefits to travelers paying the much lower ticket prices for Lite service. It compromised again by lowering the rewards of Continental's entire frequent-flier program. The results: angry travel agents and full-service customers.

Continental tried to compete in two ways at once. In trying to be low cost on some routes and full service on others, Continental paid an enormous straddling penalty. If there were no trade-offs between the two positions, Continental could have succeeded. But the absence of trade-offs is a dangerous half-truth that managers must unlearn. Quality is not always free. Southwest's convenience, one kind of high quality, happens to be consistent with low costs because its frequent departures are facilitated by a number of low-cost practices — fast gate turnarounds and automated ticketing, for example. However, other dimensions of airline quality — an assigned seat, a meal, or baggage transfer — require costs to provide.

In general, false trade-offs between cost and quality occur primarily when there is redundant or wasted effort, poor control or accuracy, or weak coordination. Simultaneous improvement of cost and differentiation is possible only when a company begins far behind the productivity frontier or when the frontier shifts outward. At the frontier, where companies have achieved current best practice, the trade-off between cost and differentiation is very real indeed.

After a decade of enjoying productivity advantages, Honda Motor Company and Toyota Motor Corporation recently bumped up against the frontier. In 1995, faced with increasing customer resistance to higher automobile prices, Honda found that the only way to produce a less-expensive car was to skimp on features. In the United States, it replaced the rear disk brakes on the Civic with lower-cost drum brakes and used cheaper fabric for the back seat, hoping customers would not notice. Toyota tried to sell a version of its best-selling Corolla in Japan with unpainted bumpers and cheaper seats. In Toyota's case, customers rebelled, and the company quickly dropped the new model.

For the past decade, as managers have improved operational effectiveness greatly, they have internalized the idea that eliminating trade-offs is a good thing.

But if there are no trade-offs companies will never achieve a sustainable advantage. They will have to run faster and faster just to stay in place.

As we return to the question, 'What is strategy?', we see that trade-offs add a new dimension to the answer. Strategy is making trade-offs in competing. The essence of strategy is choosing what *not* to do. Without trade-offs, there would be no need for choice and thus no need for strategy. Any good idea could and would be quickly imitated. Again, performance would once again depend wholly on operational effectiveness.

# Fit drives both competitive advantage and sustainability

Positioning choices determine not only which activities a company will perform and how it will configure individual activities but also how activities relate to one another. While operational effectiveness is about achieving excellence in individual activities, or functions, strategy is about *combining* activities (Figure 1.1 – see page 23).

Southwest's rapid gate turnaround, which allows frequent departures and greater use of aircraft, is essential to its high-convenience, low-cost positioning. But how does Southwest achieve it? Part of the answer lies in the company's well-paid gate and ground crews, whose productivity in turnarounds is enhanced by flexible union rules. But the bigger part of the answer lies in how Southwest performs other activities. With no meals, no seat assignment, and no interline baggage transfers, Southwest avoids having to perform activities that slow down other airlines. It selects airports and routes to avoid congestion that introduces delays. Southwest's strict limits on the type and length of routes make standardized aircraft possible: every aircraft Southwest turns is a Boeing 737.

What is Southwest's core competence? Its key success factors? The correct answer is that everything matters. Southwest's strategy involves a whole system of activities, not a collection of parts. Its competitive advantage comes from the way its activities fit and reinforce one another.

Fit locks out imitators by creating a chain that is as strong as its *strongest* link. As in most companies with good strategies, Southwest's activities complement one another in ways that create real economic value. One activity's cost, for example, is lowered because of the way other activities are performed. Similarly, one activity's value to customers can be enhanced by a company's other activities. That is the way strategic fit creates competitive advantage and superior profitability.

## *Types of fit*

The importance of fit among functional policies is one of the oldest ideas in strategy. Gradually, however, it has been supplanted on the management agenda. Rather than seeing the company as a whole, managers have turned to 'core' competencies, 'critical' resources, and 'key' success factors. In fact, fit is a far more central component of competitive advantage than most realize.

Fit is important because discrete activities often affect one another. A sophisticated sales force, for example, confers a greater advantage when the company's product embodies premium technology and its marketing approach emphasizes customer assistance and support. A production line with high levels of model variety is more valuable when combined with an inventory and order processing system that minimizes the need for stocking finished goods, a sales process equipped to explain and encourage customization, and an advertising theme that stresses the benefits of product variations that meet a customer's special needs. Such complementarities are pervasive in strategy. Although some fit among activities is generic and applies to many companies, the most valuable fit is strategy-specific because it enhances a position's uniqueness and amplifies trade-offs.[2]

There are three types of fit, although they are not mutually exclusive. First-order fit is *simple consistency* between each activity (function) and the overall strategy. Vanguard, for example, aligns all activities with its low-cost strategy. It minimizes portfolio turnover and does not need highly compensated money managers. The company distributes its funds directly, avoiding commissions to brokers. It also limits advertising, relying instead on public relations and word-of-mouth recommendations. Vanguard ties its employees' bonuses to cost savings.

Consistency ensures that the competitive advantages of activities cumulate and do not erode or cancel themselves out. It makes the strategy easier to communicate to customers, employees, and shareholders, and improves implementation through single-mindedness in the corporation.

Second-order fit occurs when *activities are reinforcing*. Neutrogena, for example, markets to upscale hotels eager to offer their guests a soap recommended by dermatologists. Hotels grant Neutrogena the privilege of using its customary packaging while requiring other soaps to feature the hotel's name. Once guests have tried Neutrogena in a luxury hotel, they are more likely to purchase it at the drugstore or ask their doctor about it. Thus Neutrogena's medical and hotel marketing activities reinforce one another, lowering total marketing costs.

In another example, Bic Corporation sells a narrow line of standard, low-priced pens to virtually all major customer markets (retail, commercial, promotional, and giveaway) through virtually all available channels. As with any variety-based positioning serving a broad group of customers, Bic emphasizes a common need (low price for an acceptable pen) and uses marketing approaches with a broad reach (a large sales force and heavy television advertising). Bic gains the benefits of consistency across nearly all activities, including product design that emphasizes ease of manufacturing, plants configured for low cost, aggressive purchasing to minimize material costs, and in-house parts production whenever the economics dictate.

Yet Bic goes beyond simple consistency because its activities are reinforcing. For example, the company uses point-of-sale displays and frequent packaging changes to stimulate impulse buying. To handle point-of-sale tasks, a company

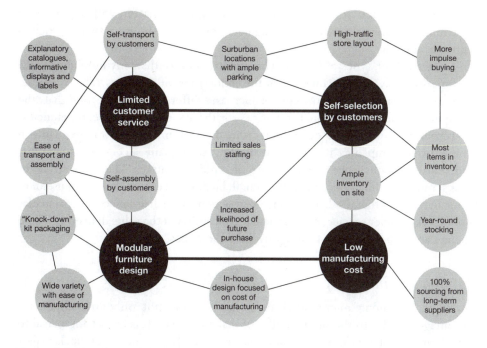

**Figure 1.1** *Mapping activity systems*

Activity-system maps, such as this one for Ikea, show how a company's strategic position is contained in a set of tailored activities designed to deliver it. In companies with a clear strategic position a number of higher-order strategic themes can be identified and implemented through clusters of tightly linked activities.

needs a large sales force. Bic's is the largest in its industry, and it handles point-of-sale activities better than its rivals do. Moreover, the combination of point-of-sale activity, heavy television advertising, and packaging changes yields far more impulse buying than any activity in isolation could.

Third-order fit goes beyond activity reinforcement to what I call *optimization of effort*. The Gap, a retailer of casual clothes, considers product availability in its stores a critical element of its strategy. The Gap could keep products either by holding store inventory or by restocking from warehouses. The Gap has optimized its effort across these activities by restocking its selection of basic clothing almost daily out of three warehouses, thereby minimizing the need to carry large in-store inventories. The emphasis is on restocking because the Gap's merchandising strategy sticks to basic items in relatively few colors. While comparable retailers achieve turns of three to four times per year, the Gap turns its inventory seven and a half times per year. Rapid restocking, moreover, reduces the cost of implementing the Gap's short model cycle, which is six to eight weeks long.[3]

Coordination and information exchange across activities to eliminate redundancy and minimize wasted effort are the most basic types of effort optimization. But there are higher levels as well. Product design choices, for example, can eliminate the need for after-sale service or make it possible for customers to perform service activities themselves. Similarly, coordination with suppliers or distribution channels can eliminate the need for some in-house activities, such as end-user training.

In all three types of fit, the whole matters more than any individual part. Competitive advantage grows out of the *entire system* of activities. The fit among activities substantially reduces cost or increases differentiation. Beyond that, the competitive value of individual activities – or the associated skills, competencies, or resources – cannot be decoupled from the system or the strategy. Thus in competitive companies it can be misleading to explain success by specifying individual strengths, core competencies, or critical resources. The list of strengths cuts across many functions, and one strength blends into others. It is more useful to think in terms of themes that pervade many activities, such as low cost, a particular notion of customer service, or a particular conception of the value delivered. These themes are embodied in nests of tightly linked activities.

## Fit and sustainability

Strategic fit among many activities is fundamental not only to competitive advantage but also to the sustainability of that advantage. It is harder for a rival to match an array of interlocked activities than it is merely to imitate a particular sales-force approach, match a process technology, or replicate a set of product features. Positions built on systems of activities are far more sustainable than those built on individual activities.

Consider this simple exercise. The probability that competitors can match any activity is often less than one. The probabilities then quickly compound to make matching the entire system highly unlikely ($0.9 \times 0.9 = 0.81$; $0.9 \times 0.9 \times 0.9 \times 0.9 = 0.66$, and so on). Existing companies that try to reposition or straddle will be forced to reconfigure many activities. And even new entrants, though they do not confront the trade-offs facing established rivals, still face formidable barriers to imitation.

The more a company's positioning rests on activity systems with second- and third-order fit, the more sustainable its advantage will be. Such systems, by their very nature, are usually difficult to untangle from outside the company and therefore hard to imitate. And even if rivals can identify the relevant interconnections, they will have difficulty replicating them. Achieving fit is difficult because it requires the integration of decisions and actions across many independent subunits.

A competitor seeking to match an activity system gains little by imitating only some activities and not matching the whole. Performance does not improve, it can decline. Recall Continental Lite's disastrous attempt to imitate Southwest.

Finally, fit among a company's activities creates pressures and incentives to improve operational effectiveness, which makes imitation even harder. Fit means that poor performance in one activity will degrade the performance in others, so that weaknesses are exposed and more prone to get attention. Conversely, improvements in one activity will pay dividends in others. Companies with strong

Table 1.1 *Alternative views of strategy*

| The implicit strategy model of the past decade | Sustainable competitive advantage |
| --- | --- |
| One ideal competitive position in the industry | Unique competitive position for the company |
| Benchmarking of all activities and achieving best practice | Activities tailored to strategy |
| Aggressive outsourcing and partnering to gain efficiencies | Clear trade-offs and choices *vis-à-vis* competitors |
| Advantages rest on a few key success factors, critical resources, core competencies | Competitive advantage arises from fit across activities |
| Flexibility and rapid responses to all competitive and market changes | Sustainability comes from the activity system, not the parts |
|  | Operational effectiveness is a given |

fit among their activities are rarely inviting targets. Their superiority in strategy and in execution only compounds their advantages and raises the hurdle for imitators.

When activities complement one another, rivals will get little benefit from imitation unless they successfully match the whole system. Such situations tend to promote winner-take-all competition. The company that builds the best activity system – Toys R Us, for instance – wins, while rivals with similar strategies – Child World and Lionel Leisure – fall behind. Thus finding a new strategic position is often preferable to being the second or third imitator of an occupied position.

The most viable positions are those whose activity systems are incompatible because of tradeoffs. Strategic positioning sets the trade-off rules that define how individual activities will be configured and integrated. Seeing strategy in terms of activity systems only makes it clearer why organizational structure, systems, and processes need to be strategy-specific. Tailoring organization to strategy, in turn, makes complementarities more achievable and contributes to sustainability.

One implication is that strategic positions should have a horizon of a decade or more, nor of a single planning cycle. Continuity fosters improvements in individual activities and the fit across activities, allowing an organization to build unique capabilities and skills tailored to its strategy. Continuity also reinforces a company's identity.

Conversely, frequent shifts in positioning are costly. Not only must a company reconfigure individual activities, but it must also realign entire systems. Some activities may never catch up to the vacillating strategy. The inevitable result of frequent shifts in strategy, or of failure to choose a distinct position in the first place, is 'me-too' or hedged activity configurations, inconsistencies across functions, and organizational dissonance.

What is strategy? We can now complete the answer to this question. Strategy is creating fit among a company's activities. The success of a strategy depends on doing many things well – not just a few – and integrating among them. If there is no fit among activities, there is no distinctive strategy and little sustainability. Management reverts to the simpler task of overseeing independent functions, and operational effectiveness determines an organization's relative performance (Table 1.1).

# Rediscovering strategy

## *The failure to choose*

Why do so many companies fail to have a strategy? Why do managers avoid making strategic choices? Or, having made them in the past, why do managers so often let strategies decay and blur?

Commonly, the threats to strategy are seen to emanate from outside a company because of changes in technology or the behavior of competitors. Although external changes can be the problem, the greater threat to strategy often comes from within. A sound strategy is undermined by a misguided view of competition, by organizational failures, and, especially, by the desire to grow.

Managers have become confused about the necessity of making choices. When many companies operate far from the productivity frontier, trade-offs appear unnecessary. It can seem that a well-run company should be able to beat its ineffective rivals on all dimensions simultaneously. Taught by popular management thinkers that they do not have to make trade-offs, managers have acquired a macho sense that to do so is a sign of weakness.

Unnerved by forecasts of hypercompetition, managers increase its likelihood by imitating everything about their competitors. Exhorted to think in terms of revolution, managers chase every new technology for its own sake (Box 1.2).

---

## Box 1.2
## Emerging industries and technologies

Developing a strategy in a newly emerging industry or in a business undergoing revolutionary technological changes is a daunting proposition. In such cases, managers face a high level of uncertainty about the needs of customers, the products and services that will prove to be the most desired, and the best configuration of activities and technologies to deliver them. Because of all this uncertainty, imitation and hedging are rampant: unable to risk being wrong or left behind, companies match all features, offer all new services, and explore all technologies.

During such periods in an industry's development, its basic productivity frontier is being established or reestablished. Explosive growth can make such times profitable for many companies, but profits will be temporary because imitation and strategic convergence will ultimately destroy industry profitability. The companies that are enduringly successful will be those that begin as early as possible to define and embody in their activities a unique competitive position. A period of imitation may be inevitable in emerging industries, but that period reflects the level of uncertainty rather than a desired state of affairs.

In high-tech industries, this imitation phase often continues much longer than it should. Enraptured by technological change itself, companies pack more features –

most of which are never used – into their products while slashing prices across the board. Rarely are trade-offs even considered. The drive for growth to satisfy market pressures leads companies into every product area. Although a few companies with fundamental advantages prosper, the majority are doomed to a rat race no one can win.

Ironically, the popular business press, focused on hot, emerging industries, is prone to presenting these special cases as proof that we have entered a new era of competition in which none of the old rules are valid. In fact, the opposite is true.

The pursuit of operational effectiveness is seductive because it is concrete and actionable. Over the past decade, managers have been under increasing pressure to deliver tangible, measurable performance improvements. Programs in operational effectiveness produce reassuring progress, although superior profitability may remain elusive. Business publications and consultants flood the market with information about what other companies are doing, reinforcing the best-practice mentality. Caught up in the race for operational effectiveness, many managers simply do not understand the need to have a strategy.

Companies avoid or blur strategic choices for other reasons as well. Conventional wisdom within an industry is often strong, homogenizing competition. Some managers mistake 'customer focus' to mean they must serve all customer needs or respond to every request from distribution channels. Others cite the desire to preserve flexibility.

Organizational realities also work against strategy. Trade-offs are frightening, and making no choice is sometimes preferred to risking blame for a bad choice. Companies imitate one another in a type of herd behavior, each assuming rivals know something they do not. Newly empowered employees, who are urged to seek every possible source of improvement, often lack a vision of the whole and the perspective to recognize trade-offs. The failure to choose sometimes comes down to the reluctance to disappoint valued managers or employees.

## The growth trap

Among all other influences, the desire to grow has perhaps the most perverse effect on strategy. Trade-offs and limits appear to constrain growth. Serving one group of customers and excluding others, for instance, places a real or imagined limit on revenue growth. Broadly targeted strategies emphasizing low price result in lost sales with customers sensitive to features or service. Differentiators lose sales to price-sensitive customers.

Managers are constantly tempted to take incremental steps that surpass those limits but blur a company's strategic position. Eventually, pressures to grow or apparent saturation of the target market lead managers to broaden the position by extending product lines, adding new features, imitating competitors' popular services, matching processes, and even making acquisitions. For years, Maytag Corporation's success was based on its focus on reliable, durable washers and dryers, later extended to include dishwashers. However, conventional wisdom emerging within the industry supported the notion of selling a full line of products. Concerned with slow industry growth and competition from broad-line appliance makers, Maytag was pressured by dealers and encouraged by customers to extend its line. Maytag expanded into refrigerators and cooking products under the Maytag brand and acquired other brands – Jenn-Air, Hardwick Stove, Hoover, Admiral, and Magic Chef – with disparate positions. Maytag has grown substantially from $684 million in 1985 to a peak of $3.4 billion in 1994, but return on sales has declined from 8% to 12% in the 1970s and 1980s to an average of less than 1% between 1989 and 1995. Cost cutting will improve this performance, but laundry and dishwasher products still anchor Maytag's profitability.

Neutrogena may have fallen into the same trap. In the early 1990s, its US distribution broadened to include mass merchandisers such as Wal-Mart Stores. Under the Neutrogena name, the company expanded into a wide variety of products – eye makeup remover and shampoo, for example – in which it was not unique and which diluted its image, and it began turning to price promotions.

Compromises and inconsistencies in the pursuit of growth will erode the competitive advantage a company had with its original varieties or target customers. Attempts to compete in several ways at once create confusion and undermine organizational motivation and focus. Profits fall, but more revenue is seen as the answer. Managers are unable to make choices, so the company embarks on a new round of broadening and compromises. Often, rivals continue to match each other until desperation breaks the cycle, resulting in a merger or downsizing to the original positioning.

## Profitable growth

Many companies, after a decade of restructuring and cost-cutting, are turning their attention to growth. Too often, efforts to grow blur uniqueness, create compromises, reduce fit, and ultimately undermine competitive advantage. In fact, the growth imperative is hazardous to strategy.

What approaches to growth preserve and reinforce strategy? Broadly, the prescription is to concentrate on deepening a strategic position rather than broadening and compromising it. One approach is to look for extensions of the strategy that leverage the existing activity system by offering features or services that rivals would find impossible or costly to match on a stand-alone basis. In other words, managers can ask themselves which activities, features, or forms of competition are feasible or less costly to them because of complementary activities that their company performs.

Deepening a position involves making the company's activities more distinctive, strengthening fit, and communicating the strategy better to those customers who should value it. But many companies succumb to the temptation to chase 'easy' growth by adding hot features, products, or services without screening them or adapting them to their strategy. Or they target new customers or markets in which the company has little special to offer. A company can often grow faster – and far more profitably – by better penetrating needs and varieties where it is distinctive than by slugging it out in potentially higher growth arenas in which the company lacks uniqueness. Carmike, now the largest theater chain in the United States, owes its rapid growth to its disciplined concentration on small markets. The company quickly sells any big-city theaters that come to it as part of an acquisition.

Globalization often allows growth that is consistent with strategy, opening up larger markets for a focused strategy. Unlike broadening domestically, expanding globally is likely to leverage and reinforce a company's unique position and identity.

Companies seeking growth through broadening within their industry can best contain the risks to strategy by creating stand-alone units, each with its own brand name and tailored activities. Maytag has clearly struggled with this issue. On the one hand, it has organized its premium and value brands into separate units with different strategic positions. On the other, it has created an umbrella appliance company for all its brands to gain critical mass. With shared design, manufacturing, distribution, and customer service, it will be hard to avoid homogenization. If a given business unit attempts to compete with different positions for different products or customers, avoiding compromise is nearly impossible.

## The role of leadership

The challenge of developing or reestablishing a clear strategy is often primarily an organizational one and depends on leadership. With so many forces at work against making choices and tradeoffs in organizations, a clear intellectual framework to guide strategy is a necessary counterweight. Moreover, strong leaders willing to make choices are essential.

In many companies, leadership has degenerated into orchestrating operational improvements and making deals. But the leader's role is broader and far more important. General management is more than the stewardship of individual functions. Its core is strategy: defining and communicating the company's unique position, making trade-offs, and forging fit among activities. The leader must provide the discipline to decide which industry changes and customer needs the company will respond to, while avoiding organizational distractions and maintaining the company's distinctiveness. Managers at lower levels lack the perspective and the confidence to maintain a strategy. There will be constant pressures to compromise, relax trade-offs, and emulate rivals. One of the leader's jobs is to teach others in the organization about strategy – and to say no. Strategy renders choices about what not to do as important as choices about what to do. Indeed, setting limits is another function of leadership. Deciding which target group of customers, varieties, and needs the company should serve is fundamental to developing a strategy. But so is deciding not to serve other customers or needs and not to offer certain features or services. Thus strategy requires constant discipline and clear communication. Indeed, one of the most important functions of an explicit, communicated strategy is to guide employees in making choices that arise because of trade-offs in their individual activities and in day-to-day decisions.

Improving operational effectiveness is a necessary part of management, but it is *not* strategy. In confusing the two, managers have unintentionally backed into a way of thinking about competition that is driving many industries toward competitive convergence, which is in no one's best interest and is not inevitable.

Managers must clearly distinguish operational effectiveness from strategy. Both are essential, but the two agendas are different.

The operational agenda involves continual improvement everywhere there are no trade-offs. Failure to do this creates vulnerability even for companies with a good strategy. The operational agenda is the proper place for constant change, flexibility, and relentless efforts to achieve best practice. In contrast, the strategic agenda is the right place for defining a unique position, making clear trade-offs, and tightening fit. It involves the continual search for ways to reinforce and extend the company's position. The strategic agenda demands discipline and continuity; its enemies are distraction and compromise.

Strategic continuity does not imply a static view of competition. A company must continually improve its operational effectiveness and actively try to shift the productivity frontier; at the same time, there needs to be ongoing effort to extend its uniqueness while strengthening the fit among its activities. Strategic continuity, in fact, should make an organization's continual improvement more effective.

A company may have to change its strategy if there are major structural changes in its industry. In fact, new strategic positions often arise because of industry changes, and new entrants unencumbered by history often can exploit them more easily. However, a company's choice of a new position must be driven by the ability to find new trade-offs and leverage a new system of complementary activities into a sustainable advantage.

## Notes

1    I first described the concept of activities and its use in understanding competitive advantage in *Competitive Advantage* (New York: The Free Press, 1985). The ideas in this article build on and extend that thinking.

2    Paul Milgrom and John Roberts have begun to explore the economics of systems of complementary functions, activities, and functions. Their focus is on the emergence of 'modern manufacturing' as a new set of complementary activities, on the tendency of companies to react to external changes with coherent bundles of internal responses, and on the need for central coordination — a strategy — to align functional managers. In the latter case, they model what has long been a bedrock principle of strategy. See Paul Milgrom and John Roberts, 'The Economics of Modern Manufacturing: Technology, Strategy,

and Organization', *American Economic Review* 80 (1990): 511–528; Paul Milgrom, Yingyi Qian, and John Roberts, 'Complementarities, Momentum, and Evolution of Modern Manufacturing', *American Economic Review* 81 (1991) 84–88; and Paul Milgrom and John Roberts, 'Complementarities and Fit: Strategy, Structure, and Organizational Changes in Manufacturing', *Journal of Accounting and Economics* 19 (March–May 1995): 179–208.

3    Material on retail strategies is drawn in part from Jan Rivkin, 'The Rise of Retail Category Killers', unpublished working paper, January 1995. Nicolaj Siggelkow prepared the case study on the Gap.

# CHAPTER 2

# Theories of Strategy

RICHARD WHITTINGTON*

Practical men, who believe themselves to be quite exempt from any intellectual influences, are usually the slaves of some defunct economist. Madmen in authority, who hear voices in the air, are distilling their frenzy from some academic scribbler of a few years back.

(Keynes 1936: 383)

## Introduction

[. . .]

Theories are important. They contain our basic assumptions about key relationships in business life. Theories tell us what to look out for, what our first steps should be, and what to expect as a result of our actions. Saving us from going back to first principles at each stage, they are actually short-cuts to action. Often these theories are not very explicit or very formal. Whether building from experience or from books, we all tend to have our own private assumptions about how things work, how to get things done. Providing the basic grounding for our behaviour, Argyris (1977) calls these assumptions 'theories of action'.

The danger of these theories is forgetting we have them. As Keynes (1936) implies, those who boast of their commonsense approach to management are very probably just following the ill-informed, half-forgotten, pseudo-scientific nostrums peddled to them in their early careers. Drawing upon his work with American senior managers, Argyris (1977) warns that nothing is more dangerous than to leave underlying assumptions hidden. Until we surface our implicit 'theories of action', we cannot test their accuracy and amend them to the conditions of the day. Those who do not actively confront their underlying assumptions are condemned to be 'prisoners of their own theories' (Argyris 1977: 119).

The point of this chapter, then, is to make explicit the assumptions that underlie . . . theories of strategy. Each theory holds very different views about our

* International Thomson Business Press for an extract from *What Is Strategy and Does It Matter?* (2nd edn) by Richard Whittington © Richard Whittington, 2001.

human capacity to think rationally and act effectively. They diverge widely in their implications for strategic management. By directly confronting these differences, you should be better able to test your own 'theories of action' and to decide finally which basic theory most closely matches your own experience and needs.

[. . .]

# The Classical approach to strategy

For Classicists, profitability is the supreme goal of business, and rational planning the means to achieve it. Dominant in the mainstream textbooks, the Classical approach draws wide disciplinary and metaphorical support. Its notions of strategy formulation are informed by the economics of eighteenth-century Scotland, while its assumptions about strategic implementation appeal back to the militaristic ideals of Ancient Greece.

For all this, the Classical approach to business strategy is still novel. The beginnings of a coherent discipline only emerged in the 1960s, with the writings of business historian Alfred Chandler (1962), theorist Igor Ansoff (1965) and the businessman Alfred Sloan (1963). These three men early established the key features of the Classical approach: the attachment to rational analysis, the separation of conception from execution, and the commitment to profit maximization.

Alfred Sloan, former President of General Motors, defined the fundamental strategic problem as positioning the firm in those markets in which maximum profits could be earned. In his great biography *My Years with General Motors*, Sloan laid down the Classical profit-orientated goal of strategy:

> the strategic aim of a business is to earn a return on capital, and if in any particular case the return in the long run is not satisfactory, the deficiency should be corrected or the activity abandoned. (1963: 49)

Sloan's (1963) biography chronicles in detail the development of the measures and methods by which, with as much cold objectivity as he could summon, he pursued this strategic aim over four decades at General Motors. Among the innovations he helped to pioneer were return on investment criteria, the decentralized divisional form and the separation of 'policy' from operations.

[. . .]

Sloan's example was highly influential. The prolific author and management consultant Peter Drucker worked for General Motors between 1943 and 1945, when the company employed half a million people. He subsequently publicized Sloan's management structures and style in two books, *The Concept of the Corporation* (1946; republished in 1973) and *Big Business* (1947). Igor Ansoff too was much impressed by Sloan, citing his statement on the strategic aim of business at the head of the first chapter of his *Corporate Strategy*, the first ever strategy textbook (a generation later, Grant 1998: 16) reproduced the same statement in his first chapter). Sloan was also closely connected with the first academic researcher of strategy, historian Alfred D. Chandler. Chandler (1962) took General Motors as one of his four central case studies in his historical account of the evolution of strategy and structure in American business; his research was financed by the Sloan Research Fund; and he was himself – full name Alfred Du Pont Chandler – connected to the family which owned a quarter of Sloan's General Motors (the Du Pont company supplied the second of his four cases).

It may not be surprising, then, that Chandler shares Sloan's faith in the superiority of the top-down, planned and rational approach to strategy-making. Chandler's (1962) own influential definition of strategy has all the characteristics of Classical strategy thought: the emphasis on the long run, the explicit and deliberate conception of goals, and the logical cascading of actions and resources from original objectives. According to Chandler, strategy is

> the determination of the basic, long-term goals and objectives of an enterprise, and the adoption of courses of action and the allocation of resources necessary for those goals. (1962: 13)

The central problem of the companies Chandler studied was how to build the organizational structures that would allow top management to focus on their strategic responsibilities. The basic reason for the success of the multidivisional structure that all four of his companies adopted in the first half of this century 'was simply that it clearly removed the executives responsible for the destiny of the entire enterprise from the more routine operational activities and so gave them the time, information, and even psychological commitment for long-term planning and appraisal' (Chandler 1962: 309). Thus was strategy formulation and control confirmed as the prime task of the top manager, strategy implementation as the responsibility of the operational managers in the divisions.

Sloan, Chandler and Ansoff did not, of course, dream up the concept of strategy from scratch. Ansoff (1965: 105) links his notion of strategy directly to both military practice and academic economics. Since then, economistic ideas about rational optimization, and militaristic expectations of hierarchical command, have continued to resonate in Classical thinking about strategy formulation and implementation.

Indeed, Bracker (1980) traces the concept of strategy to the Greek word *strategos*, 'a general', which in turn comes from roots meaning 'army' and 'lead'. Apparently, the link between military and business practice came early, when Socrates consoled Nichomachides, a Greek soldier who had lost an election to the position of general to a mere businessman. According to Bracker (1980: 219), Socrates explained to Nichomachides that the duties of a general and a businessman were equivalent: both involve planning the use of one's resources in order to meet objectives.

It is not clear that Nichomachides was consoled by this view, but anyway this military concept of business strategy was lost with the fall of the Greek city-states. There is no direct line of descent to modern business: Hoskin (1990) emphasizes the disjuncture between Greek military theory, tactical and partial in fact, and modern business strategy, long term and comprehensive in aspiration. None the less, as Hoskin (1990) finds, many of the earliest managerial systematizers of American business shared military origins, in particular training at the officer cadet school of West Point in the first half of the nineteenth century. Even today, when business strategy can claim a substantial and independent body of experience, military imagery continues to influence contemporary strategy analysis, as can be seen in the popularity of such books as James's (1985) *Business Wargames*. Certainly, the military metaphor reinforces several typical features of Classical approaches to strategy.

At the centre of the military tradition of strategy is the heroic yet slightly isolated figure of the general himself. Presiding at the top of a rigid hierarchy, it is the general who ultimately makes the decisions. From Alexander to Rommel, individual genius is critical to victory. Plans are conceived in the general's tent, overlooking the battlefield but sufficiently detached for safety. These preconceived plans are executed according to commands transmitted through obedient hierarchies to the officers and their men at the front: it is not for them to reason why, but simply to execute their orders. The men are sent to do battle, and the objective is simple: victory. Conflict, not co-operation, is the norm. The epitome of this coolly detached, sequential approach to strategy was General Colin Powell, chairman of the Joint Chiefs of Staff during the Gulf crisis. Asked how he planned to retake Iraqi-occupied Kuwait, he said: 'Our strategy for dealing with this [Iraqi] army is simple: first we are going to cut it off, then we're going to kill it' (*Sunday Times* 13 January 1991).

For the Classical theorists, this military model is complemented by an intellectual inheritance from economics. Indeed, the first academic application of the notion of strategy to business was made by two mathematical economists, von Neumann and Morgenstern (1944), in their *Theory of Games and Economic Behavior*. Since then, as Rumelt et al.'s (1991) recent view makes clear, economics has supplied the strategy field with many basic techniques and concepts – most notably Michael Porter's (1980) industry structure analysis and Oliver Williamson's (1985) concept of transaction costs in business organization. However, the most pervasive contribution of economics to strategy is the philosophical core of assumptions summed up in the ideal type of 'rational economic man' (Hollis and Nell 1975).

The ideal of rational economic man projects strategy as the product of a single entrepreneurial individual, acting with perfect rationality to maximize 'his' economic advantage. Von Neumann and Morgenstern (1944) placed this singular figure right at the heart of their conception of strategy as an elaborate 'game' of move and counter-move, bluff and counter-bluff, between competing yet interdependent businesses. Rational economic man was a necessary device. Only this reduction of the firm to a unique decision-maker would allow them to ignore internal organizational complexities; only this endowment of super-rationality would permit the sequence of mathematical calculations necessary to follow through the logics of the game.

Smuggled into Classical strategy thinking with the baggage of economics, the individualistic ideal of rational economic man goes back at least to the hard-headed economics of eighteenth-century Scotland. Hollander's (1987: 312) account of classical economics reveals how the fundamental principles of orthodox strategy thought were already present in the writings of Adam Smith. The profit-maximizing assumption is merely the economic expression of Smith's sad belief that self-interest was 'inherent in the very nature of our being'. Consequently, Smith asserted in his *Wealth of Nations* that 'each individual is continually exerting himself to find out the most advantageous employment of whatever capital he can command' – or, translated into the terms of modern accounting, each individual firm is continually exerting itself to maximize return on investment. According to Smith, our pursuit of this self-interest is governed by what he called 'prudence'. This notion of 'prudence' embodies the dual principles of 'reason' (the ability to foresee consequences and to discern advantage) and 'self-command' (the readiness to abstain from short-term opportunism in order to benefit more substantially in the long run) (Hollander 1987: 315–16). It is exactly these principles of eighteenth-century 'prudence' that are at the heart of modern long-term strategic planning.

[. . .]

The more pragmatic and self-conscious Classical thinkers hesitate over some of the economists' abstractions and the militarists' metaphors (see Grant 1998: ch. 1). Yet echoes of both continue to linger in the orthodox textbooks. Henry Mintzberg's (1990) recent critique of strategic management orthodoxy exposes this subtext with painful clarity.

By careful analysis of key texts, especially those associated with the Harvard Business School, Mintzberg (1990) identifies what he terms the 'basic premises' of Classical thought. The first premise, that strategy formation should be a controlled conscious process of thought, derives directly from the notion of rational economic man. The premise that responsibility for control and consciousness must rest with the chief executive officer – 'THE strategist', as Mintzberg (1990: 176) puts it – reflects both the individualism of economics and the military notion of the solitary general at the tip of the pyramid of command. Military notions of command also inform the premise that strategies emerge from the decision-making process fully formulated, explicit and articulated: strategies are in a sense orders for others to carry out. Thence too comes Mintzberg's (1990) last premise, that implementation is a distinct phase in the strategy process, only coming after the earlier phase of explicit and conscious formulation. It is this which underlies the image of the strategist as general in his tent, despatching orders to the front. The actual carrying-out of orders is relatively unproblematic, assured by military discipline and obedience.

In sum, the Classical approach to strategy places great confidence in the readiness and capacity of managers to adopt profit-maximizing strategies through rational long-term planning. Accordingly, the Classic texts from Ansoff (1965) to Grant (1998) furnish us with an abundant technology of matrices, formulae and flowcharts. The 'seat-of-the-pants' managerial style of William Durant at General Motors is banished to the past. Flattered by the image of Olympian detachment, lured by the promise of technique-driven success, managers are seduced into the Classical fold.

# Evolutionary perspectives on strategy

Evolutionary approaches to strategy are less confident about top management's ability to plan and act rationally. Rather than relying on managers, they expect markets to secure profit maximization. Stressing competitive processes of natural selection, Evolutionary theorists do not necessarily (prescribe rational planning methods; rather, they argue that whatever methods managers adopt, it will only be the best performers that survive. Managers need not be rational optimizers because 'evolution is nature's cost–benefit analysis' (Einhorn and Hogarth 1988: 114).

Evolutionary theorists often make an explicit parallel between economic competition and the natural law of the jungle. Bruce Henderson, founder of the Boston Consulting Group, complains:

> Classical economic theories of competition are so simplistic and sterile that they have been less contributions to understanding than obstacles. These theories postulate rational, self-interested behavior by individuals who interact through market exchanges in a fixed and static legal system of property and contracts. (1989: 143)

According to Henderson, these postulates are too abstract and unrealistic. Competition is not a matter of detached calculation but a constant struggle for survival in an overpopulated, dense and steamy jungle. He concludes (1989: 143): 'Human beings may be at the top of the ecological chain, but we are still members of the ecological community. That is why Darwin is probably a better guide to business competition than economists are.'

In fact, many economists had reached a similar conclusion long before Bruce Henderson, R.C. Hall and Hitch's (1939) simple field enquiries had discovered that business practice was far from that prescribed by the ideal of rational economic man: not only did managers fail to set output at the theoretically profit-maximizing level where marginal costs exactly equal marginal revenues, but they had no idea what their marginal cost and revenue curves were anyway. Economists adjusted to this business stupidity by letting the markets do the thinking.

Thus Alchian (1950) appealed directly to the biological principle of natural selection to propose an evolutionary theory of the firm that downgraded managerial strategy and emphasized environmental fit. The most appropriate strategies within a given market emerge as competitive processes allow the relatively better performers to survive and flourish, while the weaker performers are irresistibly squeezed out of the ecological niche. The evolution of industries typically follows the pattern of the French and United Kingdom automobile industries illustrated in Figure 2.1. As a new niche opens up, it is initially flooded by new entrants, but then overpopulation drives a process of fierce competition that allows only the most 'fit' to survive (Hannan 1997). As Milton Friedman (1953) famously argued, it hardly matters if managers do not rationally profit-maximize so long as competitive markets ensure that only those who do somehow achieve the profit-maximizing position will survive over the long run. Markets, not managers, choose the prevailing strategies within a particular environment.

The Evolutionary economists initially emphasized competition in product markets as the means of winnowing out inefficient competitors. Unfortunately, as critics such as Penrose (1952) were quick to remark, many large contemporary firms dominate the markets that are supposed to discipline them, with sufficient oligopolistic power to be well buffered against competitive pressures. For these companies, strategy is about selecting markets, rather than being selected by markets. More recent elaborations of Evolutionary theory (e.g. Pelikan 1989) have therefore emphasized other markets, especially managerial labour markets, the market for capital and the market for corporate control, as selecting the best performers for survival. In this broader view, incompetent managers are eliminated as they fail to get promoted or hired, as they find themselves unable to get

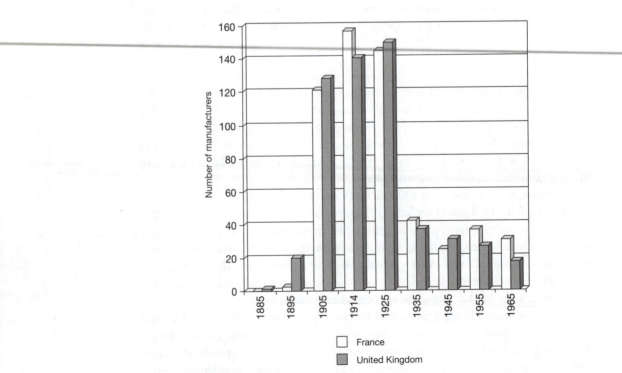

**Figure 2.1** *Populations of automobile manufacturers in France and the United Kingdom, 1885–1965* **(Hannan 1997)**

bank loans, or as falling share prices provoke either shareholder revolt or hostile takeover. Thus, by one market or another, the pressure for profit maximization is maintained.

[. . .]

Evolutionary theory has some intriguing implications for managerial strategy. Henderson (1989) draws directly from the biological 'principle of competitive exclusion' established by the Russian biologist Gause in 1934. Gause had found that when he put two small organisms of the same genus but different species in a jar with a limited supply of food, they would survive; however, if the two organisms were from the same species, with exactly the same amount of food, they would die. Coexistence is impossible if organisms make their living in an identical way. Henderson's (1989) conclusion is that business survival in a competitive environment depends on strategies of differentiation.

The challenge for strategy is that many Evolutionary theorists doubt the capacity of organizations to achieve differentiation and adaptation in a deliberate and sustainable way. As the dinosaurs found, complex biological organisms usually adapt more slowly than their environments. Human organizations are often the same. Drawing on Processual insights into the difficulties of managing change, Evolutionary theorists emphasize the limited capacity of organizations to anticipate and respond purposively to shifts in the environment. Aldrich (1979) argues that environmental fit is more likely to be the result of chance and good fortune, even error, than the outcome of deliberate strategic choice. Alchian (1950) too warns against overestimating the power of strategy. For him, firms are tossed about by unpredictable and uncontrollable market forces. Like plants which flourish because the wind blew their seeds onto the sunny side of a wall, business success is generally the result of happenstance – just being at the right place at the right time.

> Among all competitors, those whose particular conditions happened to be most appropriate for testing and adoption will be 'selected' as survivors . . . The survivors may appear to be those having *adapted* themselves to the environment, whereas the truth may well be that the environment has *adopted* them. (Alchian 1950: 213–14; emphasis in the original)

Indeed, investing in long-term strategies can be counter-productive. Organizations maximize their chances of survival in the short term by achieving perfect fit against their current environment. In a competitive environment, flexibility is evolutionarily inefficient. Strategy is too expensive; the investor in long-term strategies of innovation, diversification and change can always be undercut by the short-term, inflexible, low-cost producer. Competitive markets thus introduce a bias to strategic conservatism. According to Hannan and Freeman (1988: 25), 'Organizational selection processes favour organizations with relatively inert structures, organizations that cannot change strategy and structure as their environments change.'

Evolutionists not only insist that markets are typically too competitive for expensive strategizing and too unpredictable to outguess. They also hold that markets are too efficient to permit the creation of any sustainable advantage. In a competitive environment, elaborate strategies can only deliver a temporary advantage: competitors will be quick to imitate and erode any early benefits. Classical techniques in particular are unlikely to deliver permanent superiority. The market for such knowledge is too perfect. As McCloskey observes:

> formal methods will not earn abnormally high profits for long. The formality makes them easy to copy. Going to business school is not a way to acquire immense wealth, because it is too easy get in. (1990: 128)

The market ensures that everybody else has access to Michael Porter's (1985) writings on competitive advantage too.

For Evolutionists, then, strategy can be a dangerous delusion. Except for the minority of firms with significant market power, the prosaic conclusion of Oliver Williamson (1991: 87) is simply that 'economy is the best strategy'. The only real comparative advantage is relative efficiency. Managers must concentrate on their costs, especially the 'transaction costs' of organizing and co-ordinating. Williamson writes:

> a strategizing effort will rarely prevail if a program is burdened by significant cost excesses in production, distribution or organization. All the clever ploys and positioning, aye, all the king's horses and all the king's men, will rarely save a project that is seriously flawed in first-order economizing respects. (1991: 75)

Williamson's advice, then, is not to get distracted from the basics.

If deliberate strategizing is ineffective, then what matters is an abundance of diverse new initiatives from which the environment can select the best. Hannan and Freeman's (1988) 'population ecology' perspective suggests that overall efficiency can best be secured by ensuring a steady stream of new entrants into any organizational population, from which the relatively ill-adapted are ruthlessly selected out. Rates of new firm formation and failure, therefore, are equal and complementary indicators of economic health and dynamism. Thus the helter-skelter rise in the number of business failures in the United States – multiplying eightfold between 1980 and 1997 (Figure 2.2) – merely reflects the more effective natural selection processes brought about by competitive markets. The rise in new business start-ups over the same period has kept the American economy's 'gene pool' refreshed and replenished. It is little use trying to prop up and reform existing underperformers. Firms that are poorly adapted to current conditions should simply make way to let new businesses try their chances at achieving environmental fit. Market convert Tom Peters (1992: 618) actually applauds high business failure rates.

The Evolutionary perspective clearly has rather gloomy implications for strategy. Certainly, differentiation is a sound principle within a competitive environment, but it is doubtful whether this can be achieved deliberately or permanently. The construction of grand long-term strategies may be so much vain

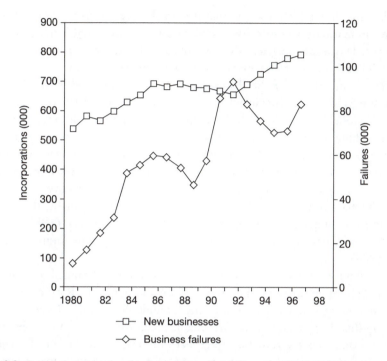

**Figure 2.2** *Darwinian America: business starts and failures in the United States* (**Economic Report to the President; www.dnb.com: note expanded coverage 1984 onwards**)

distraction; managers would do much better to get down to the modest business of making sure that what they do now is done as efficiently as possible. If managers must attempt to anticipate change, then they would be wise not to try to outguess the market by investing heavily in a single major plan. The most effective approach may be to experiment with as many different small initiatives as possible, to wait and see which flourish and which fail, and then to build on the successes whilst ruthlessly eliminating the failures. It was this Darwinian approach that guided Sony in its strategy during the 1980s, when it launched more than 160 different Walkman versions in the American market, never retaining more than about twenty versions on the market at the same time (Sanchez and Sudharshan 19 2). The Evolutionary advice, then, is that, in searching for the best strategy, it is best to let the environment do the selecting, not the managers.

# Processual approaches to strategy

Processual approaches to strategy generally share the Evolutionary scepticism about rational strategy-making, but are less confident about markets ensuring profit-maximizing outcomes. For Processualists, both organizations and markets are often sticky, messy phenomena, from which strategies emerge with much confusion and in small steps. Indeed, they argue that it is to the very imperfections of organizational and market processes that managers owe their strategies and competitive advantages. The best Processual advice is not to strive after the unattainable ideal of rational fluid action, but to accept and work with the world as it is.

The foundations for the Processual approach were laid by the innovative work of the American Carnegie School – most prominently, Richard Cyert, James March and Nobel Prize-winner Herbert Simon. Together, they advanced a model of strategy-making that is still being restated with radical claims to novelty more than four decades later. Rejecting the specious unit of rational economic man on the one hand and the perfections of competitive markets on the other, they were led to take the internal complexity of organizations seriously. Here they uncovered two of the themes that have now become fundamentals of Processual thought: the cognitive limits on rational action, since extended by Henry Mintzberg (1987, 1994) in particular; and the micro-politics of organizations, developed by Andrew Pettigrew (1973, 1985).

Aiming for a more psychologically realistic theory of human behaviour, the Carnegie School emphasized the limits of human cognition. Rational economic man is a fiction: in practice, people are only 'boundedly rational' (Cyert and March 1963). By this they mean that we are unable to consider more than a handful of factors at a time; we are reluctant to embark on unlimited searches for relevant information; we are biased in our interpretation of data; and finally we are prone to accept the first satisfactory option that presents itself, rather than insisting on the best (March and Simon 1958; Cyert and March 1963). Even momentary consideration of our everyday behaviour will probably confirm the basic plausibility of these assumptions. The result is that the environmental scanning, data analyses and calculated comparisons of strategic options advocated by Classical theorists of strategy tend always to be flawed and incomplete. This is just human nature.

The micro-political view of organizations was established by the Carnegie School's recognition of the individual interests represented in any enterprise. Firms are not united in optimizing a single utility, such as profit. Rather, they are coalitions of individuals each of whom brings their own personal objectives and cognitive biases to the organization. Organizational members bargain between each other to arrive at a set of joint goals more or less acceptable to them all. The bargaining process involves both many compromises and what Cyert and March (1963: 31) describe as 'policy sidepayments' in return for agreement. For example, the Production Director may accept a reduced investment programme in order to secure at least some new machines this year, while supporting the Technical Director's bid for a new research and development initiative in electronics just to keep her on-side. Strategy is thus the product of political compromise, not profit-maximizing calculation.

The combination of political bargaining and bounded rationality strongly favours strategic conservatism. The need for change will only be imperfectly recognized, and anyway change is suspected because it is likely to set off a period of internal civil war until a new 'dominant coalition' is established (Cyert and March

1963). Strategic behaviour therefore tends to become entrenched in the 'routines' and 'standard operating procedures' imposed by political exigency and cognitive limits. Rather than perfectly rational strategies, organizations opt simply for 'adaptive rationality', the gradual adjusting of routines as awkward messages from a dynamic environment eventually force themselves on managers' attention.

Cyert and March (1953) argued that firms can get away with these slow adjustments because, contrary to the views of the more stringent Evolutionists, markets are in fact typically quite tolerant of underperformance. Firms often enjoy sufficient market power to be able to earn reasonable profits without maximum effort. Shareholders are unable to detect this underperformance because, like everybody else, they are not rational or informed enough to know. Thus firms can build sufficient 'organizational slack' to buffer themselves against the need for strategic change, delivering just enough profits to keep everybody reasonably happy. In this sense, firms 'satisfice' rather than profit-maximize (Cyert and March 1963: 41).

This modest view of organizations and the people who run them has significant implications for strategy. The Processual perspective radically downgrades the importance of rational analysis; it limits the search for strategic flexibility; and it reduces expectations of success. In practice, strategy-makers do not strive ceaselessly for the optimal solution, but satisfy themselves with following the established routines and heuristics of the organization. Indeed, as Nelson and Winter (1982: 133) observe, 'according to the concept of strategy that has been developed by a number of investigators associated with the Harvard Business School, the fundamental heuristic imperative for top management is: Develop a strategy'.

But strategy statements themselves can become routinized heuristics, working to constrain the field of opportunity and guiding decisions into established paths. Say Nelson and Winter, in strong Processual mood:

> it is quite inappropriate to conceive of firm behavior in terms of deliberate choice from a broad menu of alternatives that some external observer considers to be 'available' opportunities for the organization. The menu is not broad, but narrow and idiosyncratic; it is built into the firm's routines, and most of the 'choosing' is also accomplished automatically by these routines. (1982: 134)

Strategies are not chosen; they are programmed.

Strategies, then, are a way in which managers try to simplify and order a world which is too complex and chaotic for them to comprehend. The regular procedures and precise quantifications of strategic planning are comforting rituals, managerial security blankets in a hostile world. Thus Weick (1990) tells the story of a Hungarian detachment that got lost in the Alps during military manoeuvres. As it snowed for two days, the soldiers despaired and laid themselves down to die in the frozen wilderness. Then suddenly one of the soldiers found a map in his pocket, the detachment took heart, and they marched confidently out of the mountains. Safe back at camp, they discovered the map was of the Pyrenees. For Weick (1990), strategic plans are often like this map: it does not matter much if they are wrong, so long as they give managers the confidence and sense of purpose to act. If the firm sits waiting for the right map, it will freeze; if it gets up and moves, it will somehow or other find direction, acquire experience and make its own opportunities (Box 2.1).

---

## Box 2.1
## Surfing the edge of chaos

The notion of 'emergence' in strategy finds increasing support in 'chaos theory', the new science of complex adaptive systems. This new science is concerned with how order tends naturally to spring from chaos. It doesn't take precise planning from the top, only a few simple rules guiding action from the bottom.

Brown and Eisenhardt (1999) give the example of 'boids' – a computer simulation of autonomous, bird-like agents. Something remarkable happens when these mindlessly moving agents are given just three simple rules: try to maintain a minimum distance from other objects, including other boids; try to match the velocity of nearby boids; and try to move to the centre of the mass of nearby boids. Regardless of their starting positions on the screen, and of the number and positioning of obstacles, the boids always end up doing the same thing: forming a flock. There's no need for leaders; order emerges naturally from myriads of small adaptive adjustments.

The point about being on the 'edge of chaos' is to have enough structure to allow for patterns to emerge, but not so much as to cause inflexibility and cost. The American company 3M allows scientists to do whatever they like with 15 per cent of their time, but within a framework that insists on taking 30 per cent of sales from products less than four years old while imposing tough targets for profit and growth. Innovative ideas – such as the Post-it or Thinsulate – bubble up from below but fall into place within a coherent strategic frame. Surfing on the edge of chaos means riding the wave – never falling behind and never falling in.

*Sources*: Brown and Eisenhardt 1999; Pascale 1999

---

In this way, the Classic sequence of formulation first, implementation second, gets reversed: strategy is discovered in action (March 1976). Alfred Sloan's (1963) distinction between 'policy creation' and 'policy execution' begins to blur. Doubting top managers' capacity to prescribe effective strategies in the splendid isolation of their executive suites, Mintzberg (1987) proposes the metaphor of strategy as 'craft'. The craftswoman is intimately involved with her materials: she shapes her clay by personal touch, imperfections inspire her to artistic improvisation, hands and mind work together in a process of constant adaptation. So should it be with strategy. In a world too complex and full of surprises to predict, the strategist needs to retain the closeness, the awareness and the adaptability of the craftsperson, rather than indulging in the hubris of grand long-range planning. For Mintzberg, crafting strategy is a continuous and adaptive process, with formation and implementation inextricably entangled.

This view of strategy is an unglamorous one: hands get dirty, steps are small and there are few bold lunges into the unknown long term. But this slow progress is not to be despised. As Lindblom (1959) claimed, there is 'a science of muddling through', involving cautious comparison of successive options and careful maintenance of consensus. The gradual adaptive approach to strategy has its own rationality, which Quinn (1980: 89) terms 'logical incrementalism'. The superior rationality of logical incrementalism lies in its acceptance of our own bounded rationality: 'Smart strategists appreciate that they cannot always be smart enough to think through everything in advance' (Mintzberg 1987: 69). Honest about his or her limits, the logical incrementalist is committed to a process of experimentation and learning.

The incrementalist approach is not necessarily a tactical one. It may be informed by an underlying logic, or 'strategic intent', that is both sufficiently clear to provide a sense of direction and sufficiently broad to allow flexibility and opportunism along the way, as for instance Komatsu's ambition simply to 'encircle Caterpillar' (Hamel and Prahalad 1989). More radically, Mintzberg and Waters (1985) suggest, the underlying strategic logic may be perceived only after the event. Strategies are often 'emergent', their coherence accruing through action and perceived in retrospect. Thus Intel's famous switch from the Dynamic Random Access Memories (DRAMs) market to its new role as a dominant player in microprocessors was achieved during the 1980s through an accumulating series of incremental investment decisions that had consistently valued the prospects of the new business more highly than the old. Yet all the while the company's explicit strategy and self-definition was still to be a 'memory company', its original business. As late as 1985, one-third of the research and development budget was still devoted to the 'strategically important' memory business, even when the company had been reduced to a negligible 2 to 3 per cent market share. As Chief Executive Officer Andy Grove observed: 'Don't ask managers "What is your strategy?" Look at what they do!' (Burgelman 1996: 423).

This incremental approach to strategy is reinforced by Processualists who emphasize the stickiness of external markets. For the 'resource-based' strategy theorists (e.g. Grant 1998), market imperfections inhibit the opportunity-maximizing strategies proposed by Classicists. The resources with which firms compete are not all to be bought and sold in markets according to the shifting matrix of strategic opportunities and threats (Collis and Montgomery 1995). Resource-based theories of the firm stress how a firm's resources include tacit skills, patterns of co-operation, and intangible assets that take time and learning to evolve. These resources cannot be traded, changed or imitated with ease (Box 2.2). The origin of a firm's competitive advantage, therefore, lies in what is unique and embedded in its resources – these constitute its core, distinctive competences (Grant 1998).

---

**Box 2.2**

## The knowledge resource

In today's knowledge-based economy, superior knowledge is likely to be the most valuable resource of all. Knowledge is valuable precisely because it is hard to manage and hard to trade. Most useful knowledge is tacit, not easily captured in managerial databases or imitated by competitors. Knowledge resides inside the heads of lower ranking staff, not in the files of top management. Knowledge is dynamic in unpredictable ways – experience and events are always adding to it, regardless of formal efforts at research and development. Knowledge is hard to trade, because the acquirer cannot know its value until it is actually used. Knowledge is often highly immobile, because embedded in the routines, culture and teams of a particular organization. For all these reasons, the value of knowledge is unlikely to diffuse away through normal processes of market competition and exchange.

Equally, all these knowledge characteristics impose constraints on the strategy process. Especially in knowledge-intensive firms, such as professional services or new technology enterprises, strategy is as likely to emerge bottom-up as top-down. After all, it is at the bottom where the knowledge lies and is continuously recreated. Top managers ignore this source of value in their strategy process at their peril.

*Sources*: Conner and Prahalad 1996; Tsoukas 1996; Zack 1999

---

In other words, the sources of sustainable superior performance lie internally, in the capacity to exploit and renew distinctive resources, rather than externally, in simply positioning the firm in the right markets. Strategy involves building on core competences, not chasing each and every opportunity. Hamel (1991: 83) accuses: 'the traditional "competitive strategy" paradigm (e.g. Porter 1980), with its focus on product-market positioning, focuses on only the last few hundred yards of what may be a skill-building marathon'. However attractive market opportunities might be, entry strategies will fail in the implementation if the firm lacks the requisite skills and resources internally or underestimates the difficulty of acquiring them externally. What matters in strategy, therefore, is the long-term construction and consolidation of distinctive internal competences. In this view, strategy becomes a patient inwardly aware process, rather than the fluid externally oriented pursuit of opportunity emphasized by Classical industry structure analyses.

Thus the Processualist focus on the imperfections of organizational and market processes yields at least four conceptions of strategy radically different from the Classical perspective: strategy may be a decision-making heuristic, a device to simplify reality into something managers can actually cope with; plans may just be managerial security blankets, providing reassurance as much as guidance; strategy may not precede action but may only emerge retrospectively, once action has taken place; strategy is not just about choosing markets and then policing performance, but about carefully cultivating internal competences. Many of the confident precepts of the Classicists are put in jeopardy: suddenly, it seems that goals are slippery and vague, long-term policy statements vain delusions, and the separation of formulation from implementation a self-serving top management myth.

For the pure Processualists of the Carnegie School, all this means that strategy is inescapably about satisficing, settling for less than the optimal. But more managerial Processualists turn the messy reality of organizations and markets to advantage. In practice, the technical sophistication of the Classicists amounts to naive idealism. It is above all by recognizing and accommodating real-world imperfections that managers can be most effective. Giving due attention to implementation, exploiting imperfect markets to build distinctive competences, cultivating flexibility for incremental adaptation – these are really the means to maximum performance.

## Systemic perspectives on strategy

Against the sometimes nihilistic propositions of Evolutionary and Processual theorists, Systemic theorists do retain faith in the capacity of organizations to plan forward and to act effectively within their environments. Where they differ from the Classicists, however, is in their refusal to accept the forms and ends of Classical rationality as anything more than historically and culturally specific phenomena. Systemic theorists insist that the rationales underlying strategy are peculiar to particular sociological contexts.

A central tenet of Systemic theory is that decision-makers are not simply detached calculating individuals interacting in purely economic transactions, but people rooted deeply in densely interwoven social systems. Granovetter's (1985) notion of social 'embeddedness' captures the sense that economic activity cannot be placed in a separate rarified sphere of impersonal financial calculation. In reality, people's economic behaviour embedded in a network of social relations that may involve their families, state, their professional and educational backgrounds, even their religion and ethnicity (Swedberg et al. 1987; Whittington 1992). These networks influence both the means and ends of action, defining what is appropriate and reasonable behaviour for their members. Behaviour that may look irrational or inefficient to the Classical theorist may be perfectly rational and efficient according to the local criteria and *modus operandi* of the particular social context.

Systemic theorists propose, therefore, that firms differ according to the social and economic systems in which they are embedded. They are not all perfect profit-maximizers, as they choose to be in Classical theory and they are obliged to be in Evolutionary theory. But nor are they just the particularistic organizations of the Processual perspective, whose idiosyncrasies are the product of internal limits and compromises. In the Systemic view, the norms that guide strategy derive not so much from the cognitive bounds of the human psyche as from the cultural rules of the local society. The internal contests of organizations involve not just the micro-politics of individuals and departments but the social groups, interests and resources of the surrounding context. The variables of the Systemic perspective include class and professions, nations and states, families and gender.

Important, therefore, to Systemic theory are differences between countries' social systems and changes within countries' social systems. As Whitley (1999) has shown for southeast Asia, prevailing forms of business may vary widely according to the local interplay of state, familial and market structures. Thus, in South Korea, a traditionally strong state has promoted the creation of the vast chaebol conglomerates; in nearby Taiwan, by contrast, the combination of an exclusionary Kuomintang state with the peculiar culture of Chinese family business has created an entrepreneurial economy of small and medium-sized firms, loosely linked by familial networks. Whitley (1991: 24) concludes: 'different kinds of enterprise structures become feasible and successful in particular social contexts, especially where cultures are homogeneous and share strong boundaries with nation states'. For all the contemporary talk of globalization, the peculiarities of local histories and local societies still matter.

Indeed, most large companies are hardly global at all. The Gestrin et al. (2000) survey of more than 200 Fortune Global 500 large corporations finds that on average roughly 60 per cent of their turnover and their assets were still concentrated in their home markets. Growth in international turnover and assets had been slow throughout the 1990s and the profit share from overseas had been disproportionately weak even before the Asian crisis of 1997–98. The world's largest international engineering conglomerates illustrate the point: only 41 per cent of General Electric's sales in 1999 were outside the United States, 35 per cent of assets and just one-third of profits (www.ge.com); at Hitachi, just 30 per cent of 1999 sales were outside Japan, 17 percent of assets, but, so depressed was the Japanese market, 69 per cent of profits (www.hitachi.co.jp). In Hu's (1992) sceptical phrase, companies like these are not so much global multinationals as domestic companies with international subsidiaries.

[. . .]

Thus even the largest multinationals can retain strong local character. As Walker (1988: 395) observes, in its image and management style 'General Motors remains a thoroughly Midwestern company.' Apple is very Californian. IKEA is Swedish. Companies – whether as competitors, customers, partners or suppliers – vary widely according to their local contexts. Rather than rising above their origins, even multinationals may be deeply influenced by the industrial cultures, class structures, politics and professional biases of their home nations.

Indeed, the very notion of 'strategy' may be culturally peculiar. Arising in the particular conditions of North America in the post-war period, the Classical conception of strategy does not always fit comfortably in other cultures. Pascale (1982) reports that the Japanese do not even have a phrase for 'corporate strategy'. 'Strategy' has strong connotations of freewill and self-control, but many cultures prefer to interpret events less as the product of deliberate human action, and more as the result of God, fate, luck or history (Boyacigiller and Adler 1991). For example, fundamentalist Muslims see life following a path pre-ordained by God, while the Chinese often explain events in terms of 'Joss', a combination of luck and fate. To these deterministic cultures, the idea of 'strategy' embodies a voluntarism that is entirely alien. Boyacigiller and Adler's (1991) analysis suggests that Classical notions of strategy are the product of a historically peculiar coincidence between the American 'can-do' culture and the steady growth and 'Pax Americana' of the 1950s and early 1960s. Strategy as a managerial practice developed in a context of cultural voluntarism and economic and political security that was uniquely favourable to long-term strategic planning.

The American origins of the strategy concept may also constrain our understanding of what strategy involves. Wilks (1990) finds that the Anglo-Saxon cultures of the United States and the United Kingdom are biased towards an individualistic free-enterprise model of strategy that denigrates explicit reliance upon the state. By contrast, the traditional nationalism of the French and German states, and the developmental role of the Japanese state, have given to the Anglo-Saxon world's major competitors industrial cultures in which the enlisting of state resources is seen as a natural and important part of strategic management (Wilks 1990). Thus national approaches to strategy can be heavily distorted by what is locally regarded as culturally legitimate.

From this perspective, the Classical and Evolutionary emphases on markets and profitability, to the exclusion of state resources and national interests, are simply the product of very particular historical and social circumstances. This is not to say that they are necessarily 'wrong'. The current sociological appreciation of the 'institutional environments' of organizations (Meyer and Rowan 1977; DiMaggio and Powell 1983) highlights the social pressures to conform to local forms of rationality. American business works within a culture which respects profit, values technical procedures and regards the free market as an article of faith. In this context, any individual business-leader who repudiates outright the forms of Classical strategy-making risks losing his or her credibility in the face of auditors, customers, financial markets and governmental regulators, all of whom can exert considerable influence on success. Whether or not formal planning in the Classical mode is economically effective, if that is how key elements of the institutional environment expect business to be done, then it is sociologically efficient to at least go through the motions. The rationality of the Classical approach to strategy may be a social construct, but nevertheless it is one that it can be dangerous to ignore.

Yet it remains important to be clear how particular conceptions of strategy reflect and reinforce the limitations of a particular society. Indeed, Shrivastava (1986) goes so far as to allege that the whole discipline of orthodox strategic management actually constitutes a self-servingly conservative political ideology. He points to how the Classic theorists' normative emphasis on top-down management and profit maximization as the ultimate unifying goal serves to reproduce the conditions of hierarchically organized capitalist society in general. The firm is typically represented as a 'co-operative system' (e.g. Barnard 1938), for whom the arrogation by top management of goal-setting and decision-making is merely a matter of administrative efficiency. Classical techniques of environmental analysis take the existing structures of society for granted and tend anyway to focus specifically on market factors, downplaying the relevance of social, cultural and political demands on the organization. Thus Michael Porter (1980: xix) blithely relegates his assumption of profit objectives to a footnote, and concentrates his industry analysis on five sets of economic forces amongst which government and labour are almost entirely lost.

Shrivastava (1986) concludes that orthodox strategic management is not a neutral, objective, scientific discipline, but an ideology that serves to normalize the existing structures of American society and universalize the goals of its dominant elite. Because it is designed to preserve the status quo, Classical strategic management traps strategists within a particularly narrow range of strategic options. To invoke state resources, or to challenge the top-down logic of strategic orthodoxy, is to play dangerously with the established social order.

The ideologies guiding strategy in different countries can be influenced strongly by different cultural traditions around the world. The American culture is hard-nosed and individualistic. In repeated surveys of international executives, Hampden-Turner and Trompenaars (1993) report that American attitudes stand out consistently from many of their competitors'. When asked whether the only goal of a company was profit, 40 per cent of American executives answered yes, against only 8 per cent from Japan and 11 per cent from Singapore. In a structured comparative analysis of American and South Korean managers' strategic decision-making criteria, project cash flow and return on investment were amongst the top three for the Americans. For the Koreans, it was sales growth and market share that were critical: cash-flow and return on investment ranked tenth and eleventh out of thirteen possible criteria (Hitt et al. 1997). In its understanding of what matters in strategy, the United States is clearly something of an outlier. But it is American practice and American research that dominate strategy textbooks world-wide.

[. . .]

More than culture is involved in defining local approaches to strategy. Differences in strategy are so enduring, and patterns so hard to change, because they are also founded on real economic, social or political conditions. Recent analyses have explored the implications for strategy of different ownership structures in particular. The detached and relatively diffuse relationships between shareholders and their companies that are taken for granted in the Anglo-Saxon economies are unusual elsewhere round the world (Scott 1997). In the Germanic economies – Germany itself, Austria, Switzerland and to a lesser extent the Netherlands and Scandinavia – banks and other financial institutions play a central and interventionist role, with long-term relationships. For example, Deutsche Bank was a prime mover in bringing its two clients together to create the merged company Daimler Benz in 1926, and three-quarters of a century later, it was still the largest shareholder in the new DaimlerChrysler company, holding 12 per cent in 1999 (Gall 1995; www.daimlerchrysler.com). Deutsche Bank also has a 9 per cent stake in the great German insurance company, Allianz, which reciprocates with a 5 per cent stake in the other direction. Although changes in German corporate law may prompt an unravelling, at the end of the twentieth century Allianz still occupied a central place in German capitalism, with substantial stakes in key utility companies, major chemicals and engineering companies, as well as the leading financial institutions. Not very much happens in German business without the Allianz or its allies having a say.

[. . .]

In China, on the other hand, 34 per cent of the nation's output and no less than 110 million workers are accounted for by state-owned firms (Bruton et al. 2000).

[. . .]

Theorists of a new 'managerial capitalism' (Marris 1964; Berle and Means 1967) suggest a growing split between ownership and control within large Western companies. Since the 1920s, firms have increasingly been governed by professional managers rather than by their true owners. These theorists accuse managers of running their firms in their own interests, sacrificing profitability for the perquisites of growth. From this Systemic perspective, then, Alfred Sloan's Classic goal of maximizing return on investment has been superseded by managerial objectives such as security, empire-building, high rewards and high status. Abundant evidence for such managerial self-interest can be found in studies of top management compensation. The continuous upward spiral of chief executive rewards in America, despite chronically poor economic performance, certainly does not suggest that top management is as unselfishly dedicated to shareholders' interests as Classical theory likes to think.

[. . .]

For practising managers, then, the special advantage of the Systemic approach lies in its heightened sociological sensitivity. By alerting individual managers to the key elements of the social systems in which they work, the Systemic approach can widen the search for resources and deepen the appreciation of competitors. Every strategist should analyse his or her particular social characteristics, and those of his or her immediate social system, in order to grasp the variety of social resources and rules of conduct available (Whittington 1992). Managers can thereby free themselves from exclusive reliance on the capitalist resources of ownership and hierarchy, and open up the political resources of the state, the network resources of ethnicity or, if male, the patriarchal resources of masculinity. Sociologically sensitized, managers can also play reflexively on the ideological resources of their profession – exploit the Classical apparatus of strategic management not just for its technical answers but also for the enhanced legitimacy won by glossy display. The value of a MBA can lie in its packaging as much as its content. As for competitors, no presumptions should be made about their strategies without analysis of their social as well as industry structures. In planning moves and counter-moves, Systemically aware managers will not assume that competitor logics are the same as their own. In international competition in particular, competitors' political power may be as important as their market power.

To conclude, the Systemic perspective challenges the universality of any single model of strategy. The objectives of strategy and the modes of strategy-making depend on the strategists' social characteristics and the social context within which they operate. From this perspective, the Classical approach emerges as culturally highly specific – after all, it originated in just two large American companies, Du Pont and General Motors, controlled by a single family during the 1920s. It may work well in certain contexts, and often the appearances at least of Classical rationality may be required anyway, but it will not translate everywhere. To insist on a socially alien form of strategy-making – whether in a Japanese *keiretsu* or a patriotic American business – is to court disaster. Moreover, to assume that your competitors or customers operate according to the same model of strategy as yourself risks substantial strategic miscalculation. A state-backed Chinese enterprise or a growth-oriented managerially controlled firm will not respond to competitive signals in the same way as a Classically run business; and, in any stand-off with an Anglo-Saxon profit-maximizer, both are likely to hold out much longer. The main message of the Systemic perspective, then, is that strategy must be sociologically sensitive.

## Conclusions

The four approaches to strategy introduced in this chapter differ widely in their advice to management. The Classical school confidently prescribes a rational, detached and sequential approach, offered as a universal norm. The Evolutionary and Processual perspectives are more cautious, each sceptical of strategists' capacity to direct strategy effectively in this rational hierarchical way. For Evolutionists, environmental change is typically too fast, too unpredictable and too implacable to anticipate and pre-empt; their advice is to concentrate on day-to-day viability while trying to keep options open. Processualists doubt whether either organizations or markets work with the ruthless efficiency that Classicists and Evolutionists respectively claim, and incline therefore towards patient strategies of incremental adjustment and cultivation of core competences. Finally, Systemic theorists take a more relativistic stance, insisting that both the ends and means of strategy depend on the character of prevailing social systems, and that therefore even the hyper-rationality of the Classical school may be appropriate in some social contexts – but only some.

The main characteristics of the four approaches are summed up in Table 2.1. For the Classical school, strategy should be formal and explicit, its objective unambiguous profit maximization. Evolutionists generally agree on the second part – for high profitability is essential to survival – but regard efforts to secure this through extravagant long-term strategies as so much futile distraction. Efficiency is the Evolutionists' watchword. Processual theorists too dismiss Classical formality, seeing strategy as 'crafted', its goals vague and any logic often only emerging in retrospect. But where Processualists find economic irrationality, Systemic analysts search for other rationalities: for them, modes of strategy are deeply embedded in particular social systems, and their processes and objectives may be perfectly rational according to the criteria of the locally dominant groups.

The main focus of each of these approaches varies accordingly. For the Classical school, success or failure is determined internally, through the quality of managerial planning, analysis and calculation. The Processualists are inward-looking too, concerned with political bargaining processes the adjustment of managerial cognitive biases and the building of core skills and competences. The two other approaches emphasize the external. Evolutionists stress the determining impact of markets, and the Darwinian processes of natural selection. Systemic theorists argue that, to understand what is really going on within the organization and amongst competitors, the strategist must be sociologically sensitive.

Table 2.1 *The four perspectives on strategy*

| | Classic | Processual | Evolutionary | Systemic |
|---|---|---|---|---|
| Strategy | Formal | Crafted | Efficient | Embedded |
| Rationale | Profit maximization | Vague | Survival | Local |
| Focus | Internal (plans) | Internal (politics/cognitions) | External (markets) | External (societies) |
| Processes | Analytical | Bargaining/learning | Darwinian | Social |
| Key influences | Economics/military | Psychology | Economics/biology | Sociology |
| Key authors | Chandler; Ansoff; Porter | Cyert and March; Mintzberg; Pettigrew | Hannan and Freeman; Williamson | Granovetter; Whitley |
| Emergence | 1960s | 1970s | 1980s | 1990s |

Table 2.1 also associates each approach with the particular decades of their emergence (cf. Mintzberg et al. 1998). The Classical approach, with its emphasis on planning and analysis, had its heyday in the 1960s, a time of steady growth and American economic and technological confidence. Faith in planning was dented hard by the largely unforeseen oil shocks of 1974 and 1979 (Wilson 1990), leaving the field open for both the Processual stress on bounded rationality and the Evolutionary awe for market forces. Evolutionary arguments gained still greater resonance with the popularity of free-market economics during the 1980s.

The most recent arrival is the Systemic approach to strategy. Although firms have always differed in their objectives and contexts, the closing of the twentieth century and the opening of the new have forced a sharper appreciation of difference. The end to the stark opposition between capitalist America and the communist Soviet bloc has allowed a more nuanced appreciation of the different textures of market economies and the rich variety of their linkages with the rest of society. The former communist economies have themselves bred a wide variety of capitalisms – from the wild Mafia capitalism of Russia to the deliberate 'red capitalism' of China. The dramatic successes – and occasionally equally dramatic failures – of Asian economies have drawn attention to the very different social structures that underlie their business systems. Even in the West, privatization has brought into the economic sphere organizations that must compete, yet which also operate with complex social and economic motives and rely upon many non-market resources. The profit-maximizing entrepreneurs and competitive markets of the textbooks are not the only reality with which strategists must contend. Competitive strategy in complex environments requires a Systemic sensitivity to the diversity of contemporary economic practices.

[. . .]

# References

Alchian, A.A. (1950) 'Uncertainty, evolution and economic theory', *Journal of Political Economy* 58: 211–21.

Aldrich, H.E. (1979) *Organizations and Environments*, Englewood Cliffs, NJ: Prentice Hall.

Ansoff, H.I. (1965) *Corporate Strategy*, Harmondsworth: Penguin.

Aoki, M. (1990) 'Towards an economic model of the Japanese firm', *Journal of Economic Literature* 24 (March): 1–27.

Argyris, C. (1977) 'Double loop learning in organizations', *Harvard Business Review* September–October: 115–25.

Baden-Fuller, C. and Stopford, J. (1994) *Rejuvenating the Mature Business*, Boston, MA: Harvard Business School Press.

Barnard, C. (1938) *The Functions of the Executive*, Boston, MA: Harvard University Press.

Berle, A.A. and Means, G.C. (1967) *The Modern Corporation and Private Property* (originally published 1932), New York: Harvest.

Biggart, N. (1989) *Charismatic Capitalism*, Chicago, IL: University of Chicago Press.

Boyacigiller, N. and Adler, N. (1991) 'The parochial dinosaur: organization science in a global context', *Academy of Management Review* 16 (2): 262–90.

Bracker, J. (1980) 'The historical development of the strategic management concept', *Academy of Management Review* 5 (2): 219–24.

Brown, S. and Eisenhardt, K. (1999) *Competing on the Edge: Strategy as Structured Chaos*, Boston: Harvard Business School Press.

Bruton, G.D., Lan, H. and Lu, Y. (2000) 'China's township and village enterprises: Kelon's competitive edge', *Academy of Management Executive* 14 (1): 19–30.

Burgelman, R.A. (1996) 'Intraorganizational ecology of strategy making and organizational adaptation: theory and field research', in J. Meindl, C. Stubbart and J. Porac (eds) *Cognition within and between Organizations*, Thousand Oaks, CA: Sage.

Chandler, A.D. (1962) *Strategy and Structure. Chapters in the History of the American Industrial Enterprise*, Cambridge, MA: MIT Press.

Collis, D.J. and Montgomery, C.A. (1995) 'Competing on resources: strategy in the 1990s', *Harvard Business Review* July–August: 119–28.

Conner, K. and Prahalad, C.K. (1996) 'A resource-based theory of the firm: knowledge versus opportunism', *Organization Science* 7 (5): 477–501.

Cyert, R.M. and March, J.G. (1956) 'Organisational factors in the theory of monopoly', *Quarterly Journal of Economics* 70 (1): 44–64.

Cyert, R.M. and March, J.G. (1963) *A Behavioural Theory of the Firm*, Englewood Cliffs, NJ: Prentice Hall.

De Wit, B. and Meyer, R. (1999) *Strategy Synthesis*, London: Thomson.

DiMaggio, P. and Powell, W.W. (1983) 'The iron cage revisited: institutional isomorphism and collective rationality in organizational fields', *American Sociological Review* 48: 147–80.

Drucker, P.E. (1946) *The Concept of the Corporation*, London: Heinemann.

Drucker, P.E. (1947) *Big Business*, London: Heinemann.

Einhorn, H.J. and Hogarth, R.M. (1988) 'Behavioural decision theory: process of judgement and choice', in D.E. Bell, H. Raiffa and A. Tversky (eds) *Decision-making: Descriptive Normative and Prescriptive Interactions*, Cambridge: Cambridge University Press.

Friedman, M. (1953) 'The methodology of positive economics', in M. Friedman, *Essays in Positive Economics*, Chicago, IL: University of Chicago Press.

Gall, L. (1995) *The Deutsche Bank, 1870–1995*, London: Weidenfeld and Nicholson.

Gestrin, M.V., Knight, R.F. and Rugman, P.M. (2000) *Templeton Global Performance Index 2000*, Oxford: Templeton College, University of Oxford.

Ghoshal, S., Bartlett, C. and Moran, P. (1999) 'A new manifesto for management', *Sloan Management Review* Spring: 9–20.

Goold, M. (1996) 'Design, planning and strategy: extra time' *California Management Review* 38 (4): 100–3.

Granovetter, M. (1985) 'Economic action and social structure: the problem of embeddedness', *American Journal of Sociology* 91 (3): 481–510.

Grant, R.M. (1991) 'The resource-based theory of competitive advantage: implications for strategy formulation', *California Management Review* 33 (3): 114–22.

Grant, R.M. (1998) *Contemporary Strategy Analysis*, Oxford: Blackwell.

Hall, R.C. and Hitch, C.J. (1939) 'Price theory and business behaviour', *Oxford Economic Papers* 2: 12–45.

Hamel, G. (1991) 'Competition for competence and interpartner learning within international alliances', *Strategic Management Journal* 12: 83–103.

Hamel, G. and Prahalad, C.K. (1989) 'Strategic intent', *Harvard Business Review* May–June: 63–76.

Hampden-Turner, C. and Trompenaars, F. (1993) *The Seven Cultures of Capitalism*, New York: Doubleday.

Hannan, M.T. (1997) 'Inertia, density and the structure of organizational populations: entries in European automobile industries, 1886–1981', *Organization Studies* 18 (2): 192–228.

Hannan, M.T. and Freeman, J. (1988) *Organizational Ecology*, Cambridge, MA: Harvard University Press.

Henderson, B.D. (1989) 'The origin of strategy', *Harvard Business Review* November–December: 139–43.

Hitt, M.A., Dacin, T.C., Tyler, B.B. and Park, D. (1997) 'Understanding the differences in Korean and US executives' strategic orientations', *Strategic Management Journal* 18 (2): 159–67.

Hollander, S. (1987) *Classical Economics*, Oxford: Blackwell.

Hollis, M. and Nell, E.J. (1975) *Rational Economic Man: A Philosophical Critique of Neo-Classical Economics*, Cambridge: Cambridge University Press.

Hoskin, K. (1990) 'Using history to understand theory: a reconceptualisation of the historical genesis of strategy', Paper presented to the European Institute for Advanced Studies in Management Workshop, Venice, October.

Hu, Y.S. (1992) 'Global or stateless corporations are national firms with international operations', *California Management Review* Winter: 115–26.

Hung, S.-C. and Whittington, R. (1997) 'Strategies and institutions: a pluralistic account of strategies in the Taiwanese computer industry', *Organization Studies* 18 (4): 551–67.

James, B.G. (1985) *Business Wargames*, Harmondsworth: Penguin.

Keynes, J.M. (1936) *The General Theory of Employment, Interest and Money*, London: Macmillan.

Knights, D. and Morgan, G. (1990) 'The concept of strategy in sociology: a note of dissent', *Sociology* 24 (3): 275–483.

Knights, D. and Morgan, G. (1991) 'Corporate strategy, organizations and subjectivity', *Organizational Studies* 12 (2): 251–73.

Lengnick-Hall, C. and Wolff, J. (1999) 'Similarities and contradictions in the core logic of three strategy research themes', *Strategic Management Journal* 20 (12): 1109–32.

Lindblom, C.E. (1959) 'The science of muddling through', *Public Administration Review* 19: 79–88.

Lowendahl, B. and Revang, O. (1998) 'Challenges to existing strategy theory in a post-industrial society', *Strategic Management Journal* 19 (8): 755–74.

Mair, A. (1999) 'Learning from Honda', *Journal of Management Studies* 36 (1): 25–46.

March, J.G. (1976) 'The technology of foolishness', in J.G. March and J.P. Olsen (eds) *Ambiguity and Choice in Organizations*, Bergen: Universitetsforlaget.

March, J.G. and Simon, H.A. (1958) *Organizations*, New York: Wiley.

Marris, R. (1964) *The Economic Theory of Managerial Capitalism*, London: Macmillan.

Mayer, M. and Whittington, R. (1999) 'Strategy, structure and "systemness": national institutions and corporate changes in France, Germany and the UK, 1950–1993', *Organization Studies* 20 (6); 933–60.

McCloskey, D.N. (1990) *If You're So Smart: the Narrative of Economic Expertise*, Chicago, IL: University of Chicago Press.

Meyer, J.W. and Rown, B. (1977) 'Institutionalized organizations: formal structure as myth and ceremony', *American Journal of Sociology* 83 (2): 340–63.

Mintzberg, H. (1987) 'Crafting strategy', *Harvard Business Review* July–August: 65–75.

Mintzberg, H. (1990) 'The design school: reconsidering the basic premises of strategic management', *Strategic Management Journal* 11: 171–95.

Mintzberg, H. (1994) *The Rise and Fall of Strategic Planning*, New York: Free Press.

Mintzberg, H., Ahlstrand, B. and Lampel, J. (1998) *Strategy Safari: a Guided Tour through the Wilds of Strategic Management*, London: Prentice Hall.

Mintzberg, H. and Waters, J.A. (1985) 'Of strategies, deliberate and emergent', *Strategic Management Journal* 6: 257–72.

Nelson, R.R. and Winter, S.G. (1982) *An Evolutionary Theory of Economic Change*, Cambridge, MA: Harvard University Press.

Pascale, R.T. (1982) 'Our curious addiction to corporate grand strategy', *Fortune* 25 January: 115–16.

Pascale, R.T. (1984) 'Perspectives on strategy: the real story behind Honda's success', *California Management Review* 24 (3): 47–72.

Pascale, R.T. (1996) 'The Honda effect', *California Management Review* 38 (4): 80–91.

Pascale, R.T. (1999) 'Surfing the edge of chaos', *Sloan Management Review* Spring: 83–92.

Pelikan, P. (1989) 'Evolution, economic competence and the market for corporate control', *Journal of Economic Behaviour and Organization* 12: 279–303.

Penrose, E.T. (1952) 'Biological analogies in the theory of the firm', *American Economic Review* 42 (5): 804–19.

Peters, T. (1992) *Liberation Management*, London: Macmillan.

Pettigrew, A.M. (1973) *The Politics of Organizational Decision-Making*, London: Tavistock.

Pettigrew, A.M. (1985) *The Awakening Giant: Continuity and Change in ICI*, Oxford: Blackwell.

Porter, M.E. (1980) *Competitive Strategy: Techniques for Analysing Industries and Firms*, New York: Free Press and Macmillan.

Porter, M.E. (1985) *Competitive Advantage: Creating and Sustaining Superior Performance*, New York: Free Press.

Porter, M.E. (1996) 'What is strategy?', *Harvard Business Review* November–December: 61–78.

Quinn, J.B. (1980) *Strategies for Change: Logical Incrementalism*, Homewood, IL: Richard D. Irwin.

Rumelt, R. (1991) 'How much does industry matter?' *Strategic Management Journal* 12 (3): 167–85.

Rumelt, R. (1996) 'The many faces of Honda', *California Management Review* 38 (4): 103–11.

Rumelt, R.P., Schendel, D. and Teece, D.J. (1991) 'Strategic management and economics', *Strategic Management Journal* 12: 5–29.

Sanchez, R. and Sudharshan, D. (1992) 'Real-time market research: learning by doing in the development of new products', in C. Karlsson (ed.) *Proceedings of the International Product Development Conference*, Brussels: European Institute for Advanced Studies in Management.

Scott, J. (1997) *Corporate Business and Capitalist Classes*, Oxford: Oxford University Press.

Shrivastava, P. (1986) 'Is strategic management ideological?', *Journal of Management* 12 (3): 363–77.

Sloan, A.P. (1963) *My Years with General Motors*, London: Sidgwick & Jackson.

Swedberg, R., Himmelstrand, W. and Brulin, G. (1987) 'The paradigm of economic sociology', *Theory and Society* 16 (2): 169–213.

Teece, D., Pisano, G. and Shuen, A. (1997) 'Dynamic capabilities and strategic management', *Strategic Management Journal* 18 (7): 509–34.

Thomsen, S. and Pedersen, T. (2000) 'Ownership structure and performance in the largest European companies', *Strategic Management Journal* 21 (6): 689–705.

Tsoukas, T. (1996) 'The firm as a distributed knowledge system: a constructionist approach', *Strategic Management Journal* 17, Winter Special Issue: 11–26.

von Neumann, J. and Morgenstern, O. (1944) *The Theory of Games and Economic Behavior*, Princeton, NJ: Princeton University Press.

Walker, R. (1988) 'The geographical organization of production systems', *Environment and Planning D: Society and Space* 6: 377–408.

Weick, K.E. (1990) 'Cartographic myths in organizations', in A. Huff (ed.) *Mapping Strategic Thought*, London: Wiley.

Whitley, R.D. (1991) 'The social construction of business systems in East Asia', *Organization Studies* 12 (1): 1–28.

Whitley, R.D. (1999) *Divergent Capitalisms*, Oxford: Oxford University Press.

Whittington, R. (1992) 'Putting Giddens into action: social systems and managerial agency', *Journal of Management Studies* 29 (6): 693–712.

Whittington, R. (1996) 'Strategy as practice', *Long Range Planning* October: 731–5.

Whittington, R. and Mayer, M. (2001) *The European Corporation: Strategy, Structure and Social Science*, Oxford: Oxford University Press.

Wilks, S. (1990) 'The embodiment of industrial culture in bureaucracy and management', in S. Clegg and S.G. Redding (eds) *Capitalism in Contrasting Cultures*, Berlin: DeGruyter.

Williamson, O.E. (1985) *The Economic Institutions of Capitalism*, New York: Free Press.

Williamson, O.E. (1991) 'Strategizing, economizing and economic organization', *Strategic Management Journal* 12: 75–94.

Wilson, I. (1990) 'The state of strategic planning: what went wrong? what goes right?', *Technological Forecasting and Social Change* 37: 103–10.

Zack, M. (1999) 'Developing a knowledge strategy', *California Management Review* 41 (3): 125–46.

# CHAPTER 3

# Of Strategies, Deliberate and Emergent

HENRY MINTZBERG AND JAMES A. WATERS*

## Introduction

How do strategies form in organizations? Research into the question is necessarily shaped by the underlying conception of the term. Since strategy has almost inevitably been conceived in terms of what the leaders of an organization 'plan' to do in the future, strategy formation has, not surprisingly, tended to be treated as an analytic process for establishing long-range goals and action plans for an organization; that is, as one of formulation followed by implementation. As important as this emphasis may be, we would argue that it is seriously limited, that the process needs to be viewed from a wider perspective so that the variety of ways in which strategies actually take shape can be considered.

For over 10 years now, we have been researching the process of strategy formation based on the definition of strategy as 'a pattern in a stream of decisions' (Mintzberg, 1972, 1978; Mintzberg and Waters, 1982, 1984; Mintzberg et al., 1986; Mintzberg and McHugh, 1985; Brunet, Mintzberg and Waters, 1986). This definition was developed to 'operationalize' the concept of strategy, namely to provide a tangible basis on which to conduct research into how it forms in organizations. Streams of behaviour could be isolated and strategies identified as patterns or consistencies in such streams. The origins of these strategies could then be investigated, with particular attention paid to exploring the relationship between leadership plans and intentions and what the organizations actually did. Using the label strategy for both of these phenomena – one called *intended*, the other *realized* – encouraged that exploration.

[ . . .]

Comparing intended strategy with realized strategy, as shown in Figure 3.1, has allowed us to distinguish *deliberate* strategies – realized as intended – from *emergent* strategies – patterns or consistencies realized despite, or in the absence of, intentions. [ . . .]

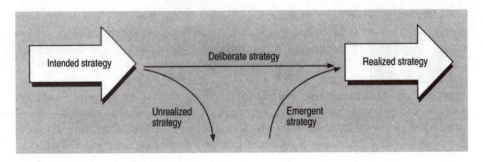

**Figure 3.1** *Types of strategies*

This paper sets out to explore the complexity and variety of strategy formation processes by refining and elaborating the concepts of deliberate and emergent
strategy. We begin by specifying more precisely what pure deliberate and pure
emergent strategies might mean in the context of organization, describing the
conditions under which each can be said to exist. What does it mean for an 'organization' – a collection of people joined together to pursue some mission in common
– to act deliberately? What does it mean for a strategy to emerge in an organization,
not guided by intentions? We then identify various types of strategies that have
appeared in our empirical studies, each embodying differing degrees of what might
be called deliberateness or emergentness. The paper concludes with a discussion of
the implications of this perspective on strategy formation for research and practice.

## Pure deliberate and pure emergent strategies

For a strategy to be perfectly deliberate – that is, for the realized strategy (pattern
in actions) to form exactly as intended – at least three conditions would seem
to have to be satisfied. First, there must have existed precise intentions in the
organization articulated in a relatively concrete level of detail, so that there can be
no doubt about what was desired before any actions were taken. Secondly, because
organization means collective action, to dispel any possible doubt about whether or
not the intentions were organizational, they must have been common to virtually all
the actors: either shared as their own or else accepted from leaders, probably in
response to some sort of controls. Thirdly, these collective intentions must have
been realized exactly as intended, which means that no external force (market,
technological, political, etc.) could have interfered with them. The environment,
in other words, must have been either perfectly predictable, totally benign, or
else under the full control of the organization. These three conditions constitute
a tall order, so that we are unlikely to find any perfectly deliberate strategies
in organizations. Nevertheless, some strategies do come rather close, in some
dimensions if not all.

For a strategy to be perfectly emergent, there must be order – consistency in action over time – in the absence of intention about it. (No consistency means no strategy or at least unrealized strategy – intentions not met.) It is difficult to imagine action in the *total* absence of intention – in some pocket of the organization if not from the leadership itself – such that we would expect the purely emergent strategy to be as rare as the purely deliberate one. But again, our research suggests that some patterns come rather close, as when an environment directly imposes a pattern of action on an organization.

Thus, we would expect to find tendencies in the directions of deliberate and emergent strategies rather than perfect forms of either. In effect, these two form the poles of a continuum along which we would expect real-world strategies to fall. Such strategies would combine various states of the dimensions we have discussed above: leadership intentions would be more or less precise, concrete and explicit, and more or less shared, as would intentions existing elsewhere in the organization; central control over organizational actions would be more or less firm and more or less pervasive; and the environment would be more or less benign, more or less controllable and more or less predictable.

Below we introduce a variety of types of strategies that fall along this continuum, beginning with those closest to the deliberate pole and ending with those most reflective of the characteristics of emergent strategy. We present these types, not as any firm or exhaustive typology (although one may eventually emerge), but simply to explore this continuum of emergentness of strategy and to try to gain some insights into the notions of intention, choice and pattern formation in the collective context we call organization.

## The planned strategy

Planning suggests clear and articulated intentions, backed up by formal controls to ensure their pursuit, in an environment that is acquiescent. In other words, here (and only here) does the classic distinction between 'formulation' and 'implementation' hold up.

In this first type, called *planned strategy*, leaders at the centre of authority formulate their intentions as precisely as possible and then strive for their implementation – their translation into collective action – with a minimum of distortion, 'surprise-free'. To ensure this, the leaders must first articulate their intentions in the form of a plan, to minimize confusion, and then elaborate this plan in as much detail as possible in the form of budgets, schedules and so on, to pre-empt discretion that might impede its realization. Those outside the planning process may act, but to the extent possible they are not allowed to decide. Programmes that guide their behaviour are built into the plan, and formal controls are instituted to ensure pursuit of the plan and the programmes.

But the plan is of no use if it cannot be applied as formulated in the environment surrounding the organization, so the planned strategy is found in an environment that is, if not benign or controllable, then at least rather predictable. Some organizations as Galbraith (1967) describes the 'new industrial states', are powerful enough to impose their plans on their environments. Others are able to predict their environments with enough accuracy to pursue rather deliberate, planned strategies. We suspect, however, that many planned strategies are found in organizations that simply extrapolate established patterns in environments that they assume will remain stable. In fact, we have argued elsewhere (Mintzberg and Waters, 1982) that strategies appear not to be *conceived* in planning processes so much as elaborated from existing visions or copied from standard industry recipes (see Grinyer and Spender, 1979); planning thus becomes programming, and the planned strategy finds its origins in one of the other types of strategies described below.

Although few strategies can be planned to the degree described above, some do come rather close, particularly in organizations that must commit large quantities of resources to particular missions and so cannot tolerate unstable environments. They may spend years considering their actions, but once they decide to act, they commit themselves firmly. In effect, they deliberate so that their strategies can be rather deliberate. Thus, we studied a mining company that had to engage in a most detailed form of planning to exploit a new ore body in an extremely remote part of Quebec. Likewise, we found a very strong planning orientation in our study of Air Canada, necessary to co-ordinate the purchase of new, expensive jet aircraft with a relatively fixed route structure.

[. . .]

## The entrepreneurial strategy

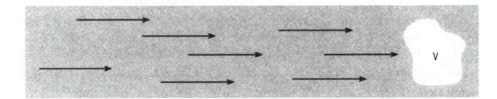

In this second type of strategy, we relax the condition of precise, articulated intentions. Here, one individual in personal control of an organization is able to impose his or her vision of direction on it. Because such strategies are rather common in entrepreneurial firms, tightly controlled by their owners, they can be called *entrepreneurial strategies*.

In this case, the force for pattern or consistency in action is individual vision, the central actor's *concept* of his or her organization's place in its world. This is coupled with an ability to impose that vision on the organization through his or her personal control of its actions (e.g. through giving direct orders to its operating personnel). Of course, the environment must again be co-operative. But entrepreneurial strategies most commonly appear in young and/or small organizations (where personal control is feasible), which are able to find relatively safe niches in their environments. Indeed, the selection of such niches is an integral part of the vision. These strategies can, however, sometimes be found in larger organizations as well, particularly under conditions of crisis where all the actors are willing to follow the direction of a single leader who has vision and will.

Is the entrepreneurial strategy deliberate? Intentions do exist. But they derive from one individual who need not articulate or elaborate them. Indeed, for reasons discussed below, he or she is typically unlikely to want to do so. Thus, the intentions are both more difficult to identify and less specific than those of the planned strategy. Moreover, there is less overt acceptance of these intentions on the part of other actors in the organization. Nevertheless, so long as those actors respond to the personal will of the leader, the strategy would appear to be rather deliberate.

In two important respects, however, that strategy can have emergent characteristics as well. First, as indicated in the previous diagram, vision provides only a general sense of direction. Within it, there is room for adaptation: the details of the vision can emerge *en route*. Secondly, because the leader's vision is personal, it can also be changed completely. To put this another way, since here the formulator is the implementor, step by step, that person can react quickly to feedback on past actions or to new opportunities or threats in the environment. He or she can thus reformulate vision, as shown in the figure below.

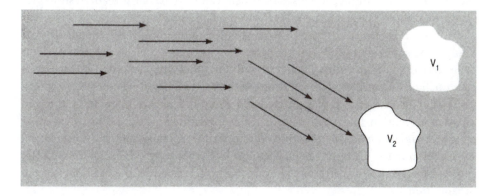

It is this adaptability that distinguishes the entrepreneurial strategy from the planned one. Visions contained in single brains would appear to be more flexible, assuming the individual's willingness to learn, than plans articulated through hierarchies, which are composed of many brains. Adaptation (and emergentness) of planned strategies are discouraged by the articulation of intentions and by the separation between formulation and implementation. Psychologists have shown that the articulation of a strategy locks it into place, impeding willingness to change it (e.g. Kiesler, 1971). The separation of implementation from formulation gives rise to a whole system of commitments and procedures, in the form of plans, programmes and controls elaborated down a hierarchy. Instead of one individual being able to change his or her mind, the whole system must be redesigned. Thus, despite the claims of flexible planning the fact is that organizations plan not to be flexible but to realize specific intentions. It is the entrepreneurial strategy that provides flexibility, at the expense of the specificity and articulation of intentions.

[. . .]

## The ideological strategy

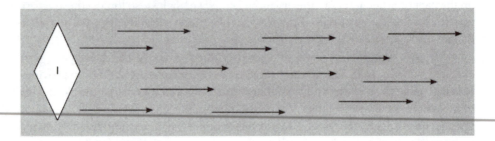

Vision can be collective as well as individual. When the members of an organization share a vision and identify so strongly with it that they pursue it as an ideology, then they are bound to exhibit patterns in their behaviour, so that clear realized strategies can be identified. These may be called *ideological strategies*.

Can an ideological strategy be considered deliberate? Since the ideology is likely to be somewhat overt (e.g. in programmes of indoctrination), and perhaps even articulated (in rough, inspirational form, such as a credo), intentions can usually be identified. The question thus revolves around whether these intentions can be considered organizational and whether they are likely to be realized as intended. In an important sense, these intentions would seem to be most clearly organizational. Whereas the intentions of the planned and entrepreneurial strategies emanate from one centre and are accepted passively by everyone else, those of the ideological strategy are positively embraced by the members of the organization.

As for their realization, because the intentions exist as a rough vision, they can presumably be adapted or changed. But collective vision is far more immutable than individual vision. All who share it must agree to change their 'collective mind'. Moreover, ideology is rooted in the past, in traditions and precedents (often the institutionalization of the vision of a departed, charismatic leader: one person's vision has become everyone's ideology). People, therefore, resist changing it. The object is to interpret 'the word', not to defy it. Finally, the environment is unlikely to impose change: the purpose of ideology, after all, is to change the environment or else to insulate the organization from it. For all these reasons, therefore, ideological strategy would normally be highly deliberate, perhaps more so than any type of strategy except the planned one.

[. . .]

## The umbrella strategy

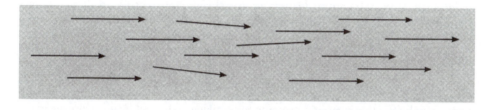

Now we begin to relax the condition of tight control (whether bureaucratic, personal or ideological) over the mass of actors in the organization and, in some cases, the condition of tight control over the environment as well. Leaders who have only partial control over other actors in an organization may design what can be called *umbrella strategies*. They set general guidelines for behaviour – define the boundaries – and then let other actors manoeuvre within them. In effect, these leaders establish kinds of umbrellas under which organizational actions are expected to fall – for example that all products should be designed for the high-priced end of the market (no matter what those products might be).

When an environment is complex, and perhaps somewhat uncontrollable and unpredictable as well, a variety of actors in the organization must be able to respond to it. In other words, the patterns in organizational actions cannot be set deliberately in one central place, although the boundaries may be established there to constrain them. From the perspective of the leadership (if not, perhaps, the individual actors), therefore, strategies are allowed to emerge, at least within these boundaries. In fact, we can label the umbrella strategy not only deliberate and emergent (intended at the centre in its broad outlines but not in its specific details), but also 'deliberately emergent' (in the sense that the central leadership intention-ally creates the conditions under which strategies can emerge).

[. . .]

We have so far described the umbrella strategy as one among a number of types that are possible. But, in some sense, virtually all real-world strategies have umbrella characteristics. That is to say, in no organization can the central leadership totally pre-empt the discretion of others (as was assumed in the planned and entre-preneurial strategies) and, by the same token, in none does a central leadership defer totally to others (unless it has ceased to lead). Almost all strategy making behaviour involves, therefore, to some degree at least, a central leadership with some sort of intentions trying to direct, guide, cajole or nudge others with ideas of their own. When the leadership is able to direct, we move towards the realm of the planned or entrepreneurial strategies; when it can hardly nudge, we move toward the realm of the more emergent strategies. But in the broad range between these two can always be found strategies with umbrella characteristics.

In its pursuit of an umbrella strategy – which means, in essence, defining general direction subject to varied interpretation – the central leadership must monitor the behaviour of other actors to assess whether or not the boundaries are being respected. In essence, like us, it searches for patterns in streams of actions. When actors, are found to stray outside the boundaries (whether inadvertently or intentionally), the central leadership has three choices: to stop them, ignore them (perhaps for a time, to see what will happen), or adjust to them. In other words, when an arm pokes outside the umbrella, you either pull it in, leave it there (although it might get wet), or move the umbrella over to cover it.

In this last case, the leadership exercises the option of altering its own vision in response to the behaviour of others. Indeed, this would appear to be the place where much effective strategic learning takes place – through leadership response to the initiatives of others. The leadership that is never willing to alter its vision in such a way forgoes important opportunities and tends to lose touch with its environment (although, of course, the one too willing to do so may be unable to sustain any central direction). The umbrella strategy thus requires a light touch, maintaining a subtle balance between proaction and reaction.

## The process strategy

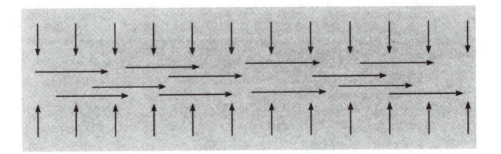

Similar to the umbrella strategy is what can be called the *process strategy*. Again, the leadership functions in an organization in which other actors must have considerable discretion to determine outcomes, because of an environment that is complex and perhaps also unpredictable and uncontrollable. But instead of trying to control strategy content at a general level, through boundaries or targets, the leadership instead needs to exercise influence indirectly. Specifically, it controls the *process* of strategy making while leaving the content of strategy to other actors. Again, the resulting behaviour would be deliberate in one respect and emergent in others: the central leadership designs the system that allows others the flexibility to evolve patterns within it.

The leadership may, for example, control the staffing of the organization, thereby determining who gets to make strategy if not what that strategy will be (all the while knowing that control of the former constitutes considerable influence over the latter). Or it may design the structure of the organization to determine the working context of those who get to make strategy.

[...]

Divisionalized organizations of a conglomerate nature commonly use process strategies: the central headquarters creates the basic structure, establishes the control systems and appoints the division managers, who are then expected to develop strategies for their own businesses (typically planned ones for reasons outlined by Mintzberg, 1979: 384–392); note that techniques such as those introduced by the Boston Consulting Group to manage the business portfolios of divisionalized companies, by involving headquarters in the business strategies to some extent, bring their strategies back into the realm of umbrella ones.

# The unconnected strategies

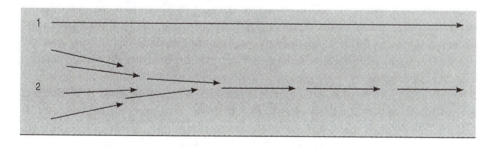

The unconnected strategy is perhaps the most straightforward one of all. One part of the organization with considerable discretion – a subunit, sometimes even a single individual – because it is only loosely coupled to the rest, is able to realize its own pattern in its stream of actions.

[...]

Unconnected strategies tend to proliferate in organizations of experts, reflecting the complexity of the environments that they face and the resulting need for considerable control by the experts over their own work, providing freedom not only from administrators but sometimes from their own peers as well. Thus, many hospitals and universities appear to be little more than collections of personal strategies, with hardly any discernible central vision or umbrella, let alone plan, linking them together. Each expert pursues his or her own strategies – method of patient care, subject of research, style of teaching. On the other hand, in organizations that do pursue central, rather deliberate strategies, even planned ones, unconnected strategies can sometimes be found in remote enclaves, either tolerated by the system or lost within it.

[. . .]

## The consensus strategy

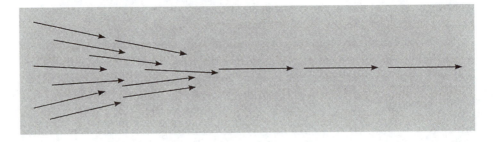

In no strategy so far discussed have we totally dropped the condition of prior intention. The next type is rather more clearly emergent. Here many different actors naturally converge on the same theme, or pattern, so that it becomes pervasive in the organizations without the need for any central direction or control. We call it the *consensus strategy*. Unlike the ideological strategy, in which a consensus forms around a system of beliefs (thus reflecting intentions widely accepted in the organization), the consensus strategy grows out of the mutual adjustment among different actors, as they learn from each other and from their various responses to the environment and thereby find a common, and probably unexpected, pattern that works for them.

In other words, the convergence is not driven by any intentions of a central management, or even by prior intentions widely shared among the other actors. It just evolves through the results of a host of individual actions. Of course, certain actors may actively promote the consensus, perhaps even negotiate with their colleagues to attain it (as in the congressional form of government). But the point is that it derives more from collective action than from collective intention.

[. . .]

## The imposed strategies

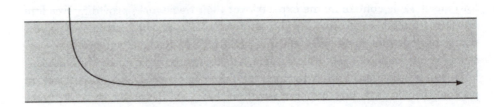

All the strategies so far discussed have derived in part at least from the will (if not the intentions) of actors within the organization. The environment has been considered, if not benign, then at least acquiescent. But strategies can be *imposed* from outside as well; that is, the environment can directly force the organization into a pattern in its stream of actions, regardless of the presence of central controls. The clearest case of this occurs when an external individual or group with a great deal of influence over the organization imposes a strategy on it. We saw this in our study of the state-owned Air Canada, when the minister who created and controlled the airline in its early years forced it to buy and fly a particular type of aircraft. Here the imposed strategy was clearly deliberate, but not by anyone in the organization. However, given its inability to resist, the organization had to resign itself to the pursuit of the strategy, so that it became, in effect, deliberate.

Sometimes, the 'environment' rather than people *per se* impose strategies on organizations, simply by severely restricting the options open to them. Air Canada chose to fly jet aeroplanes and later wide-body aeroplanes. But did it? Could any 'world class' airline have decided otherwise? Again the organization has internalized the imperative so that strategic choice becomes a moot point.

[. . .]

Reality, however, seems to bring organizations closer to a compromise position between determinism and free choice. Environments seldom pre-empt all choice, just as they seldom offer unlimited choice. That is why purely determined strategies are probably as rare as purely planned ones. Alternatively, just as the umbrella strategy may be the most realistic reflection of leadership intention, so too might the partially imposed strategy be the most realistic reflection of environmental influence. As shown in the figure below, the environment bounds what the organization can do, in this illustration determining under what part of the umbrella the organization can feasibly operate.

[. . .]

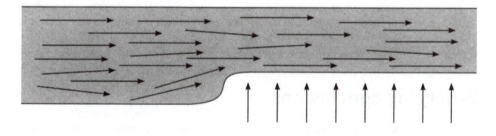

This completes our discussion of various types of strategies. Table 3.1 summarizes some of their major features.

Table 3.1 *Summary description of types of strategies*

| Strategy | Major features |
| --- | --- |
| Planned | Strategies originate in formal plans: precise intentions exist, formulated and articulated by central leadership, backed up by formal controls to ensure surprise-free implementation in benign, controllable or predictable environment; strategies most deliberate |
| Entrepreneurial | Strategies originate in central vision: intentions exist as personal, unarticulated vision of single leader, and so adaptable to new opportunities; organization under personal control of leader and located in protected niche in environment; strategies relatively deliberate but can emerge |
| Ideological | Strategies originate in shared beliefs: intentions exist as collective vision of all actors, in inspirational form and relatively immutable, controlled normatively through indoctrination and/or socialization; organization often proactive *vis-à-vis* environment; strategies rather deliberate |
| Umbrella | Strategies originate in constraints: leadership, in partial control of organizational actions, defines strategic boundaries or targets within which other actors respond to own forces or to complex, perhaps also unpredictable environment; strategies partly deliberate, partly emergent and deliberately emergent |
| Process | Strategies originate in process: leadership controls process aspects of strategy (hiring, structure, etc.), leaving content aspects to other actors; strategies partly deliberate, partly emergent (and, again, deliberately emergent) |
| Unconnected | Strategies originate in enclaves: actor(s) loosely coupled to rest of organization produce(s) patterns in own actions in absence of, or in direct contradiction to, central or common intentions; strategies organizationally emergent whether or not deliberate for actor(s) |
| Consensus | Strategies originate in consensus: through mutual adjustment, actors converge on patterns that become pervasive in absence of central or common intentions; strategies rather emergent |
| Imposed | Strategies originate in environment: environment dictates patterns in actions either through direct imposition or through implicitly pre-empting or bounding organizational choice; strategies most emergent, although may be internalized by organization and made deliberate |

# Emerging conclusions

This chapter has been written to open up thinking about strategy formation, to broaden perspectives that may remain framed in the image of it as an *a priori*, analytic process or even as a sharp dichotomy between strategies as either deliberate or emergent. We believe that more research is required on the process of strategy formation to complement the extensive work currently taking place on the content of strategies; indeed, we believe that research on the former can significantly influence the direction taken by research on the latter (and vice versa).

One promising line of research is investigation of the strategy formation process and of the types of strategies realized as a function of the structure and context of organizations. Do the various propositions suggested in this chapter, based on our own limited research, in fact hold up in broader samples, for example, that strategies will tend to be more deliberate in tightly coupled, centrally controlled organizations and more emergent in decentralized, loosely coupled ones?

It would also be interesting to know how different types of strategies perform in various contexts and also how these strategies relate to those defined in terms of specific content. Using Porter's (1980) categories, for example, will cost leadership strategies prove more deliberate (specifically, more often planned), differentiation strategies more emergent (perhaps umbrella in nature), or perhaps entrepreneurial? Or using Miles and Snow's (1978) typology, will defenders prove more deliberate in orientation and inclined to use planned strategies, whereas prospectors tend to be more emergent and more prone to rely on umbrella or process, or even unconnected, strategies? It may even be possible that highly deliberate strategy making processes will be found to drive organizations away from prospecting activities and towards cost leadership strategies whereas emergent ones may encourage the opposite postures.

The interplay of the different types of strategies we have described can be another avenue of inquiry: the nesting of personal strategies within umbrella ones or their departure in clandestine form from centrally imposed umbrellas; the capacity of unconnected strategies to evoke organizational ones of a consensus or even a planned nature as peripheral patterns that succeed and pervade the organization; the conversion of entrepreneurial strategies into ideological or planned ones as vision becomes institutionalized one way or another; the possible propensity of imposed strategies to become deliberate as they are internalized within the organization; and so on. An understanding of how these different types of strategies blend into each other and tend to sequence themselves over time in different contexts could reveal a good deal about the strategy formation process.

At a more general level, the whole question of how managers learn from the experiences of their own organizations seems to be fertile ground for research. In our view, the fundamental difference between deliberate and emergent strategy is that whereas the former focuses on direction and control – getting desired things done – the latter opens up this notion of 'strategic learning'. Defining strategy as intended and conceiving it as deliberate, as has traditionally been done, effectively precludes the notion of strategic learning. Once the intentions have been set, attention is riveted on realizing them, not on adapting them. Messages from the environment tend to get blocked out. Adding the concept of emergent strategy, based on the definition of strategy as realized, opens the process of strategy making up to the notion of learning.

Emergent strategy itself implies learning what works – taking one action at a time in a search for that viable pattern or consistency. It is important to remember that emergent strategy means, not chaos, but, in essence, *unintended order*. It is

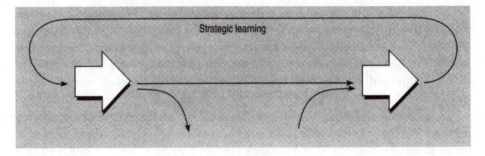

**Figure 3.2** *Strategic learning*

also frequently the means by which deliberate strategies change. As shown in Figure 3.2, in the feedback loop added to our basic diagram, it is often through the identification of emergent strategies – its patterns never intended – that managers and others in the organization come to change their intentions. This is another way of saying that not a few deliberate strategies are simply emergent ones that have been uncovered and subsequently formalized. Of course, unrealized strategies are also a source of learning, as managers find out which of their intentions do not work, rejected either by their organizations themselves or else by environments that are less than acquiescent.

We wish to emphasize that emergent strategy does not have to mean that management is out of control, only – in some cases at least – that it is open, flexible and responsive, in other words, willing to learn. Such behaviour is especially important when an environment is too unstable or complex to comprehend, or too imposing to defy. Openness to such emergent strategy enables management to act before everything is fully understood – to respond to an evolving reality rather than having to focus on a stable fantasy. For example, distinctive competence cannot always be assessed on paper *a priori*; often, perhaps usually, it has to be discovered empirically, by taking actions that test where strengths and weaknesses really lie. Emergent strategy also enables a management that cannot be close enough to a situation, or to know enough about the varied activities of its organization, to surrender control to those who have the information current and detailed enough to shape realistic strategies. Whereas the more deliberate strategies tend to emphasize central direction and hierarchy, the more emergent ones open the way for collective action and convergent behaviour.

Of course, by the same token, deliberate strategy is hardly dysfunctional either. Managers need to manage too, sometimes to impose intentions on their organizations – to provide a sense of direction. That can be partial, as in the cases of umbrella and process strategies, or it can be rather comprehensive, as in the cases of planned and entrepreneurial strategies. When the necessary information can be brought to a central place and environments can be largely understood and predicted (or at least controlled), then it may be appropriate to suspend strategic learning for a time to pursue intentions with as much determination as possible (see Mintzberg and Waters, 1984).

Our conclusion is that strategy formation walks on two feet, one deliberate, the other emergent. As noted earlier, managing requires a light deft touch – to direct in order to realize intentions while at the same time responding to an unfolding pattern of action. The relative emphasis may shift from time to time but not the requirement to attend to both sides of this phenomenon.

[. . .]

# References

Brunet, J.P., Mintzberg. H. and Waters, J. (1986) 'Does Planning Impede Strategic Thinking? The Strategy of Air Canada 1937–1976,' in Lamb, R. (ed.) *Advances in Strategic Management* (Englewood Cliffs, NJ: Prentice Hall) vol. 4.

Galbraith, J.K. (1967) *The New Industrial State* (Boston: Houghton Mifflin).

Grinyer, P.H. and Spender, J.C. (1979) *Turnaround: the Fall and Rise of the Newton Chambers Group* (London: Association Business Press).

Kiesler, C.H. (1971) *The Psychology of Commitment: Experiments Linking Behaviour to Belief* (New York: Academic Press).

Miles, R. and Snow, C. (1978) *Organizational Strategy, Structure, and Process* (New York: McGraw-Hill).

Mintzberg, H. (1972) 'Research on Strategy-making', *Proceedings of the 32nd Annual Meeting of the Academy of Management*, Minneapolis.

Mintzberg, H. (1978) 'Patterns in Strategy Formation', *Management Science*, pp. 934–48.

Mintzberg, H. (1979) *The Structuring of Organizations* (Englewood Cliffs, NJ: Prentice-Hall).

Mintzberg, H. and McHugh, A. (1985) 'Strategy Formation in Adhocracy', *Administrative Science Quarterly*.

Mintzberg, H. and Waters, J.A. (1982) 'Tracking Strategy in an Entrepreneurial Firm', *Academy of Management Journal*, pp. 465–99.

Mintzberg, H. and Waters, J.A. (1984) 'Researching the Formation of Strategies: The History of Canadian Lady, 1939–1976', in Lamb, R. (ed.) *Competitive Strategic Management* (Englewood Cliffs, NJ: Prentice Hall).

Mintzberg, H., Otis, S., Shamsie, J. and Waters, J.A. (1986) 'Strategy of Design: A Study of "Architects in Co-partnership"', in Grant, John (ed.) *Strategic Management Frontiers* (Greenwich, CT: JAI Press).

Porter, M.E. (1980) *Competitive Strategy: Techniques for Analyzing Industries and Competitors* (New York: Free Press).

# Industry Effects

This second section continues our overview of the strategy literature by introducing a fundamental distinction in strategy analysis: the focus on *external* industry characteristics versus the focus on the *internal* dynamics of the organization. As reviewed briefly in the introduction to this book, the former mainly looks at the role of industry structure in determining firm strategy and performance, while the latter looks at the role of firm-specific resources and capabilities developed inside the organization. As will become obvious by the end of the next section, these two alternative perspectives on strategy have very different views of what causes differences between firms.

Grant's first piece provides a broad overview of the effect of industry structure on firm strategy, focusing especially on Porter's 'five forces of competition' framework. In this view, strategy is about the firm creating for itself a 'market position' whereby it can defend itself from competitive forces and/or influence them in a way that places it at an advantage *vis-à-vis* its competitors and suppliers. This framework is connected to the 'structure–conduct–performance' approach of traditional industrial organization where it is assumed that the structure of an industry (e.g. how easy it is for new firms to enter) determines firm conduct/strategy (e.g. innovation strategies), and hence firm performance (e.g. profits). Grant's second piece picks up from where his first piece leaves off: by criticizing Porter's static approach for not allowing feedback effects between firm actions and the industry environment. In this second chapter, Grant introduces more dynamic ways to look at the influence of industry structure on firm strategy, for example through the industry life-cycle framework which looks at how firm strategies and industry structure co-evolve over time (structure constrains strategy but strategy changes structure). This perspective sheds light on the changing nature of Schumpetarian competition, i.e. what types of industries, or what phases in the life of a particular industry, tend to be more characterised by radical technological change.

The last reading, by Baden-Fuller and Stopford, acts as a transition to the next section. It argues that business success is determined not by the characteristics defining the industry to which the business belongs, but by the specific strategies pursued by the organization. To support their point, the authors give various examples of companies who were in 'unattractive' industries (e.g. ones with falling demand, excess capacity or low technological opportunities) but who were nevertheless able to achieve remarkable success.

## R.M. Grant: 'Analyzing the Industry Environment'

The overview piece by Grant comes from a chapter of his widely used strategy textbook *Contemporary Strategy Analysis*. Grant claims that industry analysis allows firms to focus on those aspects of the business environment that have the greatest impact on their decisions. If they try to understand everything about the environment they will suffer from information overload. The important aspects concern the characteristics of their suppliers, their competitors and their customers. Different industries will have different average profit rates depending on the characteristics of the markets they operate in. Grant introduces Porter's 'five forces of competition' framework as an example of how the influence of industry characteristics on strategy can be analyzed. At the end of the chapter, Grant outlines reasons why Porter's framework is limited. The main reason is that Porter's framework is not 'dynamic', i.e. it does not look at the interaction between firm actions and the industry environment, for example how the environment can undergo fundamental change through the innovation activities of firms. Grant's second piece considers these issues in more detail.

## R.M. Grant: 'Industry Evolution'

This second piece by Grant also comes from his textbook *Contemporary Strategy Analysis*. He presents a dynamic view of how industry structure and firm strategy co-evolve. Instead of treating industry structure as an external condition that affects firm strategy, he looks at the 'endogeneity' of industry structure: how industry structure evolves from the interaction between firm strategies and the environment. To do so, Grant presents the industry life-cycle framework, which explains how demand change and technological change over the history of an industry's life cause firm strategies and industry structure to change. For example, whereas the high entry of new firms and experimentation around different technologies and products in the *early* phase of the life-cycle causes industry structure to be relatively competitive, the fewer technological opportunities and the greater emphasis on economies of scale in the *mature* phase cause the market structure to be more stable and concentrated.

## C. Baden-Fuller and J. Stopford: 'The Firm Matters More than the Industry'

This piece comes from an excerpt from the authors' book called *Rejuvenating the Mature Business*. The authors claim that managers of mature businesses must not blame the characteristics of their industry (e.g. excess capacity, falling demand) for their problems. The fact that some firms in old industries have been able to think of innovative ways to regain competitiveness shows that it is not the industry but firm strategy that matters (a reassuring message for managers!). These firms changed the rules of the game instead of taking old rules as given. The authors organize the reading around three points. First, that a business can be successful in an industry that is not 'attractive' as defined by Porter (e.g. falling demand, severe competition from rivals). Second, that building market share is not the route to success since an increase in market share is not the cause but the *result* of good strategies. Third, that 'rejuvenating' firms or new entrants can succeed even if they have fewer resources than established incumbents. The authors use the experience of three particular firms in hostile industries to support these points.

**CHAPTER 4**

# Analyzing the Industry Environment

ROBERT M. GRANT*

[. . .]

## From environmental analysis to industry analysis

The business environment of the firm consists of all the external influences that impact a firm's decisions and performance. The problem here is that, given the vast number and range of external influences, how can managers hope to monitor, let alone analyze, environmental conditions? The starting point is some kind of system or framework for organizing information. For example, environmental influences can be classified by source into economic, technological, demographic, social, and governmental factors; or by proximity: the 'micro-environment' or 'task environment' can be distinguished from the wider influences that form the 'macro-environment'.

Though systematic, continuous scanning of the whole range of external influences might seem desirable, such extensive environmental analysis is unlikely to be cost effective and creates information overload. The Royal Dutch/Shell Group, one of the world's largest and most international enterprises, invests more heavily in the systematic monitoring and analysis of its business environment than most other companies. Its scenario analysis . . . is exceptionally far-sighted and wide-ranging in assessing its business environment. Nevertheless, the group's environmental scanning and analysis focuses on factors that are directly relevant to its strategic planning: in particular, those factors that influence the demand and supply of oil and refined products.[1]

The prerequisite for effective environmental analysis is to distinguish the vital from the merely important. Let's return to first principles. For the firm to make profit it must create value for customers. Hence, the firm must understand its

* Blackwell Publishers for an extract from *Contemporary Strategy Analysis* by Robert M. Grant © Robert M. Grant, 1998.

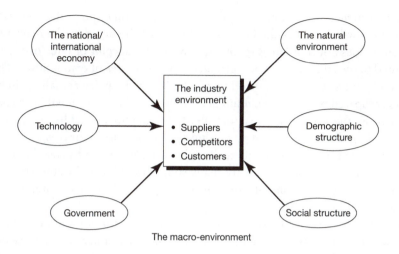

The macro-environment

**Figure 4.1** *The business environment*

customers. Second, in creating value, the firm acquires goods and services from suppliers. Hence, the firm must understand its suppliers and how to form business relationships with them. Third, the ability to generate profitability from value-creating activity depends on the intensity of competition among the firms that vie for the same value-creating opportunities. Hence, the firm must understand competition. Thus, the core of the firm's business environment is formed by its relationships with customers, suppliers, and competitors. This is the firm's industry environment.

This is not to say that macro-level factors such as general economic trends, changes in demographic structure, or social and political trends are unimportant to strategy analysis. These factors may be critical determinants of the threats and opportunities a company will face in the future. The key issue is how these more general environmental factors impact the firm's industry environment (Figure 4.1). For most firms, global warming is not a critical issue. For the producers of automobiles, oil, and electricity, it is important since government measures to restrict the production of carbon dioxide and other greenhouse gases will directly affect the demand for their products and their costs of doing business. By focusing on the industry environment, we can determine which of the macro-level influences are important for the firm and which are not.

## The determinants of industry profit: demand and competition

If the purpose of strategy is to help the firm to survive and make money, the starting point for industry analysis is: What determines the level of profit in an industry?

As already noted, business is about the creation of value for the customer. Firms create value by production (transforming inputs into outputs) or arbitrage (transferring products across time and space). Value creation requires that the price the customer is willing to pay the firm exceed the costs incurred by the firm. But value creation does not translate directly into profit. The surplus of value over cost is distributed between customers and producers by the forces of competition. The stronger the competition among producers, the lower the price actually paid by customers compared with the maximum price they would have been willing to pay In other words, the greater the proportion of the surplus gained by customers (*consumer surplus*), the less is earned by producers (*producer surplus* or *economic rent*). A single supplier of bottled water at an all-night rave can charge a price that fully exploits the dancers' thirst. If there are many suppliers of bottled water, then, in the absence of collusion, competition causes the price of bottled water to fall toward the cost of supplying it.

The surplus earned by producers over and above the minimum costs of production is not entirely captured in profits. Where an industry has powerful suppliers – monopolistic suppliers of components or employees united by a strong labor union – then a substantial part of the surplus may be appropriated by these suppliers (the profits of suppliers or premium wages of union members).

The profits earned by the firms in an industry are thus determined by three factors:

- The value of the product or service to customers
- The intensity of competition
- The relative bargaining power at different levels in the production chain.

Our industry analysis brings all three factors into a single analytic framework.

# Analyzing industry attractiveness

Table 4.1 shows the average rate of profit earned in different US industries. Some industries (such as tobacco and pharmaceuticals) consistently earn high rates of profit; others (such as iron and steel, nonferrous metals, airlines, and basic building materials) have failed to cover their cost of capital. The basic premise that underlies industry analysis is that the level of industry profitability is neither random nor the result of entirely industry-specific influences, but is determined, in part at least, by the systematic influence of *industry structure*. [. . .]

The underlying theory of how industry structure drives competitive behavior and determines industry profitability is provided by industrial organization (IO) economics. The two reference points are the theory of monopoly and the theory of perfect competition, which represent the two ends of a spectrum of industry structures. A single firm protected by barriers to the entry of new firms forms a *monopoly* in which it can appropriate in profit the full amount of the value it creates. By contrast, many firms supplying an identical product with no restrictions on entry or exit constitutes *perfect competition*: the rate of profit falls

Table 4.1  *The profitability of US manufacturing industries*

| Industry | Return on equity (1985–95) |
|---|---|
| Drugs | 19.39% |
| Food and kindred products | 13.85% |
|    of which tobacco products | 18.60% |
| Instruments and related products | 11.24% |
| Printing and publishing | 10.16% |
| Electrical and electronic equipment | 10.00% |
| Aircraft, guided missiles, and parts | 8.36% |
| Fabricated metal products | 8.15% |
| Rubber and misc. plastics products | 9.95% |
| Paper and allied products | 8.47% |
| Retail trade corporations | 8.37% |
| Petroleum and coal products | 7.88% |
| Textile mill products | 7.25% |
| Wholesale trade corporations | 5.72% |
| Stone, glass and clay products | 5.28% |
| Machinery, exc. electrical | 4.29% |
| Nonferrous metals | 4.21% |
| Motor vehicles and equipment | 2.61% |
| Iron and steel | 1.30% |
| Mining corporations | 1.24% |
| Airlines | (2.84%) |

*Source*: Federal Trade Commission

to a level that just covers firms' cost of capital. In the real world, industries fall between these two extremes. The US market for smokeless tobacco is close to being a monopoly, the Chicago grain markets are close to being perfectly competitive. Most manufacturing industries and many service industries tend to be *oligopolies*: they are dominated by a small number of major companies. Figure 4.2 identifies some key points on the spectrum. By examining the principal structural features and their interactions for any particular industry, it is possible to predict the type of competitive behavior likely to emerge and the resulting level of profitability.

## Porter's Five Forces of Competition framework

Figure 4.2 identifies four structural variables influencing competition and profitability. In practice, there are many features of an industry that determine the intensity of competition and the level of profitability. A helpful, widely used framework for classifying and analyzing these factors is the one developed by Michael Porter of Harvard Business School.[2] Porter's Five Forces of Competition framework views the profitability of an industry (as indicated by its rate of return on capital relative to its cost of capital) as determined by five sources of competitive pressure. These five forces of competition include three sources of 'horizontal' competition: competition from substitutes, competition from entrants, and

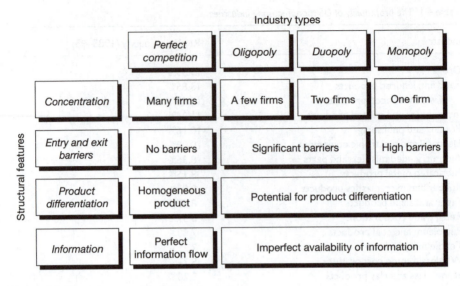

**Figure 4.2** *The spectrum of industry structures*

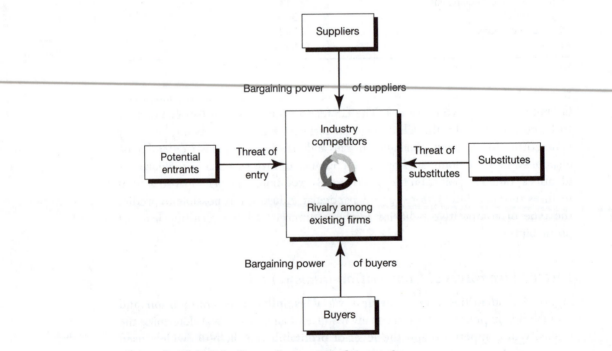

**Figure 4.3** *Porter's five forces of competition framework*

competition from established rivals; and two sources of 'vertical' competition: the bargaining power of suppliers and buyers (see Figure 4.3).

The strength of each of these competitive forces is determined by a number of key structural variables as shown in Figure 4.4.

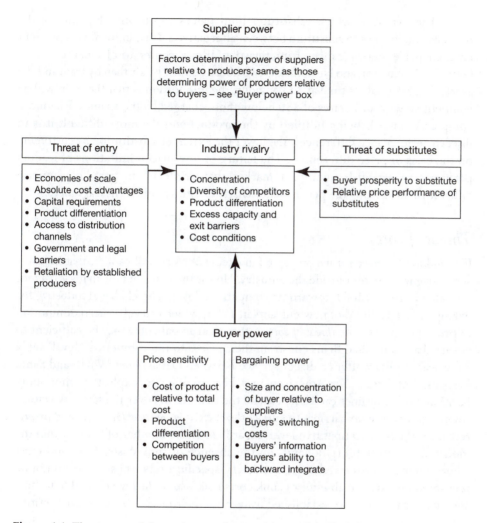

**Figure 4.4** *The structural determinants of competition and profitability within the Porter framework*

## Competition from substitutes

The price customers are willing to pay for a product depends, in part, on the availability of substitute products. The absence of close substitutes for a product, as in the case of gasoline or cigarettes, means that consumers are comparatively insensitive to price, i.e. demand is *inelastic* with respect to price. The existence of close substitutes means that customers will switch to substitutes in response to price increases for the product, i.e. demand is *elastic* with respect to price. The introduction of digital personal communication services (PCS) in the United States by Sprint Spectrum and Nextel and in the UK by Hutchinson Orange has increased the substitute competition faced by traditional cellular companies and lowered their margins.

The extent to which substitutes limit prices and profits depends on the propensity of buyers to substitute between alternatives. This, in turn, is dependent on their price–performance characteristics. If city-center to city-center travel between Washington and New York is two hours quicker by air than by train and the average traveler values time at $25 an hour, the implication is that the train will be competitive with air at fares of $50 below those charged by the airlines. The more complex the needs being fulfilled by the product and the more difficult it is to discern performance differences, the lower the extent of substitution by customers on the basis of price differences. The failure of low-priced imitations of leading perfumes to establish significant market share reflects, in part, consumers' difficulty in discerning the performance characteristics of different fragrances.

## Threat of entry

If an industry earns a return on capital in excess of its cost of capital, that industry acts a magnet to firms outside the industry. Unless the entry of new firms is barred, the rate of profit will fall toward its competitive level. The US bagel industry, for example, faced a flood of new entrants in 1996, which caused a sharp diminution of profit prospects. The *threat of entry* rather than actual entry may be sufficient to ensure that established firms constrain their prices to the competitive level. Only American Airlines offers a direct service between Dallas/Fort Worth and Santa Barbara, California. Yet American may be unwilling to exploit its monopoly position if other airlines can easily extend their routes to cover the same two cities. An industry where no barriers to entry or exit exist is *contestable*: prices and profits remain at the fully competitive level, regardless of the number of firms within the industry.[3] Contestability depends on the absence of sunk costs. *Sunk costs* exist where entry requires investment in industry-specific assets whose value cannot be recovered on exit. An absence of sunk costs makes an industry vulnerable to 'hit-and-run' entry whenever established firms raise their prices above the competitive level.

In most industries, however, new entrants cannot enter on equal terms with those of established firms. The size of the advantage of established over entrant firm (in terms of unit costs) measures the height of *barriers to entry*, which determines the extent to which the industry can, in the long run, enjoy profit above the competitive level. The principal sources of barriers to entry are: capital requirements, economies of scale, cost advantages, product differentiation, access to channels of distribution, governmental and legal barriers, and retaliation.

CAPITAL REQUIREMENTS   The capital costs of getting established in an industry can be so large as to discourage all but the largest companies. The duopoly of Boeing and Airbus in large passenger jets is protected by the prohibitive costs of establishing such a venture. In satellite television broadcasting in Britain, Rupert Murdoch's Sky TV incurred almost $1 billion in capital costs and operating losses and Robert Maxwell's British Satellite Broadcasting spent some $1.8 billion before the two merged in 1991. In other industries, entry costs can be modest. Start-up costs for franchised fast-food restaurants are around $280,000 for a Wendy's and $800,000 for a Burger King.[4]

ECONOMIES OF SCALE  In industries that are capital or research or advertising intensive, efficiency requires large-scale operation. The problem for new entrants is that they are faced with the choice of either entering on a small scale and accepting high unit costs, or entering on a large scale and running the risk of drastic underutilization of capacity while they build up sales volume. Thus, in large jet engines, economies of scale in R&D and manufacturing have caused consolidation into just three producers (General Electric, Pratt & Whitney and Rolls-Royce), which are protected by very high barriers to entry. Economies of scale in automobiles have deterred entry into that industry: recent entrants such as Ssangyong of Korea and Proton of Malaysia have incurred huge losses trying to establish themselves.

ABSOLUTE COST ADVANTAGES  Apart from economies of scale, established firms may have a cost advantage over entrants simply because they entered earlier. Absolute cost advantages tend to be associated with the acquisition of low cost sources of raw materials or economies of learning.

PRODUCT DIFFERENTIATION  In an industry where products are differentiated, established firms possess the advantages of brand recognition and customer loyalty. The percentage of US consumers loyal to a single brand varies from under 30 per cent in batteries, canned vegetables, and garbage bags, up to 61 percent in tooth-paste, 65 percent in mayonnaise, and 71 percent in cigarettes.[5] New entrants to such markets must spend disproportionately heavily on advertising and promotion to gain levels of brand awareness and brand goodwill similar to those of established companies. One study found that, compared to early entrants, late entrants into consumer goods markets incurred additional advertising and promotional costs amounting to 2.12 percent of sales revenue.[6] Alternatively, the new entrant can accept a niche position in the market or can seek to compete by cutting price. In producer goods too, reputation and close customer–supplier relationships impose similar problems for new entrants. Despite their huge financial resources, most US commercial banks have chosen to enter investment banking by means of acquiring existing investment banks.

ACCESS TO CHANNELS OF DISTRIBUTION  Whereas lack of brand awareness among consumers acts as a barrier to entry to new suppliers of consumer goods, a more immediate barrier for the new company is likely to be gaining distribution. Limited capacity within distribution channels (e.g. shelf space), risk aversion by retailers, and the fixed costs associated with carrying an additional product result in distributors' reluctance to carry a new manufacturer's product. In the United States and Britain, food and drink processors are increasingly required to make lump-sum payments to the leading supermarket chains in order to gain shelf space for a new product.

GOVERNMENTAL AND LEGAL BARRIERS   Some economists claim that the only effective barriers to entry are those created by government. In taxicabs, banking, telecommunications, and broadcasting, entry usually requires the granting of a license by a public authority. In knowledge-intensive industries, patents, copyrights, and trade secrets are major barriers to entry. Xerox Corporation's near monopoly position in the world plain-paper copier business until the mid-1970s was protected by a wall of over 2,000 patents relating to its xerography process. In industries subject to regulation and environmental and safety standards, new entrants may be at a disadvantage to established firms because compliance costs weigh more heavily on newcomers.

RETALIATION   The effectiveness of the barriers to entry also depends on the entrants' expectations as to possible retaliation by established firms. Retaliation against a new entrant may take the form of aggressive price cutting, increased advertising, sales promotion, or litigation. British Airways' retaliation against competition from Virgin Atlantic on its North Atlantic routes included not only promotional price cuts and advertising, but also a variety of 'dirty tricks' such as accessing Virgin's computer system, poaching its customers, and attacking Virgin's reputation. Southwest and other low-cost airlines have alleged that selective price cuts by American and other major airlines amounted to predatory pricing designed to drive them out of business. The likelihood of retaliation is influenced by the scale of entry. When Japanese firms first entered the US car and consumer electronics markets, they sought to avoid retaliation by introducing small products in segments that were deemed unprofitable by US producers. A successful retaliatory strategy is one that deters entry by using a threat that is credible enough to intimidate would-be entrants.[7]

THE EFFECTIVENESS OF BARRIERS TO ENTRY   Studies by Bain[8] and Mann[9] found profitability was higher in industries with 'very high entry-barriers' than in those with 'substantial' or 'moderate to low' barriers. Capital intensity and advertising are key variables that increase entry barriers and raise industry profitability.[10]

Whether barriers to entry are effective in deterring potential entrants depends on the resources of the potential entrants. Barriers that are effective for new companies may be ineffective for firms that are diversifying from other industries. George Yip found no evidence that entry barriers deterred new entry.[11] Entrants were able to successfully overcome entry barriers for one of two reasons. Some possessed resources and capabilities that permitted them to surmount barriers and compete against incumbent firms using similar strategies. American Express, for example, used its brand name to enter a broad range of financial service markets, and Mars used its strong position in confectionery to enter the ice cream market.[12] Others successfully circumvented entry barriers by adopting different strategies from those of incumbent firms. Southwest Airlines used a low-cost, 'no-frills' strategy to challenge the major US airlines. Dell Computer used direct-mail distribution and telephone-based customer service to bypass established distribution channels.

## Rivalry between established competitors

For most industries, the major determinant of the overall state of competition and the general level of profitability is competition among the firms within the industry. In some industries, firms compete aggressively – sometimes to the extent that prices are pushed below the level of costs and industry-wide losses are incurred. In others, price competition is muted and rivalry focuses on advertising, innovation, and other non-price dimensions. Six factors play an important role in determining the nature and intensity of competition between established firms: concentration, the diversity of competitors, product differentiation, excess capacity, exit barriers, and cost conditions.

CONCENTRATION   Seller concentration refers to the number and size-distribution of firms competing within a market. Seller concentration is most commonly measured by the *concentration ratio*: the combined market share of the leading producers. For example, the four-firm concentration ratio (conventionally denoted 'CR4') is the market share of the four largest producers. A market dominated by a single firm, e.g. Xerox in the US plain-paper copier market during the early 1970s, or UST in the US smokeless tobacco market, displays little competition and the dominant firm can exercise considerable discretion over the prices it charges. Where a market is dominated by a small group of leading companies (an oligopoly), price competition may also be restrained, either by outright collusion, or more commonly through 'parallelism' of pricing decisions.[13] Thus, in markets dominated by two companies, such as alkaline batteries (Duracell and Eveready), color film (Kodak and Fuji), and soft drinks (Coke and Pepsi), prices tend to be similar and competition focuses on advertising, promotion, and product development. As the number of firms supplying a market increases, coordination of prices becomes more difficult, and the likelihood that one firm will initiate price cutting increases. Despite the strong theoretical arguments, the effect of seller concentration on profitability has been hard to pin down empirically. Richard Schmalensee concludes that: 'The relation, if any, between seller concentration and profitability is weak statistically and the estimated effect is usually small.'[14]

DIVERSITY OF COMPETITORS   The ability of firms in an industry to avoid price competition also depends on their similarities in terms of origins, objectives, costs, and strategies. The cozy atmosphere of the US steel industry prior to the advent of import competition and the new mini-mills was possible because of the similarities of the companies and the outlooks of their senior managers. By contrast, the inability of OPEC to maintain prices and output quotas is a consequence of differences in objectives, production costs, language, politics and religion among member countries.

PRODUCT DIFFERENTIATION   The more similar the offerings among rival firms, the more willing customers are to substitute and the greater the incentive for firms to cut prices to increase sales. Where the products of rival firms are virtually indistinguishable, the product is a *commodity* and price is the sole basis for competition. Commodity industries such as agriculture, mining, and basic materials tend to be plagued by price wars and low profits. By contrast, in industries where products are highly differentiated (perfumes, pharmaceuticals, restaurants, management consulting services), price competition tends to be weak, even though there may be many firms competing.

EXCESS CAPACITY AND EXIT BARRIERS   Why does industry profitability tend to fall so drastically during periods of recession? The key is the balance between demand and capacity. Unused capacity encourages firms to offer price cuts to attract new business in order to spread fixed costs over a greater sales volume. Excess capacity may not be just cyclical, but part of a structural problem due to over-investment and stagnant or declining demand. In such situations, the issue is whether excess capacity will leave the industry. *Barriers to exit* are costs associated with capacity leaving an industry. Where resources are durable and specialized, and where employees are entitled to job protection, barriers to exit may be substantial.[15] Depressed profits in the European oil refining industry are the result of low demand, over-investment, and barriers to exit in the form of refinery dismantling, environmental cleanup, and employee redundancy Conversely growth industries tend to be subject to capacity shortages, which boost profitability, although cash flow in rapidly growing industries can be negative due to high rates of investment.

[. . .]

COST CONDITIONS: SCALE ECONOMIES AND THE RATIO OF FIXED TO VARIABLE COSTS   When excess capacity causes price competition, how low will prices go? The key factor is cost structure. Where fixed costs are high relative to variable costs, firms will take on marginal business at any price that covers variable cost. The consequences for profitability can be disastrous. From 1990 to 1995, the total losses of the US airline industry exceeded total profits during the previous three decades. The willingness of airlines to offer heavily discounted tickets on flights with low bookings reflects the fact that the variable costs associated with filling empty seats on a scheduled flight are close to zero. The devastating impact of excess capacity on profitability in petrochemicals, tires, steel, and memory chips is a result of high fixed costs in these businesses and the willingness of firms to accept additional business at any price that covers variable cost.

Scale economies may also encourage companies to compete aggressively on price in order to gain the cost benefits of greater volume. In consumer electronics, automobiles, and semi-conductors, the cost benefits of market leadership are powerful drivers of inter-firm competition.

## Bargaining power of buyers

The firms in an industry operate in two types of markets: in the markets for *inputs* they purchase raw materials, components, and financial and labor services from the suppliers of these factors of production; in the markets for *outputs* they sell their goods and services to customers (who may be distributors, consumers, or other manufacturers). In both markets, the relative profitability of the two parties in a transaction depends on relative economic power. Dealing first with the sales to customers, two sets of factors are important in determining the strength of buying power: buyers' price sensitivity and relative bargaining power.

BUYERS' PRICE SENSITIVITY   The extent to which buyers are sensitive to the prices charged by the firms in an industry depends upon four major factors.

- The greater the importance of an item as a proportion of total cost, the more sensitive buyers will be about the price they pay Beverage manufacturers are highly sensitive to the costs of metal cans because this is one of their largest single cost items. Conversely, most companies are not sensitive to the fees charged by their auditors, since auditing costs are such a small proportion of overall company expenses.

- The less differentiated the products of the supplying industry, the more willing the buyer is to switch suppliers on the basis of price. The manufacturers of T-shirts, light bulbs, and blank videotapes have much more to fear from Wal-Mart's buying power than do the suppliers of perfumes.

- The more intense the competition among buyers, the greater their eagerness for price reductions from their sellers. As competition in the world automobile industry has intensified, so component suppliers are subject to greater pressures for lower prices, higher quality, and faster delivery.

- The greater the importance of the industry's product to the quality of the buyer's product or service, the less sensitive are buyers to the prices they are charged. The buying power of personal computer manufacturers relative to the manufacturers of microprocessors (Intel, Motorola, Advanced Micro Devices) is limited by the critical importance of these components to the functionality of their product.

RELATIVE BARGAINING POWER   Bargaining power rests, ultimately, on refusal to deal with the other party. The balance of power between the two parties to a transaction depends on the credibility and effectiveness with which each makes this threat. The key issue is the relative cost that each party sustains as a result of the transaction not being consummated. A second issue is each party's expertise in leveraging its position through gamesmanship. Several factors influence the bargaining power of buyers relative to that of sellers.

- *Size and concentration of buyers relative to suppliers.* The smaller the number of buyers and the bigger their purchases, the greater the cost of losing one. Because of their size, health maintenance organizations (HMOs) can purchase health care from hospitals and doctors at much lower cost than can individual patients.

- *Buyers' information.* The better informed buyers are about suppliers and their prices and costs, the better they are able to bargain. Doctors and lawyers do not normally display the prices they charge, nor do traders in the bazaars of Tangier and Istanbul. Keeping customers ignorant of relative prices is an effective constraint on their buying power. But knowing prices is of little value if the quality of the product is unknown. In the markets for haircuts, interior design, and management consulting, the ability of buyers to bargain over price is limited by uncertainty over the precise attributes of the product they are buying.

- *Ability to integrate vertically.* In refusing to deal with the other party, the alternative to finding another supplier or buyer is to do-it-yourself. Large food processors such as Heinz and Campbell's Soup have reduced their dependence on the oligopolistic suppliers of metal cans by manufacturing their own. The leading retail chains have increasingly displaced their suppliers' brands with their own brand products. Backward integration need not necessarily occur – a credible threat may suffice.

Empirical evidence points to the tendency for buyer concentration to depress prices and profits in supplying industries.[16] PIMS data show that the larger the average size of customers' purchases and the larger the proportion of customers' total purchases the item represents, the lower the profitability of supplying firms.[17]

## Bargaining power of suppliers

Analysis of the determinants of relative power between the producers in an industry and their suppliers is precisely analogous to the analysis of the relationship between producers and their buyers. Since the factors that determine the effectiveness of supplier power against the buying power of the industry are the same as those that determine the power of the industry against that of its customers, they do not require a separate analysis.

Because raw materials, semi-finished products, and components tend to be commodities supplied by small companies to large manufacturing companies, their

Table 4.2 *The impact of unionization on profitability*

| | *Percentage of employees unionized* | | | | |
| --- | --- | --- | --- | --- | --- |
| | None | 1% to 35% | 35% to 60% | 60% to 75% | Over 75% |
| ROI (%) | 25 | 24 | 23 | 18 | 19 |
| ROS (%) | 10.8 | 9.0 | 9.0 | 7.9 | 7.9 |

*Source*: R.D. Buzzell and B.T. Gale, *The PIMS Principles: Linking Strategy to Performance* (New York: Free Press, 1987), p. 67

suppliers usually lack bargaining power. Hence, commodity suppliers often seek to boost their bargaining power through cartelization – e.g. OPEC, the International Coffee Organization, and farmers' marketing cooperatives. A similar logic explains labor unions.

PIMS studies of the impact of suppliers' bargaining power on firms' profitability is complex. Increasing concentration of a firm's purchases is initially beneficial since it permits certain economies of purchasing. Thereafter, increasing concentration among purchasers results in decreased profitability due to increased supplier power. Supplier power is significantly increased by forward integration into its customer's own industry. When a firm faces its suppliers as competitors within its own industry, its ROI is reduced by two percentage points. Unionization is unambiguously associated with decreasing profitability (see Table 4.2).

# Applying industry analysis

Once we understand how industry structure drives competition which, in turn, determines industry profitability, then we can apply this analysis, first, to forecasting industry profitability in the future and, second, to devising strategies to change industry structure.

## *Forecasting industry profitability*

Decisions to commit resources to a particular industry must be based on anticipated returns five to ten years in the future. Over these periods, profitability cannot be accurately forecast by projecting current industry profitability. However, we can predict changes in the underlying structure of an industry with some accuracy. Structural changes are driven by current changes in product and process technology, the current strategies of the leading players, the changes occurring in infrastructure and in related industries, and by government policies. If we understand how industry structure affects competition and profitability, we can use our projections of structural change to forecast the likely changes in industry profitability.

The first stage is to understand how past changes in industry structure have influenced competition and profitability. Box 4.1 explains deteriorating profitability of the world automobile industry in terms of the structural changes that have affected the five forces of competition. The next stage is to identify *current* structural trends and determine how these will impact the five forces of competition and resulting industry profitability. [. . .]

---

## Box 4.1

# Competition and profitability in the world automobile industry

Despite record profits earned by the US Big Three (GM, Ford, and Chrysler) from 1994 to 1997 and recovery of Japanese and German car makers in 1996–1997, the overall profitability of the world auto industry during the 1990s was dismal. During the six year period from 1990 to 1995, the average return on equity earned by the world's 10 largest car makers was 3.4 percent – substantially below their cost of equity capital. Profitability was far below the levels earned during the 1960s. What factors can explain the deterioration in industry profitability?

Substitute competition remained modest. Despite dire warnings over the imminent demise of private motoring, the automobile increased its position as the dominant-mode of personal transportation in the industrialized countries. Despite growing congestion, little shift to public transportation occurred while *telecommuting* remained in its infancy.

New entry was also limited, due mainly to the huge costs of establishing manufacturing and distribution facilities and the large scale economies in the business. New entrants during the 1980s and 1990s included Proton (Malaysia), Ssangyong and Samsung (Korea), and some small companies producing for their domestic markets.

The major force of increased competition was increased rivalry among existing car makers. At the global level, industry-concentration increased as many small and medium-sized producers were merged or acquired: in France, Peugeot and Citroen merged; Chrysler acquired AMC; VW acquired Seat and Skoda; BMW acquired Rover; Ford acquired Jaguar. Yet, looking at national markets, the picture was quite different. During the 1960s, national car makers dominated their domestic markets. The process of internationalization resulted in increased import competition and building of foreign plants, with the result that every national market featured more companies and lower concentration than three decades earlier. The US market share of the Big Three dropped from 85 to 64 percent, Fiat's share of the Italian market fell from 66 to 40 percent, Rover (formerly British Leyland) saw its UK market share decline from 40 to 11 percent; in Germany, the market share of VW and Mercedes declined from 50 to 28 percent. The leading motor vehicle manufactures in 1994 in terms of number of cars and trucks produced were as follows (figures in thousands):

| | | |
|---|---|---|
| GM | US | 8,619 |
| Ford | US | 6,462 |

| Toyota | Japan | 4,465 |
|---|---|---|
| Volkswagen | Germany | 3,299 |
| Nissan | Japan | 2,839 |
| Chrysler | US | 2,808 |
| Fiat | Italy | 2,143 |
| Peugeot | France | 1,890 |
| Renault | France | 1,761 |
| Honda | Japan | 1,765 |
| Mitsubishi | Japan | 1,529 |
| Hyundai | S. Korea | 1,255 |
| Mazda | Japan | 974 |
| Suzuki | Japan | 940 |
| Daimler-Benz | German | 930 |
| Kia | S. Korea | 691 |
| Daihatsu | Japan | 606 |
| BMW | Germany | 563 |
| VAZ | Russia | 585 |
| Daewoo | S. Korea | 523 |
| Isuzu | Japan | 456 |
| Volvo | Sweden | 448 |
| Fuji | Japan | 419 |

Not only were there more competitors, but their products were becoming increasingly similar. Increasing standardization of designs, technologies, and features resulted in different manufacturers' vehicles in each product category becoming increasingly similar. Competition was further enhanced by excess capacity. Although a strong US economy kept capacity utilization high in North America during 1995 to 1997, elsewhere the picture was less satisfactory. In Europe, capacity utilization remained low, and union agreements and political pressures presented major barriers to exit. Substantial excess capacity also existed in Japan and Korea. Worldwide, heavy investment in new plants and new process technologies was causing production capacity to grow faster than demand.

The manufacturers were also pressured by increased vertical bargaining power. The power of suppliers had increased greatly. Suppliers of components and sub-assemblies such as Bosch, TRW, Verity, Aisin Seiki, Dana, and Eaton rivaled the auto manufacturers in terms of size and multinationality. Increasingly, technology development was led by the component manufacturers, not the auto companies. At the buyer level, there were signs the auto manufacturers might be losing control over their distribution channels. In the United States, the traditional dealer system was being challenged by new 'automobile supermarkets' including Automax (owned by Circuit City) and AutoNation (owned by Republic Industries), as well as by Internet sales.

*Source*: R.M. Grant, 'The World Automobile Industry,' Georgetown School of Business, 1997.

While it is not possible to predict with any confidence the *quantitative* impact of structural changes, their *qualitative* impact is easier to assess. The main problem is the difficulty of appraising the aggregate effect of multiple structural changes where some are beneficial to profitability, others are detrimental. Thus, a key issue in the casino industry is whether the current merger wave will offset the tendency for increasing excess capacity to depress profitability. [. . .]

In other industries, there may be little ambiguity about the impact of structural changes on profitability since the main structural changes are pulling in the same direction. For example:

- It seems likely that the profitability of US network broadcasting will decline over the next ten years (1998–2007) in response to an increased number of broadcast networks (the big three – ABC, CBS, and NBC – were joined first by Fox, then by Time Warner); increased competition from substitutes such as direct satellite TV, the Internet, and video games; and increased bargaining power of production studios and local TV stations.

- The situation is similar with the issuers of bank credit cards. More competition due to increasing numbers of competitors (including non-bank issuers such as GM, GE, and AT&T), entry from various co-branders (ranging from universities and churches to clubs and airlines), lower demand due to increased consumer indebtedness, and increased substitute competition from ATM cards and electronic transactions through the Internet and other media may affect profitability.

## Strategies to alter industry structure

Understanding how the structural characteristics of an industry determine the intensity of competition and the level of profitability provides a basis for identifying opportunities for changing industry structure in order to alleviate competitive pressures. The first issue is to identify the key structural features of an industry that are responsible for depressing profitability. The second is to consider which of these structural features are amenable to change through appropriate strategic initiatives. For example:

- In consumer electronics, suppliers of leading brands (such as Sony and Pioneer) have sought to limit the buying power of discount chains by refusing to supply those chains that advertise cut prices or that do not display their products within 'an appropriate retailing environment'.

- In the European and North American oil refining industry, most firms have earned returns well below their cost of capital due to many competitors, excess capacity, and commodity products. Efforts to improve industry profitability include mergers between

BP and Mobil in Europe, between Shell and Texaco in the United States (aimed at facilitating capacity reduction), and attempts at product differentiation through performance enhancing additives to gasoline.

- Excess capacity has also been a major problem in the European petrochemicals industry. Through a series of bilateral plant exchanges, the number of companies producing each product group has been reduced and capacity rationalization has been facilitated.[18] During 1993, ICI initiated a program of plant swaps with BASF, Bayer, and Dow to reduce excess capacity in European polyurethane production.[19]

- Building entry barriers is a vital strategy for preserving high profitability in the long run. A primary goal of the American Medical Association has been to maintain the incomes of its members by controlling the numbers of doctors trained in the United States and imposing barriers to the entry of doctors from overseas.

## Defining industries: identifying the relevant market

One of the most difficult problems in industry analysis is defining the relevant industry. Suppose Jaguar, a division of Ford Motor Company, is assessing its outlook over the next ten years. In forecasting the profitability of its industry, should Jaguar consider itself part of the 'motor vehicles and equipment' industry (SIC 371), the automobile industry (SIC 3712), or the luxury car industry? Should it view its industry as national (UK), regional (Europe), or global?

The first issue is clarifying what we mean by the term 'industry'. Economists define an industry as a group of firms that supplies a market.[20] Hence, the key to defining industry boundaries is identifying the relevant market. By focusing on the relevant market, we do not lose sight of the critical relationship among firms within an industry: competition.

A market's boundaries are defined by *substitutability*, both on the demand side and on the supply side. Thus, in determining the appropriate range of products to be included in BMW's market, we should look first at substitutability on the demand side. If customers are unwilling to substitute trucks for cars on the basis of price differences, then Jaguar's market should be viewed as automobiles rather than all motor vehicles. Again if customers are willing to substitute among different types of automobiles – luxury cars, sports cars, family sedans, sport utility vehicles and station wagons – on the basis of relative price, then Jaguar's relevant market is the automobile market rather than just the luxury car market.

[. . .]

Ultimately drawing boundaries around industries and markets is a matter of judgment that must account for the purposes and context of the analysis. Substitutability tends to be higher in the long run than in the short term. Hence, if Jaguar is planning its strategy over a ten year period, its relevant business environment is the global automobile industry. If it is considering its competitive strategy over the next three years, it makes sense to focus on specific national and regional markets – the United States, Japan, the EU, and Mercosur – and on the luxury car market rather than the automobile market as a whole.

Fortunately, the precise delineation of an industry's boundaries is seldom critical to the outcome of industry analysis so long as we remain wary of external influences. Because the five forces framework includes influences from outside the industry – entrants and substitutes – the risks of defining the industry too narrowly are mitigated. For example, if we choose to identify Jaguar's industry as comprising the manufacturers of luxury cars, then we can view substitute competition as sports cars, family sedans, and sport utility vehicles, and view the manufacturers of these vehicles as potential entrants into the luxury car market.

## Beyond the Five Forces model: dynamics, game theory, and cooperation

Despite being widely used as a framework for analyzing competition and predicting profitability, Porter's Five Forces of Competition framework is not without its critics. Economists criticize its theoretical foundations. Its basis is the structure–conduct–performance approach to industrial organization economics, which has been largely displaced by game theory approaches. Researchers at McKinsey & Company have identified a number of assumptions in the structure–conduct–performance approach which do not hold in practice. For example, business relationships are not always arm's-length. Many relationships are characterized by *privilege* through affection or trust; others are *co-dependent systems* formed by webs of companies, where competition exists between webs and within webs. Thus the 'Wintel' web competes with the Apple web, while within the Wintel web, Compaq and Dell compete with one another.[21] Apart from unease over its dubious theoretical foundations, the Five Forces model is also limited by its *static* nature: it views industry structure as stable and externally determined. This determines the intensity of competition, which in turn influences the level of industry profitability. But competition is not some constrained process that determines prices and profits and leaves industry structure unchanged. Competition is a dynamic process through which industry structure itself changes through evolution and transformation. Thus, a model that does not take these features into account fails to recognize that competition changes industry structure both consciously by firms' strategic decisions and as an outcome of the resulting competitive interaction.

The essence of competition, then, is a dynamic process in which equilibrium is never reached and in the course of which industry structures are continually reformed. This is evident in the structural transformation of deregulated industries.

- By the mid-1990s, the US airline industry had developed a structure that few of the architects of deregulation had predicted. The economists of the Civil Aeronautics Board had predicted that, in the absence of government regulation of routes and fares, entry would be easy, concentration would fall, and fares would drop to their competitive levels. In practice, the industry has been shaped by the strategies of the leading players: mergers and acquisitions have increased concentration; the hub-and-spoke system has given rise to several local near-monopolies; selective price competition has driven a number of low-cost entrants into bankruptcy; and barriers to entry have been created through control of airport gates and landing slots, computer reservations systems, and frequent flyer programs.

- The privatization of British Telecom and the deregulation of the British telecommunications industry heralded a new era of intense competition and rapid and radical structural change. Competition from Mercury was soon followed by cellular phone competitors such as Vodaphone, PCS competitors such as Orange, and cable TV companies offering telephone service.

## Schumpeterian competition

Joseph Schumpeter was the first to recognize and analyze the dynamic interaction between competition and industry structure. Schumpeter focused on innovation as the central component of competition and the driving force behind industry evolution. Innovation represents a 'perennial gale of creative destruction' through which favorable industry structures – monopoly in particular – contain the seeds of their own destruction by providing incentives for firms to attack established positions through new approaches to competing. Although identified here with Schumpeter, this view of competition as a dynamic process of rivalry is associated more widely with the Austrian school of economics.[22]

The key issue raised by Schumpeter is whether we can use current industry structures as a reliable guide to the nature of competition and industry performance in the future. The relevant consideration is the speed of structural change in industry. If the pace of transformation is rapid, if entry rapidly undermines the market power of dominant firms, if innovation speedily transforms industry structure by changing process technology, by creating new substitutes, and by shifting the basis on which firms compete, then there is little merit in using industry structure as a basis for analyzing competition and profit.

Most empirical studies of changes over time in industry structure and profitability show Schumpeter's process of 'creative destruction' to be more of a breeze than a gale. Studies of United States and Canadian industry[23] have found that entry occurs so slowly that profits are undermined only slowly. One survey commented: 'the picture of the competitive process . . . is, to say the least, sluggish in the extreme'.[24] Overall, the studies show a fairly consistent picture of the rate of change of profitability and structure. Both at the firm and at the industry level, profits tend to be highly persistent in the long run.[25] Structural change – notably concentration, entry, and the identity of leading firms – also appears to be, on average, slow.[26]

Some industries, however, conform closely to Schumpeter's model. Jeffrey Williams identifies 'Schumpeterian industries' as those subject to rapid product innovation with relatively steep experience curves. In these industries, structure tends to be unstable. In computers, telecommunication services, Internet access, and electronic games, using current trends in industry structure to forecast profitability several years ahead is unreliable for two reasons: the relationship between competition and industry structure is unstable, and changes in industry structure are rapid and difficult to predict.

[. . .]

## The contribution of game theory

Central to the criticisms of Porter's Five Forces as a static framework is its failure to take full account of competitive interactions among firms . . . The essence of strategic competition is the interaction among players such that the decisions made by any one player are dependent on the actual and anticipated decisions of the other players. By relegating competition to a mediating variable that links industry structure with profitability, the Five Forces analysis offers little insight into firms' choices of whether to compete or to cooperate; sequential competitive moves; and the role of threats, promises, and commitments. Game theory has two especially valuable contributions to make to strategic management.

1 It permits the framing of strategic decisions. Apart from any theoretical value of the theory of games, the description of the game in terms of:

- Identifying the players
- Specifying each player's options
- Establishing the payoffs from every combination of options
- Defining sequences of decisions using game trees

permits us to understand the structure of the competitive situation and facilitates a systematic, rational approach to decision making.

2 Through the insight it offers into situations of competition and bargaining, game theory can predict the equilibrium outcomes of competitive situations and the consequences of strategic moves by any one player. Game theory provides penetrating insight into

central issues of strategy that go well beyond pure intuition. Simple game models (e.g. 'prisoner's dilemma') predict cooperative versus competitive outcomes, whereas more complex games permit analysis of the effects of reputation,[27] deterrence,[28] information,[29] and commitment[30] – especially within the context of multiperiod games. Particularly important for practicing managers, game theory can indicate strategies for improving the structure and outcome of the game through manipulating the payoffs to the different players.[31]

Despite the explosion of interest in game theory during the 1980s, practical applications, especially in the area of strategic management, remained limited until the 1990s. Interest in game theory has grown recently as a result of a number of practical guides to the application of the game theory's tools and insights.[32] Game theory has provided illuminating insights into a wide variety of situations, including the Cuban missile crisis of 1962,[33] President Reagan's 1981 tax cut,[34] subsidies for Airbus Industrie, the problems of OPEC in agreeing to production cuts, the competitive impact of Philip Morris's cutting cigarette prices on 'Marlboro Monday' in 1993,[35] and the auctioning of licenses of wavelengths for telecommunications by the US and New Zealand governments.[36]

One of the greatest benefits of game theory is its ability to view business interactions as comprising both competition and cooperation. A key deficiency of the Five Forces framework is in viewing rivalry and bargaining as competitive in nature. The central message of Adam Brandenburger and Barry Nalebuff's book, *Co-opetition*, is recognizing the competitive/cooperative duality of business relationships. Whereas Coca-Cola's relationship with Pepsi-Cola is essentially competitive, that between Intel and Microsoft is primarily complementary. Thus,

- A player is your *complementor* if customers value your product *more* when they have the other player's product than when they have your product alone.

- A player is your *competitor* if customers value your product *less* when they have the other player's product than when they have your product alone.

The *value net* recognizes these two types of relationship . . . It is important to recognize that a player may occupy multiple roles. Microscope and Netscape compete fiercely to dominate the market for Internet browsers. At the same time, the two companies cooperate in establishing security protocols for protecting privacy and guarding against credit card fraud on the Internet. Similarly, with customers and suppliers, though these players are essentially partners in creating value, they are also bargaining over sharing that value. The desire of competitors to cluster together – antique dealers in London's Bermondsey Market and advertising agencies on Madison Avenue – points to the complementary relations among competitors in growing the size of their market and developing its infrastructure.

The most important insights that game theory provides are its ability to identify opportunities for a player to *change the structure of a game in order to improve payoffs*.

Consider the following examples:

- *The benefits of repeated games*  A classic case of 'prisoners' dilemma' is purchasing a product where the quality cannot be easily discerned prior to purchase (e.g. a used car). The seller has an incentive to offer low quality, the buyer has an incentive to offer a low price in the likelihood that quality will be poor . . . Both parties would benefit from ensuring that the product was high quality. How can this dilemma be resolved? One answer is to change a *one period game* (single transaction) into a *repeated game* (long-term vendor relationship). Faced with the possibility of a long-term business relationship, the seller has the incentive to offer a quality product, the buyer has the incentive to offer a price that offers the seller a satisfactory return.

- *Deterrence*  The payoffs in a game can be changed through increasing the costs to other players of choices that are undesirable to the firm. By establishing the certainty that deserters would be shot, the British army made desertion a less attractive alternative for troops than advancing over no-man's-land to attack German trenches during World War I. Similarly, established airlines have sought to deter Southwest from expanding its route network by the threat of matching Southwest's fares on the new routes.

- *Bringing in competitors*  Establishing alliances and agreements with competitors can increase the value of the game by increasing the size of the market and building strength against other competitors. The key is converting win–lose (or even lose–lose) games into win–win games. When Intel developed its 8086 microprocessor, it gave up its monopoly by offering second-sourcing licenses to AMD and IBM. Although Intel was creating competition for itself, it was also encouraging the adoption of the 8086 chip by computer manufacturers (including IBM) who were concerned about overdependence on Intel. Once Intel had established its technology as the industry standard, it developed its family of 286, 386, 486, and Pentium processors and became much more restrictive over licensing. A cooperative solution was also found to Norfolk Southern's competition with CSX for control of Conrail. The 1997 bidding war was terminated when CSX and Norfolk Southern agreed to dismember and share Conrail.

Game theory permits considerable insight into the nature of situations involving interactions among multiple players. It clarifies the structure of relationships and nature of interactions among players, and it identifies the alternative actions available to different players and relates these to possible outcomes. Game theory has provided valuable decision support in negotiations and in simulating competitive patterns of action and reaction. War gaming, based on game theory principles, is a popular technique among both military planners and management consultants such as Booz Allen and Coopers & Lybrand. The weaknesses are in the ability to apply game theory to specific business situations and generate unambiguous, meaningful, and accurate predictions. Game theory is excellent in providing insights and understanding; it has been less valuable in predicting outcomes and designing strategies. [. . .]

# Opportunities for competitive advantage: identifying Key Success Factors

Our discussion of hypercompetition and game theory has taken us well beyond the confines of the Five Forces framework. Remember that the primary purpose of that model is to analyze industry attractiveness in order to forecast industry profitability. Hypercompetition explicitly recognizes that competition is a battle for competitive advantage. Game theory also focuses on positioning and maneuvering for advantage. The purpose of this section is to look explicitly at the analysis of competitive advantage . . . to identify the potential for competitive advantage within an industry in terms of the factors that determine a firm's ability to survive and prosper – its *Key Success Factors*.[37] [. . .]

To survive and prosper in an industry, a firm must meet two criteria: first, it must supply what customers want to buy, second, it must survive competition. Hence, we may start by asking two questions:

- What do our customers want?

- What does the firm need to do to survive competition?

[. . .]

To answer the first question we need to look more closely at customers of the industry and to view them, not so much as a source of bargaining power and hence as a threat to profitability, but more as the basic rationale for the existence of the industry and as the underlying source of profit. This implies that the firm must identify who its customers are, identify their needs, and establish the basis on which they select the offerings of one supplier in preference to those of another. Once we have identified the basis of customers' preference, this is just the starting point for a chain of analysis. As Table 4.3 shows, if consumers select supermarkets primarily on the basis of price, and if low prices depend on low costs, the interesting questions concern the determinants of low costs.

The second question requires that the firm examine the basis of competition in the industry. How intense is competition and what are its key dimensions? If competition in an industry is intense, then, even though the product may be highly differentiated and customers may choose on the basis of design and quality rather than price, low cost may be essential for survival. Retailers such as Harrods, Nordstrom, and Tiffany's do not compete on low prices, but in a fiercely competitive retailing sector, their prosperity depends on rigorous cost control.

Table 4.3 *Identifying Key Success Factors: some examples*

|  | What do customers want? (analysis of demand) | How does a firm survive competition? (analysis of competition) | Key success factors |
|---|---|---|---|
| Steel | Customers include auto, engineering, and container industries. Customers acutely price sensitive. Customers require product consistency and reliability of supply. Specific technical specifications required for special steels | Competition primarily on price. Competition intense due to declining demand, high fixed costs, excess capacity, low-cost imports, and exit barriers high. Transport costs high. Scale economies important | Cost efficiency through scale-efficient plants, low cost location, rapid adjustment of capacity to output, efficient use of labor. Scope for differentiation through quality service and technical factors |
| Fashion clothing | Demand fragmented by garment, style, quality, color. Customers' willingness to pay price premium for fashion, exclusivity, and quality. Mass market highly price sensitive. Retailers seek reliability and speed of supply | Low barriers to entry and exit. Low seller concentration. Few scale economies. International competition strong. Retail chains exercise strong buying power | Need to combine effective differentiation with low-cost operation. Key differentiation variables are speed of response to changing high fashions, style, reputation and quality |
| Supermarkets | Low prices. Convenient location. Wide range of products. Product range adapted to local customer preferences. Freshness of produce. Cleanliness, service, and pleasant ambience | Markets localized and concentration normally high. But customer price sensitivity encourages vigorous price competition. Exercise of bargaining power an important influence on input cost. Scale economies in operation and advertising | Low cost operation requires operational efficiency, scale efficient stores, large aggregate purchases to maximize buying power, low wage costs. Differentiation requires large stores (to allow wide product range), convenient location, easy parking |

A basic framework for identifying Key Success Factors is presented in Figure 4.5. Application of the framework to identify Key Success Factors in three industries is outlined in Table 4.3.

[. . .]

The value of success factors in formulating strategy has been scorned by some strategy scholars. Pankaj Ghemawat observes that the 'whole idea of identifying a success factor and then chasing it seems to have something in common with the ill-considered medieval hunt for the philosopher's stone, a substance that would

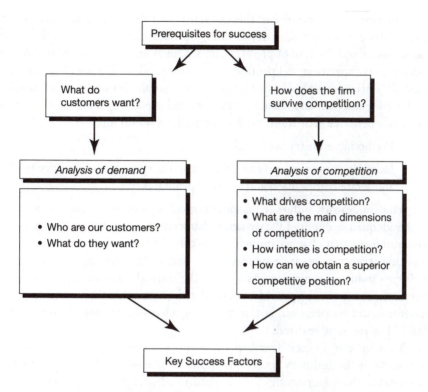

**Figure 4.5** *Identifying Key Success Factors*

transmute everything it touched into gold'.[38] The objective here in identifying Key Success Factors is less ambitious. There is no universal blueprint for a successful strategy, and even in individual industries, there is no 'generic strategy' that can guarantee superior profitability. However, each market is different in terms of what motivates customers and how competition works. Understanding these aspects of the industry environment is a prerequisite for an effective business strategy. This does not imply that firms within a industry adopt common strategies. Since every firm comprises a unique set of resources and capabilities, every firm must pursue unique key success factors.

# Summary

In this chapter, we examined concepts and frameworks to assist us in understanding the business environment of the firm. A key assumption is that to understand competition and the determinants of profitability within an industry, we are not restricted to acquiring experience-based, industry-specific learning over a long period of time. Instead, we can draw on concepts, principles, and theories that can be applied to any industry. Although every industry is unique, the patterns of competitive behavior can be explained using common analytical frameworks.

The underlying premise of this chapter is that the structural characteristics of an industry play a key role in determining the nature and intensity of the competition within it and the rate of profit it earns. Our framework for linking industry structure to competition and profitability is Porter's Five Forces of Competition model. This provides a simple, yet powerful, organizing framework for classifying the relevant features of an industry's structure and predicting their implications for competitive behavior. The framework is particularly useful for:

- Predicting industry profitability

- Indicating how the firm can influence industry structure in order to moderate competition and improve profitability.

The Porter framework suffers from some critical limitations. In particular, it does not take adequate account of the dynamic character of competition. Competition is a powerful force that changes industry structure. In hypercompetitive industries, competing strategies create a process of 'creative destruction' that continually transforms industry structure. As for the theoretical weaknesses of the Porter framework, game theory provides a broader theoretical basis for analyzing both competition and cooperation, but, in providing a basis for strategy formulation, its potential has yet to be realized.

Though the Porter framework permits analysis of competition and profitability at the industry level, our industry analysis is also directed toward understanding the opportunities for competitive advantage. Our approach has been to show that by understanding customer demand, the competitive process, and the determinants of firm-level profitability, we can identify Key Success Factors: the prerequisites for survival and success within an industry.

[. . .]

## Notes

1  See, for example, J.P. Leemhuis, 'Using Scenarios to Develop Strategies', *Long Range Planning* (April 1985): 30–37; and Pierre Wack, 'Scenarios: Shooting the Rapids', *Harvard Business Review* (November–December 1985): 139–150.

2  Michael E. Porter, *Competitive Strategy: Techniques for Analyzing Industries and Competitors* (New York: Free Press, 1980), chapter 1. For a summary, see his article, 'How Competitive Forces Shape Strategy', *Harvard Business Review* 57 (March–April 1979): 86–93.

3  W.J. Baumol, John C. Panzar, and Robert D. Willig, *Contestable Markets and the Theory of Industry Structure* (New York: Harcourt Brace Jovanovitch, 1982).

4  'Annual Franchise 500', *Entrepreneur* (January 1996).

5  'Brand Loyalty Is Rarely Blind Loyalty', *Wall Street Journal*, October 19, 1989: B1.

6  Robert D. Buzzell and Paul W. Farris, 'Marketing Costs in Consumer Goods

Industries', in *Strategy + Structure = Performance*, ed. Hans Thorelli (Bloomington, IN: Indiana University Press, 1977): 128–129.

7  Martin B. Lieberman, 'Excess Capacity as a Barrier to Entry', *Journal of Industrial Economics* 35 (June 1987): 607–627, argues that to be credible the threat of retaliation needs to be supported by excess capacity.

8  J.S. Bain, *Barriers to New Competition* (Cambridge, MA: Harvard University Press, 1956).

9  H. Michael Mann, 'Seller Concentration, Entry Barriers, and Rates of Return in Thirty Industries', *Review of Economics and Statistics* 48 (1966): 296–307.

10  See, for example, the studies by W.S. Comanor and T.A. Wilson, *Advertising and Market Power* (Cambridge: Harvard University Press, 1974); and L. Weiss, 'Quantitative Studies in Industrial Organization', in *Frontiers of Quantitative Economics*, ed. M. Intriligator (Amsterdam: North Holland, 1971).

11  George S. Yip, 'Gateways to Entry', *Harvard Business Review* 60 (September–October 1982): 85–93.

12  Guy de Jonquieres, 'Europe's New Cold Warriors', *Financial Times*, May 19, 1993: 18.

13  See 'US Probes Whether Airlines Colluded on Fare Increases', *Wall Street Journal*, December 14, 1989: B1; and 'A Tank Full of Trouble', *Economist*, December 16–22, 1989: 57.

14  Richard Schmalensee, 'Inter-Industry Studies of Structure and Performance', in *Handbook of Industrial Organization* 2, ed. Richard Schmalensee and Robert D. Willig (Amsterdam: North Holland, 1988): 976. For evidence on the impact of concentration in banking, airlines, and railroads see D.W. Carlton and J.M. Perloff, *Modern Industrial Organization* (Glenview, IL: Scott, Foresman, 1990): 383–385.

15  The problems caused by excess capacity and exit barriers are discussed in *Strategic Management of Excess Capacity*, ed. Charles Baden Fuller (Oxford: Basil Blackwell, 1990).

16  S.H. Lustgarten, 'The Impact of Buyer Concentration in Manufacturing Industries', *Review of Economics and Statistics* 57 (1975): 125–132; and Robert M. Grant, 'Manufacture–Retailer Relations: The Shifting Balance of Power', in *Business Strategy and Retailing*, ed. G. Johnson (Chichester: John Wiley & Sons, 1987).

17  Robert D. Buzzell and Bradley T. Gale, *The PIMS Principles: Linking Strategy to Performance* (New York: Free Press, 1987): 64–65.

18  See Joe Bower, *When Markets Quake* (Boston: Harvard Business School Press, 1986).

19  Paul Abrahams, 'ICI Seeks Restructure of Polyurethane Industry', *Financial Times*, July 1, 1993: 28.

20  The economist's definition of an industry can differ from normal usage of the term. For example, the US automobile industry tends to be viewed either as comprising US-owned car makers (GM, Ford, Chrysler) or US-located car makers (the Big Three plus the US subsidiaries of foreign-owned auto

companies such as Honda, Nissan, and BMW). A market-based definition would focus on all auto companies that supply the US car market wherever their plants are located.

21 Kevin Coyne, 'A Comprehensive Model for Strategy Development', paper presented at the Strategic Management Society Conference, Barcelona, October 6, 1997.

22 See Robert Jacobson, 'The Austrian School of Strategy', *Academy of Management Review* 17 (1992): 782–807; and Greg Young, Ken Smith, and Curtis Grimm, 'Austrian and Industrial Organization Perspectives on Firm-Level Competitive Activity and Performance', *Organization Science* 7 (May–June 1996): 243–254.

23 R.T. Masson and J. Shaanan, 'Stochastic Dynamic Limit Pricing: An Empirical Test', *Review of Economics and Statistics* 64 (1982): 413–422; R.T. Masson and J. Shaanan, 'Optimal Pricing and Threat of Entry: Canadian Evidence', *International Journal of Industrial Organization* 5 (1987).

24 P.A. Geroski and R.T. Masson, 'Dynamic Market Models in Industrial Organization', *International Journal of Industrial Organization* 5 (1987): 1–13.

25 Dennis C. Mueller, *Profits in the Long Run* (Cambridge: Cambridge University Press, 1986).

26 Richard Caves and Michael E. Porter, 'The Dynamics of Changing Seller Concentration', *Journal of Industrial Economics* 19 (1980): 1–15; P. Hart and R. Clarke, *Concentration in British Industry* (Cambridge: Cambridge University Press, 1980).

27 Keith Weigelt and Colin F. Camerer, 'Reputation and Corporate Strategy: A Review of Recent Theory and Applications', *Strategic Management Journal* 9 (1988): 137–142.

28 A.K. Dixit, 'The Role of Investment in Entry Deterrence', *Economic Journal* 90 (1980): 95–106.

29 P. Milgrom and J. Roberts, 'Informational Asymmetries, Strategic Behavior and Industrial Organization', *American Economic Review* 77, no. 2 (May 1987): 184–189; J. Tirole, *The Theory of Industrial Organization* (Cambridge, MA: MIT Press, 1990).

30 Pankaj Ghemawat, *Commitment: The Dynamic of Strategy* (New York: Free Press, 1991).

31 The are two outstanding introductions to the principles of game theory and their practical applications: Thomas C. Schelling, *The Strategy of Conflict*, 2nd edition (Cambridge: Harvard University Press, 1980); and A.K. Dixit and B.J. Nalebuff, *Thinking Strategically: The Competitive Edge in Business, Politics, and Everyday Life* (New York: W.W Norton, 1991).

32 Avinash K. Dixit and Barry Nalebuff, *Thinking Strategically: The Competitive Edge in Business, Politics, and Everyday Life* (New York: W.W. Norton, 1991); John McMillan, *Games, Strategies, and Managers* (New York: Oxford University Press, 1992); Adam Brandenburger and Barry Nalebuff, *Co-opetition* (New York: Doubleday, 1996).

33 Graham Allison, *Essence of Decision: Explaining the Cuban Missile Crisis* (Boston: Little, Brown, 1971).

34 A.K. Dixit and B.J. Nalebuff, *op cit.*, 131–135.

35 'Business War Games Attract Big Warriors', *Wall Street Journal*, December 22, 1994: B1.

36 'Winning the Game of Business', *Business Week*, February 11, 1985: 28.

37 The term was coined by Chuck Hofer and Dan Schendel, *Strategy Formulation: Analytical Concepts* (St Paul: West Publishing, 1977): 77, who defined Key Success Factors as 'those variables that management can influence through its decisions and that can affect significantly the overall competitive positions of the firms in an industry . . . Within any particular industry they are derived from the interaction of two sets of variables, namely, the economic and technological characteristics of the industry . . . and the competitive weapons on which the various firms in the industry have built their strategies'.

38 Pankaj Ghemawat, *Commitment: The Dynamic of Strategy* (New York: Free Press, 1991): 11.

# CHAPTER 5

# *Industry Evolution*

ROBERT M. GRANT*

> No company ever stops changing . . . Each new generation must meet changes – in
> the automotive market, in the general administration of the enterprise, and in the
> involvement of the corporation in a changing world. The work of creating goes on.
> (Alfred P. Sloan Jr, President of General Motors 1923–1937,
> Chairman 1937–1956, in *My Years with General Motors*)

[. . .]

## Introduction

The analysis of competitive advantage in the last three chapters emphasized competition as a *dynamic* process in which firms vie to gain competitive advantage only to see it eroded by imitation and innovation by rivals. The outcome of this process is an industry environment that is continually being reshaped by the forces of competition. This view of competition as a dynamic process contrasts with the *static* approach of the Porter Five Forces of Competition framework . . . which views industry structure as a stable determinant of the intensity of competition in an industry. In practice, industry structures continually evolve, driven both by the forces of competition and by fundamental changes in technology and economic growth. Firms that develop the capabilities and strategies suited to emerging industry circumstances prosper and grow; those that do not are eliminated. The issue we explore in this chapter is whether industry evolution can be anticipated. My central thesis is that, although every industry develops in a unique way, it is possible to detect some typical patterns that are the result of common driving forces. Our task is to identify patterns of industry evolution and the forces that drive them, and explore the implications for competition and competitive advantage.

* Blackwell Publishers for an extract from *Contemporary Strategy Analysis* by Robert M. Grant © Robert M. Grant, 1998.

We will examine the *industry life cycle* as a common pattern of industry development. This permits us to classify industries according to their stage of development. This raises the question, not only of the extent to which the life cycle accurately describes the evolution of different industries, but also whether there is purpose or validity in grouping diverse industries into a single category. The value of classification is in coming to grips with the key elements that determine the strategic character of an industry. The process of choosing a classification scheme and then assigning industries to different categories forces us to consider what is important about an industry. It is useful to highlight the ways in which industries are similar to one another and how they are different. Grouping industries on the basis of strategic similarities can also assist the transfer of management ideas from one industry to another. Although cigarettes, beer, processed foods, and soft drinks are very different products, the fact that they are all mature, branded, disposable consumer goods capable of international distribution provides them with strategic similarities that Philip Morris has been able to exploit.

By the time you have completed this chapter, you will be able to:

- Recognize the different stages of the industry life cycle and understand the factors that drive the process of industry evolution

- Identify the key success factors associated with industries at different stages of their life cycle

- Apply the industry life cycle to issues of strategy implementation in order to identify the organizational structures and management systems appropriate to different stages of the cycle

- Use scenarios to explore industry futures.

# The life cycle model

One of the best-known and most enduring marketing concepts is the *product life cycle*.[1] Products are born, their sales grow, they reach maturity, they go into decline, and they ultimately die. If products have life cycles, so too do the industries that produce them. The industry life cycle is the supply-side equivalent of the product life cycle. Thus, to the extent that an industry produces a range and a sequence of products, the industry life cycle is likely to be of longer duration than that of a single product. Though the 64-bit games produced by Nintendo, Sega, and Sony have a probable life cycle of a few years, the life cycle of the electronic games industry is much longer.

The life cycle is conventionally divided into four phases: introduction, growth, maturity, and decline (see Figure 5.1). Before we examine the features of each of these stages, it is important to understand the forces that are driving industry evolution. There are two factors that can be identified as fundamental to driving industry evolution: *demand growth* and the *production and diffusion of knowledge*.

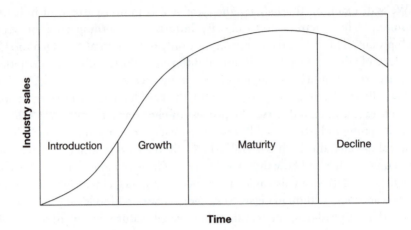

**Figure 5.1** *The industry life cycle*

## Demand growth

The life cycle and the stages within it are defined by changes in an industry's growth rate over time. The characteristic profile is an S-shaped growth curve.

- In the *introduction stage*, sales are small and the rate of market penetration is low because the industry's products are little known and customers are few. The novelty of the technology, small production scale, and lack of experience means that costs and prices are high, while quality is low. Customers for new products tend to be affluent, innovation-oriented, and risk-accepting.

- The *growth stage* is characterized by accelerating market penetration as product technology becomes more standardized and prices fall. Ownership spreads from higher-income customers to the mass market.

- The onset of the *maturity stage* is caused by increasing market saturation and slowing growth as new demand gives way to replacement demand. Once saturation is reached, demand is wholly for replacement, either direct replacement (customers replacing old products with new products) or indirect replacement (new customers replacing old customers).

- Finally, as the industry becomes challenged by new industries that produce technologically superior substitute products, the industry enters its *decline stage*.

## Creation and diffusion of knowledge

The second key force driving the industry life cycle is the creation and diffusion of knowledge. New knowledge in the form of product innovation is responsible for an industry coming into being, and the dual processes of knowledge creation and knowledge diffusion continue to drive industry evolution.

In the introduction stage, product technology advances rapidly. There is no dominant product technology, and rival technologies compete for attention. Competition is primarily between alternative technologies and design configurations. The competitive process involves the selection of the more successful from the less successful approaches, and, typically a dominant technology and design configuration emerges. This process of elimination therefore involves *standardization*.[2]

The transition from technological heterogeneity to one of increased standardization typically inaugurates the industry's growth phase. Increased standardization encourages firms to reduce costs through large-scale manufacturing methods. Hence the growth phase is associated with technology shifting from *product innovation* toward *process innovation*. Figure 5.2 shows the typical pattern.

This pattern is evident in the automobile industry. Between 1890 and 1920, cars featured a wide diversity of engine configurations and transmission designs, not to mention body designs and steering and braking systems. Ford's Model T was the first dominant design to emerge with its front-mounted, water-cooled engine, and transmission with a gearbox, wet clutch, and rearwheel drive. In the 1920s, the dominant design was refined to include an all-steel, enclosed body. During the next half century, nonconventional technologies and designs were gradually eliminated. Volkswagen's Beetle was the last mass-produced car with a rear-mounted, air-cooled engine. Renault and Citroën abandoned their distinctive technologies and designs in favor of convention. Even distinctive national differences diminished as

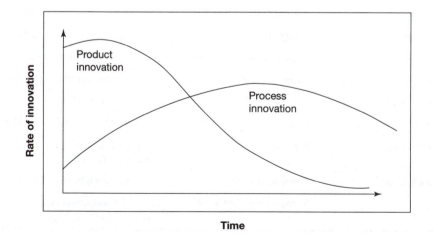

**Figure 5.2** *Product and process innovation over time*

American cars became smaller and Japanese and Italian cars became bigger. The fall of the Iron Curtain extinguished the last outposts of nonconformity: by the mid-1990s, East German two-stroke Wartburgs and Trabants were collectors' items. A growing feature of parking lots throughout the world is confused car owners searching along rows of bewilderingly similar vehicles.

Product innovation in automobiles has shifted from being radical to incremental. Most of the innovations in automobiles during the postwar era have involved the refinement of existing technologies and the application of technologies developed in other sectors (most notably the application of microelectronics and new materials such as plastics and ceramics to cars). Many product innovations have involved the adoption of features and components that were developed many years ago. Table 5.1 identifies some of these.

Once product technology and design stabilize, the challenge is to produce the product at acceptable cost and higher quality. Technological development thus shifts from product to process innovation. The success of the Model T was in Henry Ford's development of moving assembly line production with interchangeable parts. This shifted manufacturing from small-volume, craft-based workshops to huge capital-intensive plants employing large numbers of semi-skilled workers.

Table 5.1 *From option to standard: the diffusion of innovations and features in automobiles*

| Feature | Introduction | General adoption |
|---|---|---|
| Speedometer | 1901 by Oldsmobile | Circa 1915 |
| Automatic transmission | First installed in 1904 | Introduced by Packard as an option, 1938. Standard on Cadillacs and other luxury cars, early 1950s |
| Electric headlamps | GM introduced in 1908 | Became standard by 1916 |
| All steel body | Adopted by GM, 1912 | Became standard, early 1920s |
| All steel, enclosed body | Dodge, 1923 | Became standard, late 1920s |
| Radio | Appears as an option, 1923 | Standard equipment, 1946 |
| Four-wheel drive | Appears 1924 | Only limited availability by 1994 |
| Hydraulic brakes | Introduced 1924 | Became standard, 1939 |
| Shatterproof glass | First used in cars in 1927 | Standard feature in Fords, 1938 |
| Power steering | Introduced 1952 | Adopted as standard equipment, 1969 |
| Antilock brakes | Introduced 1972 | Standard on GM cars in 1991 |
| Air bags | Introduced by GM in 1974 | By 1994, most new cars equipped with air bags |

*Source*: Robert M. Grant, 'The World Automobile Industry in the 1990s', Georgetown University, miomeograph, 1994

The second revolutionary process innovation in automobile manufacturing was Toyota's system of 'lean production', involving a tightly integrated 'pull' system of production embodying just-in-time scheduling, team-based production, continuous improvement, and high levels of flexibility.

Knowledge diffusion is also important on the customer side. Over the course of the life cycle, customers become increasingly informed. As they become more knowledgeable about the performance attributes of rival manufacturers' products, so they are better able to judge value-for-money and become more price sensitive.

## How general is the life cycle pattern?

To what extent do industries conform to this life cycle pattern? The first observation is that the duration of life cycles varies from industry to industry.

- The life cycle of the railroad industry extended from the 1830s to the 1950s before entering its decline phase.

- The introduction stage of the US automobile industry lasted about 25 years from the 1890s until growth took off in 1913–1915. The growth phase lasted about 40 years. Maturity, in terms of slackening growth, set in during the mid-1950s.

- In personal computers, the introduction phase lasted only about four years before growth took off in 1978. Between 1978 and 1983 a flood of new and established firms entered the industry. Toward the end of 1984, the first signs of maturity appeared: growth stalled, excess capacity emerged, and the industry began to consolidate around a few companies. However, continued product innovation caused growth to remain strong through the late 1980s and during the 1990s.

- During the 1980s and 1990s, product life cycles became compressed. Compact discs, introduced in 1984, passed almost immediately from introduction to growth phase. By 1988, compact discs outsold conventional record albums in the United States, and by 1990, only six years since their introduction, the market appeared to be mature.

Industries also differ in their patterns of evolution. Industries supplying basic necessities such as residential construction, food processing, and clothing may never enter a decline phase because obsolescence is unlikely for such needs. Some industries may experience a rejuvenation of their life cycle. In the 1960s, the world motorcycle industry, in decline in the US and Europe, re-entered its growth phase as the influx of new Japanese bikes stimulated the recreational use of motorcycles. The TV set industry has experienced several revivals: the first caused by color TV, the second by the demand for multiple TV sets within a household, and the third spurred by the demand for computer monitors and TV video games.

High-definition TV promises a further cycle. These rejuvenations of the product life cycle are not some natural phenomenon – they are typically the result of company strategies fostering breakthrough product innovations or developing new markets for the product.

An industry is likely to be at different stages of its life cycle in different countries. Although the US auto market is in the early stages of its decline phase, markets in China, India, and Russia are in their growth phases. Multinational companies can exploit such differences: developing new products and introducing them into the advanced industrial countries, then shifting attention to other growth markets once maturity sets in. In the automobile and can-making industries, pursuing market growth phases is accompanied by shipping whole plants from North America and Western Europe to Latin America, Eastern Europe, and Asia.[3]

# Structure, competition, and success factors over the life cycle

Changes in demand growth and technology over the cycle have implications for industry structure, competition, and the sources of competitive advantage (Key Success Factors). Table 5.2 summarizes the principal features of each stage of the industry life cycle.

## Product differentiation

Emerging industries are characterized by a wide variety of product types that reflect the diversity of technologies and designs – and lack of consensus over customer requirements. Standardization during growth and maturity phases increases product uniformity with the result that a product may evolve toward commodity status unless producers are effective in developing new dimensions for differentiation, such as marketing variables, ancillary services (e.g. credit facilities, after-sales service), and product options.[4] A feature of the markets for personal computers, credit cards, securities broking, and Internet access is their increasing commodity status in which buyers select primarily on price.

## Industry structure and competition

Market growth and technological change are major determinants of the structure of manufacturing and distribution, although it is difficult to generalize about resulting industry structures. In most industries, the introduction phase is associated with a fragmented structure and diversity of products and technologies. Thus, the automobile, aircraft, and personal computer industries all went through their 'garage stages' involving numerous small start-ups. The growth stage may also attract further new entry, but soon fragmentation is counteracted by pressures for lower costs through scale efficient production. Rapid consolidation around fewer

Table 5.2 *The evolution of industry structure and competition over the life cycle*

|  | Introduction | Growth | Maturity | Decline |
|---|---|---|---|---|
| Demand | High-income buyers | Readily increasing market penetration | Mass market, replacement/ repeat buying | Customers knowledgeable |
| Technology | Competing technologies | Standardization. Rapid process innovation | Well-diffused technical knowhow: quest for technological improvements | |
| Products | Poor quality. Wide variety. Frequent design changes | Design and quality improves. Emergence of dominant design | Standardization lessens differentiation. Efforts to avoid commodtization by branding | Commodities the norm |
| Manufacturing and distribution | Short production runs. High-skilled labor content. Specialized distribution channels | Capacity shortages. Mass production. Competition for distribution | Emergence of overcapacity. Deskilling of production. Long production runs. Distributors carry fewer lines | Heavy overcapacity. Reemergence of specialty channels |
| Trade | Manufacturing shifts from advanced countries to poorer countries | | | |
| Competition | Few companies | Entry, mergers, and exits | Shakeout. Price competition increases | Price wars, exits |
| Key Success Factors | Product innovation. Establishing credible image of firm and product | Design for manufacture. Access to distribution. Building strong brand. Process innovation | Cost-efficiency through capital intensity, scale efficiency, and low input costs. High quality. Fast product development | Reduce overheads, buyer selection. Signal commitment. Rationalize capacity |

players is certainly a feature of the transition to maturity when the slowdown of market growth causes excess capacity and a 'shakeout' phase for the industry. This shakeout period may mark the onset of aggressive price competition in the industry.

Different industries have different development trends, however. Industries that begin with patent-protected new products are likely to start out as near monopolies, then become increasingly competitive. Plain-paper copiers were initially monopolized by Xerox Corporation (and its affiliates Rank Xerox and Fuji-Xerox), and it was not until the early 1980s that the industry was transformed by the entry of many competitors.

Entry barriers play a key role in the evolution of industry concentration. Where entry barriers rise due to increasing capital requirements (automobiles, commercial aircraft, telecommunications equipment) or product differentiation and access to distribution channels (soft drinks, beer, cosmetics), seller concentration is likely to increase over the life cycle. Where entry barriers fall because technology becomes more accessible or product differentiation declines, concentration may decline over time (credit cards, television broadcasting, steel, frozen foods).

The evolving structure of distribution channels also has an important influence on competition and the overall development of an industry. The typical pattern is for small-scale, specialized distribution channels to give way to larger-scale, more generalized distribution channels. At the retail level, the size of individual retail units increases and independent retailers are displaced by chains (Wal-Mart, Toys 'R' Us, Home Depot, and the like). Increasing concentration at one stage of the value chain may encourage increased concentration in other parts as firms seek *countervailing power*.[5]

## Location and international trade

The industry life cycle is associated with changes in the pattern of trade and direct investment that together result in international migration of production.[6] The life cycle theory of trade and direct investment is based on two assumptions. First, that demand for new products emerges first in the advanced industrialized countries of North America, Western Europe, and Japan and then diffuses internationally. Second, that with maturity, products require fewer inputs of technology and sophisticated skills. The result is the following development pattern:

1 New industries begin in high-income countries (traditionally the United States, but increasingly in Japan and Western Europe) because of the presence of a market and the availability of technical and scientific resources.

2 As demand grows in other markets, they are serviced initially by exports.

3 Continued growth of overseas markets and reduced need for inputs of technology and sophisticated labor skills make production attractive in newly industrialized countries. The advanced industrialized countries begin to import.

With maturity, a reduced need for skilled production workers and an increased perception of the product as a commodity, the production activity shifts increasingly to developing countries in search of low cost labor.

Thus, consumer electronics were initially produced primarily in the United States and Germany. During the early 1960s, production shifted more and more to Japan. The 1980s saw the rise of Korea, Hong Kong, and Taiwan as leading exporters. By the mid-1990s, assembly had moved to lower-wage countries such as China, the Philippines, Thailand, Mexico, and Brazil. [. . .]

## *The nature and intensity of competition*

The consequences of these structural changes over the course of the industry life cycle are for competition: first, to shift from nonprice to price competition and second, to become increasingly intense. During the introduction stage, competitors battle for technological leadership, and competition often features a diversity of technologies and designs. Heavy investments in innovation and limited sales typically make the introduction stage unprofitable, unless one firm gains a major market share through patent protection or by some other first-mover advantage. The growth phase is more conducive to profitability as market demand outstrips industry capacity, though much depends on the effectiveness of barriers to entry. With the onset of maturity, increased product standardization increases the emphasis on price competition. How intense this is depends a great deal on the capacity/demand balance and the extent of international competition. In food retailing, airlines, motor vehicles, and oil refining, maturity is associated with intense price competition and low profits. In household detergents, breakfast cereals, cosmetics, and investment banking, high levels of seller concentration and successful maintenance of product differentiation have resulted in more benign competitive circumstances. Once an industry enters its decline phase, depending on the height of exit barriers and the strength of international competition, price competition may degenerate into destructive price wars.

The pattern of changes in industry structure and competition is summarized in Figure 5.3. The consequences of these changes for profitability over the industry life cycle are shown in Table 5.3.

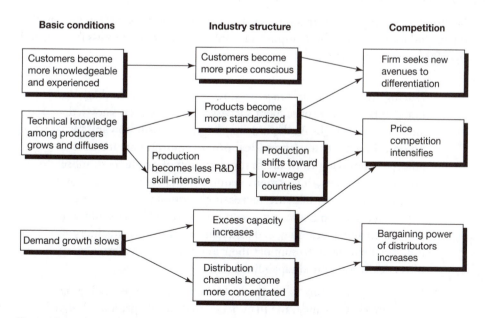

**Figure 5.3** *The driving forces of industry evolution*

Table 5.3 *Average ROI at different stages of the industry life cycle*

| | Real rate of growth | | |
| --- | --- | --- | --- |
| | Less than 3% | 3% to 6% | Over 6% |
| Growth | 22.8% | 24.4% | 24.3% |
| Maturity | 21.7% | 22.0% | 24.1% |
| Decline | 16.4% | 22.3% | |

*Note:* These results are for 6,600 business units on the PIMS database over a four year period.
*Source:* Robert D. Buzzell and Bradley T. Gale, *The PIMS Principles* (New York: Free Press, 1987): 58

Maturity in an industry usually corresponds to maturity of the individual firms. Industry membership tends to be stable with long established firms. Lack of radical innovation and limited opportunities for differentiation also lead to stability of market shares for the leading firms. This stability is partly a product of the heavy investments that leading firms have made in their market positions over long periods of time. The acquisition of experience, reputation, distribution channels, and brand recognition makes it difficult for newcomers to easily dislodge incumbents from their leadership positions. Motor vehicles, oil, chemicals, and branded consumer goods all display such stability. Upheavals in the competitive structures of mature industries are most likely the result of internationalization: new competitors from low-cost countries may undermine the market positions of long-established leaders, as in steel and shipbuilding.

## Key success factors and industry evolution

The changes in competitive structure, customer needs, and resource requirements over the industry life cycle have important implications for key success factors, and hence for business strategies.

[. . .]

- During the *introductory stage* product innovation is the basis for initial entry and for subsequent success. Soon, however, knowledge alone is not enough. As the industry begins its evolution and technological competition intensifies, other requirements for success emerge. In moving from the first generation of products to subsequent generations, investment requirements tend to grow, and financial resources become increasingly important. Capabilities in product development soon need to be matched by capabilities in manufacturing, marketing, and distribution. Hence, in an emerging industry firms need to support their innovation with a broad array of vertically integrated capabilities.

- Once the *growth stage* is reached, the key challenge is scaling up. As the market expands, the firm needs to adapt its product design and its manufacturing capability to large-scale production . . .

Investment in R&D, plant and equipment, and sales tends to be high during the growth phase. To utilize increased manufacturing capability, access to distribution becomes critical. At the same time, the tensions that organizational growth imposes create the need for internal administrative and strategic skills . . .

- With the *maturity stage*, competitive advantage is increasingly a quest for cost efficiency – or at least, this is the case in those mature industries that tend toward less and less product differentiation. The key success factors thus become the most important cost drivers within that particular industry . . . R&D, capital investment, and marketing are lower in maturity than during the growth phase.

- The transformation to the *decline phase* raises the potential for destructive price competition. Whether a firm has a competitive advantage is secondary to the importance of maintaining a stable industry environment. Hence, company strategies focus on encouraging the orderly exit of industry capacity and building a strong position in relation to residual market demand . . .

## Anticipating and shaping the future

Sustaining competitive advantage over time is not just about protecting one's position against imitation, but also about ensuring that one's competitive advantage is not rendered obsolete by changes in the industry environment. The threat to IBM in the early 1990s was not about losing its relative strengths in resources and capabilities. The problem was that changes in the market meant that its enormous investments in internal resources and capabilities (such as its technology base in semiconductors, mainframe computers, and software), its sales and marketing organization, and its customer support capabilities no longer matched industry key success factors as well as they did during the 1970s and 1980s.

The evolution of industries, and with it the changing requirements for success, creates a dilemma for the firm. The firms that are successful at one stage of the life cycle are unlikely to be successful at a subsequent stage because the resources and capabilities that provided the foundation for their success at one stage are not appropriate to the subsequent stage. Woolworth's network of medium-sized, downtown stores that had been the basis of its success during the first six decades of the twentieth century became an increasing liability as demographic and shopping trends left Woolworth stores stranded in unattractive inner-city locations.

## Managing with dual strategies

The key issue for companies to grasp is that they are competing in two time zones. Strategy is about maximizing performance under today's circumstances; it is also about developing and deploying resources and capabilities for competing in the future. Whereas strategies for the present are primarily concerned with maximizing the effectiveness of current resources and capabilities, competing in the future is concerned with redeploying existing resources and capabilities and developing, extending, and augmenting them. [. . .]

## Competing for the future

Gary Hamel and C.K. Prahalad argue that for most companies, emphasis on competing in the present means that too much management energy is devoted to preserving the past and not enough to creating the future.[7] They challenge managers with seven questions:

1 How does senior management's point of view about the future compare with that of your competitors: conventional and reactive, or distinctive and far-sighted?

2 Which business issue absorbs more senior management attention: reengineering core processes or regenerating core strategies?

3 How do your competitors view your company mostly as a rule follower or mostly as a rule maker?

4 What is your company's strength: operational efficiency or innovation and growth?

5 What is the focus of your company's advantage-building efforts: mostly catching up or mostly getting out in front?

6 What has set your transformation agenda: your competitors or your foresight?

7 Do you spend the bulk of your time as a maintenance engineer preserving the status quo or as an architect designing the future?[8]

Hamel and Prahalad develop what they describe as a 'new strategy paradigm' that emphasizes the role of strategy as a systematic and concerted approach to redefining both the company and its industry environment in the future. This compares with the conventional, more static approach which emphasizes the *fit* between the firm's strategy and, on the one hand, the industry environment and, on the other, the firm's resources and capabilities. The key is not to *anticipate* the future, but to *create* the future. [. . .]

Concern about the overly short focus of many top management teams at the expense of a longer-term strategic orientation has also been taken up by Michael Porter. Porter points to a growing tendency for companies to confuse measures and programs to promote efficiency and effectiveness with strategic decisions. Strategic decisions involve difficult-to-reverse choices over the allocation of the company's resources. The essence of strategy is choice. The strategic issues facing Apple are whether to continue its focus on developing the distinctive Macintosh computers and operating system, or to adopt the Windows/Intel standard; whether to continue developing both hardware and software, or to specialize in software; whether to maintain its independence or to seek merger. Operational effectiveness issues such as cutting administrative staff, reducing inventories, pressing suppliers for lower component prices, reengineering processes, and implementing TQM may be vitally important, but they are not strategic since they are desirable whichever strategy is adopted.[9]

[. . .]

## Summary

Strategy is about establishing direction into the future. But the future is unknown and, with accelerating changes in the world, is increasingly difficult to predict. However, some regularities are evident in terms of industries' evolutionary paths. The life cycle model provides us with some indications of how industries develop over time.

One use of the life cycle model is allowing us to classify industries according to their stage of development. This fulfills several purposes:

- It acts as a shortcut in strategy analysis. Categorizing industries and applying generalizations about the type of competition likely to emerge and the kinds of strategy likely to be effective provide a quick and useful first-cut analysis for the purposes of strategy formulation.

- Classifying an industry requires comparison with other industries. Such comparisons, by highlighting similarities and differences with other industries, can form the basis for a deeper understanding of its structure, competitive character, and sources of advantage.

- It directs attention to the forces of evolution within the industry and encourages us to anticipate and manage change.

The dual nature of strategy – maximizing competitive performance in the present while preparing for the future – is a central dilemma for strategic management. If the industry environment is subject to fundamental change, the more successful a company is in achieving fit between its resources and capabilities and the current key success factors, then the greater the difficulties of adapting to the requirements of the future. Despite Gary Hamel urging companies toward strategic revolution, the fact remains that 'core capabilities are also core rigidities'.[10]

[. . .]

# Notes

1 The concept of the product life cycle is associated with the work of Everett M. Rogers, *The Diffusion of Innovations* (New York: Free Press, 1962); and Theodore Levitt, 'Exploit the Product Life Cycle', *Harvard Business Review* (November–December 1965): 81–94. For a contemporary discussion, see Philip Kotler, *Marketing Management: Analysis, Planning, and Control*, 6th edition (Englewood Cliffs, NJ: Prentice-Hall, 1984), chapter 11.

2 This process may involve intense competition between rival technologies. The video recording industry featured competition between different technologies and formats before the emergence of the VHS format as industry standard. See Richard S. Rosenbloom and Michael A. Cusumano, 'Technological Pioneering and Competitive Advantage: The Birth of the VCR Industry', *California Management Review* 29, no. 4 (1987).

3 In the case of metal containers, see 'Crown Cork and Seal and the Metal Container Industry' (Boston: Harvard Business School, 1978).

4 In Shiv Mathur's 'transaction cycle', differentiation reemerges as products and service are recombined into new systems. See S. Mathur, 'Competitive Industrial Marketing Strategies', *Long Range Planning 17, no. 4*, 1984: 102–109.

5 J.K. Galbraith, *American Capitalism: The Concept of Countervailing Power* (Boston: Houghton Mifflin, 1952).

6 R. Vernon, 'International Investment and International Trade in the Product Cycle', *Quarterly Journal of Economics* 80 (1966): 190–207.

7 Gary Hamel and C.K. Prahalad, *Competing for the Future* (Boston: Harvard Business School, 1995).

8 Gary Hamel and C.K. Prahalad, 'Competing for the Future', *Harvard Business Review* (July–August 1994): 122–128.

9 Michael E. Porter, 'What Is Strategy?', *Harvard Business Review* (November–December 1996): 61–80.

10 Dorothy Leonard Barton, 'Core Capabilities and Core Rigidities: A Paradox in Managing New Product Development', *Strategic Management Journal* 13 (Summer 1992): 111–126.

# CHAPTER 6

# The Firm Matters More than the Industry

CHARLES BADEN-FULLER AND JOHN STOPFORD*

To rejuvenate, managers of mature businesses must reject many of their preconceived notions of what determines business success and of how value is created. Unless they jettison their baggage, they will waste time and resources following the wrong strategies, putting their organizations at risk. On the other hand, if they understand the basic economics of how value is created, they have put their foot on the first step of the staircase for rejuvenation. The Banc One story is a good place to start, for it shows that a firm can be successful in a hostile environment, that the value Banc One created came before it grew into a large bank, and that it achieved much with limited resources.

In the late 1980s and early 1990s, the US banking industry became depressed partly because of excess capacity. Retail banking became less profitable, as overborrowed consumers defaulted on their debt and savings and loan institutions were hit by scandals and incompetence. The commercial sector fared little better. Giants such as Chase Manhattan, Chemical Bank, and Citibank suffered catastrophic losses from debt to third world countries, overleveraged corporations, and loans to the property sector. Shareholders suffered as did customers who often complained that their needs were not being addressed. Nor were the troubles confined to the shores of the United States: banks based in London and Tokyo were also reeling from write-offs, slower growth, and falling margins.

At first sight, the banking industry had all the features of a hostile environment where it would be hard to grow and be consistently profitable. Yet some banks have achieved success by occupying profitable niches; others have succeeded by

* International Thomson Business Press (excluding North America) for an extract from *Rejuvenating the Mature Business* (2nd edn) by Charles Baden-Fuller and John Stopford ©Charles Baden-Fuller and John Stopford, 1999. Harvard Business School Press (North America) for an extract from *Rejuvenating the Mature Business: The Competitive Challenge* by Charles Baden-Fuller and John Stopford. Boston, MA 1994, pp. 23–40. Copyright © 1994 by the Harvard Business School Publishing Corporation. All rights reserved.

performing the basics better or differently. Banc One is an example of the latter. Focusing on the relatively prosaic markets of retail and small commercial customers, it has maintained its highly successful record of value creation and growth in the depressed banking market. While competitors have seen their capital bases eroded, Banc One has powered ahead. It achieved for its shareholders, a return on assets of 1.3 percent, considered excellent in this industry, which translates into a 14 percent post-tax return on equity for its shareholders.[1] It regularly tops the charts of bank analyst surveys; *Euromoney* rated it the best bank in the United States and the third most successful worldwide. Banc One's constituent banks have created value for customers, too; surveys show that the organization gives good service and is creative and responsive.

Banc One's success has not been based on the usual factors emphasized in textbooks. It has not sought an industry characterized by rapid growth and high profits. It did not create value by first buying market share and then exploiting its position, but rather the other way around. From humble beginnings as a small bank (third in size) in Columbus, Ohio, it has transformed itself, first building its competitive advantage on a relatively small share of the market, then capitalizing on its abilities with organic growth and growth by merger. Initially, Banc One was not well endowed. It did not have the plentiful resources of many of its bigger competitors, but it still managed to transform itself.

The success of Banc One resulted from a combination of the many factors that make up its strategy. Some have noted Banc One's focus on a few market segments – retail banking and the middle commercial market – yet these markets are not usually associated with success. Many banks serving these markets have done badly. Some have noted Banc One's emphasis on technology, yet many competitors have invested in technology and failed. Of course, careful focus and apt use of technology are part of the strategy, but both are subservient to a vital key factor: the commitment to finding ways of conducting business that differ from those of erstwhile leaders.

Banc One began by emphasizing operational efficiency, creating a capability to undertake data processing actively. After these achievements, it took on work for other banks and financial institutions as a data processor, using its great volumes and market share to exploit and further secure its competitive advantages. Banc One also emphasized service, particularly to retail and commercial customers, contrasting with the approach of many other banks, which sought to compete solely on price or failed to appreciate what customers really wanted. Again, it established an excellent reputation in the local market before its rapid growth by merger and organic expansion.

Banc One correctly sees itself as an innovator, and it has shown its forward thinking in all parts of the business by emphasizing aspects its competitors neglect. As John B. McCoy, the chairman, put it: 'One of the personalities associated with the company is John Fisher. The sense of innovation he created is pervasive. . . . One of the reasons we are so successful is that we are willing to try. . . . I can't believe the number of experiments going on inside the company.'[2]

Banc One claims that its emphasis on innovation dates back many years; the story goes that the bank was the first to install proper drive-in banking facilities in the 1950s. When John G. McCoy, father of the current chairman, took charge in 1959, he formalized the commitment to innovation by allocating 3 percent of annual profits to research and development. Many innovations have emerged since then, many small but important, some rather more noticeable. For instance, in 1966 it was the first bank outside California to link up with Bank Americard, now Visa; in 1971 it installed the first automated teller machine in the United States. More recently it innovated new methods of processing, and in 1988 initiated a number of successful designs in branch layout. Banc One's emphasis on innovation illustrates an important theme: the fallacy of simplistic, generic strategic recipes such as 'Choose a profitable industry,' 'Go for market share,' and 'Amass resources.'

## Three themes

Managers of mature businesses need to reject many of the preconceived ideas about creating value that get in the way of the rejuvenation of their firms. Some of the ideas are held close to the heart and based on a misunderstanding of the laws of economics. For example, there is no economic law which says that some industries have to be less profitable than others, or that winning market share is the route to creating value.[3] The activities of successful rejuvenators show that success is possible against seemingly difficult conditions. Cook, Richardson and Hotpoint, three rejuvenators whose stories are introduced in this chapter, illustrate three themes that we wish to address.

First, a business can be successful in an industry that seems unpromising. Our rejuvenators were successful in industries where others were doing badly. In each case, these businesses created value for their many stakeholders despite the existence of excess capacity, stable or falling overall demand, and strong competition from rivals, often those in other countries. Opportunities for progress are not measured by the *average* performance of all competitors.

Second, our firms showed that building market share is not the route to success. They showed that market share should be seen as the reward for creating added value, and that the real value in market share is in exploiting and spreading hard-won advantages. Build your competitive advantage first, then go for share.

Third, and closely related, is the realization that rejuvenating firms (or entrants) can succeed even though they are initially endowed with limited resources. Our rejuvenators became leaders by combining their resources in new ways and building new competencies from within. This method of competing has proved successful even for those vying in international markets where rivals appear to be better resourced and supported by their local governments. (See Box 6.1.)

The essence of competition in mature industries is the creation of new rules of the game, and the rejection of simplistic ideas that success is predetermined by mechanistic formulas. These themes . . . are dealt with at greater length in this chapter.

## Box 6.1

# Critical factors influencing an industry's economics

### The views of mature managers

External economic forces determine the ability to add value. In mature sectors, it is difficult for a business to achieve high profits because the firm's performance is predetermined by the industry.

Market dominance is vital to achieve success: to become more profitable, first win a large market share, then exploit the dominant position.

Leaders are immune from the competition of small followers: in international markets, only firms with large resources can win.

### The views of dynamic managers

The firm determines the industry's profits, not vice versa. Profitable industries are typically inhabited by a large number of imaginative firms, unprofitable industries by many uncreative ones. Such unprofitable industries offer great opportunities for success.

Market share should be seen as the reward for creating value and the lever to exploit advantage. Mature firms should not see market share as a way of creating advantage.

The important contests are those between different strategic approaches to the market. In these contests, small firms with limited resources can challenge the leaders.

## The industry is not to blame

Our first and central theme is that its industry is not to blame for any shortcomings in the performance of a business. Managers in mature firms often claim that the environment is the cause of their failure. They point to powerful buyers that force down prices, foreign competitors that steal customers, powerful labor unions or skill shortages that drive up labor costs, excess capacity, government legislation, and so forth. The list is long and varied. Without doubt, these factors can be troublesome and have to be managed. But the business does not have to succumb to them.

Managers in mature firms pointed out to us the texts of many strategy writers who claimed that environmental factors influence firm performance. Some even cited Michael Porter, an acknowledged authority on the subject, who said:

> The state of competition in an industry depends on five basic competitive forces . . . The strength of these forces determines the ultimate profit potential in the industry,

where profit is measured in terms of long-run return on invested capital . . . the forces range from intense in industries like tires, paper, and steel, where no firm earns spectacular returns, to relatively mild like oil-field equipment and services, cosmetics and toiletries – where high returns are quite common.[4]

While Porter adds that the forces affecting profitability can be modified, and that firms can influence them, many have taken these words to mean (incorrectly) that choice of industry matters. When it is pointed out to managers in mature firms that one or two competitors are doing well, the response is usually 'They are lucky', 'It's not really true', or 'Their success is temporary.' These managers do not seem to appreciate that looking for profitable sectors is usually a waste of time and that choosing good strategies is far more important.

For a business to rejuvenate, it must learn to ride the waves of industry misfortunes, not be sunk by them. Managers in dynamic business understand that industry forces are important to comprehend, but that the negative ones can be overcome by appropriate strategies. Managers in mature businesses feel imprisoned and powerless. The issue is not merely one of perception; it is also a question of economic reality.

The naive notion of there being 'better' or 'worse' environments received its first major body blow in the late 1980s and early 1990s, when firms were forced to reassess their diversification moves of the 1970s and early 1980s. Many firms that had failed in one industry had diversified into another sector on the basis of industry attractiveness without proper regard to the match of their capabilities with the challenges posed by the new sectors. They ingenuously thought that mastery of a new sector would be simple. Such views were even more remarkable when it was obvious that the firms' managers had not mastered their previous environment. The consequences were often disastrous; successful entry proved much harder than originally imagined. Now we are seeing much unbundling of these early 'mistakes'.

In contrast, managers of dynamic firms realize the difficulties of diversification. They realize that mastery of one sector may help a move into another, but that success is not guaranteed. The new sector may have different economics, require new skills and capabilities and new understanding. They certainly appreciate that notions of 'attractive' and 'unattractive' industries are not the basis for creating value and strategy formulation.

The statistical evidence clearly shows that the firm is critical and the industry hardly matters at all. Many economists have looked at the data on business unit performance, their samples ranging from small *ad hoc* surveys to big data bases. A brief survey of some of this work appears in Box 6.2. One of the best data bases, that developed by the US Federal Trade Commission, is comprehensive and carefully constructed. Richard Rumelt analyzed these data, and his results are as instructive as they are simple. He assessed the relative importance of four factors: the importance of industry or sector choice; the importance of firm factors – strategy; the role of ownership; and the role of unexplained factors, including luck.

## Box 6.2
# The role of industry factors determining firm performance

In 1951, Joe Bain argued that some industries had features that made them inherently more profitable than others. An economist by background, and one of the founders of the field of industrial organization, he statistically correlated the profitability of firms with their kind of industry. He found that some industries, characterized by high concentration, that is, few important players, were more profitable than others, which had low concentration. Bain's results, first published in the *Quarterly Journal of Economics* in August 1951, sparked a mountain of further work and debate.

The debate has had two parts: over whether there is an industry effect and what its implications are. After years of extensive research by more than a hundred economists, it has become clear that there was at best a small statistical relationship between profits of a business unit and its industry. Some early work had indicated that industry effects could be as large as 20 percent; that is, one-fifth of the difference between the performance of business in one industry versus another could be ascribed to choice of industry. More recently, better-quality data and better statistical work have shown that the size of the effect was smaller. Lately, there have been two important studies on US data, representing the culmination of much previous work. One was that undertaken by Richard Schmalensee and published in the *American Economic Review* in 1975. Using data collected by the US Federal Trade Commission, he argued that choice of industry contributed some 14 percent to the performance of the business. His results were based on studying data from a single year across a wide number of US industries. Richard Rumelt expanded Schmalensee's data to include other years. In his article 'How Much Does Industry Matter?' (*Strategic Management Journal*, March 1991), he showed that the choice of industry explained at best 8.3 percent of a business unit's profitability. His results seem more compelling, for Rumelt looked at effects over time, albeit a rather short period of four years. Across the water in the United Kingdom, John Cubbin ('Is It Better to Be a Weak Firm in a Strong Industry, or a Strong Firm in a Weak Industry?', Centre for Business Strategy, London Business School, no. 49) was also concerned with examining industry effects over time. In contrast to Rumelt, he used thirty years to examine industry effects. He found that over this longer period there were no persistent industry effects.

The fact that there are profitable and unprofitable industries does not necessarily mean that it is choice of industry which yields high profits. On the contrary, the Austrian and Chicago schools of economists, including Nobel Prize winner Milton Friedman, have asserted that the causality goes the other way. They suggest that some industries seem more profitable than others because profitable firms are unevenly distributed across industries. What makes firms profitable is not the industries they chose to be in, but the strategies they follow. Those industries which are apparently unprofitable are populated by large numbers of firms that are not efficient or innovative. If some industries seem to be more profitable than others, it is because more of their firms are creative, innovative, and successful.

Rumelt's findings, reported in Table 6.1, may startle the reader.[5] He found little support for the notion that the choice of industry is important. Only 8.3 percent of the differences in profitability between one business unit and another can be related to the choice of industry. By implication, more than 90 percent of profitability variations are not explained by the choice of industry, and at least half appear to be attributable to the choice of strategy. Put simply, the correct choice of strategy appears to be at least five times more important than the correct choice of industry.

Table 6.1 *Percentage of business units' profitability explained by industry and strategy factors*

| | |
|---|---|
| Choice of industry | 8.3% |
| Choice of strategy | 46.4% |
| Parent company | 0.8% |
| Not explained – random | 44.5% |

*Source*: abstracted from Richard Rumelt, 'How Much Does Industry Matter?', *Strategic Management Journal* 12, March 1991: 167–186

Readers may be skeptical of the relevance of the statistical data, which are an average over many businesses in many sectors. While willing to accept that, in general, industry factors may be unimportant, they wish to believe that in their own industry the situation may be 'different'. We examine further arguments to support our point.

# Mature industries offer good prospects for success

We think that managers of mature businesses need to rethink. Low-growth 'mature' markets or troubled industries may offer greater chances of rewards than ones that appear to be glamorous and profitable. Our reasoning is simple. In general, more profitable industries are those which are populated by more imaginative and more creative businesses. These businesses create an environment that attracts custom, grows the industry revenues, and makes the industry attractive. But creative and innovative businesses are also more fiercely competitive. To win in such environments may be difficult, as the pace of change may be rapid and the minimum standards high. In contrast, many less profitable industries are populated by sleepy, uncreative businesses that fail to innovate. In such environments, the potential for success by a creative newcomer may be greater. The demands of competition may be less exacting, and the potential for attracting customers better. (See Box 6.3.)

---

**Box 6.3**

# The industry–profit relationship

Managers of mature firms believe that the causal direction of influences on profits is as follows:

Factors affecting the industry
    ⟶ the level of firm profits

Managers of dynamic firms believe that:
  Innovation by firms
  ⟶ firm profits
        ⟶ industry profits

---

Managers in mature firms must realize that businesses do not have to follow products in their life cycle. We all know that products mature and decline; the horse and buggy, although enjoying a minor revival, does not have the popularity that it did a century ago. But products do not define a business; a business can enjoy a long life by adjusting.

For most organizations, decline in demand is the signal of lost competitiveness. In the automobile industry, the sales of European and American producers have been declining in recent years because of locally changing conditions and better, stronger foreign competition, not because of a decline in the product. The global market for cars is booming, with rapid expansion in developing and former communist countries. Automobile producers in Western Europe have discovered that such growing segments of demand as those in eastern and southern Europe can be profitably served if firms adapt.

Declining demand for a product is rare and forces businesses to create new competencies to serve related markets. This is not disastrous. Many horse-and-buggy carriage builders have evolved into highly successful service stations and farm equipment dealers.[6]

Most mature markets can be revived with better products and services. Before Xerox, the copying industry was stable and based on photography or thermal processes. The industry must have seemed to some to be mature. After xerography was developed, the market boomed. When the market appeared to mature again, the entry of Canon with small photocopiers also increased the size of the market as unexploited segments were developed. Sales of large mainframe computers have declined in recent years because of the surge in sales of powerful desktop personal computers, and smart firms have extended their capabilities from making one type of product to making another. Laptop computers have given a new boost to the computer industry. Similarly, Walkman boosted the tape recorder industry – and also transformed it. Until the entrance of Honda the motorcycle market was in steady decline. With Honda's innovations – new bicycles with attractive features sold at reasonable prices – the market revived.

Managers of mature firms must realize that businesses can be transformed with new products, new processes, new service delivery systems, and new strategies. We suggest that the growth rate of an industry is a reflection of the kinds of businesses in it, not the intrinsic nature of the environment. We do not wish to overstate our case, but rather force the reader to focus attention away from the mentality of labeling and prejudging opportunities based only on historic industry performance.

## Firms can succeed in hostile environments

William Cook is an old, established firm that makes steel castings. Its story reinforces the point that organizations can be successful in even the most hostile environments. It also sheds light on the relationship between industry conditions, firm action, and value creation. After a number of boom years that ended in 1978, most British steel casting businesses were operating at a loss. Industry sales were declining, there was excess capacity, rationalization schemes had been tried and had failed and foreign competition was emerging with great intensity. At this time Cook's resources were extremely limited. In less than ten years, Cook moved from being a barely profitable business, with only a 2 percent share of its industry, to a highly profitable business, earning an excellent rate of return, delivering high-quality service to its customers, and having more than a 30 percent share of its industry. Its actions stimulated new competitors to enter the industry to copy and rival Cook. Partly on account of all the activities of these organizations, sales stopped declining, excess capacity disappeared, and the industry looks more attractive. But, as we explain below, the sequence of events was from firm action to industry improvement, not the other way around.

In 1981, Andrew Cook took over the management of William Cook. The situation did not look good: the firm was only a small player in a big-company industry. Four rivals – F.H. Lloyd, the Weir Group, the Davy Corporation, and British Steel (then state owned) – controlled 60 percent of industry output. There were other, medium-size firms and many small firms like William Cook. The outlook was appalling. The industry had always been cyclical, but between 1975 and 1983, orders and output fell, in an unprecedented fashion, by more than 60 percent, from 268,000 metric tons to 115,000 metric tons. The average industry margin had dropped from a healthy 9 percent of sales to zero, with many large and small firms showing losses. Excess capacity was everywhere evident, for many firms had expanded at the height of the previous boom (see Table 6.2).

In the view of Andrew Cook, most firms in the industry had only themselves to blame for their problems. At the time he said, 'In the 1970s, the industry was grossly overmannered; costs were rising and only world demand sustained it. . . . The slump was good for the foundry industry. Many companies were not fit to survive.'

In 1983, at a time when capacity was more than double the level of industry sales, and its rivals were either cutting back investment or closing, Cook embarked

Table 6.2 *Output, capacity utilization, productivity, and profitability in steel castings*

|                      | 1975  | 1977 | 1979  | 1981 | 1983 | 1985 | 1987 |
| -------------------- | ----- | ---- | ----- | ---- | ---- | ---- | ---- |
| Output               | 268   | 246  | 192   | 155  | 115  | 118  | 122  |
| Capacity utilization | 100%  | 93%  | 76%   | 66%  | 58%  | 61%  | 72%  |
| Productivity         | 12.6  | 12.1 | 11.5  | 12.3 | 13.4 | 15.7 | 20.3 |
| Profitability        | 9.0   | 7.5  | −2.0  | −1.0 | 0.0  | −2.7 | n/a  |

*Note:* Output is thousands of metric tons, productivity is output in tons per person, and profitability is profit before tax as a percentage of sales

on an investment program to increase efficiency, quality, and capacity. Its stated objective was to challenge the conventional norms of the industry, especially those held by the industry leaders. Rivals thought that Cook was unwise and predicted disaster. Its plans seemed especially dangerous because its resources were limited. Although it had a stock market quotation, its shares had performed so badly that there was little opportunity to raise cash by this route and it was in a poor position to raise its debt level. Raising prices would have been impossible; its record on quality was not good, and it certainly did not have the image of a Mercedes-Benz or an IBM among its customers. Neither was it a leader technologically; it had no secret processes that would grant it an everlasting stream of income. Its ambition and resolution to win was high, a factor which . . . was important.

Conventional thinking would have suggested that Cook either milk the business or go for a high-value differentiated niche. In the castings industry, the traditional measure of differentiation was the value per ton of output, and convention suggested that there were three segments: high-value steel alloys, basic alloys, and the casting of unalloyed or basic steel. Many firms participate in the higher-valued segments. In 1981, at the beginning of its path of rejuvenation, Cook focused on the lowest-valued segment of the market. (Out of a sample of twenty-five foundries comprising more than 70 percent of the industry, Cook's value per metric ton was £931, at the bottom.)

Cook's decision to remain in the lowest price segment of the business was coupled with the decision to invest to improve company capability and quality at that low end of the market. Cook emphasized service to its customers and ensuring the right quality. These two dimensions, now commonly recognized, were not self-evident in the early 1980s. Its modest investment program aimed at improving quality and customer service yielded results very quickly. In 1984 Cook's profits rose to 10 percent of sales, while the rest of the industry recorded losses averaging 1.6 percent of sales and continued to suffer from excess capacity.

Cook did not stop there: it continued to invest in quality and service improvement. In 1985 it was the first business in the industry to win the UK government's quality award BS5750, and it had put its own operations onto a secure footing. In 1986 Cook's management felt able to expand and made a bid for the Hyde foundries, about the same size as Cook, which failed. Cook then bid for Weir's foundries, the largest in the industry. Industry members were amazed at the audacity of such a small player's seeking to take over the largest operator: most thought that Cook was mad to buy further into the troubled industry. Cook's bid succeeded, and the management set about rationalizing the Weir business, closing some parts and investing heavily in others. In 1988 Cook again bid for Hyde and this time secured the prize. By the end of 1988, Cook was the largest business in the industry, recording even better profits.

The Cook story provides an excellent illustration of how businesses can become successful in a hostile environment. Before Cook transformed itself, the castings industry was unprofitable. It is arguable that much of the lack of profitability was owing to the existing businesses' inability to compete. Because the companies could not satisfy customer requirements at a low price, orders shrank as customers were forced to buy abroad or use substitute products. Cook's improvement of quality and service levels saved the customers money and so increased the demand for the product. Like Banc One, Cook understood that features such as quality, reliability, and service could also reduce its own costs. Thus Cook generated a double advantage – higher value and lower cost. When others in the industry finally realized what Cook had done, they changed, too. They sought to catch up to Cook and invoked intense battles. The fortunes of the industry are being transformed, customers are buying, and demand has stopped declining. The causes of the transformation were principally the actions of the firms.[7]

# Large market share is the reward, not the cause of success

We believe that many managers are mistaken in the value they ascribe to market share. Enlarging market share should be seen as beneficial for a dynamic firm that wishes to leverage advantages it has won, but increasing market share is not the route to rejuvenating a mature firm. Banc One and Cook achieved significant positions in their industries after they had built new capabilities and new routines.

Cook's successful domination of the UK industry was the consequence, not the cause of its rejuvenation. In the early 1980s, Cook's business, like that of its rivals, was in bad shape. The sequence was that management first changed its own organization, seeking to improve quality and efficiency, simultaneously reducing cost. It was content to operate with a small share of the highly competitive 'low-price' segment of the market. Only when the new philosophy was ingrained, new capabilities built, new resources won, value created, and profitability established did it set about growing rapidly. Mergers were an important part of Cook's growth, and in each merger Cook set about changing the acquired business, importing Cook's best practice to leverage the benefits it had achieved.

Banc One is well known for its aggressive attitude toward growth and mergers, but this attitude came only after the organization had established its superiority. Banc One's philosophy was to first develop its capabilities, then to grow them. When Banc One undertook a merger, it was clear that the merged organizations had to change to fit the philosophy of their dynamic parent. This has been relatively easy, as the partners recognized that Banc One has many superior routines. Banc One also has a program for ensuring that the skills of its newly merged partners are learned and integrated into the rest of the Banc One network and that the cycle of improvement does not stop. It recognizes that advantages must constantly be augmented. As with all the rejuvenated firms we studied, growth is seen as a way of exploiting advantages in the virtuous cycle of improvement [. . .]

The essence of the policies of our rejuvenators was different from those adopted by the mature businesses we studied. Some of the latter had sought a way out of their troubles by merging with other mature firms rather than tackling the root causes of their problems. The consequence was to create a bigger, still mature organization with greater difficulties. Generally, these firms found that they were on a path of decline. Their growth preceded rejuvenation and had the effect of making the necessary change harder . . .

Our views on the role of market share run counter to much of the literature on strategy and what is believed in many corporate boardrooms . . . It is commonly but incorrectly held that being number one or number two in an industry gives a business unique advantages, which are greatest in industries characterized by slow growth. With a large market share, it is often argued, a business can achieve lower costs and charge higher prices than its rivals. In slow-growth markets, it is said, this may prove to be a decisive factor. Such thinking ignores the importance of innovation.

[. . .]

These widespread false beliefs appear in many guises. At one extreme are chief executives who say, 'We are only interested in industries where we hold a number one or number two position.' Such statements, if unaccompanied by an emphasis on innovation, give the wrong signal that high share leads to success. At a more mundane level, managers are encouraged to write in their plans, 'We should dominate the industry and seek success by capturing a number one position.' Again, such statements are dangerous when the writer and reader believe that share is the source, not the measure of success.

Those who advocate that large market share leads to greater profits point to the importance of several causal factors. First, large market share gives rise to the need to deliver large volumes of the service or product. Increased volume in turn gives rise to opportunities for cost savings by exploiting scale economies in production, service delivery, logistics, and marketing. Second, large market share permits a firm to benefit from experience or learning effects, which also lower costs. Third, large market share may allow a firm to charge higher prices. A product or service with a large share may seem intrinsically less risky to consumers. Finally, with a large market share, new entrants may be discouraged because they perceive the incumbent to have a substantial commitment to their industry through perceived or actual sunk costs.

From the view of mature firms, it is important to point out that these supposed benefits of large share are overrated . . . [The] way out of maturity is in innovation, and innovators realize that new ways of competing can achieve their advantages by new approaches that do not necessarily need large market share. However, those with new approaches may win market share, in which case large share is a reward for success. This Darwinian view of the market suggests that the competitive process is one in which success goes to the firm that successfully innovates.

Statistical evidence supports our view: in a large proportion of the industries studied, the firm with largest rank is not the most profitable. Often the picture is quite different; indeed according to the statistics published in Robert Buzzell and Bradley Gale – two of the strongest advocates of the value of market share – only 4 percent of the differences in profitability of one business unit versus another could be explained by differences in market share.[8] Richard Schmalensee, in his extensive study of more than 400 US manufacturing firms, found that less than 2 percent of the variations in profitability between one business and another could be explained by differences in market share.[9] Market share effects appear to be relatively unimportant across a wide sample of industries.

Growing market share is not a panacea for an organization's ills, even in mature slow-growing markets. The belief that gaining market share leads to greater profitability comes from confusing cause and effect. Many successful business have a large market share, but the causality is usually from success to share, not the other way around. Successful businesses often, but not always, grow because they have discovered an overwhelming source of competitive advantage, such as quality at low cost. Such advantages can be used to displace even the most entrenched incumbents.

## Small-share firms can challenge international players

While growing market share may be unwise before rejuvenation, should mature firms try to hang on to their market share because it has some value? The stories of Banc One and Cook show that firms with small market share can grow advantages and win. The story of Hotpoint, a moderate-size player with less than 5 percent of the European appliance market, shows how a firm can even diminish its market share and still rejuvenate in the face of intense international competition. This is a theme to which we return at length in the latter part of the book.

In the early 1960s, the appliance industry of Europe was dominated by the Italians and the Germans. Five Italian entrepreneurial firms – Zanussi, Zoppas, Ignis, Indesit, and Candy – had grown in two decades to capture more than 40 percent of all European production and sales. These Italian firms were highly profitable for many years; some, such as Ignis (acquired by Philips), Zanussi, and Indesit, had established commanding brand positions with substantial European market shares. The other major players in this period were the German firms AEG, Bauknecht, and Bosch-Siemens. Others in Europe had either established niche positions or else, like Hotpoint, were doing badly; with poor products and poor cost control, they were suffering from severe competitive pressures.

The 1980s saw a new era, and the once successful leading firms found themselves in some difficulty. The profits of Indesit and Zanussi plunged . . . and several leading German firms, especially AEG and Bauknecht, were near bankruptcy. The problems extended to the United Kingdom, where Hoover, the largest firm, also found itself in trouble.

The managers of many of the poorly-performing organizations blamed 'industry forces' for their malaise. They commissioned studies to examine the industry's economic circumstances and encouraged government departments to do the same. The main thrust of their findings was typical of many similar reports for other businesses doing badly in other industries. According to experts, the appliance industry suffered from excess capacity, barriers to exit for losing businesses, poor demand prospects, too many competitors, import competition, and subsidies.

The experts were right in what they saw: the excess capacity in the appliance industry in the 1980s was severe, demand forecasts had been too optimistic, and projected demand growth had not materialized. To make matters worse, many competitors had increased capacity to take account of the forecasted growth, so supply had grown even faster than expected demand. None of this would have been a problem if the excess supply had exited from the market, but it had not. The barriers to exit were clear: loss-making organizations owned plant that had little resale value and saw no reason to quit. Moreover, quitting involved writeoffs and payments to workers who lost their jobs. Only rich organizations could afford these expenses; most of those showing losses did not have the resources to quit. The natural barriers to exit were compounded by government policy. Since the cost of unemployment is a local or state rather than EC-level issue, each country wished to export the competitive problem or hide it by subsidizing local producers in the hope that other firms would quit.

Although the excess capacity provoked price-cutting and low margins, the prices were not low enough to keep out imports from outside the European market area. Spanish and East bloc firms continued to expand their efforts to sell in the EC market. The reports typically claimed that Spain benefited from low wages, while the East bloc countries had the benefits of both low wages and low capital costs. By any account, the reports made grim reading, and managers of most businesses used them to justify their poor profits. There were exceptions.

Chaim Schreiber at Hotpoint refused to accept the verdict that it was 'someone else's fault that we are doing badly'. He saw the problems of the industry as rooted in managerial failures, failure to build a product consumers wanted, failure to produce efficiently and distribute efficiently. Schreiber came to Hotpoint in 1974, just as the industry was going through its lowest point. He and his team rejected such previous beliefs of the industry as the importance of capturing a large sales volume. The top management team decided to cut out all sales to Continental Europe and focus effort exclusively on the United Kingdom. This reduced the sales and share of the firm in the European market – the measure used by key competitors such as Philips. In the United Kingdom, Hotpoint did not retreat to a high-price or specialist niche but concentrated its energies in selling to the mass market in competition with the other major British firm, Hoover, and the leading Continental firms from Italy and Scandinavia. This was no easy market, for prices were low and margins keen.[10]

Hotpoint's rejuvenation was initially based on reducing costs and increasing quality and flexibility. As is later documented in detail, there was first only modest investment; in time the investment grew. Ultimately, Hotpoint was able to prove that even with a small share of the European market, it could achieve lower costs, better flexibility, and better service to the customer than the strongest competitor. Hotpoint showed that adding extra value could be achieved without first increasing market share.

Under Schreiber's leadership, Hotpoint proved that all the doom-and-gloom assertions made in the public commentaries were wrong. The firm showed that the excess capacity was really 'outdated capacity' and that the low-cost imports were a signal of the inefficiency of existing producers unwilling to change. The price wars were the consequence of businesses continuing to sell models that were designed ten years earlier and had not kept pace with consumer wants. The subsidies merely propped up the inefficient; they did not threaten those which did their job properly.

Schreiber's leadership at Hotpoint was like fresh air to a stale and smoke-filled room. Hotpoint was one of the first European appliance firms to set itself the task of transformation. Like Cook in steel castings, Hotpoint did things differently, investing where others were cutting, building novel production lines and new distribution systems, and launching new products. Also like Cook, Hotpoint did not create its success in a small niche, for it was competing directly with Hoover, Indesit, and Zanussi in the mass markets of the United Kingdom. Hotpoint's transformation of profits was dramatic, as Table 6.3 indicates.

Hotpoint triggered change throughout the appliance industry. In every case, organizations went through major upheavals. By the end of the 1980s, the industry had been transformed. Old management had been removed and new managers had arrived. The structure of ownership had also altered. The resulting combinations had forced new groups: Electrolux (including Zanussi, Thorn DA, White), Whirlpool (including Philips and Bauknecht), Bosch-Siemens, Thomson, Merloni (including Scholes and Indesit), and last but not least, GEC-GE (including Hotpoint, GE Europe, Creda, and the British appliance firm, Cannon).

Table 6.3 *Hotpoint's performance*

|                        | 1975–1979 | 1980–1984 | 1985–1991 |
|------------------------|-----------|-----------|-----------|
| Profit/sales (percent) | 2.3       | 8.9       | 9.8       |

*Note:* Profit is before tax and interest

# Building resources and competitive advantage

Just as small-share firms can win, so can firms with modest resources, even when battling against international competition. In understanding the role of resources, skills, and competencies in a competitive battle, it is important to distinguish between the quantity of resources and their appropriateness. The 'resource school' of strategic thinking rightly points out that mobilizing the resource base is a critical element in an organization's success (see Box 6.4). Building and learning to deploy that base properly are elusive skills, particularly for a mature firm.

Lucky mature firms, such as Walt Disney in the 1980s, have been endowed with magnificent resources left by previous excellent management. The task for these firms is to build competencies to exploit the resources. Such a task requires a new approach to the market with the building of complementary skills and capabilities so that brands are fully exploited, intangible assets are utilized, and the people are motivated and directed to work more effectively. Managers in these firms can move along a path of rejuvenation with innovative approaches, confident that absence of resources will not inhibit their program of action.

Having substantial resources is no guarantee of success. General Motors and Ford had large financial reserves, outstanding brand reputations, excellent dealer networks, and impressive research and development laboratories. For all their resources, they are still unable to master the challenge posed by their Japanese competitors, which until recently were less well endowed They have found it hard to discard the past and build new skills. Even the relatively poorly resourced Korean producers have done better than some Western producers, making the point clear that resources alone are not sufficient for success.

More commonly, mature businesses find that their brands and reputations are of dubious value because of past poor product quality. Their intangible assets of skills and capabilities are appropriate for a bygone age, better suited to a museum than the competitive world, and their other assets have, like the family silver, long since been sold to pay debts or satisfy the needs of other stakeholders. For these organizations, we say there is hope. Renewal is possible.

Richardson is an exemplar of an organization able to grow and deploy its own resources.[11] In the late 1960s, Richardson was a small cutlery firm in Sheffield, England. It was not profitable, had neither famous brand name nor financial resources, and while its share of the UK market was small, its share of the world market was insignificant. In a little more than two decades, it has reached the number one world position in kitchen knives against competition from the Far East. Its resource base is formidable, and most of its resources were developed in-house. It has demonstrated a capacity to renew and reconstruct from within.

The background to the story, later discussed in more detail, is as follows.[12] In the late nineteenth century, the Sheffield cutlery industry was the best and strongest in the world. A large exporter of knives and forks to all parts of the world, it had

# Box 6.4
# Resource-based theories of the firm

The resource-based theories of competitive advantage, such as that of David Teece, Gary Pisano, and Amy Schuen,[1] stress the role of resources, skills, and capabilities in determining a firm's long-run health. Basic resources include access to finance, the existence of machines, skilled, intelligent employees, knowledge of products, processes, and systems, and reputation. In the battles between organizations in markets, those with superior resources appear to be at an advantage.

However, having more resources is neither necessary nor sufficient for success. Robert Grant, in 'The Resource-based Theory of Competitive Advantage', points out that many well-endowed firms find it difficult to exploit their resource bases.[2] For years the hidden assets of Walt Disney went unexploited; only when new management arrived and set about building on the resource base in the mid-1980s did the company's declining fortunes revive. IBM is clearly better resourced than many of its rivals, but this has not guaranteed it value creation. It struggles to deploy its resources effectively.[3]

Combining resources is what leads to value creation. This ability lies in the skill of the employees, the hidden routines, the systems, and the 'culture' of the business. Its effect can be powerful. As C.K. Prahalad and Gary Hamel point out, competencies such as Sony's ability to miniaturize electronics or Canon's capabilities in optics, imaging, and microprocessor controls are key to those firms' success.[4]

The ability to compete does not require large resources, but rather effective combinations and capacity to create from within. Thus it was that Microsoft rose to become one of the world's largest computer firms, Wal-Mart one of the most successful retailers, and Banc One one of the most successful bank holding companies.

## Notes

1  David Teece, Gary Pisano, and Amy Schuen, 'Dynamic Capabilities and Strategic Management', Working Paper, University of California at Berkeley, 1992.
2  Robert Grant, 'The Resource-based Theory of Competitive Advantage', *California Management Review* 33, no. 3, 1991: 114–134.
3  A point also made by G. Stalk, P. Evans, and L.E. Schulman in 'Competing on Capabilities: The New Rules of Corporate Strategy', *Harvard Business Review*, March–April 1992: 57–69.
4  C.K. Prahalad and Gary Hamel, 'The Core Competence of the Corporation', *Harvard Business Review*, May–June 1993: 79–91.

an enviable reputation for quality. In the twentieth century the situation changed, and by the early 1970s, Sheffield's position had declined greatly. The industry represented only a marginal producer on a world stage dominated by Japan, Germany, the United States, and Far Eastern manufacturers in Japan, Hong Kong, and Korea.

UK producers blamed some of their problems on unfair competition. Steel, the principal ingredient in the production of knives, cost more in the European Community (EC) than elsewhere. Because the EC cartel supported the steel producers, the 1978 price of chrome steel in the United Kingdom was £807 a metric ton, whereas similar steel was available in South Korea for £487 a metric ton. In this period, steel represented about 40 percent of the producers' sale price. At one time, the landed price for cutlery in the United Kingdom was lower per ton than the cost of buying raw unprocessed steel.

Richardson was clearly in a disadvantageous position to lead the battle against foreign competition. Although its workers were loyal, their skills were in outdated technologies and methods of operation; the managerial systems creaked badly or were nonexistent; the knowledge base of the market and the horizon of new technologies was sadly lacking. The plants were old and the customers dissatisfied. Richardson could not even rely on the local infrastructure because its immediate environment contained many hopeless businesses that were losing money and international competitive edge. By all normal accounts, the situation seemed hopeless. Many of Richardson's UK competitors had subcontracted production from low-cost overseas sources to become marketing specialists, while others retreated to craft niches, selling low volumes at high prices Neither strategy of appeasement seemed durable.

Richardson took a different approach. Its managers did not believe that the demise of the UK industry as inevitable. Despite the twin handicaps of high input prices and no established brand name, they chose to fight back. They noted that between 20 and 30 percent of imported knives came from Japan, about 10 percent from France, 10 percent from Switzerland, and more than 5 percent from Germany. These countries had neither a wage rate advantage nor always a raw material price advantage. Most continental suppliers, however, enjoyed strong consumer brand names, built up over many years of expensive advertising. Richardson's most severe competition came from Hong Kong and South Korea, which had advantages of both low wages and low steel prices.

Bryan Upton, Richardson's managing director, and his managers believed that the importers' advantages were not overwhelming and that the British businesses failed to invest in the right technologies and to make a decent product, sell it right, or present it better, and crucially failed to innovate. 'They did not deserve to survive', Upton said.

Richardson rose like a phoenix from the ruins of the UK industry by doing what the other organizations should have done. It invested in human and physical capital to improve first the process by which the product was made. The small initial investments – the resources were limited – were directed at both reducing costs and improving customer service. Remarkable progress was made quite quickly, and the better profits were reinvested in the business. The approach had to be nontraditional because of capital shortage. The managers combined optical, electronic, and mechanical technologies simply and cheaply. They also reorganized the flow of the work, especially in support services and between the traditional functions. In the course of time, Richardson developed better ways of making cheaper knives and became one of the world's lower-cost producers of blank knives. Simultaneous investments in customer service through speed and flexibility served to cement the competitive advantage over its British and foreign competitors. It chose to compete in the 'rapid response sector', where distance placed Far Eastern suppliers at a disadvantage. This, however, was not enough. Richardson went on to innovate products, including the famous Laser knife, and new marketing techniques. By the early 1990s, it had captured 15 percent of the world's knife market to be among the world's leaders. It is hard to summarize all the multiplicity of skills and resources that the organization built over a comparatively short period, but Box 6.5 gives a flavor.

---

**Box 6.5**

## The resources and capabilities created by Richardson

| **Resources** | **Capabilities** |
|---|---|
| Specialized machinery | Ability to design and build machines in-house |
| Multiskilled labor force | Ability to adapt generalized machines |
| Reputation for quality | Ability to make high-quality products at extremely low |
| Strong brand identity |    unit costs |
| Distribution network | Ability to respond rapidly to customer orders |
| Overseas factories | Ability to create and lead fashion |
| | Ability to create and cope with variety |
| | Ability to understand and then sell into diverse world |
| |    markets |

---

## Competing recipes

Organizations looking to rejuvenate should realize that the winners of today's battles have often been able to overcome their disadvantages by deploying new combinations of skills and competencies. They can become innovators and develop approaches to resolving their problems. In a competition among different approaches, the best-endowed organizations do not always win. Just as large armies can be defeated by small ones, and as David slew Goliath, so in the corporate sphere we see battles between giants and upstarts sometimes resulting in victory for organizations with modest resources.[13] Even in so-called mature industries, where incumbent strategies have evolved and been honed over long periods, new ideas displace existing leaders.

Mature firms harbor prevailing beliefs about the sources of competitive advantages. These beliefs often come from a recognition of what has worked well in the past. When firms reach maturity, the beliefs can become folklore, or even a religion. Notions that some industries are intrinsically more profitable, that share is the source of added value, or that the scale of resources, not their deployment, is the way to win, have already been attacked.

Managers in mature firms believe that their sector allows them only a few fundamental choices, or generic strategies. These are typically described as being between a low-cost strategy or a differentiated strategy. The low-cost strategy involves the sacrifice of something – speed, variety, fashion, or even quality – in order to keep costs low, the lowest in the industry. In contrast, the high-cost, differentiated strategy involves focusing on the very factors ignored by the others. Advocates of generic strategy make an implicit or explicit assertion: that opposites cannot be reconciled. According to the generic strategists, it is not possible to have both low cost and high quality, or to be low cost and fashionable, or low cost and speedy. Trying to reconcile the opposites means being stuck in the middle. This, it is suggested, is the worst of both worlds.

For a mature firm, generic strategies are a misleading way to think about the strategic future. Rejuvenating and dynamic organizations are always striving to reconcile opposites. Banc One established its premier position by rejecting orthodoxy and emphasizing aspects hitherto neglected by industry leaders. Cook won in the steel casting industry by emphasizing quality and service to customers. Hotpoint emphasized variety and quality in its approach to both its retailers and the final consumers. . . . [No] single approach works well in all industries; rather, a multiple set of approaches is necessary. The real competitive battles are fought between firms with a diversity of approaches to the market.

## Notes

1   Data as of the end of 1991.
2   R. Teitelman, 'The Magnificent McCoys', *Institutional Investor*, July 1991.
3   There is a long tradition of economists, called variously the Austrian school or the Chicago school, which have held out these views against those of other universities. In strategy, this theme was first stressed with careful evidence by W.K. Hall in 'Survival Strategies in a Hostile Environment', *Harvard Business Review*, September–October 1980: 75–85: 'Even a cursory analysis of the leading companies in the eight basic industries leads to an important observation: survival and prosperity are possible even when the business environment turns hostile and industry trends change from favorable to unfavorable. In this regard, the casual advice frequently offered to competitors

in basic industries – that is, diversify, dissolve, or be prepared for below average returns – seems oversimplified and even erroneous.'

4    M.E. Porter, *Competitive Strategy* (New York: Free Press, 1980), pp. 3–4.

5    R. Rumelt, 'How Much Does Industry Matter?', *Strategic Management Journal* 12, March 1991: 167–186. Rumelt's article, like that of R. Schmalensee, 'Do Markets Differ Much?', *American Economic Review* 75, 1985: 341–351, discusses business and industry effects. Business unit effects are the consequence of either intended or unintended strategy.

6    P. Ghemawat, B. Nalebuff, and others have written on the correct strategies for declining products, examining the optimal timing for abandonment of plant, e.g. C.W.F. Baden-Fuller, ed. *Managing Excess Capacity* (Oxford: Basil Blackwell, 1990); P. Ghemawat and B. Nalebuff, 'Exit', *Rand Journal of Economics* 16, no. 1, 1985: 184–194. Abandonment of product capacity does not mean death for the business unit Some intriguing strategies for truly declining products are explored in K. Harrigan, *Strategies for Declining Business* (Lexington, Mass.: Lexington Books, 1980).

7    Cook unwisely expanded into the United States, but found itself lacking capability and overstretched. While profitable, it has recently lost some momentum.

8    R.D. Buzzell and B.T. Gale, *The Pims Principles* (New York: Free Press, 1987).

9    Schmalensee, 'Do Markets Differ Much?'

10   For evidence on prices in the United Kingdom versus Europe, see C.W.F. Baden-Fuller and J.M. Stopford, 'Globalisation Frustrated', *Strategic Management Journal* 12, no. 7, 1991: 494–507.

11   The story of Richardson was jointly researched with Robert Grant, and many details appear in R.M. Grant and C.W.F. Baden-Fuller, *The Richardson Sheffield Story*, London Business School Case Series, 2, 1987.

12   I am grateful to Robert Grant for this information. See R.M. Grant and S. Downing, 'The UK Cutlery Industry 1974–1982: A Study of Structure Adjustment, Business Strategies and Firm Performance', Working Paper, Centre for Business Strategy, London Business School, 1985.

13   This point has been advanced by many authors, starting with Alfred Marshall and then Joseph Schumpeter, in the economics literature. In the strategy literature, there is a long tradition of emphasizing the power of new approaches. Gary Hamel and C.K. Prahalad have received much attention for their timely reminder of this fact.

# Firm Effects: Resources, Capabilities and Core Competencies

T he readings in this section explore how the internal organization of the firm affects its performance. Thus, rather than looking at how the characteristics of the industry to which the firm belongs affect its strategy and performance, the readings look at how the development and maintenance of firm-specific capabilities and competencies determine performance. This emphasis is supported by empirical studies which find that most of the variation between firm profit and growth rates occurs owing to business-specific factors and not industry-specific factors. This means that strategy matters!

We begin with the work of Edith Penrose, since her book *The Theory of the Growth of the Firm* greatly influenced researchers interested in looking at how intraorganizational factors determine firm growth. She proposes a theory of the firm that has as its focus the internal organization of the firm and the growth of firms through new products and techniques of production. Firms in her view are social organizations that produce products and services via *planning, administration and organization*. This is important because whereas traditional economic theory mainly considers the *quantity* of inputs that a firm owns, this approach considers how two firms that own the same inputs might differ greatly in their performance owing to differences in the ways that they organize, administer and plan the functioning of these inputs. How these physical and human resources are used depends on the *internal dynamics of the organization*. In fact, she claims that 'resources consist of a bundle of potential services'. The *potential* is discovered (and emerges) through the ways in which the resources are used.

The readings by Barney and by Teece et al. represent how strategy theorists have made sense of Penrose's work in the context of different debates in modern strategy theory. They refer to the ability of a firm to combine resources in an innovative and efficient way as its 'capabilities' or 'competencies'. Competencies are unique, and hence hard to imitate, because they are the results of particular combinations of different resources, i.e. a result of synergy between activities. Since competencies take time to build and since new competencies often build on old ones, firm growth can be path-dependent: tomorrow's growth depends on the previous path taken (how you got to where you are).

## E.T. Penrose: 'The Firm as an Administrative Organization'

This piece is an excerpt from Edith Penrose's classic book *The Theory of the Growth of the Firm* (1959). Penrose considers the difference between thinking of a firm in terms of the assets that it owns and thinking of a firm as an *administrative* organization which creates value by combining resources in specific ways. She suggests viewing the firm as a 'pool of resources' where resources include not just tangible resources (like machinery and research labs) but also intangible ones embodied in human resources, like skills, knowledge and the ability to interact effectively. Whereas in standard economic theory the limits to firm growth arise because of limits in market size and/or decreasing returns to scale (disadvantages to large size), in Penrose's view the limits have to do with how a firm develops its resource base and how management conceptualizes this resource base. The managers' 'mental models' and resources interact with the competitive environment and determine the firm's performance. Her work provides the basis for the 'resource-based view of the firm' which focuses on the role of firm-specific competencies and capabilities.

## J. Barney: 'Looking Inside for Competitive Advantage'

This reading appeared in the *Academy of Management Executive* in 1995. Barney argues that to develop a sustainable competitive advantage, firms must not only search for environmental opportunities (i.e. for high-opportunity, low-threat environments), but also, and especially, search for and develop their internal resources and capabilities. He claims that the S and W of traditional SWOT analysis (strengths, weaknesses, opportunities and threats) has not been given enough attention. To do so, more emphasis must be given to a firm's internal resources and capabilities. Sustainable competitive advantage, the object of strategy, is developed when resources and capabilities can add *value* to the firm, are *rare*, are hard to *imitate*, and interact with the appropriate *organizational* structure. Different examples are provided for each of these points and the 'Cola Wars' and the competitive position of the Macintosh computer are used as more detailed case studies.

## D.J. Teece, G. Pisano and A. Shuen: 'Dynamic Capabilities and Strategic Management'

This reading appeared in the *Strategic Management Journal* in 1997. It emphasizes the specific capabilities and competencies that are necessary for firms to compete in environments characterized by *rapid technological change*. The authors are concerned with how competencies and capabilities can be renewed: in order to adapt to and shape the changing business environment, firms must develop 'dynamic capabilities' which form new competencies and which apply existing ones to new situations. The reading begins by comparing the resource-based perspective of firm strategy to other perspectives (e.g. Porter's competitive forces framework, game theory, strategic conflict) and then goes on to develop the dynamic capabilities approach which builds on the work of core competencies and capabilities discussed in the previous reading. The authors claim that in order to identify new opportunities and organize production in the most efficient way possible, firms must develop technological, organizational and managerial processes within the firm. This is different from 'strategizing' which instead focuses on defending one's position from rivals, for example via barriers to entry (as maintained by the competitive forces approach). The authors underline the implications of this approach for the dynamics of 'path-dependency' (when your future path depends on *how* you got to your current standing).

# CHAPTER 7

# The Firm as an Administrative Organization

EDITH T. PENROSE*

So far as I know, no economist has as yet attempted a general theory of the growth of firms. This seems to me so very strange that I am sure anyone attempting it should indeed watch his (or her) step, for naturally there is always a good reason for what economists do or do not do. Perhaps such a theory is impossible to construct, unnecessary, trivial, or outside the pale of economics proper. I do not know, but I offer this study in the hope that all four possibilities will be rejected.

We shall be concerned with the growth of firms, and only incidentally with their size. The term 'growth' is used in ordinary discourse with two different connotations. It sometimes denotes merely increase in amount; for example, when one speaks of 'growth' in output, exports, sales. At other times, however, it is used in its primary meaning implying an increase in size or an improvement in quality as a result of a *process* of development, akin to natural biological processes in which an interacting series of internal changes leads to increases in size accompanied by changes in the characteristics of the growing object. Thus the terms 'economic growth' and 'economic development' are often used interchangeably where 'growth' implies not only an increase in the national product but also a progressive changing of the economy. 'Growth' in this second sense often also has the connotation of 'natural' or 'normal' – a process that will occur whenever conditions are favourable because of the nature of the 'organism'; size becomes a more or less incidental result of a continuous on-going or 'unfolding' process.

But this is not the way the size of firms is looked at in traditional economic analysis, which examines the advantages and disadvantages of *being* a particular size and explains movement from one size to another in terms of the net advantages of different sizes. Growth becomes merely an adjustment to the size appropriate to given conditions; there is no notion of an *internal* process of *development* leading to

* Oxford University Press for an extract from *The Theory of the Growth of the Firm* by Edith Penrose © Edith T. Penrose Estate, 1959.

cumulative movements in any one direction. Still less is there any suggestion that there may be advantages in *moving* from one position to another quite apart from the advantages of *being* in a different position. It is often presumed that there is a 'most profitable' size of firm and that no further explanation than the search for profit is needed of how and why firms reach that size. Such an approach to the explanation of the size of firms will be rejected in this study; it will be argued that size is but a by-product of the process of growth, that there is no 'optimum', or even most profitable, size of firm. As we shall see, traditional theory has always had trouble with the limits to the size of firms, and I think we shall find the source of the trouble.

[. . .]

A comprehensive theory of the growth of the firm must explain several qualitatively different kinds of growth and must take account not only of the sequence of changes created by a firm's own activities but also of the effect of changes that are external to the firm and lie beyond its control. Not all of these things can be discussed at the same time, however, without creating such a serious confusion between very different types of causal relationships that the discussion degenerates into a generalized description of a sequence of events that appears largely fortuitous and to have been introduced for the convenience of a pre-determined conclusion, like the coincidences of a poorly constructed detective story. Hence the development of the theory must proceed in stages.

After a discussion of the characteristics of the business firm, its functions, and the factors influencing its behaviour, we shall turn to an examination of the forces inherent in the nature of firms which at the same time create the possibilities for, provide the inducements to, and limit the amount of the expansion they can undertake or even plan to undertake in any given period of time. It will then be shown that this limit is by its nature temporary, that in the very process of expansion the limit recedes, and that after the completion of an optimum plan for expansion a new 'disequilibrium' has been created in which a firm has new inducements to expand further even if all external conditions (including the conditions of demand and supply) have remained unchanged.

In all of the discussion the emphasis is on the internal resources of a firm – on the productive services available to a firm from its own resources, particularly the productive services available from management with experience within the firm. It is shown not only that the resources with which a particular firm is accustomed to working will shape the productive services its management is capable of rendering (where management is defined in the broadest sense), but also that the experience of management will affect the productive services that all its other resources are capable of rendering. As management tries to make the best use of the resources available, a truly 'dynamic' interacting process occurs which encourages con-tinuous growth but limits the rate of growth. In order to focus attention on the crucial role of a firm's 'inherited' resources, the environment is treated, in the first instance, as an 'image' in the entrepreneur's mind of the possibilities and restrictions with which he is confronted, for it is, after all, such an 'image' which in fact determines a man's behaviour; whether experience confirms expectations is another story. Even 'demand' as seen by a firm is largely conditioned by the productive services available to it, and hence the 'direction of expansion' – the products a firm becomes interested in producing – can be analyzed with reference to the relationship between its resources and its own view of its competitive position.

[. . .]

## The firm in theory

[. . .]

In a private enterprise industrial economy the business firm is the basic unit for the organization of production. The greater part of economic activity is channelled through firms. The patterns of economic life, including the patterns of consumption as well as of production, are largely shaped by the multitude of individual decisions made by the businessmen who guide the actions of the business units we call firms. The very nature of the economy is to some extent defined in terms of the kind of firms that compose it, their size, the way in which they are established and grow, their methods of doing business, and the relationships between them. In consequence, the firm has always occupied a prominent place in economic analysis. It is a complex institution, impinging on economic and social life in many directions, comprising numerous and diverse activities, making a large variety of significant decisions, influenced by miscellaneous and unpredictable human whims, yet generally directed in the light of human reason.[1]

[. . .]

The 'theory of the firm' – as it is called in the literature – was constructed for the purpose of assisting in the theoretical investigation of one of the central problems of economic analysis – the way in which prices and allocation of resources among different uses are determined. It is but part of the wider theory of value, indeed one of its supporting pillars, and its vitality is derived almost exclusively from its connection with this highly developed, and still basically unchallenged general system for the economic analysis of the problem of price determination and resource allocation.[2] In this context only those aspects of the behaviour of firms are considered that are relevant to the problems that the wider theory is designed to solve.

[. . .]

## The limits to 'size'

The conditions of equilibrium analysis require that there be something to prevent the indefinite expansion of output of the individual 'firm' defined in the above manner. In the model of the firm in 'pure' competition, the limit to output is found only in the assumption that the cost of producing the individual product must rise after a point as additional quantities of it are produced; in the model of the firm in 'monopolistic' competition, the limit is partly found in falling revenue as additional quantities of the product are sold. Without some such limit to the output of a given product – which, in this context, means to the size of the firm – no determinate 'equilibrium position' can be posited in static theory.

Thus, regardless of the specific framework of their particular theories, economists have looked to the limitations of management (causing increasing long-run costs of production) or of the market (causing decreasing revenue from sales), or to uncertainty about future prospects (causing both increasing cost of larger outputs and decreasing revenue from larger sales because of the necessity of making allowance for risk) to provide a limit to the size of firm.[3]

[. . .]

The notion that the market limits the size of firms follows from the assumption that a firm is tied to given products, that a specific group of markets governs its possibilities of expansion. If this assumption is dropped, however, one is dealing with a different concept of the 'firm' and a different type of analysis becomes more appropriate. With a different concept of the firm one can recognize that a 'firm', when appropriate resources are available, can produce anything for which a demand can be found or created, and it becomes a matter of taste or convenience whether one speaks of the 'market' or of the resources of the firm itself as the consideration limiting its expansion.

[. . .]

# The function and nature of the industrial firm

Probably it would be generally agreed that the primary economic function of an industrial firm is to make use of productive resources for the purpose of supplying goods and services to the economy in accordance with plans developed and put into effect within the firm. The essential difference between economic activity inside the firm and economic activity in the 'market' is that the former is carried on within an administrative organization, while the latter unit is not. [. . .]

One important aspect of the definition of the firm for our purposes, then, involves its role as an autonomous administrative planning unit, the activities of which are interrelated and are co-ordinated by policies which are framed in the light of their effect on the enterprise as a whole.

[. . .]

It is evident that there will be great variations in the number, range, and nature of the tasks of the central management of different firms, depending on the structure of the firm, the preferences and ambitions of the top management group, and the extent to which the firm is faced with external changes which require action not provided for under existing arrangements. In an unchanging environment, for example, an established firm that had succeeded in creating optimum administrative procedures and framing an optimum set of policies could operate successfully without any overt acts of 'central management' at all; even new appointments could conceivably be made according to established regulations. Managerial and supervisory functions could be carried on by appropriate officials on different levels in the firm within the framework provided by the administrative organization and existing policy 'directives'. In such circumstances, the administrative problem is 'solved' once an appropriate administrative structure has been established.

Adaptation to change poses somewhat different problems. One type of problem is the adjustment to 'short-run' conditions – the day-to-day, month-to-month decisions required in operations – and another is the adjustment to 'long-run' changes and the making of 'long-range 'policies. While undoubtedly no clear dividing line can be drawn between the two types of problem, the former certainly requires many decisions that cannot be individually 'cleared' with central management in the large firm; in consequence, organizational structures and procedures have been evolved which not only permit the making of such decisions on almost all administrative 'levels' in the firm but also ensure at the same time a high degree of consistency among decisions. Similarly, techniques and procedures have been created to enable central management to deal with the longer-run problems without excessive congestion at the top.

## Size and administration co-ordination

The question has often been raised and is still debated, whether a firm can get 'too big' to enable both kinds of problem to be efficiently handled. At one time it was almost universally agreed that such a point would be reached as a firm grew in size, that management or 'co-ordination' was a 'fixed factor' which would necessarily give rise to diminishing returns and increasing costs of operation at some point. Behind this notion lay the common-sense deduction that consistency of behaviour requires 'single-minded' direction which is clearly limited in its possible scope simply because the capacity of any human being is finite. The conclusion that the limited capacity of the individual will limit the size of firms has not, however, been supported by events – at least not in any clearly discernible way. Now it seems likely that this 'single-mindedness' can be achieved through an appropriate form of organization inherited from the past and operated by people, also inherited from the past, who share a common tradition, who are accustomed to the organization and to each other, and who thus form an entity which works with sufficient consistency and efficiency in broad areas to make unnecessary any one individual having to comprehend and direct its detailed working. It is this capacity of the firm to alter its administrative structure in such a way that non-routine managerial decisions requiring real judgment can be made by large numbers of different people within the firm without destroying the firm's essential unity, that makes it so difficult to say with confidence that there is a point where a firm is too big or too complex to be efficiently managed.

[. . .]

Apparently what has happened as firms have grown larger is not that they have become inefficient, but that with increasing size both the managerial function and the basic administrative structure have undergone fundamental changes which profoundly affect the nature of the 'organism' itself. The differences in the administrative structure of the very small and the very large firms are so great that in many ways it is hard to see that the two species are of the same genus. We say they are because they both fulfil the same function, yet they certainly fulfil it differently, and it may be that in time the differences will become so great that we should consider in what sense they can both be called industrial 'firms'. In other words, I think the question whether firms can get 'too big' for efficiency is the wrong question, for there is no reason to assume that as the large firms grow larger and larger they will become inefficient; it is much more likely that their organization will become so different that we must look on them differently; we cannot define a caterpillar and then use the same definition for a butterfly.

[. . .]

## The firm as a collection of productive resources

The cohesive character that an administrative organization imparts to the activities of the people operating within it provides the justification for separating for analytical purposes such a group from all other groups. The activities of the group which we call an industrial firm are further distinguished by their relation to the use of productive resources for the purpose of producing and selling goods and services. Thus, a firm is more than an administrative unit; it is also a collection of productive resources the disposal of which between different uses and over time is determined by administrative decision. When we regard the function of the private business firm from this point of view, the size of the firm is best gauged by some measure of the productive resources it employs.

The physical resources of a firm consist of tangible things – plant, equipment, land and natural resources, raw materials, semi-finished goods, waste products and by-products, and even unsold stocks of finished goods. Some of these are quickly and completely used up in the process of production, some are durable in use and continue to yield substantially the same services for a considerable period of time, some are transformed in production into one or more intermediate products which themselves can be considered as resources of the firm once they are produced, some are acquired directly in the market, and some that are produced within the firm can neither be purchased nor sold outside the firm. All of them are things that the firm buys, leases, or produces, part and parcel of a firm's operations and with the uses and properties of which the firm is more or less familiar.

There are also human resources available in a firm – unskilled and skilled labour, clerical, administrative, financial, legal, technical, and managerial staff. Some employees are hired on long-term contracts and may represent a substantial investment on the part of the firm. For some purposes these can be treated as more or less fixed or durable resources, like plant or equipment; even though they are not 'owned' by the firm, the firm suffers a loss akin to a capital loss when such employees leave the firm at the height of their abilities. Such human resources may well be on the payroll for considerable periods of time even though their services cannot be adequately used at the time. This may sometimes be true also of daily or weekly workers. They, too, may often be considered as a permanent 'part' of the firm, as resources the loss of whose services would involve a cost – or lost opportunity – to the firm.

Strictly speaking, it is never *resources* themselves that are the 'inputs' in the production process, but only the *services* that the resources can render.[4] The services yielded by resources are a function of the way in which they are used – exactly the same resource when used for different purposes or in different ways and in combination with different types or amounts of other resources provides a different service or set of services. The important distinction between resources and services is not their relative durability; rather it lies in the fact that resources consist of a bundle of potential services and can, for the most part, be defined independently of their use, while services cannot be so defined, the very word 'service' implying a function, an activity. As we shall see, it is largely in this distinction that we find the source of the uniqueness of each individual firm.

[. . .]

# The productive opportunity of the firm and the 'entrepreneur'

[. . .]

The business firm, as we have defined it, is both an administrative organization and a collection of productive resources; its general purpose is to organize the use of its 'own' resources together with other resources acquired from outside the firm for the production and sale of goods and services at a profit; its physical resources yield services essential for the execution of the plans of its personnel, whose activities are bound together by the administrative framework within which they are carried on. The administrative structure of the firm is the creation of the men who run it; the structure may have developed rather haphazardly in response to immediate needs as they arose in the past, or it may have been shaped largely by conscious attempts to achieve a 'rational' organization; it may consist of no more than one or two men who divide the task of management; or it may be so elaborate that its complete ramifications cannot even be depicted in the most extensive chart. In any event, there need be nothing 'fixed' about it; it can, in principle, always be adapted to the requirements of the firm – expanded, modified, and elaborated as the firm grows and changes.

The productive activities of such a firm are governed by what we shall call its 'productive opportunity', which comprises all of the productive possibilities that its 'entrepreneurs' see and can take advantage of.[5] A theory of the growth of firms is essentially an examination of the changing productive opportunity of firms; in order to find a limit to growth, or a restriction on the rate of growth, the productive opportunity of a firm must be shown to be limited in any period.

[. . .]

# The managerial limit

[. . .]

Of the three classes of explanation why there may be a limit to the growth of firms – managerial ability, product or factor markets, and uncertainty and risk – the first refers to conditions within the firm, the second to conditions outside the firm, and the third is a combination of internal attitudes and external conditions. In this chapter we shall be concerned with the analysis of the fundamental and inescapable limits to the amount of expansion a firm can undertake at a given time when there is no rigid external barrier to its expansion, but we shall temporarily ignore expansion through acquisition and merger, reserving that for separate discussion.

[. . .]

Expansion does not take place automatically; on the contrary, the composition and extent of an expansion programme, as well as its execution, must be planned. Planning implies on the one hand a purpose, and on the other, the organization of resources to accomplish this purpose in some desired manner. Specifically, the creation of an 'optimum' plan for expansion requires that the resources available to a firm, whether already acquired by the firm or obtainable in the market, be used to 'best' advantage.[6] It is obvious that if all necessary productive services, including managerial and entrepreneurial services, were available in unlimited amounts at constant prices, and if demand for products were infinitely elastic, no 'best' plan could be constructed: a larger plan would always be better than a smaller one. It follows that there must be some limiting consideration to which the plan is anchored.

The assumption that a firm can obtain in the market any type of resource or quality of management implies that the specialized resources or managerial abilities it may need to take advantage of market opportunities are available to it. We assume that there are numerous opportunities for profitable production open to the individual firm. Nevertheless, the firm cannot, and in general will not attempt to, extend its expansion plans, and with them its 'management team', in an effort to take advantage of *all* such opportunities. It *cannot* do so because the very nature of a firm as an administrative and planning organization requires that the *existing* responsible officials of the firm at least know and approve, even if they do not in detail control all aspects of, the plans and operations of the firm; it *will not* even try to do so if the officials of the firm are themselves concerned to maintain its character as an organized unit.

[. . .]

Since there is plainly a *physical* maximum to the number of things any individual or group of individuals can do, there is clearly some sort of limit to the rate at which even the financial transactions of individuals or groups can be expanded. In the present discussion, however, we are dealing with the rate of expansion of the firm as an administrative and planning organization. It follows that the existing officials of such an organization must have something to do with any operations that are to be treated as an expansion of that organization's operations; for to call a group of activities which are unconnected with a given organization an expansion of that organization is a contradiction in terms. This being so, the capacities of the *existing* managerial personnel of the firm necessarily set a limit to the expansion of that firm in any given period of time, for it is selfevident that such management cannot be hired in the market-place.

Businessmen commonly refer to the managerial group as a 'team', and the use of this word implies that management in some sense works as a unit. An administrative group is something more than a collection of individuals; it is a collection of individuals who have had experience in working together, for only in this way can 'teamwork' be developed. Existing managerial personnel provide services that cannot be provided by personnel newly hired from outside the firm, not only because they make up the administrative organization which cannot be expanded except by their own actions, but also because the experience they gain from working within the firm and with each other enables them to provide services that are uniquely valuable for the operations of the particular group with which they are associated.

These are services which make possible a working relationship between particular individuals making decisions and taking action in a particular environment, and they determine the efficiency and confidence with which action can be taken by the group as a whole. Unless such services are provided by its members, the group cannot function as a unit. It is for this reason that it is impossible for a firm to expand efficiently beyond a certain point merely by drawing up a management 'blueprint' for an extensive organization and then proceeding to hire people to fill the various positions and carry out the functions laid down in detailed 'job descriptions'.

If a group is to gain experience in working together, it must have work to do. The total amount of work to be done at any time in a firm depends on the size of the firm's operations, which is in turn limited by the plans and actions of the past and thus by the managerial resources existing at the time the plans were made. Hence not only does existing management limit the amount of new management that can be hired (after all the services of existing management are required even to greet, let alone to install and instruct, the new personnel) but the plans put into effect by past management limit the rate at which newly hired personnel can gain the requisite experience. Extensive planning requires the co-operation of many individuals who have confidence in each other, and this, in general, requires knowledge of each other. Individuals with experience within a given group cannot be hired from outside the group, and it takes time for them to achieve the requisite experience. It follows, therefore, that if a firm deliberately or inadvertent expands its organization more rapidly than the individuals in the expanding organization can obtain the experience with each other and with the firm that is necessary for the effective operation of the group, the efficiency of the firm will suffer, even if optimum adjustments are made in the administrative structure; in extreme cases this may lead to such disorganization that the firm will be unable to compete efficiently in the market with other firms, and a period of 'stagnation' may follow.[7]

There is nothing novel about the suggestion that there are difficulties attendant upon the rapid expansion of the activities of a group of individuals bound together by intricate and delicate relationships. In a general way the notion has frequently been put forward in the literature. I am giving so much attention to it in order to emphasize the significance of the experience gained by the personnel of a firm operating in a particular environment. In one form or another the experience of a firm's managerial group plays a crucial role in the whole process of expansion, for the process by which experience is gained is properly treated as a process creating new productive services available to the firm.

. . . [A] distinction was made [earlier] between resources and productive services. Managerial services of the type described here are as much productive services in a firm as are the services of engineers in the physical production process; and they are a necessary part of the 'inputs' of which the productive activities of a firm are composed. Of all the various kinds of productive services, managerial services are the only type which every firm, because of its very nature as an administrative organization, must make use of. Since the services from 'inherited' managerial resources control the amount of new managerial resources that can be absorbed, they create a fundamental and inescapable limit to the amount of expansion a firm can undertake at any time.

[. . .]

If the argument is accepted that a firm will expand only in accordance with plans for expansion and that the extent of these plans will be limited by the size of the experienced managerial group, then it is evident that as plans are completed and put into operation, managerial services absorbed in the planning processes will be gradually released and become available for further planning.

[. . .]

In most circumstances one would expect new managerial services to be created in the process of expansion and to remain available to the firm. Any substantial expansion normally involves both acquisition of new personnel and promotion and redistribution of the old. Not infrequently a new subdivision of managerial organization is effected and a further decentralization of managerial functions takes place.

[. . .]

# The continuing availability of unused productive services

Resources include the physical things a firm buys, leases, or produces for its own use, and the people hired on terms that make them effectively part of the firm. Services, on the other hand, are the contributions these resources can make to the productive operations of the firm. A resource, then, can be viewed as a bundle of possible services.

For any given scale of operations a firm must possess resources from which it can obtain the productive services appropriate to the amounts and types of product it intends to produce. Some of the services will be obtained from resources already under the control of the firm in the form of fixed plant and equipment, more or less permanent personnel, and inventories of materials and goods in process; others will be obtained from resources the firm acquires in the market as occasion demands. Although the 'inputs' in which the firm is interested are productive services, it is *resources* that, with few exceptions, must be acquired in order to obtain services. For the most part, resources are only obtainable in discrete amounts, that is to say, a 'bundle' of services must be acquired even if only a 'single' service should be wanted.[8] The amount and kind of productive services obtainable from each *class* of resource are different, and sometimes, particularly with respect to personnel, the amount and kind of service obtainable from each *unit* within a resource-class are different. Having acquired resources for actual and contemplated operations, a firm has an incentive to use as profitably as possible the services obtainable from each unit of each type of resource acquired.

It follows, therefore, that as long as expansion can provide a way of using the services of its resources more profitably than they are being used, a firm has an incentive to expand; or alternatively, so long as any resources are not used fully in current operations, there is an incentive for a firm to find a way of using them more fully. Unused productive services available from existing resources are a 'waste', sometimes an unavoidable waste (that is to say, it may not pay to try to use them) but they are 'free' services which, if they can be used profitably, may provide a competitive advantage for the firm possessing them.

[. . .]

# The firm as a pool of resources

[. . .]

[A] firm is essentially a pool of resources the utilization of which is organized in an administrative framework. In a sense, the final products being produced by a firm at any given time merely represent one of several ways in which the firm could be using its resources, an incident in the development of its basic potentialities. Over the years the products change, and there are numerous firms to-day which produce few or none of the products on which their early reputation and success were based.

Their basic strength has been developed above or below the end-product level as it were – in technology of specialized kinds and in market positions. Within the limits set by the rate at which the administrative structure of the firm can be adapted and adjusted to larger and larger scales of operation, there is nothing inherent in the nature of the firm or of its economic function to prevent the indefinite expansion of its activities.

[. . .]

## Notes

1   I hope I shall be forgiven if, on occasion, I endow the firm itself with human attributes, considering it, not as a 'legal person', but, by analogy, as an 'economic person' (although not necessarily as the 'economic man'). This fiction permits me to speak of the 'firm', rather than its managers or executives, acting in this way or that, and facilitates exposition in those cases where no distinction is required between the firm and the men who run it.

2   Consequently the various attacks on the theory of the firm, whether they come from theorists emphasizing the effect of uncertainty or from investigators of the actual behaviour of firms, have failed to dislodge it from its key position in economic theory. To do so, even for the competitive case, would, as Hicks has pointed out, involve the 'wreckage' of 'the greater part of general equilibrium theory', which can hardly be accepted until something better has been evolved to take its place. J.R. Hicks, *Value and Capital* (Oxford: Clarendon Press, 2nd edn., 1946), p. 84.

3   The effect of uncertainty is not always put in these terms – see, for example, M. Kalecki, 'The Principle of Increasing Risk', *Economica* vol. IV (New Series) Nov. 1937; pp. 440–447 – but most formulations can usually be expressed in terms of 'corrected' cost and revenue estimates.

4   I am avoiding the use of the term 'factor of production' precisely because it makes no distinction between resources and services, sometimes meaning the one and sometimes the other in economic literature.

5   The term 'entrepreneur' throughout this study is used in a functional sense to refer to individuals or groups within the firm providing entrepreneurial services, whatever their position or occupational classification may be. Entrepreneurial services are those contributions to the operations of a firm which relate to the introduction and acceptance on behalf of the firm of new ideas, particularly with respect to products, location, and significant changes in technology, to the acquisition of new managerial personnel, to fundamental changes in the administrative organization of the firm, to the raising of capital, and to the making of plans for expansion, including the choice of method of expansion. Entrepreneurial services are contrasted with managerial services, which relate to the execution of entrepreneurial ideas and proposals and to the supervision of existing operations. The same individuals may, and more often

than not probably do, provide both types of service to the firm. The 'management' of a firm includes individuals supplying the entrepreneurial services as well as those supplying managerial services, but the 'competence of management' refers to the way in which the managerial function is carried out while the 'enterprise of management' refers to the entrepreneurial function. The nature of the organization of a firm and the relationships between the individuals within it have often as important an influence on the competence and enterprise of management and on the kinds of decisions taken as do the inherent characteristics of the individuals themselves. The influence of 'organizational structure' has been particularly stressed by the 'organization theorists'. See, for example R.M. Cyert and J.G. March, 'Organization Structure and Pricing Behavior in an Oligopolistic Market', *American Economic Review*, Vol. XLV, No. 1 (Mar. 1955), pp. 129–139.

6 The judgment regarding which of several alternative possibilities is 'best' will, of course, for any given firm be influenced by the attitude of the firm's entrepreneurs towards risk and by their ideas about the kind of action appropriate to their firm. We need not inquire into these things for the present but merely assume that they remain unchanged from one planning period to the next.

7 One student of industrial organization has noted that 'business enterprise today (as we must not cease to observe) is a corporate manifestation and its capacity to cope with larger outputs is not fixed but expands with its structure – and depends on the relation . . . between the governing members of the corporation . . . Some firms will fail with size because of management, if the immediate jump in size which they attempt is too great; or if the management is incapable of adapting its structure': P. Sargant Florence, *The Logic of British and American Industry* (London: Routledge and Kegan Paul, 1953), p. 64.

8 Even those raw materials which are in principle finely divisible must usually be acquired in minimum-sized bundles because to acquire less than the 'standard unit' is usually disproportionately expensive. However, this type of indivisibility is probably not of much practical importance.

# CHAPTER 8

# Looking Inside for Competitive Advantage

JAY B. BARNEY*

## Executive Overview

S trategic managers and researchers have long been interested in understanding sources of competitive advantage for firms. Traditionally, this effort has focused on the relationship between a firm's environmental opportunities and threats on the one hand, and its internal strengths and weaknesses on the other. Summarized in what has come to be known as SWOT (Strengths, Weaknesses, Opportunities, and Threats) analysis, this traditional logic suggests that firms that use their internal strengths in exploiting environmental opportunities and neutralizing environmental threats, while avoiding internal weaknesses, are more likely to gain competitive advantages than other kinds of firms.[1]

This simple SWOT framework points to the importance of both external and internal phenomena in understanding the sources of competitive advantage. To date, the development of tools for analyzing environmental opportunities and threats has proceeded much more rapidly than the development of tools for analyzing a firm's internal strengths and weaknesses. To address this deficiency, this chapter offers a simple, easy-to-apply approach to analyzing the competitive implications of a firm's internal strengths and weaknesses.

The history of strategic management research can be understood as an attempt to 'fill in the blanks' created by the SWOT framework; i.e. to move beyond suggesting that strengths, weaknesses, opportunities, and threats are important for understanding competitive advantage to suggest models and frameworks that can be used to analyze and evaluate these phenomena. Michael Porter and his associates have developed a number of these models and frameworks for analyzing

* Academy of Management for 'Looking Inside for Competitive Advantage' by Jay B. Barney © *Academy of Management Executive*, 1995.

environmental opportunities and threats.[2] Porter's work on the 'five forces model', the relationship between industry structure and strategic opportunities, and strategic groups can all be understood as an effort to unpack the concepts of environmental opportunities and threats in a theoretically rigorous, yet highly applicable way.

However, the SWOT framework tells us that environmental analysis – no matter how rigorous – is only half the story. A complete understanding of sources of competitive advantage requires the analysis of a firm's internal strengths and weaknesses as well.[3] The importance of integrating internal with environmental analyses can be seen when evaluating the sources of competitive advantage of many firms. Consider, for example,

- WalMart, a firm that has, for the last twenty years, consistently earned a return on sales twice the average of its industry;

- Southwest Airlines, a firm whose profits continued to increase, despite losses at other US airlines that totaled almost $10 billion from 1990 to 1993; and

- Nucor Steel, a firm whose stock price continued to soar through the 1980s and '90s, despite the fact that the market value of steel companies has remained flat or fallen during the same time period.[4]

These firms, and many others, have all gained competitive advantages – despite the unattractive, high threat, low opportunity environments within which they operate. Even the most careful and complete analysis of these firms' competitive environments cannot, by itself, explain their success. Such explanations must also include these firms' internal attributes – their strengths and weaknesses – as sources of competitive advantage. Following more recent practice, internal attributes will be referred to as *resources* and *capabilities* throughout the following discussion.[5]

A firm's resources and capabilities include all of the financial, physical, human, and organizational assets used by a firm to develop, manufacture, and deliver products or services to its customers. Financial resources include debt, equity, retained earnings, and so forth. Physical resources include the machines, manufacturing facilities, and buildings firms use in their operations. Human resources include all the experience, knowledge, judgment, risk taking propensity, and wisdom of individuals associated with a firm. Organizational resources include the history, relationships, trust, and organizational culture that are attributes of groups of individuals associated with a firm, along with a firm's formal reporting structure, explicit management control systems, and compensation policies.

In the process of filling in the 'internal blanks' created by SWOT analysis, managers must address four important questions about their resources and capabilities: (1) the question of value, (2) the question of rareness, (3) the question of imitability, and (4) the question of organization.

# The question of value

To begin evaluating the competitive implications of a firm's resources and capabilities, managers must first answer the question of value: Do a firm's resources and capabilities add value by enabling it to exploit opportunities and/or neutralize threats?

The answer to this question, for some firms, has been yes. Sony, for example, has a great deal of experience in designing, manufacturing, and selling miniaturized electronic technology. Sony has used these resources to exploit numerous market opportunities, including portable tape players, portable disc players, portable televisions, and easy-to-hold 8mm video cameras. 3M has used its skills and experience in substrates, coatings, and adhesives, along with an organizational culture that rewards risk taking and creativity, to exploit numerous market opportunities in office products, including invisible tape and Post-It™ Notes. Sony's and 3M's resources – including their specific technological skills and their creative organizational cultures – made it possible for these firms to respond to, and even create, new environmental opportunities.

Unfortunately, for other firms, the answer to the question of value has been no. For example, USX's long experience in traditional steel-making technology and the traditional steel market made it almost impossible for USX to recognize and respond to fundamental changes in the structure of the steel industry. Because they could not recognize new opportunities and threats, USX delayed its investment in, among other opportunities, thin slab continuous casting steel manufacturing technology. Nucor Steel, on the other hand, was not shackled by its experience, made these investments early, and has become a major player in the international steel industry. In a similar way, Sears was unable to recognize or respond to changes in the retail market that had been created by WalMart and specialty retail stores. In a sense, Sears' historical success, along with a commitment to stick with a traditional way of doing things, led it to miss some significant market opportunities.[6]

Although a firm's resources and capabilities may have added value in the past, changes in customer tastes, industry structure, or technology can render them less valuable in the future. General Electric's capabilities in transistor manufacturing became much less valuable when semiconductors were invented. American Airlines' skills in managing their relationship with the Civil Aeronautics Board (CAB) became much less valuable after airline deregulation. IBM's numerous capabilities in the mainframe computing business became less valuable with the increase in power, and reduction in price, of personal and mini computers. One of the most important responsibilities of strategic managers is to constantly evaluate whether or not their firm's resources and capabilities continue to add value, despite changes in the competitive environment.

Some environmental changes are so significant that few, if any, of a firm's resources remain valuable in any environmental context.[7] However, this kind of radical environmental change is unusual. More commonly, changes in a firm's environment may reduce the value of a firm's resources in their current use, while leaving the value of those resources in other uses unchanged. Such changes might even *increase* the value of those resources in those other uses. In this situation, the critical issue facing managers is: how can we use our traditional strengths in new ways to exploit opportunities and/or neutralize threats?

Numerous firms have weathered these environmental shifts by finding new ways to apply their traditional strengths. AT&T had developed a reputation for providing high-quality long distance telephone service. It moved rapidly to exploit this reputation in the newly competitive long distance market by aggressively marketing its services against MCI, Sprint, and other carriers. Also, AT&T had traditional strengths in research and development with its Bell Labs subsidiary. To exploit these strengths in its new competitive context, AT&T shifted Bell Labs' mission from basic research to applied research, and then leveraged those skills by forming numerous joint ventures, acquiring NCR, and other actions. Through this process, AT&T has been able to use some of its historically important capabilities to try to position itself as a major actor in the global telecommunications and computing industry.

Another firm that has gone through a similar transformation is the Hunter Fan Company. Formed in 1886, Hunter Fan developed the technology it needed to be the market share leader in ceiling fans used to cool large manufacturing facilities. Unfortunately, the invention of air conditioning significantly reduced demand for industrial fans, and Hunter Fan's performance deteriorated rapidly. However, in the 1970s, rising energy prices made energy conservation more important to home owners. Since ceiling fans can significantly reduce home energy consumption, Hunter Fan was able to move quickly to exploit this new opportunity. Of course, Hunter Fan had to develop some new skills as well, including brass-plating capabilities and new distribution networks. However, by building on its traditional strengths in new ways, Hunter Fan has become a leader in the home ceiling fan market.[8]

By answering the question of value, managers link the analysis of internal resources and capabilities with the analysis of environmental opportunities and threats. Firm resources are not valuable in a vacuum, but rather are valuable only when they exploit opportunities and/or neutralize threats. The models developed by Porter and his associates can be used to isolate potential opportunities and threats that the resources a firm controls can exploit or neutralize.

Of course, the resources and capabilities of different firms can be valuable in different ways. This can be true, even if firms are competing in the same industry. For example, while both Rolex and Timex manufacture watches, they exploit very different valuable resources. Rolex emphasizes its quality manufacturing, commitment to excellence, and high-status reputation in marketing its watches. Timex emphasizes its high-volume, low-cost manufacturing skills and abilities. Rolex exploits its capabilities in responding to demand for very expensive watches; Timex exploits its resources in responding to demand for practical, reliable, low-cost timekeeping.

# The question of rareness

That a firm's resources and capabilities are valuable is an important first consideration in understanding internal sources of competitive advantage. However, if a particular resource and capability is controlled by numerous competing firms, then that resource is unlikely to be a source of competitive advantage for any one of them. Instead, valuable but common (i.e. not rare) resources and capabilities are sources of competitive parity. For managers evaluating the competitive implications of their resources and capabilities, these observations lead to the second critical issue: How many competing firms already possess these valuable resources and capabilities?

Consider, for example, two firms competing in the global communications and computing industries: NEC and AT&T. Both these firms are developing many of the same capabilities that are likely to be needed in these industries over the next decade. These capabilities are clearly valuable, although – since at least these two firms, and maybe others, are developing them – they may not be rare. If they are not rare, they cannot – by themselves – be sources of competitive advantage for either NEC or AT&T. If either of these firms is to gain competitive advantages, they must exploit resources and capabilities that are different from the communication and computing skills they are *both* cited as developing. This may be part of the reason why AT&T recently restructured its telecommunications and computer businesses into separate firms.[9]

While resources and capabilities must be rare among competing firms in order to be a source of competitive advantage, this does not mean that common, but valuable, resources are not important. Indeed, such resources and capabilities may be essential for a firm's survival. On the other hand, if a firm's resources are valuable and rare, those resources may enable a firm to gain at least a temporary competitive advantage. WalMart's skills in developing and using point-of-purchase data collection to control inventory have given it a competitive advantage over K-Mart, a firm that until recently has not had access to this timely information. Thus, for many years, WalMart's valuable point-of-purchase inventory control systems were rare, at least relative to its major US competitor, K-Mart.[10]

# The question of imitability

A firm that possesses valuable and rare resources and capabilities can gain, at least, a temporary competitive advantage. If, in addition, competing firms face a cost disadvantage in imitating these resources and capabilities, firms with these special abilities can obtain a sustained competitive advantage. These observations lead to the question of imitability: Do firms without a resource or capability face a cost disadvantage in obtaining it compared to firms that already possess it?

Obviously, imitation is critical to understanding the ability of resources and capabilities to generate sustained competitive advantages. Imitation can occur in at least two ways: duplication and substitution. Duplication occurs when an imitating firm builds the same kinds of resources as the firm it is imitating. If one firm has a competitive advantage because of its research and development skills, then a duplicating firm will try to imitate that resource by developing its own research and development skills. In addition, firms may be able to substitute some resources for other resources. If these substitute resources have the same strategic implications and are no more costly to develop, then imitation through substitution will lead to competitive parity in the long run.

So, when will firms be at a cost disadvantage in imitating another's resources and capabilities, either through duplication or substitution? While there are numerous reasons why some of these internal attributes of firms may be costly to imitate, most of these reasons can be grouped into three categories: the importance of history in creating firm resources; the importance of numerous 'small decisions' in developing, nurturing, and exploiting resources; and the importance of socially complex resources.

## The importance of history

As firms evolve, they pick up skills, abilities, and resources that are unique to them, reflecting their particular path through history. These resources and capabilities reflect the unique personalities, experiences, and relationships that exist in only a single firm. Before the Second World War, Caterpillar was one of several medium-sized firms in the heavy construction equipment industry struggling to survive intense competition. Just before the outbreak of war, the Department of War (now the Department of Defense) concluded that, in order to pursue a global war, they would need one worldwide supplier of heavy construction equipment to build roads, air strips, army bases, and so forth. After a brief competition, Caterpillar was awarded this contract and, with the support of the Allies, was able to develop a worldwide service and supply network for heavy construction equipment at very low cost.

After the war, Caterpillar continued to own and operate this worldwide service and supply network. Indeed, Caterpillar management still advertises their ability to deliver any part, for any piece of Caterpillar equipment, to any place in the world, in under two days. By using this valuable capability, Caterpillar was able to become the dominant firm in the heavy construction equipment industry. Even today, despite recessions and labor strife, Caterpillar remains the market share leader in most categories of heavy construction equipment.[11]

Consider the position of a firm trying to duplicate Caterpillar's worldwide service and supply network, at the same cost as Caterpillar. This competing firm would have to receive the same kind of government support that Caterpillar received during the Second World War. This kind of government support is very unlikely.

It is interesting to note that at least one firm in the heavy construction equipment industry has begun to effectively compete against Caterpillar: Komatsu. However, rather than attempting to duplicate Caterpillar's service and supply network, Komatsu has attempted to exploit its own unique design and manufacturing resources by building machines that do not break down as frequently. Since Komatsu's machines break down less frequently, Komatsu does not require as extensive a worldwide service and supply network as Caterpillar. In this sense, Komatsu's special design and manufacturing skills in building machines that break down less frequently may be a strategic substitute for Caterpillar's worldwide service and supply network.[12]

In general, whenever the acquisition or development of valuable and rare resources depends upon unique historical circumstances, those imitating these resources will be at a cost disadvantage building them. Such resources can be sources of sustained competitive advantage.

## The importance of numerous small decisions

Strategic managers and researchers are often enamored with the importance of 'Big Decisions' as determinants of competitive advantage. IBM's decision to bring out the 360 series of computers in the 1960s was a 'Big Decision' that had enormous competitive implications until the rise of personal computers. General Electric's decision to invest in the medical imaging business was a 'Big Decision' whose competitive ramifications are still unfolding. Sometimes such 'Big Decisions' are critical in understanding a firm's competitive position. However, more and more frequently, a firm's competitive advantage seems to depend on numerous 'small decisions' through which a firm's resources and capabilities are developed and exploited. Thus, for example, a firm's competitive advantage in quality does not depend just upon its announcing that it is seeking the Malcolm Baldridge Quality Award. It depends upon literally hundreds of thousands of decisions made each day by employees in the firm – small decisions about whether or not to tighten a screw a little more, whether or not to share a small idea for improvement, or whether or not to call attention to a quality problem.[13] From the point of view of sustaining a competitive advantage, 'small decisions' have some advantages over 'Big Decisions.' In particular, small decisions are essentially invisible to firms seeking to imitate a successful firm's resources and capabilities. 'Big Decisions', on the other hand, are more obvious, easier to describe, and, perhaps, easier to imitate. While competitors may be able to observe the consequences of numerous little decisions, they often have a difficult time understanding the sources of the advantages.[14] A case in point is The Mailbox, Inc., a very successful firm in the bulk mailing business in the Dallas-Ft. Worth market. If there was ever a business where it seems unlikely that a firm would have a sustained competitive advantage, it is bulk mailing. Firms in this industry gather mail from customers, sort it by postal code, and then take it to the post office to be mailed. Where is the competitive advantage here? And yet, The Mailbox has enjoyed an enormous market share advantage in the Dallas-Ft. Worth area for several years. Why?

When asked, managers at The Mailbox have a difficult time describing the sources of their sustained advantages. Indeed, they can point to *no* 'Big Decisions' they have made to generate this advantage. However, as these managers begin to discuss their firm, what becomes clear is that their success does not depend on doing a few big things right, but on doing lots of little things right. The way they manage accounting, finance, human resources, production, or other business functions, separately, is not exceptional. However, to manage all these functions so well, and so consistently over time is truly exceptional. Firms seeking to compete against The Mailbox will not have to imitate just a few internal attributes; they will have to imitate thousands, or even hundreds of thousands of such attributes — a daunting task indeed.[15]

## The importance of socially complex resources

A final reason that firms may be at a cost disadvantage in imitating resources and capabilities is that these resources may be socially complex. Some physical resources (e.g. computers, robots, and other machines) controlled by firms are very complex. However, firms seeking to imitate these physical resources need only purchase them, take them apart, and duplicate the technology in question. With just a couple of exceptions (including the pharmaceutical and specialty chemicals industries), patents provide little protection from the imitation of a firm's physical resources.[16] On the other hand, socially complex resources and capabilities — organizational phenomena like reputation, trust, friendship, teamwork and culture — while not patentable, are much more difficult to imitate. Imagine the difficulty of imitating Hewlett Packard's (HP) powerful and enabling culture. One of the most important components of HP's culture is that it supports and encourages teamwork and cooperation, even across divisional boundaries. HP has used this socially complex capability to enhance the compatibility of its numerous products, including printers, plotters, personal computers, mini-computers, and electronic instruments. By cooperating across these product categories, HP has been able to almost double its market value, all without introducing any radical new products or technologies[17]

In general, when a firm's resources and capabilities are valuable, rare, and socially complex, those resources are likely to be sources of sustained competitive advantage. One firm that apparently violates this assertion is Sony. Most observers agree that Sony possesses some special management and coordination skills that enables it to conceive, design, and manufacture high quality, miniaturized consumer electronics. However, it appears that every time Sony brings out a new miniaturized product, several of its competitors quickly duplicate that product, through reverse engineering, thereby reducing Sony's technological advantage. In what way can Sony's socially complex miniaturization skills be a source of sustained competitive advantage, when most of Sony's products are quickly imitated?

The solution to this paradox depends on shifting the unit of analysis from the performance of Sony's products over time to the performance of Sony over time. After it introduces each new product, Sony experiences a rapid increase in sales and profits associated with that product. However, this leads other firms to reverse engineer the Sony product and introduce their own version. Increased competition leads the sales and profits associated with the new product to be reduced. Thus, at the level of individual products introduced by Sony, Sony apparently enjoys only very short-lived competitive advantages.

However, by looking at the total returns earned by Sony across all of its new products over time, the source of Sony's sustained competitive advantage becomes clear. By exploiting its capabilities in miniaturization, Sony is able to constantly introduce new and exciting personal electronics products. No one of these products generate a sustained competitive advantage. However, over time, across several such product introductions, Sony's capability advantages do lead to a sustained competitive advantage.[18]

## The question of organization

A firm's competitive advantage potential depends on the value, rareness, and imitability of its resources and capabilities. However, to fully realize this potential, a firm must also be organized to exploit its resources and capabilities. These observations lead to the question of organization: Is a firm organized to exploit the full competitive potential of its resources and capabilities?

Numerous components of a firm's organization are relevant when answering the question of organization, including its formal reporting structure, its explicit management control systems, and its compensation policies. These components are referred to as *complementary resources* because they have limited ability to generate competitive advantage in isolation. However, in combination with other resources and capabilities, they can enable a firm to realize its full competitive advantage.[19]

Much of Caterpillar's sustained competitive advantage in the heavy construction industry can be traced to its becoming the sole supplier of this equipment to Allied forces in the Second World War. However, if Caterpillar's management had not taken advantage of this opportunity by implementing a global formal reporting structure, global inventory and other control systems, and compensation policies that created incentives for its employees to work around the world, then Caterpillar's potential for competitive advantage would not have been fully realized. These attributes of Caterpillar's organization, by themselves, could not be a source of competitive advantage; i.e. adopting a global organizational form was only relevant for Caterpillar because it was pursuing a global opportunity. However, this organization was essential for Caterpillar to realize its full competitive advantage potential.

In a similar way, much of WalMart's continuing competitive advantage in the discount retailing industry can be attributed to its early entry into rural markets in the southern United States. However, to fully exploit this geographic advantage, WalMart needed to implement appropriate reporting structures, control systems, and compensation policies. We have already seen that one of these components of

WalMart's organization – its point-of-purchase inventory control system – is being imitated by K-Mart, and thus, by itself, is not likely to be a source of sustained competitive advantage. However, this inventory control system has enabled WalMart to take full advantage of its rural locations by decreasing the probability of stock outs and by reducing inventory costs.

While a complementary organization enabled Caterpillar and WalMart to realize their full competitive advantage, Xerox was prevented from taking full advantage of some of its most critical valuable, rare, and costly-to-imitate resources and capabilities because it lacked such organizational skills. Through the 1960s and early 1970s, Xerox invested in a series of very innovative technology development research efforts. Xerox managed this research effort by creating a stand alone research laboratory (Xerox PARC, in Palo Alto, California), and by assembling a large group of highly creative and innovative scientists and engineers to work there. Left to their own devices, these scientists and engineers developed an amazing array of technological innovations, including the personal computer the 'mouse', windows-type software, the laser printer, the 'paperless office', ethernet, and so forth. In retrospect, the market potential of these technologies was enormous. Moreover, since these technologies were developed at Xerox PARC, they were rare. Finally, Xerox may have been able to gain some important first mover advantages if they had been able to translate these technologies into products, thereby increasing the cost to other firms of imitating these technologies.

Unfortunately, Xerox did not have an organization in place to take advantage of these resources. For example, no structure existed whereby Xerox PARC's innovations could become known to managers at Xerox. Indeed, most Xerox managers – even many senior managers – were unaware of these technological developments through the mid-1970s. Once they finally became aware of them, very few of the innovations survived Xerox's highly bureaucratic product development process – a process where product development projects were divided into hundreds of minute tasks, and progress in each task was reviewed by dozens of large committees. Even those innovations that survived the product development process were not exploited by Xerox managers. Management compensation at Xerox depended almost exclusively on maximizing current revenue. Short-term profitability was relatively less important in compensation calculations, and the development of markets for future sales and profitability was essentially irrelevant. Xerox's formal reporting structure, its explicit management control systems, and its compensation policies were all inconsistent with exploiting the valuable, rare, and costly-to-imitate resources developed at Xerox PARC. Not surprisingly, Xerox failed to exploit any of these potential sources of sustained competitive advantage.[20]

This set of questions can be applied in understanding the competitive implications of phenomena as diverse as the 'cola wars' in the soft drink industry and competition among different types of personal computers.

# The competitive implications of the 'Cola Wars'

Almost since they were founded, Coca-Cola, Inc. and PepsiCo Inc. have battled each other for market share in the soft drink industry. In many ways, the intensity of these 'cola wars' increased in the mid-1970s with the introduction of PepsiCo's 'Pepsi Challenge' advertising campaign. While significant advertising and other marketing expenditures have been made by both these firms, and while market share has shifted back and forth between them over time, it is not at all clear that these efforts have generated competitive advantages for either Coke or Pepsi.

Obviously, market share is a very valuable commodity in the soft drink industry. Market share translates directly into revenues, which, in turn, has a large impact on profits and profitability. Strategies pursued by either Coke or Pepsi designed to acquire market share will usually be valuable.

But are these market share acquisition strategies rare or does either Coca-Cola or Pepsi have a cost advantage in implementing them? Both Coca-Cola and PepsiCo are marketing powerhouses; both have enormous financial capabilities and strong management teams. Any effort by one to take share away can instantly be matched by the other to protect that share. In this sense, while Coke's and Pepsi's share acquisition strategies may be valuable, they are not rare, nor does either Coke or Pepsi have a cost advantage in implementing them. Assuming that these firms are appropriately organized (a reasonable assumption), then the cola wars should be a source of competitive parity for these firms.

This has, apparently, been the case. For example, Pepsi originally introduced its 'Pepsi Challenge' advertising campaign in the Dallas-Ft. Worth market. After six months of the Pepsi Challenge – including price discounts, coupon campaigns, numerous celebrity endorsements, and so on – Pepsi was able to double its share of the Dallas-Ft. Worth market from 7% to 14%. Unfortunately, the retail price of Pepsi's soft drinks, after six months of the Pepsi Challenge, was approximately one half the pre-challenge level. Thus Pepsi doubled its market share, but cut its prices in half – exactly the result one would expect in a world of competitive parity.[21]

It is interesting to note that both Coca-Cola and Pepsi are beginning to recognize the futility of going head to head against an equally skilled competitor in a battle for market share to gain competitive advantages. Instead, these firms seem to be altering both their market share and other strategies. Coke, through its Diet Coke brand name, is targeting older consumers with advertisements that use personalities from the '50s, '60s, and '70s (e.g. Elton John and Gene Kelly). Pepsi continues its focus on attracting younger drinkers with its 'choice of a new generation' advertising campaigns. Coke continues its traditional focus on the soft drink industry, while Pepsi has begun diversifying into fast food restaurants and other related businesses. Coke has extended its marketing efforts internationally, whereas Pepsi focuses mostly on the market in the United States (although it is beginning to alter this strategy). In all these ways, Coke and Pepsi seem to be moving away from head-to-head competition for market share, and moving towards exploiting *different* resources.

## The competitive position of the Macintosh computer

Building on earlier research conducted by Xerox PARC, Apple Computer developed and marketed the first user-friendly alternative to DOS-based personal computers, the Macintosh. Most Macintosh users have a passion for their computers that is usually reserved for personal relationships. Macintosh users shake their heads and wonder why DOS-based computer users don't wake up and experience the 'joy of Macintosh.'

The first step in analyzing the competitive position of the Macintosh is to evaluate whether or not 'user friendliness' in a personal computer is valuable; i.e. does it exploit an environmental opportunity and/or neutralize an environmental threat? While user friendliness is not a requirement of all personal computer users, it is not unreasonable to conclude that many of these computer users, other things being equal, would prefer working on a user friendly machine compared with a user unfriendly machine. Thus, the Macintosh computer does seem to respond to a real market opportunity.

When the Macintosh was first introduced, was user friendliness rare? At that time, DOS-based machines were essentially the only alternative to the Macintosh, and DOS-based software, in those early days, was anything but user friendly. Thus, the Macintosh was apparently both valuable and rare, and thus a source of at least a temporary competitive advantage for Apple.

Was the user-friendliness of the Macintosh costly to imitate? At first, it seemed likely that user-friendly software would rapidly be developed for DOS-based machines, and thus that the user-friendly Macintosh would only enjoy a temporary competitive advantage. However, history has shown that user friendliness was not easy to imitate.

Imitation of the user-friendly Macintosh by DOS-based machines was slowed by a combination of at least two factors. First, the Macintosh hardware and software system had originally been developed by teams of software, hardware, and production engineers all working in Apple Computer. The teamwork, trust, commitment, and enthusiasm that these Apple employees enjoyed while working on Macintosh technology was difficult for other computer firms to duplicate, since most of those firms specialized either in hardware design and manufacturing (e.g. IBM) or software development (e.g. Microsoft, Lotus). In other words, the socially complex resources that Apple was able to bring to bear in the Macintosh project were difficult to duplicate in vertically non-integrated computer hardware and software firms.

Second, Apple management had a different conception of the personal computer and its future than did managers at IBM and other computer firms. At

IBM, for example, computers had traditionally meant mainframe computers, and mainframe computers were expected to be complicated and difficult to operate. User friendliness was never an issue in IBM mainframes (users of IBM's JCL know the truth of that assertion!), and thus was not an important concern when IBM entered into the personal computer market. However, at Apple, computers were Jobs' and Wozniak's toys – a hobby, to be used for fun. If management's mindset is that 'computers are supposed to be fun', then it suddenly becomes easier to develop and build user-friendly computers.

Obviously, these two mindsets – IBM's 'computers are complex tools run by technical specialists' versus Apple's 'computers are toys for everyone' – were deeply embedded in the cultures of these two firms, as well as those firms that worked closely with them. Such mindsets are socially complex, slow to change, and difficult to imitate. It took some time before the notion that a computer should be (or even could be) easy to use came to prominence in DOS-based systems.[22] Only recently, after almost ten years (an eternity in the rapidly changing personal computer business), has user-friendly software for DOS-based machines been developed. With the introduction of Windows by Microsoft, the rareness of Macintosh's user friendliness has been reduced, as has been the competitive advantage that Macintosh had generated.

Interestingly, just as Windows software was introduced, Apple began to radically change its pricing and product development strategies. First Apple cut the price of the Macintosh computer, reflecting the fact that user friendliness was not as rare after Windows as it was before Windows. Second, Apple seems to have recognized the need to develop new resources and capabilities to enhance their traditional user-friendly strengths. Rather than only competing with other hardware and software companies, Apple has begun developing strategic alliances with several other computer firms, including IBM and Microsoft. These alliances may help Apple develop the resources and capabilities they need to remain competitive in the personal computer industry over the next several years.

## The management challenge

In the end, this discussion reminds us that sustained competitive advantage cannot be created simply by evaluating environmental opportunities and threats, and then conducting business only in high-opportunity, low-threat environments. Rather, creating sustained competitive advantage depends on the unique resources and capabilities that a firm brings to competition in its environment. To discover these resources and capabilities, managers must look inside their firm for valuable, rare and costly-to-imitate resources, and then exploit these resources through their organization.

# Notes

1 The original SWOT framework was proposed and developed by E. Learned, C. Christiansen, K. Andrews, and W. Guth in *Business Policy* (Homewood, IL: Irwin, 1969). Though the field of strategic management has evolved a great deal since then, this fundamental SWOT framework, as an organizing principle, has remained unchanged. See for example Michael Porter, 'The Contributions of Industrial Organization to Strategic Management', *Academy of Management Review*, 6, 1981, 609–620; and Jay Barney, 'Firm Resources and Sustained Competitive Advantage', *Journal of Management*, 17, 1991, 99–120.

2 Porter's work is described in detail in M. Porter, *Competitive Strategy* (New York, NY: Free Press, 1980), and M. Porter, *Competitive Advantage* (New York, NY: Free Press, 1985).

3 A variety of different authors have begun to explore the competitive implications of a firm's internal strengths and weaknesses. Building on some seminal insights by Edith Penrose [*The Theory of the Growth of the Firm* (New York, NY: Wiley, 1959)], this work has come to be known as the Resource-Based View of the Firm. Resource-based scholarly work includes: Birger Wernerfelt, 'A Resource-Based View of the Firm', *Strategic Management Journal*, 5, 1984, 171–180; Richard Rumelt, 'Toward a Strategic Theory of the Firm', in R. Lamb (ed.), *Competitive Strategic Management* (Englewood Cliffs, NJ: Prentice-Hall, 1984), 556–570; Jay Barney, 'Strategic Factor Markets', *Management Science*, 41, 1980, 1231–1241; and Jay Barney, 'Organizational Culture: Can It Be A Source of Sustained Competitive Advantage?' *Academy of Management Review*, 11, 1986, 791–800. The framework developed in this article draws most closely from Jay Barney, 'Firm Resources and Sustained Competitive Advantage', *op. cit.*

4 For more detailed discussions of the internal resources and capabilities of these firms, see Pankaj Ghemewat, 'WalMart Stores' Discount Operations', Case No. 9-387-018 (Harvard Business Schoo, 1986); S. Chakravarty, 'Hit 'Em Hardest with the Mostest', *Forbes*, 148, September 16, 1991, 48–54; and Pankaj Ghemawat, 'Nucor at a Crossroad', Case No. 9-793-039 (Harvest Business School, 1992).

5 Different terms have been used to describe these internal phenomena, including core competencies (C.K. Prahalad and Gary Hamel, 'The Core Competence of the Organization', *Harvard Business Review*, 90, 1990, 79–93), firm resources (Birger Wernerfelt, *op. cit.*, and Jay B. Barney, 'Firm Resources and Sustained Competitive Advantage') and firm capabilities (George Stalk, Phillip Evans, and Lawrence Shulman, 'Competing on Capabilities: The New Rules of Corporate Strategy', *Harvard Business Review*, March–April, 1992, 57–69). While distinctions among these terms can be drawn, for our purposes they can, and will, be used interchangeably.

6 For details, see B. Schlender, 'How Sony Keeps the Magic Going', *Fortune*, 125, February 24, 1992, 76–84; L. Krogh, J. Praeger, D. Sorenson, and

J. Tomlinson, 'How 3M Evaluates Its R&D Programs', *Research Technology Management*, 31, November/December, 1988, 10–14; Richard Rosenbloom, 'Continuous Casting Investments at USX Corporation', Case No. 9-392-232 (Harvard Business School, 1990); and Cynthia Montgomery, 'Sears, Roebuck and Co. in 1989', Case No. 9-391-147 (Harvard Business School, 1989).

7   This kind of environmental or technological shift is called a Schumpeterian revolution, and firms in this setting have little systematic hope of gaining competitive advantages, unless the competitive environment shifts again, although they can be lucky. See Jay B. Barney, 'Types of Competitors and the Theory of Strategy: Toward an Integrative Framework', *Academy of Management Review*, 1986, 791–800.

8   For a discussion of AT&T's attempt to develop new resources and capabilities, see D. Kirkpatrick, 'Could AT&T Rule the World?' *Fortune*, 127, May 17, 1993, 54–56. Hunter Fan's experience was described through personal communication with managers there, and in a publication celebrating Hunter Fan's 100th anniversary in 1986.

9   Prahalad and Hamel's 1990 discussion of NEC's attempt to develop the resources needed to compete in the global telecommunications and computer industry is insightful, especially in comparison to Kirkpatrick's discussion of AT&T's efforts in *Fortune*.

10  WalMart's point of purchase inventory control system and the impact of WalMart's rural stores on its performance, are described in Ghemewat, *op. cit.*, 1986. K-Mart's inventory control response to WalMart is described in L. Steven's 'Front Line Systems', *Computerworld*, 26, 1992, 61–63.

11  See M.G. Rukstad and J. Horn, 'Caterpillar and the Construction Equipment Industry in 1988', Case No. 9-389-097 (Harvard Business School, 1989).

12  Komatsu's response to Caterpillar's competitive advantage is described in C.A. Bartlett and U.S. Rangan, 'Komatsu Ltd', Case No. 9-385-277 (Harvard Business School, 1985).

13  See Richard Blackburn and Benson Rosen, 'Total Quality and Human Resources Management: Lessons Learned from Baldridge Award-winning Companies', *Academy of Management Executive*, 7, 1993, 49–66.

14  These invisible assets have been described by H. Itami, *Mobilizing Invisible Assets* (Cambridge, MA: Harvard University Press, 1987).

15  Personal communication.

16  See E. Mansfield, 'How Rapidly Does New Industrial Technology Leak Out?' *Journal of Industrial Economics*, 34, 1985, 217–223; and E. Mansfield, M. Schwartz, and S. Wagner, 'Imitation Costs and Patents: An Empirical Study', *Economic Journal*, 91, 1981, 907–918.

17  See S.K. Yoder, 'A 1990 Reorganization at Hewlett Packard Already Is Paying Off', *Wall Street Journal*, July 22, 1991, Section Ak, 1+. This is not to suggest that socially complex resources and capabilities do not change and evolve in an organization. They clearly do. Nor does this suggest that managers can never radically alter a firm's socially complex resources and capabilities. Such

transformational leaders do seem to exist, and do have an enormous impact on these resources in a firm. Managers such as the late Mike Walsh at Tenneco, Lee Iacocca at Chrysler, and Jack Welch at General Electric apparently have been such leaders. However, this kind of leadership is a socially complex phenomenon, and thus very difficult to imitate. Even if a leader in one firm can transform its socially complex resources and capabilities, it does not necessarily mean that other firms will be able to imitate this feat at the same cost. The concept of transformational leaders is discussed in N. Tichy, *The Transformational Leader* (New York, NY: Wiley, 1986).

18  See Schlender, *op. cit.*

19  See Raphael Amit and Paul Schoemaker, 'Strategic Assets and Organizational Rent', *Strategic Management Journal*, 14, 1993, 33–46; David Teece. 'Profitting From Technological Innovation', *Research Policy*, 15, 1986, 285–305; and Ingemar Dierickx and Karel Cool, 'Asset Stock Accumulation and Sustainability of Competitive Advantage', *Management Science*, 35, 1989, 1504–1511, for a discussion of complementary resources and capabilities. Of course, complementary organizational resources are part of a firm's overall resource and capability base, and thus the competitive implications of these resources could be evaluated using the questions of value, rareness, and imitability. However, the question of organization is included in this discussion to emphasize the particular importance of complementary organizational resources in enabling a firm to fully exploit its competitive advantage potential.

20  Xerox's organizational problems with Xerox PARC are described, in detail, in David T. Kearns and David A. Nadler, *Prophets in the Dark* (New York, NY: Harper Collins, 1992); Douglas K. Smith and Robert C. Alexander, *Fumbling the Future* (New York, NY: William Morrow, 1988); and L. Hooper, 'Xerox Tries to Shed Its Has Been Image with a Big New Machine', *Wall Street Journal*, September 20, 1990, Section A, 1+.

21  See A.E. Pearson and C.L. Irwin, 'Coca-Cola vs. Pepsi-Cola (A)', Case No. 9-387-108 (Harvard Business School, 1988), for a discussion of the cola wars, and their competitive implications for Coke and Pepsi.

22  See D.B. Yoffie, 'Apple Computer – 1992', Case No. 9-792-081 (Harvard Business School, 1992), for a complete discussion of Apple, IBM, and Apple's new strategies for the 1990s.

# CHAPTER 9

# Dynamic Capabilities and Strategic Management

DAVID J. TEECE, GARY PISANO AND AMY SHUEN*

[. . .]

## Introduction

The fundamental question in the field of strategic management is how firms achieve and sustain competitive advantage.[1] We confront this question here by developing the dynamic capabilities approach, which endeavors to analyze the sources of wealth creation and capture by firms. The development of this framework flows from a recognition by the authors that strategic theory is replete with analyses of firm-level strategies for sustaining and safeguarding extant competitive advantage, but has performed less well with respect to assisting in the understanding of how and why certain firms build competitive advantage in regimes of rapid change. Our approach is especially relevant in a Schumpeterian world of innovation-based competition, price/performance rivalry, increasing returns, and the 'creative destruction' of existing competences. The approach endeavors to explain firm-level success and failure. We are interested in building a better theory of firm performance, as well as informing managerial practice.

[. . .]

The dominant paradigm in the field during the 1980s was the competitive forces approach developed by Porter (1980). This approach, rooted in the structure–conduct–performance paradigm of industrial organization (Mason, 1949; Bain, 1959), emphasizes the actions a firm can take to create defensible positions against competitive forces. A second approach, referred to as a strategic conflict approach (e.g. Shapiro, 1989), is closely related to the first in its focus on product market imperfections, entry deterrence, and strategic interaction. The strategic conflict approach uses the tools of game theory and thus implicitly views competitive

* John Wiley & Sons Limited for 'Dynamic Capabilities and Strategic Management' by David J. Teece, G. Pisano and A. Shuen © *Strategic Management Journal*, 1997.

outcomes as a function of the effectiveness with which firms keep their rivals off balance through strategic investments, pricing strategies, signaling, and the control of information. Both the competitive forces and the strategic conflict approaches appear to share the view that rents flow from privileged product market positions.

Another distinct class of approaches emphasizes building competitive advantage through capturing entrepreneurial rents stemming from fundamental firm-level efficiency advantages. These approaches have their roots in a much older discussion of corporate strengths and weaknesses; they have taken on new life as evidence suggests that firms build enduring advantages only through efficiency and effectiveness, and as developments in organizational economics and the study of technological and organizational change become applied to strategy questions. One strand of this literature, often referred to as the 'resource-based perspective', emphasizes firm-specific capabilities and assets and the existence of isolating mechanisms as the fundamental determinants of firm performance (Penrose, 1959; Rumelt, 1984; Teece, 1984; Wernerfelt, 1984).[2] This perspective recognizes but does not attempt to explain the nature of the isolating mechanisms that enable entrepreneurial rents and competitive advantage to be sustained.

Another component of the efficiency-based approach is developed in this paper. Rudimentary efforts are made to identify the dimensions of firm-specific capabilities that can be sources of advantage, and to explain how combinations of competences and resources can be developed, deployed, and protected. We refer to this as the 'dynamic capabilities' approach in order to stress exploiting existing internal and external firm-specific competences to address changing environments. Elements of the approach can be found in Schumpeter (1942), Penrose (1959), Nelson and Winter (1982), Prahalad and Hamel (1990), Teece (1976, 1986a, 1986b, 1988) and in Hayes, Wheelwright, and Clark (1988): Because this approach emphasizes the development of management capabilities, and difficult-to-imitate combinations of organizational, functional and technological skills, it integrates and draws upon research in such areas as the management of R&D, product and process development, technology transfer, intellectual property, manufacturing, human resources, and organizational learning. Because these fields are often viewed as outside the traditional boundaries of strategy, much of this research has not been incorporated into existing economic approaches to strategy issues. As a result, dynamic capabilities can be seen as an emerging and potentially integrative approach to understanding the newer sources of competitive advantage.

We suggest that the dynamic capabilities approach is promising both in terms of future research potential and as an aid to management endeavoring to gain competitive advantage in increasingly demanding environments.

[. . .]

# Models of strategy emphasizing the exploitation of market power

## Competitive forces

The dominant paradigm in strategy at least during the 1980s was the competitive forces approach. Pioneered by Porter (1980), the competitive forces approach views the essence of competitive strategy formulation as 'relating a company to its environment . . . [T]he key aspect of the firm's environment is the industry or industries in which it competes.' Industry structure strongly influences the competitive. rules of the game as well as the strategies potentially available to firms.

In the competitive forces model, five industry-level forces – entry barriers, threat of substitution, bargaining power of buyers, bargaining power of suppliers, and rivalry among industry incumbents – determine the inherent profit potential of an industry or subsegment of an industry. The approach can be used to help the firm find a position in an industry from which it can best defend itself against competitive forces or influence them in its favor (Porter, 1980: 4).

This 'five-forces' framework provides a systematic way of thinking about how competitive forces work at the industry level and how these forces determine the profitability of different industries and industry segments. The competitive forces framework also contains a number of underlying assumptions about the sources of competition and the nature of the strategy process. To facilitate comparisons with other approaches, we highlight several distinctive characteristics of the framework.

Economic rents in the competitive forces framework are monopoly rents (Teece, 1984). Firms in an industry earn rents when they are somehow able to impede the competitive forces (in either factor markets or product markets) which tend to drive economic returns to zero. Available strategies are described in Porter (1980). Competitive strategies are often aimed at altering the firm's position in the industry *vis-àvis* competitors and suppliers. Industry structure plays a central role in determining and limiting strategic action.

Some industries or subsectors of industries become more 'attractive' because they have structural impediments to competitive forces (e.g. entry barriers) that allow firms better opportunities for creating sustainable competitive advantages. Rents are created largely at the industry or subsector level rather than at the firm level. While there is some recognition given to firmspecific assets, differences among firms relate primarily to scale. This approach to strategy reflects its incubation inside the field of industrial organization and in particular the industrial structure school of Mason and Bain[3] (Teece, 1984).

## Strategic conflict

The publication of Carl Shapiro's 1989 article, confidently titled 'The Theory of Business Strategy', announced the emergence of a new approach to business strategy, if not strategic management. This approach utilizes the tools of game theory to analyze the nature of competitive interaction between rival firms. The main thrust of work in this tradition is to reveal how a firm can influence the behavior and actions of rival firms and thus the market environment.[4] Examples of such moves are investment in capacity (Dixit, 1980), R&D (Gilbert and Newberry, 1982), and advertising (Schmalensee, 1983). To be effective, these strategic moves require irreversible commitments.[5] The moves in question will have no effect if they can be costlessly undone. A key idea is that by manipulating the market environment, a firm may be able to increase its profits.

[. . .]

We have a particular view of the contexts in which the strategic conflict literature is relevant to strategic management. Firms that have a tremendous cost or other competitive advantage *vis-à-vis* their rivals ought not be transfixed by the moves and countermoves of their rivals. Their competitive fortunes will swing more on total demand conditions, not on how competitors deploy and redeploy their competitive assets. Put differently, when there are gross asymmetrics in competitive advantage between firms, the results of game-theoretic analysis are likely to be obvious and uninteresting. The stronger competitor will generally advance, even if disadvantaged by certain information asymmetries. To be sure, incumbent firm can be undone by new entrants with a dramatic cost advantage, but no 'gaming' will overturn that outcome. On the other hand, if firms' competitive positions are more delicately balanced, as with Coke and Pepsi, and United Airlines and American Airlines, then strategic conflict is of interest to competitive outcomes. Needless to say, there are many such circumstances, but they are rare in industries where there is rapid technological change and fast-shifting market circumstances.

In short, where competitors do not have deep-seated competitive advantages, the moves and countermoves of competitors can often be usefully formulated in game-theoretic terms. However, we doubt that game theory can comprehensively illuminate how Chrysler should compete against Toyota and Honda, or how United Airlines can best respond to Southwest Airlines since Southwest's advantage is built on organizational attributes which United cannot readily replicate.[6] Indeed, the entrepreneurial side of strategy – how significant new rent streams are created and protected – is largely ignored by the game-theoretic approach. Accordingly, we find that the approach, while important, is most relevant when competitors are closely matched[7] and the population of relevant competitors and the identity of their strategic alternatives can be readily ascertained. Nevertheless, coupled with other approaches it can sometimes yield powerful insights.

However, this research has an orientation that we are concerned about in terms of the implicit framing of strategic issues. Rents, from a game-theoretic perspective, are ultimately a result of managers' intellectual ability to 'play the game'. The adage of the strategist steeped in this approach is 'do unto others before they do unto you'. We worry that fascination with strategic moves and Machiavellian tricks will distract managers from seeking to build more enduring sources of competitive advantage. The approach unfortunately ignores competition as a process involving the development, accumulation, combination, and protection of unique skills and capabilities. Since strategic interactions are what receive focal attention, the impression one might receive from this literature is that success in the marketplace is the result of sophisticated plays and counterplays, when this is generally not the case at all.[8]

In what follows, we suggest that building a dynamic view of the business enterprise – something missing from the two approaches we have so far identified – enhances the probability of establishing an acceptable descriptive theory of strategy that can assist practitioners in the building of long-run advantage and competitive flexibility. Below, we discuss first the resource-based perspective and then an extension we call the dynamic capabilities approach.

# Models of strategy emphasizing efficiency

## *Resource-based perspective*

The resource-based approach sees firms with superior systems and structures being profitable not because they engage in strategic investments that may deter entry and raise prices above long-run costs, but because they have markedly lower costs, or offer markedly higher quality or product performance. This approach focuses on the rents accruing to the owners of scarce firm-specific resources rather than the economic profits from product market positioning.[9] Competitive advantage lies 'upstream' of product markets and rests on the firm's idiosyncratic and difficult-to-imitate resources.[10]

One can find the resources approach suggested by the earlier preanalytic strategy literature. A leading text of the 1960s (Learned et al., 1969) noted that 'the capability of an organization is its demonstrated and potential ability to accomplish against the opposition of circumstance or competition, whatever it sets out to do. Every organization has actual and potential strengths and weaknesses; it is important to try to determine what they are and to distinguish one from the other.' Thus what a firm can do is not just a function of the opportunities it confronts; it also depends on what resources the organization can muster.

[. . .]

New impetus has been given to the resource-based approach by recent theoretical developments in organizational economics and in the theory of strategy, as well as by a growing body of anecdotal and empirical literature[11] that highlights the importance of firm-specific factors in explaining firm performance. Cool and Schendel (1988) have shown that there are systematic and significant performance differences among firms which belong to the same strategic group within the US pharmaceutical industry. Rumelt (1991) has shown that intraindustry differences in profits are greater than interindustry differences in profits, strongly suggesting the importance of firm-specific factors and the relative unimportance of industry effects.[12] Jacobsen (1988) and Hansen and Wernerfelt (1989) made similar findings.

A comparison of the resource-based approach and the competitive forces approach (discussed earlier in the paper) in terms of their implications for the strategy process is revealing. From the first perspective, an entry decision looks roughly as follows: (1) pick an industry (based on its 'structural attractiveness'); (2) choose an entry strategy based on conjectures about competitors' rational strategies; (3) if not already possessed, acquire or otherwise obtain the requisite assets to compete in the market. From this perspective, the process of identifying and developing the requisite assets is not particularly problematic. The process involves nothing more than choosing rationally among a well-defined set of investment alternatives. If assets are not already owned, they can be bought. The resource-based perspective is strongly at odds with this conceptualization.

From the resource-based perspective, firms are heterogeneous with respect to their resources/capabilities/endowments. Further, resource endowments are 'sticky': at least in the short run, firms are to some degree stuck with what they have and may have to live with what they lack.[13] This stickiness arises for three reasons. First, business development is viewed as an extremely complex process.[14] Quite simply, firms lack the organizational capacity to develop new competences quickly (Dierickx and Cool, 1989). Secondly, some assets are simply not readily tradeable, for example, tacit know-how (Teece, 1976, 1980) and reputation (Dierickx and Cool, 1989). Thus, resource endowments cannot equilibrate through factor input markets. Finally, even when an asset can be purchased, firms may stand to gain little by doing so. As Barney (1986) points out, unless a firm is lucky, possesses superior information, or both, the price it pays in a competitive factor market will fully capitalize the rents from the asset.

Given that in the resources perspective firms possess heterogeneous and sticky resource bundles, the entry decision process suggested by this approach is as follows: (1) identify your firm's unique resources; (2) decide in which markets those resources can earn the highest rents; and (3) decide whether the rents from those assets are most effectively utilized by (a) integrating into related market(s), (b) selling the relevant intermediate output to related firms, or (c) selling the assets themselves to a firm in related businesses (Teece, 1980, 1982).

[. . .]

[The] resource-based perspective also invites consideration of managerial strategies for developing new capabilities (Wernerfelt, 1984). Indeed, if control over scarce resources is the source of economic profits, then it follows that such issues as skill acquisition, the management of knowledge and know-how (Shuen, 1994), and learning become fundamental strategic issues. It is in this second dimension, encompassing skill acquisition, learning, and accumulation of organizational and intangible or 'invisible' assets (Itami and Roehl, 1987), that we believe lies the greatest potential for contributions to strategy.

## *The dynamic capabilities approach: overview*

The global competitive battles in high-technology industries such as semi-conductors, information services, and software have demonstrated the need for an expanded paradigm to understand how competitive advantage is achieved. Well-known companies like IBM, Texas Instruments, Philips, and others appear to have followed a 'resource-based strategy' of accumulating valuable technology assets, often guarded by an aggressive intellectual property stance. However, this strategy is often not enough to support a significant competitive advantage. Winners in the global marketplace have been firms that can demonstrate timely responsiveness and rapid and flexible product innovation, coupled with the management capability to effectively coordinate and redeploy internal and external competences. Not surprisingly, industry observers have remarked that companies can accumulate a large stock of valuable technology assets and still not have many useful capabilities.

We refer to this ability to achieve new forms of competitive advantage as 'dynamic capabilities' to emphasize two key aspects that were not the main focus of attention in previous strategy perspectives. The term 'dynamic' refers to the capacity to renew competences so as to achieve congruence with the changing business environment; certain innovative responses are required when time-to-market and timing are critical, the rate of technological change is rapid, and the nature of future competition and markets difficult to determine. The term 'capabilities' emphasizes the key role of strategic management in appropriately adapting, integrating, and reconfiguring internal and external organizational skills, resources, and functional competences to match the requirements of a changing environment.

One aspect of the strategic problem facing an innovating firm in a world of Schumpeterian competition is to identify difficult-to-imitate internal and external competences most likely to support valuable products and services. Thus, as argued by Dierickx and Cool (1989), choices about how much to spend (invest) on different possible areas are central to the firm's strategy. However, choices about domains of competence are influenced by past choices. At any given point in time, firms must follow a certain trajectory or path of competence development. This path not only defines what choices are open to the firm today, but also puts bounds around what its internal repertoire is likely to be in the future. Thus, firms, at various points in time, make long-term, quasi-irreversible commitments to certain domains of competence.[15]

The notion that competitive advantage requires both the exploitation of existing internal and external firm-specific capabilities, and developing new ones is partially developed in Penrose (1959), Teece (1982), and Wernerfelt (1984). However, only recently have researchers begun to focus on the specifics of how some organizations first develop firm-specific capabilities and how they renew competences to respond to shifts in the business environment.[16] These issues are intimately tied to the firm's business processes, market positions, and expansion paths. Several writers have recently offered insights and evidence on how firms can develop their capability to adapt and even capitalize on rapidly changing environments.[17] The dynamic capabilities approach seeks to provide a coherent framework which can both integrate existing conceptual and empirical knowledge, and facilitate prescription. In doing so, it builds upon the theoretical foundations provided by Schumpeter (1934), Penrose (1959), Williamson (1975, 1985), Barney (1986), Nelson and Winter (1982), Teece (1988), and Teece et al. (1994).

# Toward a dynamic capabilities framework

## *Terminology*

In order to facilitate theory development and intellectual dialogue, some acceptable definitions are desirable. We propose the following.

FACTORS OF PRODUCTION   These are 'undifferentiated' inputs available in disaggregate form in factor markets. By undifferentiated we mean that they lack a firm-specific component. Land, unskilled labor, and capital are typical examples. Some factors may be available for the taking, such as public knowledge. In the language of Arrow, such resources must be 'non-fugitive.'[18] Property rights are usually well defined for factors of production.

RESOURCES[19]   Resources are firm-specific assets that are difficult if not impossible to imitate. Trade secrets and certain specialized production facilities and engineering experience are examples. Such assets are difficult to transfer among firms because of transactions costs and transfer costs, and because the assets may contain tacit knowledge.

ORGANIZATIONAL ROUTINES/COMPETENCES   When firm-specific assets are assembled in integrated clusters spanning individuals and groups so that they enable distinctive activities to be performed, these activities constitute organizational routines and processes. Examples include quality, miniaturization, and systems integration. Such competences are typically viable across multiple product lines, and may extend outside the firm to embrace alliance partners.

CORE COMPETENCES   We define those competences that define a firm's fundamental business as core. Core competences must accordingly be derived by looking across the range of a firm's (and its competitors) products and services.[20] The value of core competences can be enhanced by combination with the appropriate complementary assets. The degree to which a core competence is distinctive depends on how well endowed the firm is relative to its competitors, and on how difficult it is for competitors to replicate its competences.

DYNAMIC CAPABILITIES   We define dynamic capabilities as the firm's ability to integrate, build, and reconfigure internal and external competences to address rapidly changing environments. Dynamic capabilities thus reflect an organization's ability to achieve new and innovative forms of competitive advantage given path dependencies and market positions (Leonard-Barton, 1992).

PRODUCTS   End products are the final goods and services produced by the firm based on utilizing the competences that it possesses. The performance (price, quality, etc.) of a firm's products relative to its competitors at any point in time will depend upon its competences (which over time depend on its capabilities)

## Markets and strategic capabilities

Different approaches to strategy view sources of wealth creation and the essence of the strategic problem faced by firms differently. The competitive forces framework sees the strategic problem in terms of industry structure, entry deterrence, and positioning; game-theoretic models view the strategic problem as one of inter-action between rivals with certain expectations about how each other will behave;[21] resource-based perspectives have focused on the exploitation of firm-specific assets. Each approach asks different, often complementary questions. A key step in building a conceptual framework related to dynamic capabilities is to identify the foundations upon which distinctive and difficult-to-replicate advantages can be built, maintained, and enhanced.

A useful way to vector in on the strategic elements of the business enterprise is first to identify what is not strategic. To be strategic, a capability must be honed to a user need[22] (so there is a source of revenues), unique (so that the products/services produced can be priced without too much regard to competition) and difficult to replicate (so profits will not be competed away). Accordingly, any assets or entity which are homogeneous and can be bought and sold at an established price cannot be all that strategic (Barney, 1986). What is it, then, about firms which undergirds competitive advantage?

To answer this, one must first make some fundamental distinctions between markets and internal organization (firms). The essence of the firm, as Coase (1937) pointed out, is that it displaces market organization. It does so in the main because inside the firms one can organize certain types of economic activity in ways one cannot using markets. This is not only because of transaction costs, as Williamson (1975, 1985) emphasized, but also because there are many types of arrangements where injecting high-powered (market like) incentives might well be quite destructive of cooperative activity and learning.[23] Inside an organization, exchange cannot take place in the same manner that it can outside an organization, not just because it might be destructive to provide high-powered individual incentives, but because it is difficult if not impossible to tightly calibrate individual contribution to a joint effort. Hence, contrary to Arrow's (1969) view of firms as quasi markets, and the task of management to inject markets into firms, we recognize the inherent limits and possible counter-productive results of attempting to fashion firms into simply clusters of internal markets. In particular, learning and internal technology transfer may well be jeopardized.

Indeed, what is distinctive about firms is that they are domains for organizing activity in a nonmarket-like fashion. Accordingly, as we discuss what is distinctive about firms, we stress competences/capabilities which are ways of organizing and getting things done which cannot be accomplished merely by using the price system to coordinate activity.[24] The very essence of most capabilities/competences is that they cannot be readily assembled through markets (Teece, 1982, 1986a; Zander and Kogut, 1995). If the ability to assemble competences using markets is what is meant by the firm as a nexus of contracts (Fama, 1980), then we unequivocally state that the firm about which we theorize cannot be usefully modeled as a nexus of contracts. By 'contract' we are referring to a transaction undergirded by a legal agreement, or some other arrangement which clearly spells out rights, rewards, and responsibilities. Moreover, the firm as a nexus of contracts suggests a series of bilateral contracts orchestrated by a coordinator. Our view of the firm is that the organization takes place in a more multilateral fashion, with patterns of behavior and learning being orchestrated in a much more decentralized fashion, but with a viable headquarters operation.

The key point, however, is that the properties of internal organization cannot be replicated by a portfolio of business units amalgamated just through formal contracts as many distinctive elements of internal organization simply cannot be replicated in the market. That is, entrepreneurial activity cannot lead to the immediate replication of unique organizational skills through simply entering a market and piecing the parts together overnight. Replication takes time, and the replication of best practice may be illusive. Indeed, firm capabilities need to be understood not in terms of the organizational structures and managerial processes which support productive activity. By construction, the firm's balance sheet contains items that can be valued, at least at original market prices (cost). It is necessarily the case, therefore, that the balance sheet is a poor shadow of a firm's distinctive competences. That which is distinctive cannot be bought and sold short of buying the firm itself, or one or more of its subunits.

There are many dimensions of the business firm that must be understood if one is to grasp firm-level distinctive competences/capabilities. In this paper we merely identify several classes of factors that will help determine a firm's distinctive competence and dynamic capabilities. We organize these in three categories: processes, positions, and paths. The essence of competences and capabilities is embedded in organizational processes of one kind or another. But the content of these processes and the opportunities they afford for developing competitive advantage at any point in time are shaped significantly by the assets the firm possesses (internal and market) and by the evolutionary path it has adopted/inherited. Hence organizational processes, shaped by the firm's asset positions and molded by its evolutionary and co-evolutionary paths, explain the essence of the firm's dynamic capabilities and its competitive advantage.

# Processes, positions, and paths

We thus advance the argument that the competitive advantage of the firm lies with its managerial and organizational processes, shaped by its (specific) asset position, and the paths available to it.[25] By managerial and organizational processes, we refer to the way things are done in the firm, or what might be referred to as its routines, or patterns of current practice and learning. By position we refer to its current specific endowments of technology, intellectual property, complementary assets, customer base, and its external relations with suppliers and complementors. By paths we refer to the strategic alternatives available to the firm, and the presence or absence of increasing returns and attendant path dependencies.

Our focus throughout is on asset structures for which no ready market exists, as these are the only assets of strategic interest. A final section focuses on replication and imitation, as it is these phenomena which determine how readily a competence or capability can be cloned by competitors, and therefore distinctiveness of its competences and the durability of its advantage.

The firm's processes and positions collectively encompass its competences and capabilities. A hierarchy of competences/capabilities ought to be recognized, as some competences may be on the factory floor, some in the R&D labs, some in the executive suites, and some in the way everything is integrated. A difficult-to-replicate or difficult-to-imitate competence was defined earlier as a distinctive competence. As indicated, the key feature of distinctive competence is that there is not a market for it, except possibly through the market for business units. Hence competences and capabilities are intriguing assets as they typically must be built because they cannot be bought.

## *Organizational and managerial processes*

Organizational processes have three roles: coordination/integration (a static concept); learning (a dynamic concept); and reconfiguration (a transformational concept). We discuss each in turn.

COORDINATION/INTEGRATION  While the price system supposedly coordinates the economy,[26] managers coordinate or integrate activity inside the firm. How efficiently and effectively internal coordination or integration is achieved is very important (Aoki, 1990).[27] Likewise for external coordination.[28] Increasingly, strategic advantage requires the integration of external activities and technologies. The growing literature on strategic alliances, the virtual corporation, and buyer–supplier relations and technology collaboration evidences the importance of external integration and sourcing.

There is some field-based empirical research that provides support for the notion that the way production is organized by management inside the firm is the source of differences in firms' competence in various domains. For example, Garvin's (1988) study of 18 room air-conditioning plants reveals that quality performance was not related to either capital investment or the degree of automation of the facilities. Instead, quality performance was driven by special organizational routines. These included routines for gathering and processing information, for linking customer experiences with engineering design choices, and for coordinating factories and component suppliers.[29] The work of Clark and Fujimoto (1991) on project development in the automobile industry also illustrates the role played by coordinative routines. Their study reveals a significant degree of variation in how different firms coordinate the various activities required to bring a new model from concept to market. These differences in coordinative routines and capabilities seem to have a significant impact on such performance variables as development cost, development lead times, and quality. Furthermore, Clark and Fujimoto tended to find significant firm-level differences in coordination routines and these differences seemed to have persisted for a long time. This suggests that routines related to coordination are firm-specific in nature.

Also, the notion that competence/capability is embedded in distinct ways of coordinating and combining helps to explain how and why seemingly minor technological changes can have devastating impacts on incumbent firms' abilities to compete in a market. Henderson and Clark (1990), for example, have shown that incumbents in the photolithographic equipment industry were sequentially devastated by seemingly minor innovations that, nevertheless, had major impacts on how systems had to be configured. They attribute these difficulties to the fact that systems-level or 'architectural' innovations often require new routines to integrate and coordinate engineering tasks. These findings and others suggest that productive systems display high interdependency, and that it may not be possible to change one level without changing others. This appears to be true with respect to the 'lean production' model (Womack et al. 1991) which has now transformed the Taylor or Ford model of manufacturing organization in the automobile industry.[30] Lean production requires distinctive shop floor practices and processes as well as distinctive higher-order managerial processes. Put differently, organizational processes often display high levels of coherence, and when they do, replication may be difficult because it requires systemic changes throughout the organization and also among interorganizational linkages, which might be very hard to effectuate. Put differently, partial imitation or replication of a successful model may yield zero benefits.[31]

[. . .]

Recognizing the congruences and complementarities among processes, and between processs and incentives, is critical to the understanding of organizational capabilities. In particular, they can help us explain why architectural and radical innovations are so often introduced into an industry by new entrants. The incumbents develop distinctive organizational processes that cannot support the new technology, despite certain overt similarities between the old and the new. The frequent failure of incumbents to introduce new technologies can thus be seen as a consequence of the mismatch that so often exists between the set of organizational processes needed to support the conventional product/service and the requirements of the new. Radical organizational reengineering will usually be required to support the new product, which may well do better embedded in a separate subsidiary where a new set of coherent organizational processes can be fashioned.[32]

LEARNING   Perhaps even more important than integration is learning. Learning is a process by which repetition and experimentation enable tasks to be performed better and quicker. It also enables new production opportunities to be identified.[33] In the context of the firm, if not more generally, learning has several key characteristics. First, learning involves organizational as well as individual skills.[34] While individual skills are of relevance, their value depends upon their employment, in particular organizational settings. Learning processes are intrinsically social and collective and occur not only through the imitation and emulation of individuals, as with teacher–student or master–apprentice, but also because of joint contributions to the understanding of complex problems.[35] Learning requires common codes of communication and coordinated search procedures. Second, the organizational knowledge generated by such activity resides in new patterns of activity, in 'routines', or a new logic of organization. As indicated earlier, routines are patterns of interactions that represent successful solutions to particular problems. These patterns of interaction are resident in group behavior, though certain subroutines may be resident in individual behavior. The concept of dynamic capabilities as a coordinative management process opens the door to the potential for interorganizational learning. Researchers (Doz and Shuen, 1990; Mody, 1993) have pointed out that collaborations and partnerships can be a vehicle for new organizational learning, helping firms to recognize dysfunctional routines, and preventing strategic blindspots.

RECONFIGURATION AND TRANSFORMATION   In rapidly changing environments, there is obviously value in the ability to sense the need to reconfigure the firm's asset structure, and to accomplish the necessary internal and external transformation (Amit and Schoemaker, 1993; Langlois, 1994). This requires constant surveillance of markets and technologies and the willingness to adopt best practice. In this regard, benchmarking is of considerable value as an organized process for accomplishing such ends (Camp, 1989). In dynamic environments, narcissistic organizations are likely to be impaired. The capacity to reconfigure and transform is itself a learned organizational skill. The more frequently practiced, the easier accomplished.

Change is costly and so firms must develop processes to minimize low pay-off change. The ability to calibrate the requirements for change and to effectuate the necessary adjustments would appear to depend on the ability to scan the environment, to evaluate markets and competitors, and to quickly accomplish reconfiguration and transformation ahead of competition. Decentralization and local autonomy assist these processes. Firms that have honed these capabilities are sometimes referred to as 'high-flex'.

## Positions

The strategic posture of a firm is determined not only by its learning processes and by the coherence of its internal and external processes and incentives, but also by its specific assets. By specific assets we mean for example its specialized plant and equipment. These include its difficult-to-trade knowledge assets and assets complementary to them, as well as its reputational and relational assets. Such assets determine its competitive advantage at any point in time. We identify several illustrative classes.

TECHNOLOGICAL ASSETS   While there is an emerging market for know-how (Teece, 1981), much technology does not enter it. This is either because the firm is unwilling to sell it[36] or because of difficulties in transacting in the market for know-how (Teece, 1980). A firm's technological assets may or may not be protected by the standard instruments of intellectual property law. Either way, the ownership protection and utilization of technological assets are clearly key differentiators among firms. Likewise for complementary assets.

COMPLEMENTARY ASSETS   Technological innovations require the use of certain related assets to produce and deliver new products and services. Prior commercialization activities require and enable firms to build such complementarities (Teece, 1986b). Such capabilities and assets, while necessary for the firm's established activities, may have other uses as well. These assets typically lie downstream. New products and processes can either enhance or destroy the value of such assets (Tushman, Newman, and Romanelli, 1986). Thus the development of computers enhanced the value of IBM's direct sales force in office products, while disk brakes rendered useless much of the auto industry's investment in drum brakes.

FINANCIAL ASSETS   In the short run, a firm's cash position and degree of leverage may have strategic implications. While there is nothing more fungible than cash, it cannot always be raised from external markets without the dissemination of considerable information to potential investors. Accordingly, what a firm can do in short order is often a function of its balance sheet. In the longer run, that ought not be so, as cash flow ought be more determinative.

REPUTATIONAL ASSETS   . . . Reputations often summarize a good deal of information about firms and shape the responses of customers, suppliers, and competitors . . . However, in our view, reputational assets are best viewed as an intangible asset that enables firms to achieve various goals in the market.
[. . .]

STRUCTURAL ASSETS   . . . The degree of hierarchy and the level of vertical and lateral integration are elements of firm-specific structure. Distinctive governance modes can be recognized (e.g. multiproduct, integrated firms; high 'flex' firms;

virtual corporations; conglomerates), and these modes support different types of innovation to a greater or lesser degree. For instance, virtual structures work well when innovation is autonomous; integrated structures work better for systemic innovations.

INSTITUTIONAL ASSETS  Environments cannot be defined in terms of markets alone . . . [Institutions] themselves are a critical element of the business environment. Regulatory systems, as well as intellectual property regimes, tort laws, and antitrust laws, are also part of the environment. So is the system of higher education and national culture. There are significant national differences here, which is just one of the reasons geographic location matters (Nelson, 1994). Such assets may not be entirely firm specific; firms of different national and regional origin may have quite different institutional assets to call upon because their institutional/policy settings are so different.

MARKET (STRUCTURE) ASSETS  . . . [Market] position in regimes of rapid technological change is often extremely fragile. This is in part because time moves on a different clock in such environments.[37] Moreover, the link between market share and innovation has long been broken, if it ever existed (Teece, 1996) . . . Strategy should be formulated with regard to the more fundamental aspects of firm performance, which we believe are rooted in competences and capabilities and shaped by positions and paths.

ORGANIZATIONAL BOUNDARIES  An important dimension of 'position' is the location of a firm's boundaries. Put differently, the degree of integration (vertical, lateral, and horizontal) is of quite some significance . . . When specific assets or poorly protected intellectual capital are at issue, pure market arrangements expose the parties to recontracting hazards or appropriability hazards. In such circumstances, hierarchical control structures may work better than pure arms-length contracts.

## Paths

PATH DEPENDENCIES  Where a firm can go is a function of its current position and the paths ahead. Its current position is often shaped by the path it has traveled. In standard economics textbooks, firms have an infinite range of technologies from which they can choose and markets they can occupy. Changes in product or factor prices will be responded to instantaneously, with technologies moving in and out according to value maximization criteria. Only in the short run are irreversibilities recognized. Fixed costs – such as equipment and overheads – cause firms to price below fully amortized costs but never constrain future investment choices. 'Bygones are bygones.' Path dependencies are simply not recognized. This is a major limitation of microeconomic theory.

The notion of path dependencies recognizes that 'history matters'. Bygones are rarely bygones, despite the predictions of rational actor theory. Thus a firm's previous investments and its repertoire of routines (its 'history') constrain its future behavior.[38] This follows because learning tends to be local. That is, opportunities for learning will be 'close in' to previous activities and thus will be transaction and production specific (Teece, 1988). This is because learning is often a process of trial, feedback, and evaluation. If too many parameters are changed simultaneously, the ability of firms to conduct meaningful natural quasi experiments is attenuated. If many aspects of a firm's learning environment change simultaneously, the ability to ascertain cause–effect relationships is confounded because cognitive structures will not be formed and rates of learning diminist as a result. One implication is that many investments are much longer term than is commonly thought.

The importance of path dependencies is amplified where conditions of increasing returns to adoption exist. This is a demand-side phenomenon, and it tends to make technologies and products embodying those technologies more attractive the more they are adopted. Attractiveness flows from the greater adoption of the product amongst users, which in turn enables them to become more developed and hence more useful. Increasing returns to adoption has many sources including network externalities (Katz and Shapiro, 1985), the presence of complementary assets (Teece, 1986b) and supporting infrastructure (Nelson, 1996), learning by using (Rosenberg, 1982), and scale economies in production and distribution. Competition between and amongst technologies is shaped by increasing returns. Early leads won by good luck or special circumstances (Arthur, 1983) can become amplified by increasing returns. This is not to suggest that first movers necessarily win. Because increasing returns have multiple sources, the prior positioning of firms can affect their capacity to exploit increasing returns. Thus, in Mitchell's (1989) study of medical diagnostic imaging, firms already controlling the relevant complementary assets could in theory start last and finish first.

In the presence of increasing returns, firms can compete passively, or they may complete strategically through technology-sponsoring activities.[39] The first type of competition is not unlike biological competition amongst species, although it can be sharpened by managerial activities that enhance the performance of products and processes. The reality is that companies with the best products will not always win, as chance events may cause 'lock-in' on inferior technologies (Arthur, 1983) and. may even in special cases generate switching costs for consumers. However, while switching costs may favor the incumbent, in regimes of rapid technological change switching costs can become quickly swamped by switching benefits. Put differently, new products employing different standards often appear with alacrity in market environments experiencing rapid technological change, and incumbents can be readily challenged by superior products and services that yield switching benefits. Thus the degree to which switching costs cause 'lock-in' is a function of factors such as user learning, rapidity of technological change, and the amount of ferment in the competitive environment.

TECHNOLOGICAL OPPORTUNITIES The concept of path dependencies is given forward meaning through the consideration of an industry's technological opportunities. It is well recognized that how far and how fast a particular area of industrial activity can proceed is in part due to the technological opportunities that lie before it. Such opportunities are usually a lagged function of foment and diversity in basic science, and the rapidity with which new scientific breakthroughs are being made.

However, technological opportunities may not be completely exogenous to industry, not only because some firms have the capacity to engage in or at least support basic research, but also because technological opportunities are often fed by innovative activity itself. Moreover, the recognition of such opportunities is affected by the organizational structures that link the institutions engaging in basic research (primarily the university) to the business enterprise. Hence, the existence of technological opportunities can be quite firm specific.

Important for our purposes is the rate and direction in which relevant scientific frontiers are being rolled back. Firms engaging in R&D may find the path dead ahead closed off, though breakthroughs in related areas may be sufficiently close to be attractive. Likewise, if the path dead ahead is extremely attractive, there may be no incentive for firms to shift the allocation of resources away from traditional pursuits. The depth and width of technological opportunities in the neighborhood of a firm's prior research activities thus are likely to impact a firm's options with respect to both the amount and level of R&D activity that it can justify. In addition, a firm's past experience conditions the alternatives management is able to perceive. Thus, not only do firms in the same industry face 'menus' with different costs associated with particular technological choices, they also are looking at menus containing different choices.[40]

## Assessment

The essence of a firm's competence and dynamic capabilities is presented here as being resident in the firm's organizational processes, that are in turn shaped by the firm's assets (positions) and its evolutionary path. Its evolutionary path, despite managerial hubris that might suggest otherwise, is often rather narrow.[41] What the firm can do and where it can go are thus rather constrained by its positions and paths. Its competitors are likewise constrained. [. . .]

The parameters we have identified for determining performance are quite different from those in the standard textbook theory of the firm, and in the competitive forces and strategic conflict approaches to the firm and to strategy.[42] [. . .]

[The] firm in our conceptualization is much more than the sum of its parts — or a team tied together by contracts.[43] Indeed, to some extent individuals can be moved in and out of organizations and, so long as the internal processes and structures remain in place, performance will not necessarily be impaired. A shift in the environment is a far more serious threat to the firm than is the loss of key individuals, as individuals can be replaced more readily than organizations can be transformed. Furthermore, the dynamic capabilities view of the firm would suggest that the behavior and performance of particular firms may be quite hard to replicate, even if its coherence and rationality are observable. This matter and related issues involving replication and imitation are taken up in the section that follows.

## Replicability and imitatability of organizational processes and positions

Thus far, we have argued that the competences and capabilities (and hence competitive advantage) of a firm rest fundamentally on processes, shaped by positions and paths. However, competences can provide competitive advantage and generate rents only if they are based on a collection of routines, skills, and complementary assets that are difficult to imitate.[44] A particular set of routines can lose their value if they support a competence which no longer matters in the marketplace, or if they can be readily replicated or emulated by competitors. Imitation occurs when firms discover and simply copy a firm's organizational routines and procedures. Emulation occurs when firms discover alternative ways of achieving the same functionality.[45]

### Replication

To understand imitation, one must first understand replication. Replication involves transferring or redeploying competences from one concrete economic setting to another. Since productive knowledge is embodied, this cannot be accomplished by simply transmitting information. Only in those instances where all relevant knowledge is fully codified and understood can replication be collapsed into a simple problem of information transfer. Too often, the contextual dependence of original performance is poorly appreciated, so unless firms have replicated their systems of productive knowledge on many prior occasions, the act of replication is likely to be difficult (Teece, 1976). Indeed, replication and transfer are often impossible absent the transfer of people, though this can be minimized if investments are made to convert tacit knowledge to codified knowledge. Often, however, this is simply not possible.

In short, competences and capabilities, and the routines upon which they rest, are normally rather difficult to replicate.[46] Even understanding what all the relevant routines are that support a particular competence may not be transparent. Indeed, Lippman and Rumelt (1992) have argued that some sources of competitive advantage are so complex that the firm itself, let alone its competitors, does not understand them.[47] As Nelson and Winter (1982) and Teece (1982) have explained, many organizational routines are quite tacit in nature. Imitation can also be hindered by the fact few routines are 'stand-alone'; coherence may require that a change in one set of routines in one part of the firm (e.g. production) requires changes in some other part (e.g. R&D). [. . .]

At least two types of strategic value flow from replication. One is the ability to support geographic and product line expansion. To the extent that the capabilities in question are relevant to customer needs elsewhere, replication can confer value.[48] Another is that the ability to replicate also indicates that the firm has the foundations in place for learning and improvement. Considerable empirical evidence supports the notion that the understanding of processes, both in production and in management, is the key to process improvement. In short, an organization cannot improve that which it does not understand. Deep process understanding is often required to accomplish codification. Indeed, if knowledge is highly tacit, it indicates that underlying structures are not well understood, which limits learning because scientific and engineering principles cannot be as systemically applied.[49] Instead, learning is confined to proceeding through trial and error, and the leverage that might otherwise come from the application of scientific theory is denied.

## Imitation

Imitation is simply replication performed by a competitor. If self-replication is difficult, imitation is likely to be harder. In competitive markets, it is the ease of imitation that determines the sustainability of competitive advantage. Easy imitation implies the rapid dissipation of rents.

Factors that make replication difficult also make imitation difficult. Thus, the more tacit the firm's productive knowledge, the harder it is to replicate by the firm itself or its competitors. When the tacit component is high, imitation may well be impossible, absent the hiring away of key individuals and the transfers of key organization processes.

However, another set of barriers impedes imitation of certain capabilities in advanced industrial countries. This is the system of intellectual property rights, such as patents, trade secrets, and trademarks, and even trade dress.[50] Intellectual property protection is of increasing importance in the United States, as since 1982 the legal system has adopted a more pro-patent posture. Similar trends are evident outside the United States. Besides the patent system, several other factors cause there to be a difference between replication costs and imitation costs. The observability of the technology or the organization is one such important factor. Whereas vistas into product technology can be obtained through strategies such as reverse engineering, this is not the case for process technology, as a firm need not expose its process technology to the outside in order to benefit from it.[51] Firms with product technology, on the other hand, confront the unfortunate circumstances that they must expose what they have got in order to profit from the technology. Secrets are thus more protectable if there is no need to expose them in contexts where competitors can learn about them.

[. . .]

We use the term appropriability regimes to describe the ease of imitation. Appropriability is a function of both the ease of replication and the efficacy of intellectual property rights as a barrier to imitation. Appropriability is strong when both a technology is inherently difficult to replicate and the intellectual property system provides legal barriers to imitation. When it is inherently easy to replicate and intellectual property protection is either unavailable or ineffectual, then appropriability is weak. Intermediate conditions also exist.

## Conclusion

The four paradigms discussed above are quite different, though the first two have much in common with each other (strategizing) as do the last two (economizing). But are these paradigms complementary or competitive? According to some authors, 'the resource perspective complements the industry analysis framework' (Amit and Schoemaker, 1993: 35). While this is undoubtedly true, we think that in several important respects the perspectives are also competitive. While this should be recognized, it is not to suggest that there is only one framework that has value. Indeed, complex problems are likely to benefit from insights obtained from all of the paradigms we have identified plus more. The trick is to work out which frameworks are appropriate for the problem at hand. Slavish adherence to one class to the neglect of all others is likely to generate strategic blindspots. The tools themselves then generate strategic vulnerability. [. . .]

### Efficiency vs market power

The competitive forces and strategic conflict approaches generally see profits as stemming from strategizing – that is, from limitations on competition which firms achieve through raising rivals' costs and exclusionary behavior (Teece, 1984). The competitive forces approach in particular leads one to see concentrated industries as being attractive – market positions can be shielded behind entry barriers and rivals' costs can be raised. It also suggests that the sources of competitive advantage lie at the level of the industry, or possibly groups within an industry. In text book presentations, there is almost no attention at all devoted to discovering, creating, and commercializing new sources of value.

The dynamic capabilities and resources approaches clearly have a different orientation. They see competitive advantage stemming from high-performance routines operating 'inside the firm', shaped by processes and positions. Path dependencies (including increasing returns) and technological opportunities mark the road ahead. Because of imperfect factor markets, or more precisely the nontradability of 'soft' assets like values, culture, and organizational experience, distinctive competences and capabilities generally cannot be acquired; they must be built. This sometimes takes years – possibly decades. In some cases, as when the competence is protected by patents, replication by a competitor is ineffectual as a means to access the technology. The capabilities approach accordingly sees definite limits on strategic options, at least in the short run. Competitive success occurs in part because of policies pursued and experience and efficiency obtained in earlier periods.

Competitive success can undoubtedly flow from both strategizing and economizing,[52] but along with Williamson (1991) we believe that 'economizing is more fundamental than strategizing . . . or put differently, that economy is the best strategy'.[53] Indeed, we suggest that, except in special circumstances, too much 'strategizing' can lead firms to underinvest in core competences and neglect dynamic capabilities, and thus harm long-term competitiveness.

[. . .]

# Notes

1   For a review of the fundamental questions in the field of strategy, see Rumelt, Schendel, and Teece (1994).

2   Of these authors, Rumelt may have been the first to self-consciously apply a resource perspective to the field of strategy. Rumelt (1984: 561) notes that the strategic firm 'is characterized by a bundle of linked and idiosyncratic resources and resource conversion activities'. Similarly, Teece (1984: 95) notes: 'Successful firms possess one or more forms of intangible assets, such as technoiogical or managerial know-how. Over time, these assets may expand beyond the point of profitable reinvestment in a firm's traditional market. Accordingly, the firm may consider deploying its intangible assets in different product or geographical markets, where the expected returns are higher, if efficient transfer modes exist'. Wernerfelt (1984) was early to recognize that this approach was at odds with product market approaches and might constitute a distinct paradigm of strategy.

3   In competitive environments characterized by sustainable and stable mobility and structural barriers, these forces may become the determinants of industry-level profitability. However, competitive advantage is more complex to ascertain in environments of rapid technological change where specific assets owned by heterogeneous firms can be expected to play a larger role in explaining rents.

4   The market environment is all factors that influence market outcomes (prices, quantities, profits) including the beliefs of customers and of rivals, the number of potential technologies employed, and the costs or speed with which a rival can enter the industry.

5   For an excellent discussion of committed competition in multiple contexts, see Ghemawat (1991).

6   Thus even in the air transport industry game-theoretic formulations by no means capture all the relevant dimensions of competitive rivalry. United Airlines' and United Express's difficulties in competing with Southwest

Airlines because of United's inability to fully replicate Southwest's opeation capabilities is documented in Gittel (1995).

7　When closely matched in an aggregate sense, they may nevertheless display asymmetries which game theorists can analyze.

8　The strategic conflict literature also tends to focus practitioners on product market positioning rather than on developing the unique assets which make possible superior product market positions (Dierickx and Cool, 1989).

9　In the language of economics, rents flow from unique firm-specific assets that cannot readily be replicated, rather than from tactics which deter entry and keep competitors off balance. In short, rents are Ricardian.

10　Teece (1982: 46) saw the firm as having 'a variety of end products which it can produce with its organizational technology'.

11　Studies of the automobile and other industries displayed differences in organization which often underlay differences amongst firms. (See, for example, Womack, Jones, and Roos, 1991; Hayes and Clark, 1985; Barney, Spender and Reve, 1994; Clark and Fujimoto, 1991; Henderson and Cockburn, 1994; Nelson, 1991; Levinthal and Myatt, 1994.)

12　Using FTC line of business data, Rumelt showed that stable industry effects account for only 8 percent of the variance in business unit returns. Furthermore, only about 40 percent of the dispersion in industry returns is due to stable industry effects.

13　In this regard, this approach has much in common with recent work on organizational ecology (e.g. Freeman and Boeker, 1984) and also on commitment (Ghemawat, 1991: 17–25).

14　Capability development, however, is not really analyzed.

15　Deciding, under significant uncertainty about future states of the world, which long-term paths to commit to and when to change paths is the central strategic problem confronting the firm. In this regard, the work of Ghemawat (1991) is highly germane to the dynamic capabilities approach to strategy.

16　See, for example, Iansiti and Clark (1994) and Henderson (1994).

17　See Hayes et al. (1988), Prahalad and Hamel (1990), Dierickx and Cool (1989), Chandler (1990), and Teece (1993).

18　Arrow (1996) defines fugitive resources as ones that can move cheaply amongst individuals and firms.

19　We do not like the term 'resource' and believe it is misleading. We prefer to use the term firm-specific asset. We use it here and to try and maintain links to the literature on the resource-based approach which we believe is important.

20　Thus Eastman Kodak's core competence might be considered imaging, IBM's might be considered integrated data processing and service, and Motorola's untethered communications.

21　In sequential move games, each player looks ahead and anticipates his rival's future responses in order to reason back and decide action, i.e. look forward, reason backward.

22  Needless to say, users need not be the current customers of the enterprise. Thus a capability can be the basis for diversification into new product markets.

23  Indeed, the essence of internal organization is that it is a domain of unleveraged or low-powered incentives. By unleveraged we mean that rewards are determined at the group or organization level, not primarily at the individual level, in an effort to encourage team behavior, not individual behavior.

24  We see the problem of market contracting as a matter of coordination as much as we see it a problem of opportunism in the face of contractual hazards. In this sense, we are consonant with both Richardson (1960) and Williamson (1975, 1985).

25  We are implicitly saying that fixed assets, like plant and equipment which can be purchased off-the-shelf by all industry participants, cannot be the source of a firm's competitive advantage. In as much as financial balance sheets typically reflect such assets, we point out that the assets that matter for competitive advantage are rarely reflected in the balance sheet, while those that do not are.

26  The coordinative properties of markets depend on prices being 'sufficient' upon which to base resource allocation decisions.

27  Indeed, Ronald Coase, author of the pathbreaking 1937 article 'The nature of the firm', which focused on the costs of organizational coordination inside the firm as compared to across the market, half a century later has identified as critical the understanding of 'why the costs of organizing particular activities differs among firms' (Coase, 1988: 47). We argue that a firm's distinctive ability needs to be understood as a reflection of distinctive organizational or coordinative capabilities. This form of integration (i.e. inside business units) is different from the integration between business units; they could be viable on a stand-alone basis (external integration). For a useful taxonomy, see Iansiti and Clark (1994).

28  Shuen (1994) examines the gains and hazards of the technology make-vs.-buy decision and supplier codevelopment.

29  Garvin (1994) provides a typology of organizational processes.

30  Fujimoto (1994: 18–20) describes key elements as they existed in the Japanese auto industry as follows: 'The typical volume production system of effective Japanese makers of the 1980s (e.g. Toyota) consists of various intertwined elements that might lead to competitive advantages. Just-in-Time (JIT), Jidoka (automatic defect detection and machine stop), Total Quality Control (TQC), and continuous improvement (Kaizen) are often pointed out as its core subsystems. The elements of such a system include inventory reduction mechanisms by Kanban system: levelization of production volume and product mix (heijunka); reduction of 'muda' (non-value adding activities), 'mura' (uneven pace of production) and muri (excessive workload); production plans based on dealers' order volume (genyo seisan); reduction of die set-up time and lot size in stamping operation; mixed model assembly; piece-by-piece transfer of parts between machines (ikko-nagashi); flexible

task assignment for volume changes and productivity improvement (shojinka); multi-task job assignment along the process flow (takotei-mochi); U-shape machine layout that facilitates flexible and multiple task assignment, on-the-spot inspection by direct workers (tsukurikomi); fool-proof prevention of defects (poka-yoke); real-time feedback of production troubles (andon); assembly line stop cord; emphasis on cleanliness, order and discipline on the shop floor (5-S); frequent revision of standard operating procedures by supervisors; quality control circles; standardized tools for quality improvement (e.g. 7 tools for QC, QC story); worker involvement in preventive maintenance (Total Productive Maintenance); low cost automation or semi-automation with just-enough functions); reduction of process steps for saving of tools and dies, and so on. The human-resource management factors that back up the above elements include stable employment of core workers (with temporary workers in the periphery); long-term training of multi-skilled (multi-task) workers; wage system based in part on skill accumulation; internal promotion to shop floor supervisors; cooperative relationships with labor unions; inclusion of production supervisors in union members; generally egalitarian policies for corporate welfare, communication and worker motivation. Parts procurement policies are also pointed out often as a source of the competitive advantage.

31  For a theoretical argument along these lines, see Milgrom and Roberts (1990).

32  See Abernathy and Clark (1985).

33  For a useful review and contribution, see Levitt and March (1988).

34  Levinthal and March, (1993), Mahoney (1995) and Mahoney and Pandian (1992) suggest that both resources and mental models are intertwined in firm-level learning.

35  There is a large literature on learning, although only a small fraction of it deals with organizational learning. Relevant contributors include Levitt and March (1988), Argyris and Schon (1978), Levinthal and March (1981), Nelson and Winter (1982), and Leonard-Barton (1995).

36  Managers often evoke the 'crown jewels' metaphor. That is, if the technology is released, the kingdom will be lost.

37  For instance, an Internet year might well be thought of as equivalent to 10 years on many industry clocks, because as much change occurs in the Internet business in a year that occurs in say the auto industry in a decade.

38  For further development, see Bercovitz, de Figueiredo, and Teece (1996).

39  Because of huge uncertainties, it may be extremely difficult to determine viable strategies early on. Since the rules of the game and the identity of the players will be revealed only after the market has begun to evolve, the pay-off is likely to lie with building and maintaining organizational capabilities that support flexibility. For example, Microsoft's recent about-face and vigorous pursuit of Internet business once the NetScape phenomenon became apparent is impressive, not so much because of its organizational capacity to effectuate a strategic shift.

40    This is a critical element in Nelson and Winter's (1982) view of firms and technical change.

41    We also recognize that the processes, positions, and paths of customers also matter. See our discussion above on increasing returns, including customer learning and network externalities.

42    In both the firm is still largely a black box. Certainly, little or no attention is given to processes, positions, and paths.

43    See Alchian and Demsetz (1972).

44    We call such competences distinctive. See also Dierickx and Cool (1989) for a discussion of the characteristics of assets which make them a source of rents.

45    There is ample evidence that a given type of competence (e.g. quality) can be supported by different routines and combinations of skills. For example, the Garvin (1988) and Clark and Fujimoto (1991) studies both indicate that there was no one 'formula' for achieving either high quality or high product development performance.

46    See Szulanski's (1995) discussion of the intrafirm transfer of best practice. He quotes a senior vice president of Xerox as saying 'you can see a high performance factory or office, but it just doesn't spread. I don't know why'. Szulanski also discusses the role of benchmarking in facilitating the transfer of best practice.

47    If so, it is our belief that the firm's advantage is likely to fade, as luck does run out.

48    Needless to say, there are many examples of firms replicating their capabilities inappropriately by applying extant routines to circumstances where they may not be applicable, e.g. Nestlé's transfer of developed-country marketing methods for infant formula to the Third World (Hartley, 1989). A key strategic need is for firms to screen capabilities for their applicability to new environments.

49    Different approaches to learning are required depending on the depth of knowledge. Where knowledge is less articulated and structured, trial and error and learning-by-doing are necessary, whereas in mature environments where the underlying engineering science is better understood, organizations can undertake more deductive approaches or what Pisano (1994) refers to as 'learning-before-doing'.

50    Trade dress refers to the 'look and feel' of a retail establishment, e.g. the distinctive marketing and presentation style of The Nature Company.

51    An interesting but important exception to this can be found in second sourcing. In the microprocessor business, until the introduction of the 386 chip, Intel and most other merchant semi producers were encouraged by large customers like IBM to provide second sources, i.e. to license and share their proprietary process technology with competitors like AMD and NEC. The microprocessor developers did so to assure customers that they had sufficient manufacturing capability to meet demand at all times.

52 Phillips (1971) and Demsetz (1974) also made the case that market concentration resulted from the competitive success of more efficient firms, and not from entry barriers and restrictive practices.

53 We concur with Williamson that economizing and strategizing are not mutually exclusive. Strategic ploys can be used to disguise inefficiencies and to promote economizing outcomes, as with pricing with reference to learning curve costs. Our view of economizing is perhaps more expansive than Williamson's as it embraces more than efficient contract design and the minimization of transactions costs. We also address production and organizational economies, and the distinctive ways that things are accomplished inside the business enterprise.

# References

Abernathy, W.J. and K. Clark (1985). 'Innovation: Mapping the winds of creative destruction', *Research Policy*, 14, pp. 3–22.

Alchian, A.A. and H. Demsetz (1972). 'Production, information costs, and economic organization', *American Economic Review*, 62, pp. 777–795.

Amit, R. and P. Schoemaker (1993). 'Strategic assets and organizational rent', *Strategic Management Journal* 14(1), pp. 33–46.

Aoki, M. (1990). 'The participatory generation of information rents and the theory of the firm'. In M. Aoki, B. Gustafsson and O.E. Williamson (eds.), *The Firm as a Nexus of Treaties*. Sage, London, pp. 26–52.

Argyris, C. and D. Schon (1978). *Organizational Learning*. Addison-Wesley, Reading, MA.

Arrow, K. (1969). 'The organization of economic activity. Issues pertinent to the choice of market vs. nonmarket allocation'. In *The Analysis and Evaluation of Public Expenditures: The PPB System, 1*. US Joint Economic Committee, 91st Session. US Government Printing Office, Washington, DC, pp. 59–73.

Arthur, W.B. (1983) 'Competing technologies and lock-in by historical events: The dynamics of allocation under increasing returns', working paper WP-83–90, International Institute for Applied Systems Analysis, Laxenburg, Austria.

Bain, J.S. (1959). *Industrial Organization*. Wiley, New York.

Barney, J.B. (1986). 'Strategic factor markets: Expectations, luck, and business strategy', *Management Science* 32(10), pp. 1231–1241.

Barney, J.B., J.-C. Spender and T. Reve (1994). *Crafoord Lectures*, vol. 6. Chartwell-Bratt, Bromley, UK and Lund University Press, Lund, Sweden.

Bercovitz, J.E.L., J.M. de Figueiredo and D.J. Teece (1996). 'Firm capabilities and managerial decision-making: A theory of innovation biases'. In R. Garud, P. Nayyar and Z. Shapira (eds.), *Innovation: Oversights and Foresights*. Cambridge University Press, Cambridge, UK pp. 233–259.

Camp, R. (1989). *Benchmarking: The Search for Industry Best Practices that Lead to Superior Performance*. Quality Press, Milwaukee, WI.

Chandler, A.D., Jr. (1990). *Scale and Scope: The Dynamics of Industrial Competition*. Harvard University Press, Cambridge, MA.

Clark, K. and T. Fujimoto (1991). *Product Development Performance: Strategy, Organization and Management in the World Auto Industries*. Harvard Business School Press, Cambridge, MA.

Coase, R. (1937). 'The nature of the firm', *Economica*, 4, pp. 386–405.

Coase, R. (1988). 'Lecture on the Nature of the Firm, III', *Journal of Law, Economics and Organization*, 4, pp. 33–47.

Cool, K. and D. Schendel (1988). 'Performance differences among strategic group members', *Strategic Management Journal*, 9(3), pp. 207–223.

Demsetz, H. (1974). 'Two systems of belief about monopoly'. In H. Goldschmid, M. Mann and J.F. Weston (eds.), *Industrial Concentration: The New Learning*. Little, Brown, Boston, MA, pp. 161–184.

Dierickx, I. and K. Cool (1989). 'Asset stock accumulation and sustainability of competitive advantage', *Management Science*, 35(12), pp. 1504–1511.

Dixit, A. (1980). 'The role of investment in entry deterrence', *Economic Journal*, 90, pp. 95–106.

Doz, Y. and A. Shuen (1990). 'From intent to outcome: A process framework for partnerships', INSEAD working paper.

Fama, E.F. (1980). 'Agency problems and the theory of the firm', *Journal of Political Economy*, 88, pp. 288–307.

Freeman, J. and W. Boeker (1984). 'The ecological analysis of business strategy'. In G. Carroll and D. Vogel (eds.), *Strategy and Organization*. Pitman, Boston, MA, pp. 64–77.

Fujimoto, T. (1994). 'Reinterpreting the resource-capability view of the firm: A case of the development-production systems of the Japanese automakers', draft working paper, Faculty of Economics, University of Tokyo.

Garvin, D. (1988). *Managing Quality*. Free Press, New York.

Garvin, D. (1994). 'The processes of organization and management', Harvard Business School working paper #94–084.

Ghemawat, P. (1991). *Commitment: The Dynamics of Strategy*. Free Press, New York.

Gilbert, R.J. and D.M.G. Newberry (1982). 'Preemptive patenting and the persistence of monopoly', *American Economic Review*, 72, pp. 514–526.

Gittell, J.H. (1995). 'Cross functional coordination, control and human resource systems: Evidence from the airline industry', unpublished Ph.D. thesis, Massachusetts Institute of Technology.

Hansen, G.S. and B. Wernerfelt (1989). 'Determinants of firm performance: The relative importance of economic and organizational factors', *Strategic Management Journal*, 10(5), pp. 399–411.

Hartley, R.F. (1989). *Marketing Mistakes*. Wiley, New York.

Hayes, R. and K. Clark (1985). 'Exploring the sources of productivity differences at the factory level'. In K. Clark, R.H. Hayes and C. Lorenz (eds.), *The Uneasy Alliance: Managing the Productivity–Technology Dilemma*. Harvard Business School Press, Boston, MA, pp. 151–188.

Hayes, R.S. Wheelwright and K. Clark (1988). *Dynamic Manufacturing: Creating the Learning Organization*. Free Press, New York.

Henderson, R.M. (1994). 'The evolution of integrative capability: Innovation in cardiovascular drug discovery', *Industrial and Corporate Change*, 3(3), pp. 607–630.

Henderson, R.M. and K.B. Clark (1990). 'Architecture innovation: The reconfiguration of existing product technologies and the failure of established firms', *Administrative Science Quarterly*, 35, pp. 9–30.

Henderson, R.M. and I. Cockburn (1994). 'Measuring competence? Exploring firm effects in pharmaceutical research, *Strategic Management Journal*, Summer Special Issue, 15, pp. 63–84.

Iansiti, M. and K.B. Clark (1994). 'Integration and dynamic capability: Evidence from product development in automobiles and mainframe computers', *Industrial and Corporate Change*, 3(3), pp. 557–605.

Itami, H. and T.W. Roehl (1987). *Mobilizing Invisible Assets*. Harvard University Press, Cambridge, MA.

Jacobsen, R. (1988). 'The persistence of abnormal returns', *Strategic Management Journal*, 9(5), pp. 415–430.

Katz, M. and C. Shapiro (1985). 'Network externalities, competition and compatibility', *American Economic Review*, 75, pp. 424–440.

Langlois, R. (1994). 'Cognition and capabilities: Opportunities seized and missed in the history of the computer industry', working paper, University of Connecticut. Presented at the conference on Technological Oversights and Foresights, Stern School of Business, New York University, 11–12 March 1994.

Learned, E., C. Christensen, K. Andrews and W. Guth (1969). *Business Policy: Text and Cases*. Irwin, Homewood, IL.

Leonard-Barton, D. (1995). *Wellsprings of Knowledge*. Harvard Business School Press, Boston, MA.

Levinthal, D. and J. March (1981). 'A model of adaptive organizational search', *Journal of Economic Behavior and Organization*, 2, pp. 307–333.

Levinthal, D.A. and J.G. March (1993). 'The myopia of learning', *Strategic Management Journal*, Winter Special Issue, 14, pp. 95–112.

Levinthal, D. and J. Myatt (1994). 'Co-evolution of capabilities and industry: The evolution of mutual fund processing', *Strategic Management Journal*, Winter Special Issue, 15, pp. 45–62.

Levitt, B. and J. March (1988). 'Organizational learning', *Annual Review of Sociology*, 14, pp. 319–340.

Lippman, S.A. and R.P. Rumelt (1992). 'Demand uncertainty and investment in industry-specific capital', *Industrial and Corporate Change* 1(1), pp. 235–262.

Mahoney, J. (1995). 'The management of resources and the resources of management', *Journal of Business Research*, 33(2), pp. 91–101.

Mahoney, J.T. and J.R. Pandian (1992). 'The resource-based view within the conversation of strategic management', *Strategic Management Journal*, 13(5), pp. 363–380.

Mason, E. (1949). 'The current state of the monopoly problem in the US', *Harvard Law Review*, 62, pp. 1265–1285.

Milgrom, P. and J. Roberts (1990). 'The economics of modern manufacturing: Technology, strategy, and organization', *American Economic Review*, 80(3), pp. 511–528.

Mitchell, W. (1989). 'Whether and when? Probability and timing of incumbents' entry into emerging industrial subfields', *Administrative Science Quarterly*, 34, pp. 208–230.

Mody, A. (1993). 'Learning through alliances', *Journal of Economic Behavior and Organization*, 20(2), pp. 151–170.

Nelson, R.R. (1991). 'Why do firms differ, and how does it matter? *Strategic Management Journal*, Winter Special Issue, 12, pp. 61–74.

Nelson, R.R. (1994). 'The co-evolution of technology, industrial structure, and supporting institutions', *Industrial and Corporate Change*, 3(1), pp. 47–63.

Nelson, R. (1996). 'The evolution of competitive or comparative advantage: A preliminary report on a study'. WP-96-21, International Institute for Applied Systems Analysis, Laxemberg, Austria.

Nelson, R. and S. Winter (1982). *An Evolutionary Theory of Economic change*. Harvard University Press, Cambridge, MA.

Penrose, E. (1959). *The Theory of the Growth of the Firm*. Basil Blackwell, London.

Phillips, A.C. (1971). *Technology and Market Structure*. Lexington Books, Toronto.

Pisano, G. (1994). 'Knowledge integration and the locus of learning: An empirical analysis of process development', *Strategic Management Journal*, Winter Special Issue, 15, pp. 85–100.

Porter, M.E. (1980). *Competitive Strategy*. Free Press, New York.

Prahalad, C.K. and G. Hamel (1990). 'The core competence of the corporation', *Harvard Business Review*, 68(3), pp. 79–91.

Richardson, G.B.H. (1960, 1990). *Information and Investment*. Oxford University Press, New York.

Rosenberg, N. (1982). *Inside the Black Box: Technology and Economics*. Cambridge University Pres, Cambridge, MA.

Rumelt, R.P. (1984). 'Towards a strategic theory of the firm'. In R.B. Lamb (ed.), *Competitive Strategic Management*. Prentice-Hall, Englewood Cliffs, NJ, pp. 556–570.

Rumelt, R.P. (1991). 'How much does industry matter?', *Strategic Management Journal*, 12(3), pp. 167–185.

Rumelt, R.P., D. Schendel and D. Teece (1994). *Fundamental Issues in Strategy*. Harvard Business School Press, Cambridge, MA.

Schmalensee, R. (1983). 'Advertising and entry deterrence: An exploratory model', *Journal of Political Economy*, 91(4), pp. 636–653.

Schumpeter, J.A. (1934). *Theory of Economic Development*. Harvard University Press, Cambridge, MA.

Schumpeter, J.A. (1942). *Capitalism, Socialism, and Democracy*. Harper, New York.

Shapiro, C. (1989). 'The theory of business strategy', *RAND Journal of Economics*, 20(1), pp. 125–137.

Shuen, A. (1994). 'Technology sourcing and learning strategies in the semiconductor industry', unpublished Ph.D. dissertation, University of California, Berkeley.

Szulanski, G. (1995). 'Unpacking stickiness: An empirical investigation of the barriers to transfer best practice inside the firm', *Academy of Management Journal*, Best Papers Proceedings, pp. 437–441.

Teece, D.J. (1976). *The Multinational Corporation and the Resource Cost of International Technology Transfer*. Ballinger, Cambridge, MA.

Teece, D.J. (1980). 'Economics of scope and the scope of the enterprise', *Journal of Economic Behavior and Organization*, 1, pp. 223–247.

Teece, D.J. (1981). 'The market for know-how and the efficient international transfer of technology', *Annals of the Academy of Political and Social Science*, 458, pp. 81–96.

Teece, D.J. (1982). 'Towards an economic theory of the multiproduct firm', *Journal of Economic Behavior and Organization*, 3, pp. 39–63.

Teece, D.J. (1984). 'Economic analysis and strategic management', *California Management Review*, 26(3), pp. 87–110.

Teece, D.J. (1986a). 'Transactions cost economics and the multinational enterprise', *Journal of Economic Behavior and Organization*, 7, pp. 21–45.

Teece, D.J. (1986b). 'Profiting from technological innovation', *Research Policy*, 15(6), pp. 285–305.

Teece, D.J. (1988). 'Technological change and the nature of the firm'. In G. Dosi, C. Freeman, R. Nelson, G. Silverberg and L. Soete (eds.), *Technical Change and Economic Theory*. Pinter Publishers, New York, pp. 256–281.

Teece, D.J. (1993). 'The dynamics of industrial capitalism: Perspectives on Alfred Chandler's *Scale and Scope* (1990)', *Journal of Economic Literature*, 31(1), pp. 199–225.

Teece, D.J. (1996) 'Firm organization, industrial structure, and technological innovation', *Journal of Economic Behavior and Organization*, 31, pp. 193–224.

Teece, D.J., R. Rumelt, G. Dosi and S. Winter (1994). 'Understanding corporate coherence: Theory and evidence', *Journal of Economic Behavior and Organization*, 23, pp. 1–30.

Tushman, M.L., W.H. Newman and E. Romanelli (1986). 'Convergence and upheaval: Managing the unsteady pace of organizational evolution', *California Management Review*, 29(1), pp. 29–44.

Wernerfelt, B. (1984). 'A resource-based view of the firm', *Strategic Management Journal*, 5(2), pp. 171–180.

Williamson, O.E. (1975). *Markets and Hierarchies*. Free Press, New York.

Williamson, O.E. (1985). *The Economic Institutions of Capitalism*. Free Press, New York.

Williamson, O.E. (1991). 'Strategizing, economizing, and economic organization', *Strategic Management Journal*, Winter Special Issue, 12, pp. 75–94.

Womack, J., D. Jones and D. Roos (1991). *The Machine that Changed the World*. Harper-Perennial, New York.

Zander, U. and B. Kogut (1995). 'Knowledge and the speed of the transfer and imitation of organizational capabilities: An empirical test', *Organization Science*, 6(1), pp. 76–92.

# Strategic Innovation and Firm Size

This section continues the discussion on capabilities and competencies by focusing on a particular type of organizational capability: the capability to 'innovate'. The readings argue that technological and organizational innovation depend on firm-specific characteristics like firm size and the internal organization of the firm, as well as on the characteristics of the innovation itself, like the degree of change that the innovation brings about (e.g. radical versus incremental innovation) or on the particular stage in the industry life-cycle in which it emerges.

A question that has been examined by economists and business strategists for many years is whether it is large or small firms that are better innovators. Joseph Schumpeter's (1883–1950) work on technological innovation provided many interesting insights into this question, which later inspired the work of evolutionary economists who are interested in how activities related to technological change cause differences between firms to arise and how competitive selection pressures 'winnow in' on those differences (Nelson and Winter, 1982). The reasons why large size can be advantageous for innovation include: biases in capital markets which give preference to large firms owing to the greater stability of their internally generated funds; higher returns from research and development (R&D) owing to greater volume over which to spread costs of research and financial planning; and the lower risk incurred from any one R&D project owing to the more diversified portfolios of large firms. The reasons why small firms may have advantages in innovation include: their greater managerial control and flexibility since research in large labs may become over-organized; their greater flexibility and motivation to foresee future changes in demand and technology; and their ability to attract scientists and entrepreneurs who are disillusioned by large bureaucratic firms. Empirical evidence suggests that there is no one answer to whether it is small or large firms which are more innovative. The relationship between firm size and innovation is sensitive to various factors such as the type of industry being considered, the underlying knowledge base of the technology, and the specific phase in the industry life-cycle. Thus, the appropriate question is not 'Do large or small firms have greater advantages in the innovation process?', but rather 'Under which circumstances do large or small firms have the relative innovative advantage?' For example, some studies have found that small firms have a relative advantage in innovation when innovation is radical as opposed to incremental, when the environment is characterized by strong uncertainty, and when production is skill intensive rather than capital intensive (Acs and Audretsch, 1987). All of these conditions tend to hold in the early phase of the industry life-cycle (e.g. high uncertainty due to volatile changes in demand, prices and technological change). Since these conditions change over time, we should expect the relative advantage of large and small firms to change over time.

This discussion provides insights into the question encountered in the reading by Porter in Chapter 1. Are decisions based on operational efficiency (doing existing things better) not strategic? The readings in this section suggest that under certain conditions (often those in which large firms have advantages in innovation), operational efficiency may be a good strategy to pursue. However, since those conditions will eventually change, it is always important to keep an eye out for new ways of operating (new products, new markets, new distribution channels, etc.). The last reading claims that one way for established firms to maintain their lead is to make sure that they do not lose their capacity to question the status quo. This is because although current success is built upon existing rules, those same rules may embody the seeds for future failure when the conditions they are based on change.

## W.J. Abernathy and K. Wayne: 'Limits of the Learning Curve'

This reading appeared in the *Harvard Business Review* in 1974. The authors look at the trade-off between strategies that are aimed at doing existing things better and strategies that are aimed at doing altogether different things. They claim that the consequence of pursuing strategies based only on process improvements, like economies of scale, is the loss in the ability to make real innovative changes.

Hence strategies which pursue a learning curve (i.e. which focus on decreasing costs through increasing volume) are strategic as long as the technological environment is stable. But conditions favouring efficient, high-volume, established operations are different from those that stimulate innovation: when consumer tastes are changing and new technological opportunities appear, concentration on scale may create an internal inertia that prevents the firm from adapting to change. The authors use the experience of the Ford Motor Company in the late 1920s to support their points.

## R.M. Henderson and K.B. Clark: 'Architectural Innovation: the Reconfiguration of Existing Product Technologies and the Failure of Established Firms'

The reading by Henderson and Clark appeared in the *Administrative Science Quarterly* in 1990. The authors argue that while it is true that radical innovations may render the competencies developed by established firms obsolete, even minor incremental innovations can wipe away the advantages of incumbents. This is so when changes affect product 'architecture', i.e. when the linkages between the parts of a product change without changing the parts. Since architectural knowledge tends to be embedded in the structure and information-processing procedures of organizations, the need to make architectural changes is less obvious than the need to make changes to the parts. This, combined with the fact that incumbent firms by definition have more invested in existing structures, gives them a disadvantage in implementing architectural innovations. The authors warn established firms to beware of becoming too wed to the established communication channels. To prepare for the uncertain future, engineers must constantly learn not only about (new) components but also and especially about new links between components and hence the architecture of the product.

## C. Markides: 'Strategic Innovation in Established Companies'

The reading by Markides appeared in the *Sloan Management Review* in 1998. Markides approaches the topic of innovation from a different viewpoint than the previous two readings. Whereas the two other readings look at innovation through incremental/radical changes in actual production structures and/or in final products, Markides looks at 'strategic innovation' through the ways that firms are able to change the rules of the game in their industry, i.e. fundamental reconceptualization of what the business is all about. He claims that although both small and large firms must be able to do this, it is much harder for large firms. The need for strategic innovation is less obvious to established firms because they are already successful in the industry. They find it difficult to strategically innovate because of factors like structural and cultural inertia. And here is the trickiest part of all: precisely because established firms are complacent owing to their current success, they cannot rely on their current financial condition to act as a signal that changes must be made. Current profits are built on past strategies. If current strategies are outdated, then future profits will soon reflect this. Once current profits finally fall, it might be too late to regain competitiveness. Thus companies must not wait for the crisis before implementing changes. They must institutionalize questioning attitudes and create positive crises which ask questions.

## References

Acs, Z.J. and Audretch, D.B. (1987) 'Innovation, market structure and firm size', *Review of Economics and Statistics*, LXIX (4): 567–74.

Nelson, R.R. and Winter, S.G. (1982) *An Evolutionary Theory of Economic Change*. Cambridge, MA: Harvard University Press.

# CHAPTER 10

# Limits of the Learning Curve

WILLIAM J. ABERNATHY AND KENNETH WAYNE*

[. . .]

Many companies have built successful marketing and production strategies around the learning curve – the simple but powerful concept that product costs decline systematically by a common percentage each time that volume doubles. The learning-curve relationship is important in planning because it means that increasing a company's product volume and market share will also bring cost advantages over the competition.

However, other results that are not planned, foreseen, or desired may grow out of such a market penetration/cost reduction progression. Reduced flexibility, a loss of innovative capability, and higher overhead may accompany efforts to cut costs.

A manager failing to consider the possible outcome of following a cost-minimizing strategy may find himself with few competitive options once he reaches the point where decelerating volume expansion prevents him from obtaining further significant cost reduction.

But if he can identify the likely consequences in advance, he can either anticipate them in his plans or choose an alternative strategy. In this article we analyze those consequences and conclude that management cannot expect to receive the benefits of cost reduction provided by a steep learning-curve projection and at the same time expect to accomplish rapid rates of product innovation and improvement in product performance. Managers should realize that the two achievements are the fruits of different strategies.

Proponents of the learning curve have developed the relationships between volume growth and cost reduction through the use of two distinct but related approaches:

1 The learning curve (also called the progress function and start-up function) shows that *manufacturing costs* fall as volume rises. It has typically been developed for standardized products like airframes and cameras.

* *Harvard Business Review* for an extract from 'Limits of the Learning Curve' by William J. Abernathy and Kenneth Wayne, Sept/Oct 1974. Copyright © 1974 by the Harvard Business School Publishing Corporation.

2 The experience curve traces declines in the *total costs* of a product line over extended periods of time as volume grows. Typically, it includes a broader range of costs that are expected to drop than does the learning curve, but disregards any product or process design changes introduced during the period of consideration. [. . .]

The two approaches are sufficiently similar for many purposes of planning and analysis. [. . .]

## Hard strategic questions

Evidence on cost decreases in a wide range of products, including semiconductors, petrochemicals, automobiles, and synthetic fibers, supports the notion that total product costs, as well as manufacturing costs, decline by a constant and predictable percentage each time volume doubles. Because this volume/cost relationship is reliable and quantifiable, it has appeal as a strategic planning tool for use in marketing and financial planning, as well as in production. Moreover, a strategy that seeks the largest possible market share at the earliest possible date can gain not only market penetration but also advantages over competitors who have failed to reach equal volume.

Examples of the economic effects of the learning curve can be found everywhere. The price of ferromagnetic memory cores for computers plunged from 5 cents per bit (unit of memory) in 1965 to less than a half cent in 1973, thereby significantly reducing the costs of computers. In less than two decades of production DuPont reduced the cost of rayon fiber from 53 cents a pound to 17 cents (values not adjusted for inflation). Airframe costs can drop more than 50% per pound during the three to five years of a high-volume production run if the manufacturer can control the rate of modification and sustain volume production.

In considering examples of independent action by one corporation, the most important is that of the Ford Motor Company in its early years. (The Ford example actually shows an experience curve, but the point it makes is equally valid for a learning-curve situation.) During an initial period of less than two years, the average price of a Ford automobile was reduced from more than $5,000 to about $3,000 through the introduction of a dominant product, the Model T. Then, as Figure 10.1 shows on a logarithmic scale, the company cut the price of the Model T to less than $900 following an 85% experience curve. (To underline the contrasts in price, all the figures are translated into 1958 dollars.)

During this time span wages were increased more than threefold, the working day was reduced by fiat from ten hours to eight, the moving assembly line was invented, and one of the nation's largest industrial complexes (River Rouge) was created entirely out of retained earnings. We shall return to the Ford case shortly.

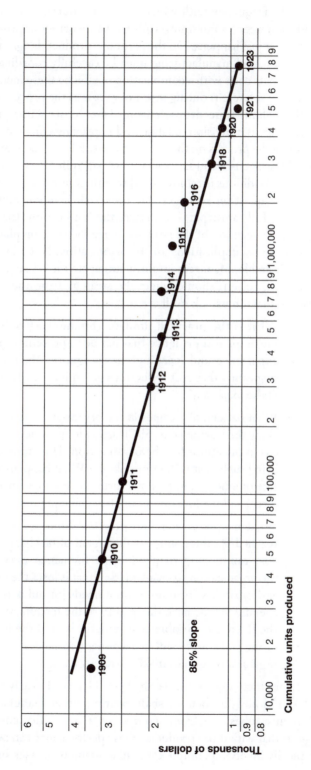

**Figure 10.1** *Price of Model T, 1909–1923 (average list price in 1958 dollars)*

215

The frequency with which this cost reduction/volume increase pattern is found, in practice sometimes leads to the incorrect impression that the learning-curve effect just happens. On the contrary, product design, marketing, purchasing, engineering, and manufacturing must be carefully coordinated and managed. The producer cuts costs with a combination of effects; these include spreading overhead over larger volume, reducing inventory costs as the process becomes more rational and throughput time drops, cutting labor costs with, process improvements, achieving greater division of labor, and improving efficiency through greater famil-iarity with the process on the part of the work force and management. The impetus toward lower costs and higher volume is fragile, however, and if any one of the necessary conditions is removed, a discontinuous return to higher costs may result.

The question management must ask in undertaking such a strategy is whether it fully anticipates or desires the implications that accompany results or that follow execution of the strategy. After the start-up phase, doubling of volume has tremendous implications for the organization. Not all the changes it undergoes may be desirable. Management must anticipate the consequences so that it can plan for them, or else it should reject the strategy from the beginning. Some of the questions that it must ask itself are:

- What is the practical limit to volume/cost reduction? Much of the empirical evidence that has been presented in support of the experience and learning curves ignores their limits, implicitly suggesting that cost reductions go on forever. How long can bene-fits be expected?

- What pattern of changes in the organization accompanies progress along the learning curve? Clearly, a long sequence of cost reduction has implications for the organization. How must it be changed to bring such cost reductions about? What happens to overhead, the rate of innovation, manufacturing technology, inventory, the work force, and the investment in plant and equipment?

- What happens when the practical limits of cost reduction are reached? At this point, can the organization change its strategy from cost minimizing to product-performance maximizing? Or has the organization so changed itself that it loses the vitality, flexibility, and capability for innovation it needs for quick response? In more specific terms, have the quality of the manufacturing technology, the fixed and variable cost structures, and the innovative powers of the work force and management deteriorated so much that the organization cannot make a strategy change?

To explore these questions, we shall consider Ford's early experience, particularly with the Model T. Then we shall examine other manufacturing cases — such as TV picture tubes, electronic components, and office equipment. The evidence suggests that with those products whose performance can be improved significantly — typically involving complex manufacturing processes such as use of electronic equipment machinery – the incidence of product innovation establishes the limit to the learning curve.

The consequence of intensively pursuing a cost-minimization strategy is a reduced ability to make innovative changes and to respond to those introduced by competitors – although the amount of loss seems to depend on the degree to which the manufacturer follows such a strategy, and its intensity. The problem of strategy choice, then, is balancing the hoped-for advantages from varying degrees of cost reduction against a consequent loss in flexibility and ability to innovate.

## From Model T to Model A

At Ford, the experience curve did not continue indefinitely; it governed only the Model T era. Then Ford abandoned it for a performance-maximizing strategy by which the company tried to improve performance year by year at an ever higher product price. The product was the Model A. However, Ford's long devotion to the experience-curve strategy made the transition to another strategy difficult and very costly.

[. . .]

Because manufacturing costs vary directly with weight, a comparison of the two trend lines in different periods is revealing. After the Model T was discontinued in 1927, Ford raised the price of its car from year to year, in contrast to the earlier period. The increases were due mainly to design changes which were made to enhance comfort, performance, and safety, but which required more and more expensive materials and caused the price per pound to rise steadily. Considered over a number of years, these systematic annual changes represent a trade-off in favor of size, weight, and performance, as opposed to price.

. . . [After] an initial period in which several models were offered at the same time, the product line was consolidated in 1909 to the Model T. Ford's objective was to reduce the price of the automobile and thereby increase volume and market share. Before the Model T was conceived, when the least expensive Ford car was priced at $850 and tires alone cost more than $60 a set, Henry Ford announced plans to sell autos at $400 – although, he told reporters, 'It will take some time to figure what we can do.'

By 1907, after the death of the former company president and the expulsion of dissident stockholder-managers who advocated high-priced cars, attention turned to product cost reduction. The company felt confident in taking this step because of its success with the relatively inexpensive Model N in 1907 and later with the Model T, which was clearly a superior product.[1]

The company accomplished savings by building modern plants, extracting higher volume from the existing plant, obtaining economies in purchased parts, and gaining efficiency through greater division of labor. By 1913 these efforts had reduced production throughput times from 21 days to 14. Later, production was speeded further through major process innovations like the moving assembly line in motors and radiators and branch assembly plants. At times, however, labor turnover reportedly ran as high as 40% per month.[2]

Up to this point, Ford had achieved economies without greatly increasing the rate of capital intensity. To sustain the cost cuts, however, the company embarked on a policy of backward and further forward integration in order to reduce transportation and raw materials costs, improve reliability of supply sources, and control dealer performance. The rate of capital investment showed substantial increases after 1913, rising from 11 cents per sales dollar that year to 22 cents by 1921. The new facilities that were built or acquired included blast furnaces, logging operations and saw mills, a railroad, weaving mills, coke ovens, a paper mill, a glass plant, and a cement plant.

Throughput time was slashed to four days[3] and the inventory level cut in half, despite the addition of large raw materials inventories. The labor hours required of unsalaried employees per 1,000 pounds of vehicle delivered fell correspondingly some 60% during this period, in spite of the additions to the labor force resulting from the backward integration thrust and in spite of substantial use of Ford employees in factory construction.

Constant improvements in the production process made it more integrated, more mechanized, and increasingly paced by conveyors. Consequently, the company felt less need for management in planning and control activities. The percentage of salaried workers was cut from nearly 5% of total employment for 1913 to less than 2% by 1921; these reductions in Ford personnel enabled the company to hold in line the burgeoning fixed-cost and overhead burden.

The strategy of cost minimization single-mindedly followed with the Model T was a spectacular success. But the changes that accompanied it carried the seeds of trouble that affected the organization's ability to vary its product, alter its cost structure, and continue to innovate.

## Cost of transition

In its effort to keep reducing Model T costs while wages were rising, Ford continued to invest heavily in plant, property, and equipment. These facilities even included coal mines, rubber plantations, and forestry operations (to provide wooden car parts). By 1926, nearly 33 cents in such assets backed each dollar of sales, up from 20 cents just four years earlier, thereby increasing fixed costs and raising the break-even point.

In the meantime, the market was changing. In the early 1920s, consumer demand began shifting to a heavier, closed body and to more comfort. Ford's chief rival, General Motors, quickly responded to this shift with new designs. Ford's response, was to add features to the Model T which gradually increased the weight; between 1915 and 1925 the weight of the car actually gained by nearly 25%, while engine power remained the same.

But the rate of product improvement halted the steady reduction of costs. Nevertheless, to maintain market growth Ford further cut the list price along the experience-curve formula. This created a severe margin squeeze, particularly when unit sales began falling after 1923. As the rate of design changes accelerated and wage levels continued to rise, manufacturing costs loomed ever larger in the retail price. In 1926, the manufacturing costs of some models reached 93% of list price, and some models were actually sold to dealers at prices below costs. (See Table 10.1 for sales, manufacturing, and other data on Ford during the critical two decades.) Ford, unbeatable at making one product efficiently, was vulnerable to GM's strategy of quality and competition via superior vehicle performance. As Alfred Sloan, architect of GM's strategy, later wrote:

> Mr. Ford . . . had frozen his policy in the Model T . . . preeminently an open-car design. With its light chassis, it was unsuited to the heavier closed body, and so in less than two years [by 1923] the closed body made the already obsolescing design of the Model T noncompetitive as an engineering design . . .
>
> The old [GM] strategic plan of 1921 was vindicated to a 'T', so to speak, but in a surprising way as to the particulars. The old master had failed to master change . . . His precious volume, which was the foundation of his position, was fast disappearing. He could not continue losing sales and maintain his profits. And so, for engineering and market reasons, the Model T fell . . . In May 1927 . . . he shut down his great River Rouge plant completely and kept it shut down for nearly a year to retool, leaving the field to Chevrolet unopposed and opening it up for Mr. Chrysler's Plymouth. Mr. Ford regained sales leadership again in 1929, 1930, and 1935, but, speaking in terms of generalities, he had lost the lead to General Motors.[4]

A company that had developed and introduced eight new models during a four-year period, before undertaking the cost-minimization strategy, had subsequently so specialized its work force, process technology, and management that it consumed nearly a year in model development and changeover. As an illustration of its specialization, in the course of the model change Ford lost $200 million, replaced 15,000 machine tools and rebuilt 25,000 more, and laid off 60,000 workers in Detroit alone.

So we see that when costs could not be reduced as fast as they were added through design changes, the experience-curve formula became inoperative. While this sequence should give pause to managers who wish to apply the experience curve to make product-line changes, it does not invalidate the principle of the learning curve, which assumes a standardized product.

## Decline of innovation

The sequence of evolutionary development in product and process during the period of the cost-minimization strategy and the subsequent strategy transition is paralleled in the pattern of major Ford innovations. Figure 10.2 plots the frequency and significance of Ford-initiated innovations by type of application: product innovation, process innovation, and transfer of process technology to or from

Table 10.1  Ford vital statistics, 1910–1931

| Year | Motor vehicles sales (in thousands of units) | % of market share | % of employees salaried | Labor rate (in $ per hour) | Manufacturing cost as % of list price* | Direct labor hours per vehicle*† | Fixed assets per $ sales | Labor hours per vehicle | Profit (loss) (in millions of dollars)‡ |
|---|---|---|---|---|---|---|---|---|---|
| 1910 | 32 | 10.7 | 6.9 | 0.25 | | | | 232 | $15 |
| 1911 | 70 | 20.3 | 3.5 | 0.23 | | | | 265 | 21 |
| 1912 | 170 | 22.1 | 5.5 | 0.23 | | | 0.10 | 95 | 40 |
| 1913 | 203 | 39.6 | 4.9 | 0.27 | 41 | 66 | 0.11 | 152 | 75 |
| 1914 | 308 | 48.0 | 5.7 | 0.55 | 40 | 42 | 0.15 | 79 | 90 |
| 1915 | 501 | 43.4 | 4.5 | 0.55 | | | 0.19 | 72 | 74 |
| 1916 | 735 | 38.6 | 4.4 | 0.55 | | | 0.15 | 84 | 178 |
| 1917 | 664 | 46.1 | 3.2 | 0.61 | 79 | 47 | 0.16 | 106 | 51 |
| 1918 | 498 | 43.5 | 3.5 | 0.66 | | | 0.22 | 133 | 95 |
| 1919 | 941 | 46.9 | 3.0 | 0.76 | | | 0.26 | 100 | 140 |
| 1920 | 463 | | 2.9 | 0.84 | 70 | 49 | 0.27 | 267 | 64 |
| 1921 | 971 | 55.4 | 1.9 | 0.87 | | | 0.22 | 102 | 125 |
| 1922 | 1,307 | | 1.4 | 0.82 | 60 | 31 | 0.20 | 125 | 237 |
| 1923 | 2,019 | 47.5 | 1.1 | 0.85 | | | 0.19 | 125 | 193 |
| 1924 | 1,929 | | 1.2 | 0.83 | 62 | 35 | 0.25 | 140 | 214 |
| 1925 | 1,920 | 41.5 | 1.2 | | | | 0.27 | 160 | 219 |
| 1926 | 1,563 | | 1.4 | 0.87 | 93 | 69 | 0.33 | 178 | 132 |
| 1927 | 424 | 10.6 | 1.5 | 0.87 | | | 0.81 | 475 | (65) |
| 1928 | 750 | | 2.0 | | | | 0.84 | 375 | (143) |
| 1929 | 1,870 | 32.0 | 2.1 | 0.92 | 86 | 80 | 0.40 | 182 | 175 |
| 1930 | 1,432 | | 2.8 | | | | 0.54 | 210 | 113 |
| 1931 | 731 | 26.2 | 4.0 | | 69 | 40 | 1.06 | 290 | (97) |

* For Model T Touring Car 1913–1926, Model A Tudor 1929 and 1931.
† Computed from direct labor cost for models specified above and from Ford labor rates.
‡ In constant 1958 dollars.

Sources: Ford Archives; Federal Trade Commission, Report on the Motor Vehicle Industry, 76th Congress, First Session (1940), House Document 468. Missing figures are not

associated industries. The new methods and designs are those claimed by Ford. For our analysis, four independent industry experts evaluated the importance of each one and rated it on a scale of 1 to 5. The innovations range in significance from the introduction of the plastic steering wheel (index average of 1) in 1921 to the invention of the power-driven final assembly line (index of 5) in 1914. The vertical axis in the figure provides a sum of the average points assigned to significant developments by two-year intervals in Ford's history.

The figure indicates that the intensity of innovative activity is closely related to major events in the unfolding of the cost-minimization strategy. During the Model T period the activity shows a ripple effect. Installation of new product applications occurs in clusters with new model development and then declines in frequency as the design is standardized, efficiency is refined, and the process is integrated into operations. Process innovations rise to a peak after the period of product innovation, as the manufacturer rationalizes the process and reduces costs. (Compare the peak designated circled 1 with the peak designated squared 1, circled 2 with squared 2, and so on.) As the manufacturer works out these problems, he transfers process technology following the thrust into backward integration, and a third peak of activity occurs (triangled 2, triangled 3, and so on).

The figure suggests not only that the nature of innovation changes, but also that the intensity of innovative activity diminishes. Ford produced only one new product application or process technique during the seven years after 1932 that rated as high on the scale as 4 — the development of transfer machines. This step toward further automation took place in 1937.

The changes introduced to trim costs altered the innovative activity in two ways. First, after 1926 the types of innovation peaked coincidentally. As operations became more elaborate and systemslike, product and process change developed intimate linkages; many different elements had to be altered simultaneously to introduce change. This relationship implies a high cost of change. Secondly, the nature of product innovation shifted. In the early years, a new model meant a complete transformation involving major innovation. Later, model change became an annual affair, and innovation centered on new features available across model lines rather than on new models. For instance, the V-8 engine, whose development appears as a substantial cluster of innovations in Figure 10.2, was produced without substantial alterations for 18 years.

Not surprisingly, the third class of innovation, technology transfers, increased in frequency through the period under consideration. This class had particularly long-term value at Ford since it improved the manufacturing capability. Many of these transfers were accomplished in Ford's newly integrated feeder operations, such as one where technology was applied to produce plate glass continuously.

Ford's experience demonstrates the important link between innovation and strategy. Innovation is not the pacing element; it is part of the strategy. Ford's choice of strategy made innovation more costly and a more serious organizational problem. Unfortunately, the cost-cutting drives also led to weakening of the

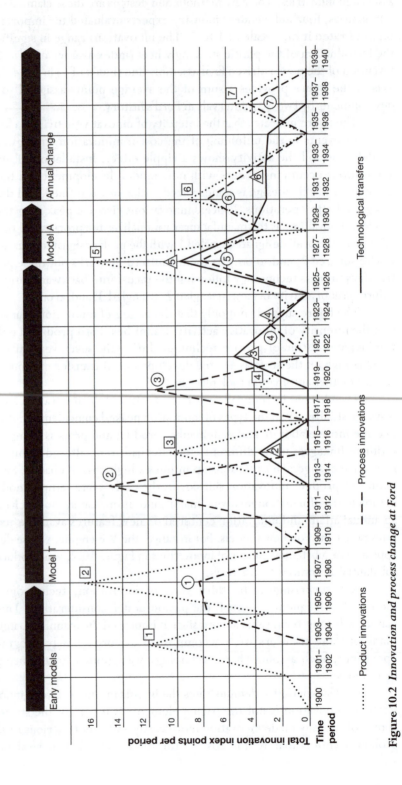

**Figure 10.2** *Innovation and process change at Ford*

······ Product innovations          —— Process innovations

—— Technological transfers

resources (the salaried employees) needed to initiate and carry out innovation. It is not surprising that the company took nearly a year to change over to the Model A.

With its new model, Ford rose again. Combining the old philosophy of cost reduction with the appeal of an entirely new car boasting demonstrably high performance, the company wrestled the major market share from GM in 1930. But its market share fell once more. Indeed, Chrysler, a distinct third among auto makers during the 1920s, held second place ahead of Ford during most of the Depression.

As it turned out, the company's highly specialized production process lacked the balance to handle the new product; for example, the company had overcapacity in wood (the Model T had many wooden parts) but undercapacity in glass and body parts manufacturing. Moreover, as indicated by the data in Table 10.1, Ford never regained the high levels of labor and capital productivity of its heyday. Despite extensive investments in new plant and equipment, even in the highest volume year for the Model A (1929), 40 cents in plant and equipment assets were required per dollar of sales, and nearly 80 hours of direct labor were required per vehicle.

Ford did not improve on these figures until the late 1940s, when new management restructured the company and made heavy plant investments. From the time it introduced the Model A, Ford was compelled to compete on the basis of product quality and performance – a strategy in which it was not skilled.

## Airframes, computers, and so on

The Ford case provides a spectacular example of one company's action in pursuing a cost-minimization strategy to its end. Although this is an extreme case in terms of strategy choices and investment magnitudes, the same forces and consequences can be found at stake in other industries. In some cases these forces and consequences are evident when a rapid rate of product change retards the inauguration of the learning curve, and in other cases the difficulties terminate the downward trend. Consider:

- Douglas Aircraft, once an extremely successful, high-volume aircraft manufacturer, was forced into a merger in 1967 with the McDonnell Company by financial problems whose roots lay in poor control of airframe production costs under fast-shifting conditions. On the assumption that it could reduce the costs of its new jet model following a learning-curve formula, Douglas had made certain commitments on delivery dates and prices to airline customers. But continued modification of its plans disrupted, as *Fortune* put it, 'the normal evolution of the all-important learning curve'.[5]

- International Business Machines' schedules to deliver its new 360 series of computers a decade ago were thrown out of kilter. IBM's

1965 annual report described the situation this way: 'Although our production of System 360 is building up rapidly and equipment shipped has been performing well, we had problems . . . As a result we found it necessary in October to advise customers of delays from our originally planned delivery schedules. The basic building blocks in the System/360 circuitry are advanced new micro-electronic circuit modules requiring totally new manufacturing concepts.' The snag was attributable to the company's efforts to attain high-volume production while it was undertaking major product innovation.

- The price of TV picture tubes followed the experience-curve pattern from the introduction of television in the late 1940s until 1963, the average unit price dropping from $34 to $8 (in terms of 1958 dollars). The advent of color TV ended the pattern, as the price for both black-and-white and color TV tubes shot up to $51 by 1966. Then the experience curve reasserted itself; the price dropped to $48 in 1968, $37 in 1970, and $36 in 1972. The transition was less traumatic than is sometimes the case because the innovation was foreseen and the new product was sufficiently similar to the old one that manufacturers could apply their estab-lished techniques and facilities in making the color tube.

- In some cases radically new technology or the cost of transition has forced many of the 'old' manufacturers out of the business. Such has been the case in the shift from vacuum tubes to transistors, from manual to electric typewriters, and from mechanical calculators to electronic machines. The major producers of textile machinery for rug manufacturing, like Lansdowne and Crompton & Knowles, found their markets taken from them by the advent of the new tufting technology in carpets.

The contrary relationship between product innovation and efficiency exists not only in instances where the impetus for change comes about after a long and successful production run, as in the Ford case and in that of Volkswagen more recently. It can also be found when the change is an unintended continuation of uncertainty following new model introduction, as happened in the foregoing airframe and computer examples.

## Common elements of change

To consider the sort of changes that can accompany a cost-minimizing strategy, it is useful to abstract that aspect of the Ford case. The kinds of changes that took place can be grouped into six categories – product, capital equipment and process technology, task characteristics and process structure, scale, material inputs, and labor.

*Product*   Standardization increases, models change less frequently, and the product line offers less diversity. As the implementation of the strategy continues, the total contribution improves with acceptance of lower margins accompanying larger volume.

*Capital equipment and process technology*   Vertical integration expands and specialization in process equipment, machine tools, and facilities increases. The rate of capital investment rises while the flexibility of these investments declines.

*Task characteristics and process structure*   The throughput time improves and the division of labor is extended as the production process is rationalized and oriented more toward a line-flow operation. The amount of direct supervision decreases as the labor input falls.

*Scale*   The process is segmented to take advantage of economies of scale. Facilities offering economies of scale, such as engine plants, are centralized as volume rises, while others, like assembly plants, are dispersed to trim transportation costs. Spreading the higher overhead over larger volume gains savings.

*Material inputs*   Through either vertical integration or capture of sources of supply, material inputs come under control. Costs are reduced by forcing suppliers to develop materials that meet process needs and by directly reducing processing costs.

*Labor*   The heightening rationalization of the process leads to greater specialization in labor skills and may ultimately lessen workers' pride in their jobs and concern for product quality. Process changes alter the skills requirements from the flexibility of the craftsman to the dexterity of the operative.

The same pattern of change in the six categories that characterizes the Ford history also describes periods of major cost reduction in other industries. For example, as light-bulb manufacturing progressed from a manual process to an almost entirely automated one, a similar pattern of product development, process elaboration, increase in capital intensity, and so on, was evident.[6] In areas as diverse as furniture manufacturing and commercial building construction, the problems of improving productivity and achieving innovation often hinge on changes similar in thrust to those at Ford. Life-cycle studies of international trade in many products, such as chemicals and petrochemicals, demonstrate a coordinated pattern of change involving product characteristics, scale, and price competition that is consistent with the Ford case.

Studies of manufacturing technology yield a common finding for electronics, chemical, and metal-working companies, among others, that certain conditions in a company, like its supervisory structure, product-line diversity, and utilization of technology, relate to characteristics of the manufacturing process. More specifically, manufacturers with more efficient line flows have different ratios of supervisory personnel to the work force, different levels of authority, less product diversity, and greater product standardization than manufacturers with more flexible production process structures.

## Risks of success

In analyzing the difficulties of Ford and other companies, we are not arguing that the pursuit of a cost-minimization strategy is inappropriate. The failure of many companies, particularly small, innovative ones, can be traced to their inability to make the transition to high volume and cost efficiency. Nevertheless, management needs to recognize that conditions stimulating innovation are different from those favoring efficient, high-volume, established operations.

While there must be a theoretical limit to the amount by which costs can ultimately be reduced, a manufacturer reaches the practical limit first. However, the practical limit is not reached because he has exhausted his means of cutting costs; it is rather determined by the market's demand for product change, the rate of technological innovation in the industry, and competitors' ability to use product performance as the basis for competing.

In determining how the learning-curve strategy should be pursued, management must realize that the risk of misjudging the limit rises directly with the successful continuation of the strategy. There are two reasons for this seemingly paradoxical development: first, the market becomes increasingly vulnerable to performance competition and second, attempts to continue reducing costs diminish the organization's ability to respond to this kind of competition.

The market becomes more vulnerable to performance competition because the company must stake out an ever-larger market share to maintain a constant, significant rate of cost cutting. Demand must be doubled each time in order to realize the same proportional cost reduction. As the market expands, it becomes harder to hold together and the competition is better able to segment it 'from the top', with a superior product or customized options. Once this action is taken, the company on the learning curve must either abandon the all-important volume bases of scale or introduce a major product improvement. Either step, or both, ends the cost-reduction sequence.

The unfortunate implication is that product innovation is the enemy of cost efficiency, and vice versa. To make the learning curve evolve successfully, the manufacturer needs a standard product. Under conditions of rapid product change, he cannot slash unit output costs.

## Managing technology

The role expected of technology is critical in the formulation of manufacturing strategy. Many a company has sailed into the unknown, trailing glowing reports about the R&D under way in its laboratories and the new products it is developing. Yet too often the promises in annual reports to stockholders and in news releases are never realized. The problem hinges on difficulties in recognizing that a shift in strategy has a pervasive effect *across* the organization's functional areas. The production department cannot follow a program of cost reduction along the learning curve at the same time that R&D or the marketing people are going full steam ahead into new ventures that change the nature of the product.

When a new product born of technology fails, management is often chided because it assertedly marketed the product poorly. The problem may have come, however, from management's failure to realize that its capabilities to handle innovation had weakened. Foresight is a matter of judging the challenge in terms of altered capabilities as well as technological changes and market forces. In the Ford case the difficulties arose as much from what the organization did to itself as from GM's actions. The ability to switch to a different strategy seems to depend on the extent to which the organization has become specialized in following one strategy and on the magnitude of change it must face. An extreme in either factor can spell trouble.

Very little is known about how to plan for this type of technological change. But we can point to two courses of action that some major companies have followed in avoiding the problems we have described. One is to maintain the efforts to continue development of the existing high-volume product lines. This requires setting the industry pace in periodically inaugurating major product changes while stressing cost reduction via the learning curve between model changes. This course of action – which IBM has followed in computers – is obviously a costly option which only companies with large resources should undertake. It amounts to a decision to maintain comparatively less efficient operations overall.

The second course of action is to take a decentralized approach in which separate organizations or plants in the corporate framework adopt different strategies within the same line of business. Several corporations in high-technology industries have taken this approach with success. One organization in the company will pursue profits with a traditional product, like rayon, to the limit of the experience curve. At the same time a new, different organization will undertake the development of innovative (perhaps even competitive) products or processes, such as nylon. In taking this tack, some companies have shut down old plants and started up new ones instead of mingling different capabilities that are at various stages of their development.[7]

Neither of these courses of action will suit the needs of every organization, but some means of dealing with the issue of technological change and strategy transitions should be included in strategic planning.

# Notes

1    Allan Nevins, *Ford: The Times, the Man, the Company* (New York, Scribner, 1954), Chapter XII.

2    Keith Sward, *The Legend of Henry Ford* (New York, Rinehart, 1948), p. 51.

3    See *Factory Facts from Ford* (Detroit, Ford Motor Company, 1924).

4    Alfred P. Sloan, Jr., *My Years With General Motors* (New York, Doubleday, 1964), pp. 162–163.

5    John Mecklin, 'Douglas Aircraft's Stormy Flight Plan', *Fortune*, December 1966, p. 258.

6    See James R. Bright, *Automation and Management* (Boston, Division of Research, Harvard Business School, 1958).

7    For more on this approach, see Wickham Skinner, 'The Focused Factory', HBR May–June 1974, p. 113.

# CHAPTER 11

# Architectural Innovation: the Reconfiguration of Existing Product Technologies and the Failure of Established Firms

REBECCA M. HENDERSON AND KIM B. CLARK*

[. . .]

The distinction between refining and improving an existing design and introducing a new concept that departs in a significant way from past practice is one of the central notions in the existing literature on technical innovation (Mansfield, 1968; Moch and Morse, 1977; Freeman, 1982). Incremental innovation introduces relatively minor changes to the existing product, exploits the potential of the established design, and often reinforces the dominance of established firms . . . Although it draws from no dramatically new science, it often calls for considerable skill and ingenuity and, over time, has very significant economic consequences . . . Radical innovation, in contrast, is based on a different set of engineering and scientific principles and often opens up whole new markets and potential applications . . . Radical innovation often creates great difficulties for established firms . . . and can be the basis for the successful entry of new firms or even the redefinition of an industry.

Radical and incremental innovations have such different competitive consequences because they require quite different organizational capabilities. Organizational capabilities are difficult to create and costly to adjust (Nelson and Winter, 1982; Hannan and Freeman, 1984). Incremental innovation reinforces the capabilities of established organizations, while radical innovation forces them to ask

* *Administrative Science Quarterly* for 'Architectural Innovation: The Reconfiguration of Existing Product Technologies and the Failure of Established Firms' by Rebecca M. Henderson and Kim B. Clark, vol 35, no 1 © *Administrative Science Quarterly*, March 1990.

a new set of questions, to draw on new technical and commercial skills, and to employ new problem-solving approaches (Burns and Stalker, 1966; Hage, 1980; Ettlie, Bridges, and O'Keefe, 1984; Tushman and Anderson, 1986).

The distinction between radical and incremental innovation has produced important insights, but it is fundamentally incomplete. There is growing evidence that there are numerous technical innovations that involve apparently modest changes to the existing technology but that have quite dramatic competitive consequences (Clark, 1987). The case of Xerox and small copiers and the case of RCA and the American radio receiver market are two examples.

Xerox, the pioneer of plain-paper copiers, was confronted in the mid-1970s with competitors offering copiers that were much smaller and more reliable than the traditional product. The new products required little new scientific or engineering knowledge, but despite the fact that Xerox had invented the core technologies and had enormous experience in the industry, it took the company almost eight years of missteps and false starts to introduce a competitive product into the market. In that time Xerox lost half of its market share and suffered serious financial problems (Clark, 1987).

In the mid-1950s engineers at RCA's corporate research and development center developed a prototype of a portable, transistorized radio receiver. The new product used technology in which RCA was accomplished (transistors, radio circuits, speakers, tuning devices), but RCA saw little reason to pursue such an apparently inferior technology. In contrast, Sony, a small, relatively new company, used the small transistorized radio to gain entry into the US market. Even after Sony's success was apparent, RCA remained a follower in the market as Sony introduced successive models with improved sound quality and FM capability. The irony of the situation was not lost on the R&D engineers: for many years Sony's radios were produced with technology licensed from RCA, yet RCA had great difficulty matching Sony's product in the marketplace (Clark, 1987).

Existing models that rely on the simple distinction between radical and incremental innovation provide little insight into the reasons why such apparently minor or straightforward innovations should have such consequences. [. . .]

# Conceptual framework

## Component and architectural knowledge

In this paper, we focus on the problem of product development, taking as the unit of analysis a manufactured product sold to an end user and designed, engineered, and manufactured by a single product-development organization. We define innovations that change the way in which the components of a product are linked together, while leaving the core design concepts (and thus the basic knowledge underlying the components) untouched, as 'architectural' innovation.[1] This is the kind of innovation that confronted Xerox and RCA. It destroys the usefulness of a firm's architectural knowledge but preserves the usefulness of its knowledge about the product's components.

This distinction between the product as a whole – system – and the product in its parts – the components – has a long history in the design literature (Marples, 1961; Alexander, 1964). For example, a room fan's major components include the blade, the motor that drives it, the blade guard, the control system, and the mechanical housing. The overall architecture of the product lays out how the components will work together. Taken together, a fan's architecture and its components create a system for moving air in a room.

A component is defined here as a physically distinct portion of the product that embodies a core design concept (Clark, 1985) and performs a well-defined function. In the fan, a particular motor is a component of the design that delivers power to turn the fan. There are several design concepts one could use to deliver power. The choice of one of them – the decision to use an electric motor, for example – establishes a core concept of the design. The actual component – the electric motor – is then a physical implementation of this design concept.

The distinction between the product as a system and the product as a set of components underscores the idea that successful product development requires two types of knowledge. First, it requires component knowledge, or knowledge about each of the core design concepts and the way in which they are implemented in a particular component. Second, it requires architectural knowledge, or knowledge about the ways in which the components are integrated and linked together into a coherent whole. The distinction between architectural and component knowledge, or between the components themselves and the links between them, is a source of insight into the ways in which innovations differ from each other.

## Types of technological change

The notion that there are different kinds of innovation, with different competitive effects, has been an important theme in the literature on technological innovation since Schumpeter (1942). Following Schumpeter's emphasis on creative destruction, the literature has characterized different kinds of innovations in terms of their impact on the established capabilities of the firm. This idea is used in Figure 11.1, which classifies innovations along two dimensions, The horizontal dimension captures an innovation's impact on components, while the vertical .captures its impact on the linkages between components.[2] There are, of course, other ways to characterize different kinds of innovation. But given, the focus here on innovation and the development of new products, the framework outlined in Figure 11.1 is useful because it focuses on the impact of an innovation on the usefulness of the existing architectural and component knowledge of the firm.

Framed in this way, radical and incremental innovation are extreme points along both dimensions. Radical innovation establishes a new dominant design and, hence, a new set of core design concepts embodied in components that are linked together in a new architecture. Incremental innovation refines and extends an

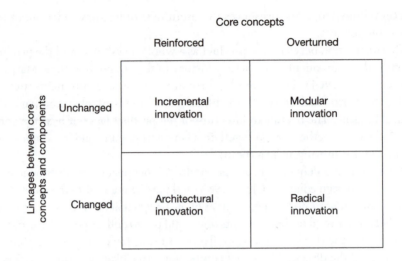

**Figure 11.1** *A framework for defining innovation*

established design. Improvement occurs in individual components, but the under-lying core design concepts, and the links between them, remain the same.

Figure 11.1 shows two further types of innovation: innovation that changes only the core design concepts of a technology and innovation that changes only the relationships between them. The former is a modular innovation, such as the replacement of analog with digital telephones. To the degree that one can simply replace an analog dialing device with a digital one, it is an innovation that changes a core design concept without changing the product's architecture. Our concern, however, is with the last type of innovation shown in the matrix: innovation that changes a product's architecture but leaves the components, and the core design concepts that they embody, unchanged.

The essence of an architectural innovation is the reconfiguration of an established system to link together existing components in a new way. This does not mean that the components themselves are untouched by architectural innovation. Architectural innovation is often triggered by a change in a component – perhaps size or some other subsidiary parameter of its design – that creates new interactions and new linkages with other components in the established product. The important point is that the core design concept behind each component – and the associated scientific and engineering knowledge – remain the same.

We can illustrate the application of this framework with the example of the room air fan. If the established technology is that of large, electrically powered fans, mounted in the ceiling, with the motor hidden from view and insulated to dampen the noise, improvements in blade design or in the power of the motor would be incremental innovations. A move to central air conditioning would be a radical innovation. New components associated with compressors, refrigerants, and their associated controls would add whole new technical disciplines and new inter-relationships. For the maker of large, ceiling-mounted room fans, however, the introduction of a portable fan would be an architectural innovation. While the primary components would be largely the same (e.g. blade, motor, control system), the architecture of the product would be quite different. There would be significant changes in the interactions between components. The smaller size and the co-location of the motor and the blade in the room would focus attention on new types of interaction between the motor size, the blade dimensions, and the amount of air that the fan could circulate, while shrinking the size of the apparatus would probably introduce new interactions between the performance of the blade and the weight of the housing.

The distinctions between radical, incremental, and architectural innovations are matters of degree. The intention here is not to defend the boundaries of a particular definition, particularly since there are several other dimensions on which it may be useful to define radical and incremental innovation. The use of the term architectural innovation is designed to draw attention to innovations that use many existing core design concepts in a new architecture and that therefore have a more significant impact on the relationships between components than on the technologies of the components themselves. The matrix in Figure 11.1 is designed to suggest that a given innovation may be less radical or more architectural, not to suggest that the world can be neatly divided into four quadrants.

These distinctions are important because they give us insight into why established firms often have a surprising degree of difficulty in adapting to architectural innovation. Incremental innovation tends to reinforce the competitive positions of established firms, since it builds on their core competencies (Abernathy and Clark, 1985) or is 'competence enhancing' (Tushman and Anderson ,1986). In the terms of the framework developed here, it builds on the existing architectural and component knowledge of an organization. In contrast, radical innovation creates unmistakable challenges for established firms, since it destroys the usefulness of their existing capabilities. In our terms, it destroys the usefulness of both architectural and component knowledge (Cooper and Schendel, 1976; Daft, 1982; Tushman and Anderson, 1986).

Architectural innovation presents established firms with a more subtle challenge. Much of what the firm knows is useful and needs to be applied in the new product, but some of what it knows is not only not useful but may actually handicap the firm. Recognizing what is useful and what is not, and acquiring and applying new knowledge when necessary, may be quite difficult for an established firm because of the way knowledge – particularly architectural knowledge – is organized and managed.

## The evolution of component and architectural knowledge

Two concepts are important to understanding the ways in which component and architectural knowledge are managed inside an organization. The first is that of a dominant design. Work by Abernathy and Utterback (1978), Rosenberg (1982), Clark (1985), and Sahal (1986) and evidence from studies of several industries show that product technologies do not emerge fully developed at the outset of their commercial lives (Mansfield, 1977). Technical evolution is usually characterized by periods of great experimentation followed by the acceptance of a dominant design. The second concept is that organizations build knowledge and capability around the recurrent tasks that they perform (Cyert and March, 1963; Nelson and Winter, 1982). Thus one cannot understand the development of an organization's innovative capability or of its knowledge without understanding the way in which they are shaped by the organization's experience with an evolving technology.

The emergence of a new technology is usually a period of considerable confusion. There is little agreement about what the major subsystems of the product should be or how they should be put together. There is a great deal of experimentation (Burns and Stalker, 1966; Clark, 1985). For example, in the early days of the automobile industry, cars were built with gasoline, electric, or steam engines, with steering wheels or tillers, and with wooden or metal bodies (Abernathy, 1978).

These periods of experimentation are brought to an end by the emergence of a dominant design (Abernathy and Utterback, 1978; Sahal, 1986). A dominant design is characterized both by a set of core design concepts that correspond to the major functions performed by the product (Marples, 1961; Alexander, 1964; Clark, 1985) and that are embodied in components and by a product architecture that defines the ways in which these components are integrated (Clark, 1985; Sahal, 1986). It is equivalent to the general acceptance of a particular product architecture and is characteristic of technical evolution in a very wide range of industries (Clark, 1985). A dominant design often emerges in response to the opportunity to obtain economies of scale or to take advantage of externalities (David, 1985; Arthur, 1988). For example, the dominant design for the car encompassed not only the fact that it used a gasoline engine to provide motive force but also that it was connected to the wheels through a transmission and a drive train and was mounted on a frame rather than on the axles. A dominant design incorporates a range of basic choices about the design that are not revisited in every subsequent design. Once the dominant automobile design had been accepted, engineers did not reevaluate the decision to use a gasoline engine each time they developed a new design. Once any dominant design is established, the initial set of components is refined and elaborated, and progress takes the shape of improvements in the components within the framework of a stable architecture.

This evolutionary process has profound implications for the types of knowledge that an organization developing a new product requires, since an organization's knowledge and its information-processing capabilities are shaped by the nature of the tasks and the competitive environment that it faces (Lawrence and Lorsch, 1967; Galbraith, 1973).[3]

In the early stages of a technology's history, before the emergence of a dominant design, organizations competing to design successful products experiment with many different technologies. Since success in the market turns on the synthesis of unfamiliar technologies in creative new designs, organizations must actively develop both knowledge about alternate components and knowledge of how these components can be integrated. With the emergence of a dominant design, which signals the general acceptance of a single architecture, firms cease to invest in learning about alternative configurations of the established set of components. New component knowledge becomes more valuable to a firm than new architectural knowledge because competition between designs revolves around refinements in particular components. Successful organizations therefore switch their limited attention from learning a little about many different possible designs to learning a great deal about the dominant design. Once gasoline-powered cars had emerged as the technology of choice, competitive pressures in the industry strongly encouraged organizations to learn more about gasoline-fired engines. Pursuing refinements in steam- or electric-powered cars became much less attractive. The focus of active problem solving becomes the elaboration and refinement of knowledge about existing components within a framework of stable architectural knowledge (Dosi, 1982; Clark, 1985).

Since in an industry characterized by a dominant design, architectural knowledge is stable, it tends to become embedded in the practices and procedures of the organization. Several authors have noted the importance of various institutional devices like frameworks and routines in completing recurring tasks in an organization (Galbraith, 1973; Nelson and Winter, 1982; Daft and Weick, 1984). The focus in this paper, however, is on the role of communication channels, information filters, and problem-solving strategies in managing architectural knowledge.

CHANNELS, FILTERS, AND STRATEGIES An organization's communication channels, both those that are implicit in its formal organization (A reports to B) and those that are informal ('I always call Fred because he knows about X'), develop around those interactions within the organization that are critical to its task (Galbraith, 1973; Arrow, 1974). These are also the interactions that are critical to effective design. They are the relationships around which the organization builds architectural knowledge. Thus an organization's communication channels will come to embody its architectural knowledge of the linkages between components that are critical to effective design. For example, as a dominant design for room fans emerges, an effective organization in the industry will organize itself around its conception of the product's primary components, since these are the key subtasks of the organization's design problem (Mintzberg, 1979; von Hippel, 1990). The organization may create a fan-blade group, a motor group, and so on. The communication channels that are created between these groups will reflect the organization's knowledge of the critical interactions between them. The fact that those working on the motor and the fan blade report to the same supervisor and meet weekly is an embodiment of the organization's architectural knowledge about the relationship between the motor and the fan blade.

The information filters of an organization also embody its architectural knowledge. An organization is constantly barraged with information. As the task that it faces stabilizes and becomes less ambiguous, the organization develops filters that allow it to identify immediately what is most crucial in its information stream (Arrow, 1974; Daft and Weick, 1984). The emergence of a dominant design and its gradual elaboration molds the organization's filters so that they come to embody parts of its knowledge of the key relationships between the components of the technology. For instance, the relationships between the designers of motors and controllers for a room fan are likely to change over time as they are able to express the nature of the critical interaction between the motor and the controller in an increasingly precise way that allows them to ignore irrelevant information. The controller designers may discover that they need to know a great deal about the torque and power of the motor but almost nothing about the materials from which it is made. They will create information filters that reflect this knowledge.

As a product evolves, information filters and communication channels develop and help engineers to work efficiently, but the evolution of the product also means that engineers face recurring kinds of problems, Over time, engineers acquire a store of knowledge about solutions to the specific kinds of problems that have arisen in previous projects. When confronted with such a problem, the engineer does not reexamine all possible alternatives but, rather, focuses first on those that he or she has found to be helpful in solving previous problems. In effect, an organization's problem-solving strategies summarize what it has learned about fruitful ways to solve problems in its immediate environment (March and Simon, 1958; Lyles and Mitroff, 1980; Nelson and Winter, 1982). Designers may use strategies of this sort in solving problems within components, but problem-solving strategies also reflect architectural knowledge, since they are likely to express part of an organization's knowledge about the component linkages that are crucial to the solution of routine problems. An organization designing fans might learn over time that the most effective way to design a quieter fan is to focus on the interactions between the motor and the housing.

The strategies designers use, their channels for communication, and their information filters emerge in an organization to help it cope with complexity. They are efficient precisely because they do not have to be actively created each time a need for them arises. Further, as they become familiar and effective, using them becomes natural. Like riding a bicycle, using a strategy, working in a channel, or employing a filter does not require detailed analysis and conscious, deliberate execution. Thus the operation of channels, filters, and strategies may become implicit in the organization.

Since architectural knowledge is stable once a dominant design has been accepted, it can be encoded in these forms and thus becomes implicit. Organizations that are actively engaged in incremental innovation, which occurs within the context of stable architectural knowledge, are thus likely to manage much of their architectural knowledge implicitly by embedding it in their communication channels, information filters, and problem-solving strategies. Component knowledge, in contrast, is more likely to be managed explicitly because it is a constant source of incremental innovation.

## Problems created by architectural innovation

Differences in the way in which architectural and component knowledge are managed within an experienced organization give us insight into why architectural innovation often creates problems for established firms. These problems have two sources. First, established organizations require significant time (and resources) to identify a particular innovation as architectural, since architectural innovation can often initially be accommodated within old frameworks. Radical innovation tends to be obviously radical – the need for new modes of learning and new skills becomes quickly apparent. But information that might warn the organization that a particular innovation is architectural may be screened out by the information filters and communication channels that embody old architectural knowledge. Since radical innovation changes the core design concepts of the product, it is immediately obvious that knowledge about how the old components interact with each other is obsolete. The introduction of new linkages, however, is much harder to spot. Since the core concepts of the design remain untouched, the organization may mistakenly believe that it understands the new technology. In the case of the fan company, the motor and the fan-blade designers will continue to talk to each other. The fact that they may be talking about the wrong things may only become apparent after there are significant failures or unexpected problems with the design.

The development of the jet aircraft industry provides an example of the impact of unexpected architectural innovation. The jet engine initially appeared to have important but straightforward implications for airframe technology. Established firms in the industry understood that they would need to develop jet engine expertise but failed to understand the ways in which its introduction would change the interactions between the engine and the rest of the plane in complex and subtle ways (Miller and Sawyers, 1968; Gardiner, 1986). This failure was one of the factors that led to Boeing's rise to leadership in the industry.

This effect is analogous to the tendency of individuals to continue to rely on beliefs about the world that a rational evaluation of new information should lead them to discard (Kahneman, Slovic, and Tversky, 1982). Researchers have commented extensively on the ways in which organizations facing threats may continue to rely on their old frameworks – or in our terms on their old architectural knowledge – and hence misunderstand the nature of a threat. They shoehorn the bad news, or the unexpected new information, back into the patterns with which they are familiar (Lyles and Mitroff, 1980; Dutton and Jackson, 1987; Jackson and Dutton, 1988).

Once an organization has recognized the nature of an architectural innovation, it faces a second major source of problems: the need to build and to apply new architectural knowledge effectively. Simply recognizing that a new technology is architectural in character does not give an established organization the architectural knowledge that it needs. It must first switch to a new mode of learning and then invest time and resources in learning about the new architecture (Louis and Sutton, 1989). It is handicapped in its attempts to do this, both by the difficulty all organizations experience in switching from one mode of learning to another and by the fact that it must build new architectural knowledge in a context in which some of its old architectural knowledge may be relevant.

An established organization setting out to build new architectural knowledge must change its orientation from one of refinement within a stable architecture to one of active search for new solutions within a constantly changing context. As long as the dominant design remains stable, an organization can segment and specialize its knowledge and rely on standard operating procedures to design and develop products. Architectural innovation, in contrast, places a premium on exploration in design and the assimilation of new knowledge. Many organizations encounter difficulties in their attempts to make this type of transition (Argyris and Schön, 1978; Weick, 1979; Hedberg, 1981; Louis and Sutton, 1989). New entrants, with smaller commitments to older ways of learning about the environment and organizing their knowledge, often find it easier to build the organizational flexibility that abandoning old architectural knowledge and building new requires.

Once an organization has succeeded in reorientating itself, the building of new architectural knowledge still takes time and resources. This learning may be quite subtle and difficult. New entrants to the industry must also build the architectural knowledge necessary to exploit an architectural innovation, but since they have no existing assets, they can optimize their organization and information-processing structures to exploit the potential of a new design. Established firms are faced with an awkward problem. Because their architectural knowledge is embedded in channels, filters, and strategies, the discovery process and the process of creating new information (and rooting out the old) usually takes time. The organization may be tempted to modify the channels, filters, and strategies that already exist rather than to incur the significant fixed costs and considerable organizational friction required to build new sets from scratch (Arrow, 1974). But it may be difficult to identify precisely which filters, channels, and problem-solving strategies need to be modified, and the attempt to build a new product with old (albeit modified) organizational tools can create significant problems.

The problems created by an architectural innovation are evident in the introduction of high-strength-low-alloy (HSLA) steel in automobile bodies in the 1970s. The new materials allowed body panels to be thinner and lighter but opened up a whole new set of interactions that were not contained in existing channels and strategies. One automaker's body-engineering group, using traditional methods, designed an HSLA hood for the engine compartment. The hoods, however, resonated and oscillated with engine vibrations during testing. On further investigation, it became apparent that the traditional methods for designing hoods worked just fine with traditional materials, although no one knew quite why. The knowledge embedded in established problem-solving strategies and communication channels was sufficient to achieve effective designs with established materials, but the new material created new interactions and required the engineers to build new knowledge about them.

Architectural innovation may thus have very significant competitive implications. Established organizations may invest heavily in the new innovation, interpreting it as an incremental extension of the existing technology or under-estimating its impact on their embedded architectural knowledge. But new entrants to the industry may exploit its potential much more effectively, since they are not handicapped by a legacy of embedded and partially irrelevant architectural knowledge.

[. . .]

# Conclusions

[. . .]

The ideas developed here could also be linked to those of authors such as Abernathy and Clark (1985), who have drawn a distinction between innovation that challenges the technical capabilities of an organization and innovation that challenges the organization's knowledge of the market and of customer needs. Research could also examine the extent to which these insights are applicable to problems of process innovation and process development. [. . .]

The concept of architectural innovation and the related concepts of component and architectural knowledge have a number of important implications. These ideas not only give us a richer characterization of different types of inno-vation, but they open up new areas in understanding the connections between innovation and organizational capability. The paper suggests, for example, that we need to deepen our understanding of the traditional distinction between innovation that enhances and innovation that destroys competence within the firm, since the essence of architectural innovation is that it both enhances and destroys competence, often in subtle ways.

An architectural innovation's effect depends in a direct way on the nature of organizational learning. This paper not only underscores the role of organizational learning in innovation but suggests a new perspective on the problem. Given the evolutionary character of development and the prevalence of dominant designs, there appears to be a tendency for active learning among engineers to focus on improvements in performance within a stable product architecture. In this context, learning means learning about components and the core concepts that underlie them. Given the way knowledge tends to be organized within the firm, learning about changes in the architecture of the product is unlikely to occur naturally.

Learning about changes in architecture – about new interactions across components (and often across functional boundaries) – may therefore require explicit management and attention. But it may also be that learning about new architectures requires a different kind of organization and people with different skills. An organization that is structured to learn quickly and effectively about new component technology may be ineffective in learning about changes in product architecture. What drives effective learning about new architectures and how learning about components may be related to it are issues worth much further research.

These ideas also provide an intriguing perspective from which to understand the current fashion for cross-functional teams and more open organizational environments. These mechanisms may be responses to a perception of the danger of allowing architectural knowledge to become embedded with tacit or informal linkages.

To the degree that other tasks performed by organizations can also be described as a series of interlinked components within a relatively stable framework, the idea of architectural innovation yields insights into problems that reach beyond product development and design. To the degree that manufacturing, marketing, and finance rely on communication channels, information filters, and problem-solving strategies to integrate their work together, architectural innovation at the firm level may also be a significant issue.

Finally, an understanding of architectural innovation would be useful to discussions of the effect of technology on competitive strategy. Since architectural innovation has the potential to offer firms the opportunity to gain significant advantage over well-entrenched, dominant firms, we might expect less-entrenched competitor firms to search actively for opportunities to introduce changes in product architecture in an industry. The evidence developed here and in other studies suggests that architectural innovation is quite prevalent. As an interpretive lens, architectural innovation may therefore prove quite useful in understanding technically based rivalry in a variety of industries.

## Notes

We include here only the theoretical basis of the argument included in the original article. Although it provides an excellent illustration of the argument, we have omitted the empirical study, carried out by the authors, on the semiconductor photolithographic alignment equipment industry.

1   In earlier drafts of this paper we referred to this type of innovation as 'generational'. We are indebted to Professor Michael Tushman for his suggestion of the term 'architectural'.
2   We are indebted to one of the anonymous *ASO* reviewers for the suggestion that we use this matrix.
3   For simplicity, we will assume here that organizations can be assumed to act as boundedly rational entities, in the tradition of Arrow (1974) and Nelson and Winter (1982).

# References

Abernathy, William J. 1978 The Productivity Dilemma: Roadblock to Innovation in the Automobile Industry. Baltimore: Johns Hopkins University Press.

Abernathy, William J., and Kim Clark 1985 'Innovation: Mapping the winds of creative-destruction'. Research Policy, 14: 3–22.

Abernathy, William J., and James Utterback 1978 'Patterns of industrial innovation'. Technology Review, June–July: 40–47.

Alexander, Christopher 1964 Notes on the Synthesis of Form. Cambridge, MA: Harvard University Press.

Argyris, Chris, and Donald Schön 1978 Organizational Learning. Reading, MA: Addison-Wesley.

Arrow, Kenneth 1974. The Limits of Organization, New York: Norton.

Arthur, Brian 1988 'Competing technologies: An overview'. In Giovanni Dosi et al. (eds.), Technical Change and Economic Theory: 590–607. New York: Columbia University Press.

Burns, Tom and George Stalker 1966 The Management of Innovation. London: Tavistock.

Clark, Kim B. 1985 'The interaction of design hierarchies and market concepts in technological evolution'. Research Policy, 14: 235–251.

Clark, Kim B. 1987 'Managing technology in international competition: The case of product development in response to foreign entry'. In Michael Spence and Heather Hazard (eds.), International Competitiveness: 27–74. Cambridge, MA: Ballinger.

Cooper, Arnold C., and Dan Schendel 1976 'Strategic response to technological threats'. Business Horizons, 19: 61–69.

Cyert, Richard M., and James G. March 1963 A Behavioural Theory of the Firm. Englewood Cliffs, NJ: Prentice-Hall.

Daft, Richard L. 1982 'Bureaucratic versus nonbureaucratic structure and the process of innovation and change'. In Samuel B. Bacharach (ed.), Research in the Sociology of Organizations, 1: 129–166. Greenwich, CT: JAI Press.

Daft, Richard L., and Karl E. Weick 1984 'Towards a model of organizations as interpretation systems'. Academy of Management Review, 9: 284–295.

David, Paul A. 1985 'Clio and the economics of QWERTY'. American Economic Review, 75: 332–337.

Dosi, Giovanni 1982 'Technological paradigms and technological trajectories: A suggested interpretation of the determinants and directions of technical change'. Research Policy, 11: 147–162.

Dutton, Jane E., and Susan E. Jackson 1987 'Categorizing strategic issues: Links to organizational action'. Academy of Management Review, 12: 76–90.

Ettlie, John E., William P. Bridges, and Robert D. O'Keefe 1984 'Organizational strategy and structural differences for radical vs. incremental innovation'. Management Science, 30: 682–695.

Freeman, Christopher 1982 The Economics of Industrial Innovation, 2nd edn. Cambridge MA: MIT Press.

Galbraith, Jay 1973 Designing Complex Organizations. Reading, MA: Addison-Wesley.

Gardiner, J. P. 1986 'Design trajectories for airplanes and automobiles during the past fifty years'. In Christopher Freeman (ed.), Design Innovation and Long Cycles in Economic Development: 121–141. London: Francis Pinter.

Hage, Jerald 1980 Theories of Organization. New York: Wiley Interscience.

Hannan, Michael T., and John Freeman 1984 'Structural inertia and organizational change'. American Sociological Review, 49: 149–164.

Hedberg, Bo L. T. 1981 'How organizations learn and unlearn'. In P. C. Nystrom and W. H. Starbuck (eds.), Handbook of Organizational Design, 1: 3–27. New York: Oxford University Press.

Jackson, Susan E., and Jane E. Dutton 1988 'Discerning threats and opportunities'. Administrative Science Quarterly, 33: 370–387.

Kahneman, David, Paul Slovic, and Amos Tversky 1982 Judgment under Uncertainty: Heuristics and Biases. Cambridge: Cambridge University Press.

Lawrence, Paul R., and Jay W. Lorsch 1967 Organization and Environment: Managing Differentiation and Integration. Homewood, IL: Irwin.

Louis, Meryl R., and Robert I. Sutton 1989 'Switching cognitive gears: From habits of mind to active thinking'. Working Paper, School of Industrial Engineering, Stanford University.

Lyles, Majorie A., and Ian I. Mitroff 1980 'Organizational problem formulation: An empirical study'. Administrative Science Quarterly, 25: 102–119.

Mansfield, Edwin 1968 Industrial Research and Technical Innovation. New York: Norton.

Mansfield, Edwin 1977 The Production and Application of New Industrial Technology. New York: Norton.

March, James G., and Herbert A. Simon 1958 Organizations. New York: Wiley.

Marples, David L. 1961 'The decisions of engineering design'. IEEE Transactions on Engineering Management, EM.8 (June): 55–71.

Miller, Ronald, and David Sawyers 1968 The Technical Development of Modern Aviation. New York: Praeger.

Mintzberg, Henry 1979 The Structuring of Organizations. Englewood Cliffs, NJ: Prentice-Hall.

Moch, Michael, and Edward V. Morse 1977 'Size, centralization and organizational adoption of innovations'. American Sociological Review, 42: 716–725.

Nelson, Richard, and Sidney Winter 1982 An Evolutionary Theory of Economic Change. Cambridge, MA: Harvard University Press.

Rosenberg, Nathan 1982 Inside the Black Box: Technology and Economics. Cambridge: Cambridge University Press.

Sahal, Devendra 1986 'Technological guideposts and innovation avenues'. Research Policy, 14: 61–82.

Schumpeter, Joseph A. 1942 Capitalism, Socialism and Democracy. Cambridge: MA: Harvard University Press.

Tushman, Michael L., and Philip Anderson 1986 'Technological discontinuities and organizational environments'. Administrative Quarterly, 31: 439–465.

von Hippel, Eric 1990 'Task partitioning: An innovation process variable'. Research Policy (in press).

Weick, Karl E. 1979 'Cognitive processes in organizations'. In B. M. Staw and L. L. Cummings (eds.), Research in Organizational Behavior, 1: 41–47. Greenwich, CT: JAI Press.

# CHAPTER 12

# Strategic Innovation in Established Companies

CONSTANTINOS MARKIDES*

[. . .]

In May 1959, when Harry Cunningham became president of Kresge, the variety store chain (originally founded in 1897) was second only to Woolworth. In the next few years, Cunningham transformed Kresge (with 803 stores in operation) into the largest discount store in the United States and renamed it Kmart. The decision was a particularly difficult one because, as Cunningham explained, 'Discounting at the time had a terrible odor . . . If I had announced my intentions ahead of time, I never would have made president.'[1] Yet the move into discounting rejuvenated the company, and by 1976, Kmart had almost twice the sales volume of Woolworth and was only second behind Sears in general merchandise retailers.

From 1984 to 1985, Intel decided to exit from the dynamic random access memory (DRAM) business and wholly embrace microchips based on the x86CISC architecture. The decision completed the company's transformation from a memory company into a microprocessor company – a move so radical that a mid-level manager commented: 'It was kind of like Ford getting out of cars.'[2] The move put Intel on an exponential growth curve; in 1996, the company announced record profits of $5.2 billion on sales of $20.8 billion.

In 1989, when Denis Cassidy took over as chairman of the Boddington Group PLC, the company was a vertically integrated beer producer that owned a brewery, wholesalers, and pubs throughout the United Kingdom. In the next two years, Cassidy set about transforming the company into a 'hospitality' organization. He sold the brewery and diversified into restaurants, homes for the elderly, and hotels, while keeping the portfolio of large managed pubs. 'The decision to sell the brewery was a painful one, especially since the brewery has been part of us for more than 200 years,' Cassidy explained. But the move resulted in the creation of

* Massachusetts Institute of Technology for 'Strategic Innovation in Established Companies' by Costantinos Markides, *MIT Sloan Management Review*, Spring 1998. Copyright © 1998 by Massachusetts Institute of Technology. All rights reserved.

enormous shareholder value, especially when compared with the strategies of other regional brewers in the United Kingdom.

In 1989, Peter Schou, CEO of a small Danish bank called Lan & Spar, set about transforming the bank from a general-purpose, traditional savings bank into a focused, low-cost direct bank. The bank targeted professional retail customers and encouraged them to do their banking via phone, fax, and mail. Within three years, its market share had tripled. By 1997, the direct bank had evolved into the world's first on-line, real-time PC bank and was also trying an Internet-based version. These changes have helped Lan & Spar move from forty-second in Denmark to tenth, and the bank is consistently ranked first or second in profitability every year.

These stories are more than successful examples of corporate turnarounds (such as Harley-Davidson). They are more than inspired stories of dramatic improvements in the existing business (like IBM). And they are more than successful internal venturing decisions (à la mobile phones at Ericsson) or successful attempts to add another business to the existing product portfolio (like HP moving into digital photography). These are all examples of what I call strategic innovation: a fundamental reconceptualization of what the business is all about that, in turn, leads to a dramatically different way of playing the game in an existing business.

Strategic innovation is difficult to achieve, evidenced by the fact that only a small number of firms (for example, Dell Computers, CNN, IKEA, the Body Shop, First Direct, MTV, Southwest Airlines, Canon, and USA Today) can claim to be successful strategic innovators. What is even more interesting, however, is that within this select group of companies lies an even smaller and more select subset of companies: strategic innovators who are also established industry leaders. All evidence suggests that most strategic innovations come from outsiders, rarely from established players. In this article, I use successful strategic innovations by established companies – such as the four stories above – to explain how long-time industry players can overcome the obstacles and improve their chances of becoming strategic innovators.

While I explore how an established company can achieve strategic innovation, whether the company should pursue and implement the innovation is another matter. This is a separate decision that requires its own thought process. To clarify this point, suppose that, like IBM or American Airlines, you are an established industry player with a substantial market share position. This means that you have already taken a position in your industry and are making a lot of money. Now, suppose that a new position emerges, created by players such as Dell Computer or Southwest Airlines. Should you abandon your current position for the new one? Alternatively, can you occupy both positions simultaneously?

The answers to these questions are not easy. For example, should American Airlines abandon the hub-and-spoke system to adopt Southwest Airlines' direct system? Alternatively, can it possibly play both games simultaneously?[3] Similarly, should IBM give up its extensive distribution channels of dealers and direct salespeople to move into the mail-order business like Dell Computers? Alternatively, can it join the mail-order game while simultaneously playing its current game through its dealers? Won't this damage its relationships with the dealers.[4] Should Barclays Bank shut down its extensive branch network to follow Midlands Bank into telephone banking? Alternatively, can it organize itself to play both games efficiently? My purpose here is not to explore these questions.[5] Rather, I take the position of an established firm that wants to discover a new strategic position (that is, strategically innovate) and ask the question: how can this firm identify a new strategic position?

## Overcoming obstacles

In any industry, companies have to take a position on three strategic issues: who is going to be the customer? What products or services should we offer to the chosen customer? How can we offer these products or services in a cost-efficient way?[6] The answers to the 'who–what–how' questions form the backbone of any company's strategy. In fact, some will argue that they are the strategy of a company.[7] Over time, different companies make different choices on these three dimensions, and before long, the industry gets 'filled' – that is, most possible customer segments are taken care of, most products and services are being offered in one form or another, and most possible distribution or manufacturing methods or technologies are being utilized. In fact, this filling up of the industry space by enough competitors eventually leads to industry maturity.

As I explained in an earlier *SMR* article, strategic innovation takes place when a company identifies gaps in industry positioning, goes after them, and the gaps grow to become the new mass market.[8] By gaps, I mean: (1) new customer segments emerging, or customer segments that existing competitors neglect; (2) new customer needs emerging, or existing customer needs that existing competitors do not serve well; and (3) new ways of producing, delivering, or distributing existing (or new) products or services to existing (or new) customer segments. These gaps tend to emerge for various reasons, such as changing consumer tastes and preferences, changing technologies, changing government policies, and so on. The gaps can be created by external changes or proactively by the company itself.

The majority of companies that strategically innovate by identifying and exploiting new who–what–how positions in the business tend to be entrepreneurial start-ups (for example, the Body Shop, CNN, Dell Computers, or IKEA) or new market entrants (for example, Canon or National Bank of Scotland). It is rare to find a strategic innovator that is also an established industry big player – a fact that hints at the difficulties of risking a sure thing for uncertainty.

The generic issue of innovation (not only strategic) by established companies is the subject of numerous studies.[9] Compared to new entrants or niche players, established companies find it hard to innovate because of structural and cultural inertia, internal politics, complacency, fear of cannibalizing existing products, fear of destroying existing competencies, satisfaction with the status quo, and a general lack of incentive to abandon a certain present (which is profitable) for an uncertain future.

In addition, since there are fewer industry leaders than potential new entrants, the chance that the innovator will emerge from the ranks of industry leaders is small.

Given all these barriers to innovation, it is understandable why there are not more strategic innovators emerging from the ranks of established players. Yet Intel, Kresge, and Boddington were all established industry players that conceptualized their businesses in an entirely different way and thus started playing the game in a totally different way.[10]

What we can learn from these firms is how established companies overcome obstacles to innovation. In general, established players face four types of obstacles:

1  I am having a good time in my little part of the world and making good money. Why should I change?

2  Even if I recognize the need to change (and, in particular, to change my strategy or who–what–how position), what shall I change into?

3  Even when I see a possible new position emerging, how do I know that it's going to be a winner? What if I jump into it and it turns out to be a mistake?

4  Even if I decide to jump, how do I make sure that my employees (who have vested interests in maintaining the status quo) jump with me? Can I manage two industry positions simultaneously or do I have to relinquish the old for the new? And if I can have both positions, how do I organize to manage the old and the new simultaneously?

Based on my research on strategic innovation by established industry players, I explore some tactics for overcoming the four obstacles to innovation.

# How to overcome the inertia of success

You will never discover new lands if you don't venture outside the safety of the harbor. Similarly, you will never discover new ways of playing the game if you don't question the way you currently play. A prerequisite for strategic innovation is a fundamental questioning of the way we do business today. It means actively thinking about the business and perhaps mentally experimenting with a few 'whys' and 'what ifs'. This is difficult for any company to do but it is almost impossible for a successful one.

Successful companies 'know' that the way they play the game is the right way. After all, they have all those profits to prove it. Not only do they find it difficult to question their way of doing business, but their natural reaction is to dismiss alternative ways even when they see competitors trying something new. For example, it took Xerox at least twenty years to recognize Canon as a serious threat and respond. It took Caterpillar even longer to face up to Komatsu.

Unfortunately, advising companies to question their way of playing the game and think of alternative ways, especially when they are successful, is fruitless. They simply do not do it, even though they know and agree with the principle. It's like advising people that they should not wait to get sick before visiting a doctor, but that they should do so every few months. Although most human beings agree with these sentiments, few actually do it. The same is true with companies: even though few managers disagree with the need to fundamentally question the way they do business before a crisis strikes, few do it.

Suppose your company goes through the experience depicted in Figure 12.1: a history of growth and profitability and then a sudden change of fortune and a financial crisis at point B. Given this scenario, when are you most likely to seriously question the way you operate? If you are at all typical of the majority of companies, you would probably start thinking about change around point B, and then start doing something about it after things get even worse, right in the middle of the crisis. Why change when everything seems to be going so well and the company is enjoying record profits?

Needless to say, trying to change in the middle of a crisis is the worst time to do so. It is much better to think about the business in a proactive, long-term way when times are good, probably at point A. Established companies that want to strategically innovate must take the time to question the way they do business, especially when they are successful. They should not wait for a crisis to start contemplating the future.

The ideal scenario is the pattern in Figure 12.2: well before the company gets into trouble, it actively rejuvenates itself at point X, which allows it to embark on another growth curve. Just when the new growth curve is about to taper off, the company rejuvenates itself again at point Y, once again embarking on another growth curve, and so on.[11] (As I point out later, an organization can identify where it is on the curve – and decide whether the moment for rejuvenation has arrived – by monitoring not only its financial health but also its strategic health; and it can successfully rejuvenate itself by creating internal 'positive crises', that is, by creating challenges that have been 'sold' to the rest of the organization.) Although

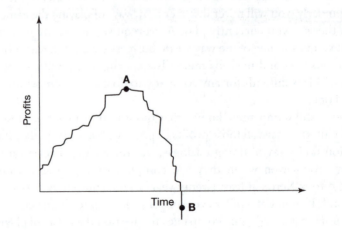

**Figure 12.1** *Financial versus strategic health*

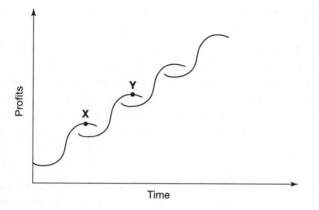

**Figure 12.2** *Rejuvenating the organization*

this scenario looks utopian, there are companies that have gone through such an evolution. Hewlett-Packard made rejuvenating transitions in moving from instruments to computers, from minicomputer-based technology to micro-processor-based technology, and finally, from computers to desktop publishing. Motorola went from consumer electronics to semiconductors and now tele-communications. Johnson & Johnson has moved from consumer products to pharmaceuticals. 3M has changed business at least three times so far – from mining to sandpaper to tapes and so on. Microsoft is attempting such a transition by moving into an Internet-based world, and General Electric is trying to move heavily into services and out of manufacturing.[12]

Unfortunately, such examples are rare. Most companies do not question their way of doing business until a crisis hits them. How did the strategic innovators succeed in overcoming the inertia of success and fundamentally question their way of doing business? I identified two interrelated approaches:

- They monitored not only their financial health but also their strategic health for early warning signals before the crisis came.

- They artificially created a positive crisis to galvanize the organization into active thinking. More importantly, because the positive crisis they created usually took the form of a new challenge for the organi-zation, they took the time to sell the challenge to all employees.

## Monitoring strategic health

Strategic health refers to a company's future health that could be different from today (as measured by its financial health). Many companies appear to be very profitable (for example, IBM in 1990), only to discover two to three years later that they are facing a crisis. Conversely, many companies that appear today to be in financial difficulties (for example, IBM in 1994) are really ready to embark on a period of growth and profitability.

This implies that there is often a difference between a company's financial and strategic health, and that financial health may not be a good predictor of the future. This, in turn, implies that a company needs to monitor not only its financial health but also its strategic health. The company must find measures or indicators that are like early warning systems. Two to three years before a crisis, they indicate that something is not going well and the company needs to make a correction.[13]

Consider, again, the case of Boddington. In 1989, Denis Cassidy's decision to sell the brewery was not very well received by several board members who were part of Boddington's founding family. One family member remarked: 'The brewery has been part of our company since our founding in 1774; you cannot sell it!' The strategic reorientation went ahead anyway (not without casualties), and all measures suggest that it was a great success. Why did Cassidy undertake such a dramatic change in the first place? After all, the company was financially doing quite well at the time. He rationalized his decision:

> At the time I took over, the company was still profitable. So, if you only looked at the numbers, there was nothing to worry about. However, when you looked at our business over time, you could tell that something fundamental was happening. For example, consumption of traditional English ale (the traditional lukewarm English 'beer' and Boddington's mainstream product) went from 85 percent of the population in 1950 to less than 45 percent in 1988. What took its place? Imported beer which could be drunk cold. It's as if the consumer was telling us that our product was not wanted any more. Making the situation even more serious was the fact that the Mergers and Monopolies Commission (MMC) was about to announce its decision on the brewing industry. We all expected that the decision would require big brewers to unbundle their vertical integration by divesting their captive pub operations. These fundamental changes in the industry required action, even though we were still quite profitable.

The Boddington story highlights two emerging points in all the cases of strategic innovators that I examined. First, this particular manager decided to strategically innovate, even though his company was financially healthy. What motivated him to act was the state of the company's strategic health. He worried that financial problems might surface in the future. What allowed him to 'see' the future were several indicators of strategic health: customer dissatisfaction, structural change in the industry, and deregulation. Additional indicators of strategic health that other strategic innovators used include trends over time in the financial health of the company, employee morale, innovation and new products in the pipeline, customer satisfaction as well as distributor and supplier feedback, changes in the industry and the company's fit with the new environment, and the company's financial health relative to its best competitors.

Second, it is one thing to get an early warning that trouble is brewing and another thing to decide what to do about it and then do it. This is where strong leadership comes in: being able to see a different future and having the courage to abandon the status quo for something uncertain.

# Creating positive crises

A second tactic the strategic innovators used to overcome the organization's natural inertia of success was to convince all employees that the current performance was good but not good enough. They achieved this not by denying how well the organization was currently doing but by developing a new challenge that made the current performance appear inadequate. Their purpose was to galvanize everybody into active thinking – to question how they worked, what they did, and what they had to do differently to respond to the new challenge. In a sense, the CEO created a positive crisis by saying: 'I know we are doing quite well, but our goal now is not to just do well but to aim for the moon. Can we achieve that?'

The notion of creating a stretching goal is not new.[14] However, the key word is 'convince': what distinguished the successful strategic innovators is the time and effort that went into selling the new challenge to everybody. People started thinking actively and started questioning the status quo only after they 'bought' the new challenge. How did the successful innovators succeed in selling the challenge to so many people?

The selling process consists of three steps. First, the company must communicate and explain its objective so that there comes a point when everybody says, 'I know what we are trying to achieve and I understand why.' People cannot get excited about anything unless they first know what it is that the company is aiming to achieve and why.

Second, the company should make the objective realistic and achievable so that people say, 'Yes, I think we can achieve this objective.' This is more difficult than it sounds. Usually, ambitious and stretching goals and objectives are needed to generate excitement. Yet these are exactly the goals that tend to generate disbelief and dismissal as unrealistic and unachievable. Somehow, these ambitious goals need to become believable to employees. A few early victories (manufactured, if necessary) can help a lot in generating belief.

Third, people must move from rational acceptance of an objective to emotional commitment. At the end of this magical jump, people should be saying: 'Yes, I know what the objective is, I understand why we are aiming for such an objective, I believe we can achieve it, and I am personally committed to it.' This jump is extremely difficult to accomplish, and various tactics are needed to pull it off, among them:

- Make people feel part of an elite group that is difficult for others to enter. Reinforce the team feeling through symbols and rituals.

- Create a credible enemy for the team.

- Create positive and negative incentives to promote the chosen objective.

- Allow people to develop the objective themselves and empower them to carry it out. Lead by example.

- Keep communicating and reminding people of the objective.

# Change into what?

The second obstacle facing established companies is that, even when they know that their current profitability will not last and they see the need to change, they don't always see what to change into. This is a problem that every company, not just established players, faces. Therefore, the five generic steps to identifying strategic positioning gaps that I described in my previous article are applicable here: an established company must continuously question the answers it has given to the who–what–how questions and must question the definition of its business.[15] Here, I highlight two specific tactics that established companies in particular can use to achieve innovation in their strategic thinking and planning: (1) challenge the accepted strategic planning process, and (2) institutionalize a questioning attitude.

## *Challenge the strategic planning process*

Companies that are able and willing to start their thinking at different starting points are more likely to escape existing assumptions and stereotypes and to see or discover something new. Therefore, established players that have adopted a certain strategic planning process must find a way to go through the process from many different possible angles.

In practice, established companies are constantly preoccupied with how they need to compete in their business without ever questioning the who and the what. They spend all their time finding ways to improve their operations (such as reengineering the business or restructuring the operations) and not enough time questioning who their customers are and what they really want. New or small companies start with a clean slate and are therefore more likely to see new customer segments or new customer needs emerging. Only by shifting some of their emphasis away from the how and more toward the who and the what can established companies succeed in discovering new customers and new products or services.

To identify strategic positioning gaps, thinking through the 'who–what–how' questions in different order may prove to be particularly useful. For example:

1  A company can define first which customers it will target (who), determine what these customers want (what), and then decide how to satisfy these needs (how).

2  Alternatively, it can start by deciding what products or services it will offer (what) and, based on that, decide who will want to buy these products (who) and how it will produce and deliver them (how).

3  In another approach, the company can start with its existing core competencies (how) and, based on those, decide what products and services to offer (what) and to whom (who).

There is no right or wrong way. However, every company has a dominant way of thinking. An established company able to abandon that and experiment by starting its thinking at different places has a better chance of finding something new and innovative. Any attempt to create strategy must force managers to use as many approaches as possible.

## Institutionalize a questioning attitude

The second tactic for discovering new strategic positions is to create an innovative culture. The underlying logic for this tactic is that what creates behavior in organizations is the underlying 'context' or 'environment' of that organization. By environment, I mean four things: the firm's culture, its incentives, its structure, and its people. If people are to be more innovative, the environment must promote innovation. A company that wants to create a questioning attitude in its people must first ask: 'What kind of culture, incentives, structure, and people do we need to create this behavior?'[16]

Successful strategic innovators have done exactly this. They have designed the appropriate environment that encourages and promotes a questioning attitude. As a result, continuous questioning of the status quo and continuous experimentation just happen.

What kind of environment promotes this kind of behavior? At Lan & Spar Bank in Denmark, the CEO knows the name and background of all 250 employees and spends more than 50 percent of his time mixing and talking with them. He acts quickly on new ideas from employees and gives small gifts or monetary rewards to some. 3M Company expects employees to spend 15 percent of their time on unauthorized projects. If a project reaches the new venture stage, it is spun off as a separate division, with the entrepreneur as divisional president. MCI encourages people to take calculated risks, and top management fosters a culture that questions everything. As a result, whereas in most companies people are afraid to make mistakes, at MCI, people are afraid of not making mistakes! At the Body Shop, every employee has access to the DODGI (Department of Damn Good Ideas) and can discuss ideas with senior managers.

These are only a few examples of tactics that promote innovation. An enormous amount of literature exists to help managers institutionalize innovation in their companies.[17] However, if so much is known about creating an innovative organization, why is strategic innovation by established firms the exception rather than the rule? The main reason for this is that even though many companies know how to achieve innovation, very few actually do it, primarily because top management has no incentive to change the status quo. What, then, differentiated the successful strategic innovators in this study from the rest? Strategic innovators not only institutionalized a questioning attitude (through a variety of tactics), but, no matter how successful they had been, they always found ways to shake up the system every few years.

What these innovators seem to know is that it doesn't matter how actively you question your way of doing things or how much you encourage this kind of behavior in the organization. Eventually, the system will reach blissful stability, characterized by contentment, satisfaction with success, managerial overconfidence or even arrogance, strong but monolithic culture, strong institutional memory that allows the company to operate on automatic pilot, and strong internal political coalitions. Inevitably, success will breed unyielding mental models that, in turn, produce passive thinking. These things will happen no matter how successful you have been in institutionalizing a questioning attitude. This implies that every few years, something must stir things up again and destabilize the system all over again.

The successful innovators were not afraid to destabilize a smooth-running machine and to do so periodically but continuously. How did they do it? The development of positive crises, especially challenges sold to the rest of the organization, is a powerful mechanism to destabilize the system and start the thinking process again. Equally powerful is the arrival of new blood at the top, a new leader unconstrained by the past and ready to challenge the status quo. In most of the examples of strategic innovation at established companies, the innovation occurred with the arrival of a new CEO, such as Walter Haas at Levi's, Denis Cassidy at Boddington's, Harry Cunningham at Kmart, Peter Schou at Lan & Spar Bank, Jack Welch at GE, Colin Marshall at British Airways, and Lou Gerstner at IBM. Even Intel's decision to exit the DRAMs memory business was made after Andrew Grove asked CEO Gordon Moore to consider what new management would do if he and Moore were replaced.[18]

This point has serious implications. The current CEO may find it extremely difficult to break away from the past and transform the company. But even if a new CEO succeeds in transforming a company once, what is the chance that the same CEO will be able to do it again in a few years? What is the chance that an Andrew Grove or a Jack Welch or a Bill Gates will be able to transform their companies two or three times in their lifetime? It takes a great leader indeed to fundamentally question his or her mental models continuously and escape the trappings of success more than once. If that is the case, CEOs need to develop the ability to move on so that new blood can take their place. Alternatively, companies must be willing to remove their leaders (especially if they are very successful) to an advisory role, so they can still have the successful CEO's knowledge and experience while receiving an infusion of new blood at the same time.

## Will it be a winner?

The third obstacle facing established companies is the uncertainty surrounding new strategic positions. At any given time, a company does not know which of its many bright ideas will succeed; nor does it know which core competencies will be essential for the future.

How do successful strategic innovators decide which core competencies they should build and which new ideas they should place bets on? How do they know if the strategic position they have just come up with or the numerous positions they see other companies creating will be winners? If you are Revlon, how do you know that the Body Shop's idea for environmentally friendly cosmetics will catch on? If you are IBM, how do you know that Dell's idea of selling personal computers direct to individuals will succeed? If you are Perdue, how do you know that consumers will accept your idea of differentiating chickens?

The simple answer to this question is that you don't know. A company should be willing to experiment with new ideas and see if they work out. But, should a company place bets on anything and everything that moves? To answer these questions, consider why the capitalist system won over the socialist system.[19] In the socialist system, somebody tries to decide beforehand what is a good idea and then allocate resources accordingly. In the capitalist system, on the other hand, no central coordinating mechanism exists. Nobody tries to outsmart the market. Instead, multiple bets (i.e. initiatives) are made, and through some selection process (which is not necessarily efficient), winners and losers emerge. The capitalist system is certainly wasteful, but it is the best engine of progress so far designed.

What characterizes successful strategic innovators is their ability to incorporate the essential features of the capitalist system into their organizations. They have purposefully created internal variety (even at the expense of efficiency) and then allowed the outside market to decide the winners and losers. Thus, within many strategic innovators is the harmonious coexistence of often conflicting features (i.e. variety) that are continuously tested in the market and, if found wanting, are eliminated without too much debate.

The Leclerc organization in France illustrates vividly how successful strategic innovators create the necessary internal variety and then let the market decide what wins and what loses. At any given time, 1,000 experiments are taking place within Leclerc, all within certain accepted parameters, all at the initiative of an individual. Nobody really knows which will succeed. But from this experimentation, winners do emerge: the practices and products that consumers choose as winners. The winners are quickly picked by the rest of the organization and inevitably become part of the day-to-day business.[20]

[. . .]

## How to organize?

The final obstacle for any strategic innovator is the implementation of a new idea. Established firms face two unique challenges:

1 Because the strategic innovation will compete with the established
   business for managerial attention and resources, the managers of an
   established firm must convince everyone of the need and usefulness
   of the new idea if it is to have any chance of success.

2 Because the strategic innovation will be different from the status quo, it needs its own institutional support. The organization cannot simply export its current strategy, culture, systems, and processes into the strategic innovation. A completely new setup is required, which raises the issue of harmonious coexistence of the old and the new.[21]

For example, consumer goods companies such as Unilever and Procter & Gamble face the threat of generic, unbranded products entering their markets. Major supermarkets offer their own brands of products ranging from colas to soaps and detergents. These distributor-owned brands have made significant inroads in most European countries and the United States and account for 20 percent to 50 percent market share. Their success is based on their recipe of good quality at low prices.

The challenge facing companies like Unilever and P&G is whether to offer their own generic products along with their more well-known brands. However, even if they do decide to get into this business, another challenge awaits them: Unilever's or P&G's organizational setup is now geared toward innovation and the development of branded products. This setup requires a certain organizational culture, structure, incentives, systems, and processes, all of which support a differentiation strategy. On the other hand, generic products compete on price and require a lowcost strategy, which needs a totally different setup.

How can Unilever or P&G develop a setup that supports the differentiation and low-cost strategies at the same time? This is a situation that established firms contemplating a new strategic position face: how to make the new strategic position coexist harmoniously with their existing business. At the same time, they have to worry about a second challenge: how to manage the transition from the old to the new.

Strategic innovators usually respond to the first challenge by setting up a separate organizational unit to support the new strategic innovation. For example, Midlands Bank established its banking unit, First Direct, as a totally different subsidiary. Similarly, Direct Insurance is a separate unit within the Royal Bank of Scotland.

Even though this solution is quite efficient, it is not without problems.[22] Once a company sets up a separate unit, the challenge is how to integrate the two so that they work together. What distinguishes successful innovators is not that they ask or even demand integration. Rather, they create a context that encourages and supports integration.

What kind of context or environment promotes integration? At Leclerc, the strong family culture and the founder's motivating vision both act as the glue that holds everything together. Lan & Spar Bank regularly uses team-based incentives and rewards while letting information flow quickly and uninterrupted. Unilever often transfers managers across subsidiaries and national boundaries. 3M uses cross-functional teams and shares information at regular company conferences. At Bank One, business integrators travel from one branch to another exchanging ideas and best practice.

There is an almost unlimited number of tactics and practices that an organization can use to achieve integration.[23] The problem usually is not lack of tactics or ideas; it is lack of will to put the tactics into practice.

The second challenge facing strategic innovators is far more difficult – how to manage the transition from the old to the new. When questioned about why his bank was not moving into direct banking, the CEO of a British bank replied: 'I see that direct banking is the future. But what do you want me to do, shut down 1,000 branches and fire 20,000 people overnight?' His solution is to move from the old to the new slowly: let the two systems coexist but, over time, allocate resources to the new so that it grows at the expense of the old. This minimizes the trauma of change but has its own weaknesses in that it allows the supporters of the status quo – or the managers whose interests lie with the status quo – to sabotage the transition. The solution is strong leadership from the top.

# Conclusion

When it comes to strategic innovation, the big challenge for small firms or new entrants is coming up with new strategic ideas. On the other hand, the big challenge for established companies is organizational: they need to develop the culture, mind-set, and underlying environment to continually question current success while promoting continual experimentation. Underpinning all the successful strategic innovators examined was a specific mind-set that encouraged dissatisfaction with the status quo and demanded ongoing soul searching. Ultimately, those companies that strive for self-renewal will succeed in the long term.

# Notes

1   'K Mart Has to Open Some New Doors on the Future', Fortune, 1977, p. 144.
2   R.A. Burgelman and A.S. Grove, 'Strategic Dissonance', California Management Review, volume 38, Winter 1996, pp. 8–28 (quote from p. 15).
3   The answer, according to Michael Porter, is no. He describes how Continental Airlines tried to play both games by maintaining its position as a full service airline while creating a new service dubbed Continental Lite to imitate the strategy of Southwest. This venture failed, suggesting that 'positioning trade-offs deter straddling or repositioning, because competitors that engage in those approaches undermine their strategies and degrade the value of their existing activities.' See: M. Porter, 'What Is Strategy?', Harvard Business Review, volume 74, November–December 1996, pp. 61–78 (quote from p. 69).
4   Earlier attempts by IBM to play both games simultaneously (through a direct-sales operation called Ambra) had failed. For a fascinating discussion on how IBM, Compaq, and HP are now trying to imitate Dell's position (without

abandoning their current position), see: D. Kirkpatrick, 'Now Everyone in PCs Wants to Be Like Mike', Fortune, 8 September 1997, pp. 47–48.

5   See C. Markides, Crafting Strategy: A Journey into the Mind of the Strategist (Boston: Harvard Business School Press, forthcoming).

6   See D. Abell, Defining the Business: The Starting Point of Strategic Planning (Englewood Cliffs, New Jersey: Prentice-Hall, 1980).

7   Porter (1996).

8   C. Markides, 'Strategic Innovation', Sloan Management Review, volume 38, Spring 1997, pp. 9–23.

9   See, for example: M. Tushman and P Anderson, 'Technological Discontinuities and Organizational Environments', Administrative Science Quarterly, volume 31, 1986, pp. 439–465; R. Henderson and K. Clark, 'Architectural Innovation: The Reconfiguration of Existing Product Technologies and the Failure of Established Firms', Administrative Science Quarterly, volume 35, 1990, pp. 9–30; A. Meyer, G. Brooks, and J. Goes, 'Environmental Jolts and Industry Revolutions: Organizational Responses to Discontinuous Change', Strategic Management Journal, volume 11, 1990, pp. 93–110; and D. Leonard-Barton, 'Core Capabilities and Core Rigidities: A Paradox in Managing New Product Development', Strategic Management Journal, volume 13, 1992, pp. 111–125.

10  The other firms that form the backbone for this article include British Airways, Midlands Bank, Hewlett-Packard, Leclerc Supermarkets (in France), 3M, Royal Bank of Scotland, Tesco, Lan & Spar Bank (in Denmark), Douwe Egberts (in the Netherlands), and Hanes Corporation.

11  For similar concepts, see: C. Handy, The Empty Raincoat (London: Basic Books, 1994); C. Markides, 'Business Is Good? Time for Change!', London Business School Alumni News, Spring 1994, p. 15; and Burgelman and Grove (1996).

12  See 'Jack Welch's Encore', Business Week, 28 October 1996, pp. 42–50.

13  The importance of monitoring the organization's strategic health to anticipate (rather than react to) change is also emphasized in: M. Tushman, W. Newman, and E. Romanelli, 'Convergence and Upheaval: Managing the Unsteady Pace of Organizational Evolution', California Management Review, volume 26, Fall 1986, pp. 29–44; and C. Markides, 'Strategic Management: An Overview', in S. Crainer, ed., Financial Times Handbook of Management (London: Financial Times, Pitman Publishing, 1995), pp. 126–135.

14  See, for example: G. Hamel and C.K. Prahalad, 'Strategic Intent', Harvard Business Review, volume 67, May–June 1989, pp. 63–76; and J. Collins and J. Porras, Built to Last: Successful Habits of Visionary Companies (New York: Harper Business, 1994).

15  Markides (1997).

16  The notion that the underlying 'structure' of the system creates the behavior in that system has been the subject of a large amount of literature in the systems dynamics field. See, for example: J. Forrester, Principles of Systems,

second edition (Portland, Oregon: Productivity Press, 1968); and A. Van Ackere, E. Larsen, and J. Morecroft, 'Systems Thinking and Business Process Redesign', European Management Journal, volume 11, 1993, pp. 412–423. For a more managerial angle, see: C. Bartlett and S. Ghoshal, 'Rebuilding Behavioral Context: Turn Process Reengineering into People Reengineering', Sloan Management Review, volume 37, Fall 1995, pp. 11–23.

17    The literature on this topic is huge. As a start, see: R. Burgelman and L. Sayles, Inside Corporate Innovation: Strategy, Structure, and Managerial Skills (New York: Free Press, 1986); R.M. Kanter, The Change Masters (New York: Simon & Schuster, 1984); M. Tushman and W. Moore, eds., Readings in the Management of Innovation, second edition (New York: Harper Business, 1988); D. Miller, 'The Icarus Paradox: How Exceptional Companies Bring about Their Own Downfall,' Business Horizons, volume 35, 1992, pp. 24–35; and S. Ghoshal and C. Bartlett, 'Changing the Role of Top Management: Beyond Structure to Processes', Harvard Business Review, volume 73, January–February 1995, pp. 86–96.

18    Burgelman and Grove (1996), p. 20.

19    R. Nelson, 'Capitalism as an Engine of Progress', Research Policy, volume 19, 1990, pp. 193–214.

20    For a supporting discussion, see: M. Tushman and C. O'Reilly III, 'Ambidextrous Organizations: Managing Evolutionary and Revolutionary Change', California Management Review, volume 38, Summer 1996, pp. 8–30; Burgelman and Grove (1996); and Bartlett and Ghoshal (1995).

21    This same point is also discussed in: Tushman and O'Reilly (1996); and Burgelman and Grove (1996).

22    See, for example: Burgelman and Sayles (1986).

23    See, for example: S. Ghoshal and C. Bartlett, 'Rebuilding Behavioral Context: A Blueprint for Corporate Renewal', Sloan Management Review, volume 37, Winter 1996, pp. 23–36.

# Organizational Structure, Learning and Knowledge Management

The readings in this section explore the ways that organizations can be structured and changed through time so as to increase their ability to learn and to manage new knowledge. Knowledge is the ability to process information, so unlike information it cannot simply be bought: it must be developed over time. In different ways, the readings explain why this development requires costly investments and why it is subject to positive feedback: those firms able to create dynamic organizational structures, able to learn today, will learn more tomorrow. The message in the readings is particularly pertinent today when many popular strategy recipes seem to imply that all that matters is the ability to 'think differently' and to 'lead not follow', without emphasizing the particular organizational and financial investments that must be made for this to take place.

The first reading, by Teece, explores the work of Alfred Chandler, an economic historian whose study of the role of economies of scale and scope in creating competitive advantage has important implications for today's managers (especially those that focus only on flexibility). Teece's review provides an excellent connection between Chandler's work and the 'resource-based' perspective of strategy outlined in Section 3. Chandler highlights the important role of managerial strategy by illustrating how those firms with superior technology will not succeed if they do not combine it with strategies aimed at investments in economies of scale and scope and the creation of efficient organizational structures. The second reading, by Cohen and Levinthal, argues that the ability of organizations to recognize the value of new information and to absorb it into their structures, what they call its 'absorptive capacity', depends on the organization's development of prior related knowledge. The authors consider the determinants of the cognitive structure of an organization and how the process of knowledge creation is cumulative and hence path-dependent. The last reading, by Carlisle, pays special attention to the role of human relationships: knowledge creation is driven by the co-operative and creative interaction between its members, so firm strategy must be geared towards stimulating that interaction in an innovative way. Those firms that focus too much on technology and markets ignore the fact that knowledge, unlike information, cannot be bought but must be developed, and that development requires a strategy.

# D.J. Teece: 'The Dynamics of Industrial Capitalism: Perspectives on Alfred Chandler's *Scale and Scope*'

The reading by Teece appeared in the *Journal of Economic Literature* in 1993. Teece reviews the work of historian Alfred Chandler, widely recognized for his comparative accounts of the historical development of managerial capitalism. The main point in *Scale and Scope* is one that should be welcomed by students of strategy. Chandler claims that the competitiveness of firms, industries and countries depends not so much on the structure of markets and technologies as on the organizational strategies of managers: it is business organizations that shape markets and technology, not vice versa. He defines strategy as the determination of the basic long-term goals and objectives of an enterprise, and the adoption of courses of action and the allocation of resources necessary for achieving these goals. He outlines specific types of investments that must be made for these goals to be achieved and compares the fate of firms in different countries (US, Britain, Germany) depending on whether they made these investments. Those firms that are able to make the necessary investment in scale and scope will build first mover advantages associated with learning and incumbency effects. Teece uses the points raised in Chandler to draw connections with the resource-based and competence-based theory of the firm developed in Section 3.

# W.M. Cohen and D.A. Levinthal: 'Absorptive Capacity: a New Perspective on Learning and Innovation'

This reading appeared the *Administrative Science Quarterly* in 1990. Cohen and Levinthal argue that the ability of organizations to recognize the value of new information and to absorb it into their structures, what they call 'absorptive capacity', depends on the organizations' development of *prior related knowledge*. It is this prior experience which enables firms to 'learn how to learn' and without it they miss out on the potential benefits from activities like joint ventures in R&D. It is not important that prior knowledge be closely related to the current new information since what matters is the firm's ability to learn (i.e. learning to learn) and its ability to adapt to new information. The firm's diversity of experience in production and research is important since it increases the chances that the new information that arrives can be understood and interpreted creatively. Hence 'absorptive capacity' is a result, or by-product, of the firm's active engagement in learning activities. The authors consider the determinants of the cognitive structure of an organization and how the process of knowledge creation is cumulative and hence path-dependent: those firms that have developed a significant body of knowledge will be better learners and hence develop more knowledge in the future.

# Y. Carlisle: 'Strategic Thinking and Knowledge Management'

This piece was written for an Open University course on knowledge management. The field of knowledge management draws on insights from the resource-based theory of the firm (developed in Section 3) to study how knowledge is created and maintained in organizations. Knowledge, unlike information, is dynamic, always undergoing change: information can be bought but knowledge, used to interpret information, must be created over time. Not all firms are able to develop knowledge. For example, although large firms might be in the best position to purchase quality information (e.g. larger R&D laboratories), they will not necessarily be the best at interpreting this information in creative and innovative ways if their large size makes them too bureaucratic and inertial. To support this point, Carlisle uses the experience of small firms that were able to attack the lead of established firms even though the latter spent much more money on information and communication technologies. The focus on knowledge instead of information has a concrete implication for management strategies. Whereas the message for managers that emerges from 'transaction cost' economies and the treatment of 'asymmetric information' in standard economic theory is that managers must monitor and control the opportunistic behaviour of the organization's members (usually in a top-down way owing to the assumption of opportunistic behaviour), the message for managers that emerges from the 'knowledge-based approach' is that managers must develop a more horizontal, less controlling structure which allows more co-operative interaction and enables the creativity of the organization's members to blossom.

# The Dynamics of Industrial Capitalism: Perspectives on Alfred Chandler's Scale and Scope

DAVID J. TEECE*

This review essay is about a major treatise on modern capitalism by Alfred D. Chandler, one of the great authorities on business history. *Scale and Scope: The Dynamics of Industrial Capitalism* (1990) is a monumental work that answers important questions about managerial behavior and business institutions – the heart of the capitalist system of organization. The book ought to influence, if not shape, the research agenda for work in business history, industrial organization, the theory of the firm, and economic change for decades to come. In one powerful sweep it has also helped rebalance the literature on processes of wealth generation in capitalist society by displaying how the competitiveness of nations has depended in an important way upon the organizational and financial capabilities of firms, and their supporting institutions. Professor Chandler recounts the history of how managers in the United States, Britain, and Germany built the organizations and took the risks of investment necessary to capture the economies of scale and scope opened up by the technological innovations of the second industrial revolution. His thesis is not that markets shape business organization as is commonly supposed in economic theorizing; rather it is that business organizations shape markets. The implication of this *tour de force* is that much of what is in the textbooks in mainstream microeconomics, industrial organization, and possibly growth and development ought to be revised, in some cases relegated to the appendices, if economic analysis is to come to grips with the essence of productivity improvement and wealth generation in advanced industrial economies. It challenges much current economic orthodoxy enough so that most will choose to sidestep rather than deal with the ramifications.

　　[. . .]

* *Journal of Economic Literature* for 'The Dynamics of Industrial Capitalism: Perspectives on Alfred Chandler's Scale and Scope' by David J. Teece © *Journal of Economic Literature*, 1993.

# Major themes and propositions in *Scale and Scope*

In *Scale and Scope* Chandler examines the beginnings and subsequent growth of managerial capitalism in the United States, Germany, and Great Britain through the lens of what he considers then and now to be its basic institution, the modern industrial enterprise (p. 3). The period covered is from the 1870s through the 1960s, with brief references to the 1970s and 1980s. The individual companies studied were the 200 largest manufacturing firms in each of the three countries, using the sources familiar to business historians – company and individual histories, monographs, investment directories, published company and government reports, secondary sources, and archival records (p. 10). Chandler uses these sources in each country to examine what in the United States he labels *competitive managerial capitalism*, in Britain *personal capitalism*, and in Germany, *cooperative managerial capitalism* (pp. 11–12). What we receive is numerous case studies woven together into an insightful comparative study of the development of industrial capitalism with the firm put center stage. Various charts and statistical tables help track the firms that are the main actors during the periods studied.

Chandler's implicit thesis is that firms and markets evolve together to shape industrial outcomes. A perspective that relies on markets only as the lens through which to understand industrial development is likely to be seriously flawed. Rather, the strategic and organizational choices made by managers – choices not necessarily dictated by markets and technologies – shape if not determine both firm level and national economic performance.

The framework Chandler advances to interpret the beginnings and the evolutionary paths of each form of capitalism is his own unique blend of organizational economics. He recognizes that the modern industrial firm is basically an organization that has developed the capacity, through complex hierarchy, to make the activities and operations of the whole enterprise more than the sum of the parts (p. 15). The purpose of managerial hierarchy is to capture scale and scope economies within and among functions through planning and coordination (p. 17). Some systems and structures accomplish this better than others.

During the last quarter of the 19th century, major innovations made in the processes of production created many new industries and transformed old ones. Technological advances during this period were scale dependent and capital dependent and organizational innovations (as described by Chandler) were needed to exploit these scale-dependent advances (p. 21). Many older labor-intensive industries, including textiles, lumber, furniture, printing, and publishing, were largely unaffected. Capturing the economies available in new industries was not an automatic process. It came by

> improving and rearranging inputs; by using new or greatly improved machinery, furnaces, stills, and other equipment; by reorienting the processes of production within the plant; by placing the several intermediary processes employed in making

a final product within a single works; and by increasing the applications of energy (particularly that generated by fossil fuel). (p. 22)[1]

It required coordination and control, exercised through organizational structures and systems designed by management.[2]

Indeed, Chandler argues that it required new forms of industrial enterprise – organizational innovation – to take advantage of the opportunities which were afforded by new technologies. In Chandler's framework, *investment* in capital intensive production facilities of sufficient size to capture scale and scope economies and in supporting managerial systems was key to the creation of the modern industrial enterprise.

> The critical entrepreneurial act was not the invention – or even the commercialization – of a new or greatly improved product or process. Instead it was the construction of a plant of the optimal size required to exploit fully the economies of scale or those of scope, or both. (p. 26)

To Chandler, marketplace success involved three essential steps by top management: (1) the investment in production facilities large enough to achieve the cost advantages of scale and scope; (2) investment in product-specific marketing, distribution, and purchasing networks; (3) recruiting and organizing of the managers needed to supervise and coordinate functional activities and allocate resources for future production and distribution. The entrepreneurs first to perform these three critical steps 'acquired powerful competitive advantages' – what Chandler defines as first-mover advantages associated with learning and incumbency effects (p. 34). Latecomers had to make larger investments to compete, and they also had to deal with the added risk flowing from the competitive strengths and moves of the incumbents.[3]

# Competitive managerial capitalism in the United States

Chandler sets out to explain why the modern, integrated, multi-unit enterprise appeared in greater numbers and attained a greater size in a shorter period of time in the United States than in Europe. He finds the answer related in part to the large size of the US market, integrated by the railroad and the telegraph, a story told in more detail in the *Visible Hand* (1977), and partly due to its competitive characteristics. The railroads pioneered modern management in the 1850s and later, through bills of lading, intercompany billing, equipment identification and management, cost accounting, pricing, and so forth. But in *Scale and Scope* the essential thesis is that

> between the 1850s and the 1880s the transportation and communications networks established the technological and organizational base for the exploitation

of economies of scale and scope in the processes of production and distribution. (p. 58)

The entrepreneurial response in distribution preceded that in production because innovation in distribution was primarily organizational, not technological. The reasons for the decline of commission agents and the growth of full line, full service wholesalers and mass retailers is not entirely clear from Chandler's analysis.[4] Many of the names of the mass retailers that emerged after the Civil War are still familiar today and include Macy's, Lord & Taylor, Strawbridge & Clothier, John Wanamaker, Marshall Field, and Emporium. Montgomery Ward and Sears Roebuck came to dominate the rural market, relying heavily on mail-order operations. These houses build administrative systems to handle more transactions a day than most traditional merchants could handle in a lifetime.

The new forms of transportation and communication eventually created an even greater revolution in production, stimulating impressive technological as well as organizational changes.

> The laying down of railroad and telegraph systems precipitated a wave of industrial innovation in Western Europe and the United States far more wide ranging than that which had occurred in Britain at the end of the eighteenth century. This wave has been properly termed by historians the Second Industrial Revolution. (p. 62)

[They] involved systemic innovations in oil refining, steel, machinery, glass, artificial dyes, fibers, fertilizers, and food processing. But for the potential of these innovations to be realized, entrepreneurs had to make the three pronged investment.[5]

In industries where only one or two pioneering enterprises made the three pronged investment, these enterprises quickly dominated the market. More often, however, the modern industrial enterprise in the United States appeared after merger or acquisition (p. 71). This in turn was often preceded by efforts to manage capacity utilization by fixing prices and output. Cartel agreements in the United States were, however, extremely unstable because, as in Britain, contractual agreements in restraint of trade could not be enforced in courts of law. Moreover, after 1890 the passage of the Sherman Act made what was previously unenforceable quite illegal. The Sherman Act 'was to have a profound impact on the evolution of modern industrial enterprises in the U.S.' (p. 72). [. . .]

While some mergers initially created little more than federations out of previously independent companies, Chandler asserts that 'nearly all the mergers that lasted did so only if they successfully exploited the economics of scale and (to a much lesser extent) those of scope' (p. 78).

The merger movement is to Chandler the most important single episode in the evolution of the modem industrial enterprise in the United States from the 1880s to the 1940s as it permitted the rationalization of American industries in a way that did not begin in Britain and Germany until the 1920s. Moreover, nationwide consolidation tended to reduce family control, which in turn facilitated putting representatives of investment banks and other financial institutions, often important in arranging financing for mergers and acquisitions, on the boards of American industrial enterprises for the first time. However, the influence of the financiers waned as the companies were able to finance long-term investment as well as current operations from retained earnings, and the influence of management correspondingly increased.[6]

By World War I managerial capitalism had taken root in America, and the companies that were 'the first to make the essential, interrelated, three pronged investments in production, distribution, and management remained the leaders from the 1880s to the 1940s' (p. 91), not only in the United States but also, Chandler argues, in Britain and Germany. To support this proposition for the United States, Chandler provides industry-by-industry reviews in Chapters 4 through 6. He shows how the Standard Oil Company came to lead, not just domestically, but in Europe where it obtained an early and significant advantage through exports of kerosene from the US (strong demand for gasoline came only after 1900). Standard's unprecedented throughputs provided the foundation for its low cost position, as the railroads offered lower rates to J.D. Rockefeller to get Standard's business than they did to Rockefeller's competitors. The favorable transportation rates in turn helped Rockefeller form the Standard Oil Alliance, which attempted to set price and output levels in the industry. The coming of oil pipelines, a technological innovation in transportation which the Alliance first saw as a threat, required massive investment but, by dramatically lowering transportation costs, helped provide the foundation for transforming the Alliance into a trust because it supported larger scale refineries which in turn required consolidation of refining capacity. But the enterprise was so successful that it was able to create 'several of the world's largest industrial fortunes, not only for the Rockefellers but also for their close associates, including the Harknesses, Payne, Henry Flagler, and others' (p. 94).

The Standard Oil breakup of 1911 split the company along functional lines, with only Standard of New Jersey and Standard of California remaining vertically integrated; those left without an integrated structure set about trying to create one. 'Successful challengers were those that made the interrelated three-pronged investments' (p. 104) and included Sun, Phillips, Sinclair, and Gulf. Meanwhile, long before World War II, salaried managers, not the founders or the founders' families, were in control of the Standard Oil companies – members of the Rockefeller family were generally not involved, even on the board of directors. In contrast to the history on the European continent, 'no investment banker ever played a significant, ongoing role as a decision maker in a major American oil company' (p. 104).

Chandler describes the evolution of many other important industries, including machinery, electrical equipment, industrial chemicals, rubber, paper, cement, and steel. Steel is of particular interest, not just because of its overall importance to the economy in this period, but because, as Chandler puts it, 'the most effective first mover sold out'. The first mover was Andrew Carnegie who understood, as did Henry Ford and John D. Rockefeller, the significance of high capacity utilization – '"hard driving" as Carnegie termed it' (p. 128).[7]

[. . .]

Carnegie, while not the first to install new technologies like the Bessemer converter, was the first to build a large, vertically integrated facility, the Edgar Thomson Works in Pittsburgh, which remained for decades the largest steel works in the world. The large investments made by Carnegie and Illinois Steel enabled unit costs and prices to fall dramatically.[8] Carnegie also pursued an integration strategy, first backwards into iron ore and coke. He then threatened a forward integration strategy into fabricated products like wire, rail, tubes, and hoops. The investment banker J. Pierpont Morgan, who had extensive ties to the fabricators, including Federal Steel, who would be threatened by this move, offered to buy Carnegie Steel at Carnegie's price. In 1900 he merged Carnegie Steel and Federal Steel, the two leaders in the steel industry, and then in the following year negotiated to merge or acquire secondary producers, thereby establishing the world's largest industrial corporation, US Steel.

[. . .]

US industrial firms, once they had honed their organizational capabilities and begun generating significant cash flow, continued to expand through investment abroad and through diversification. Where the dynamics of growth rested on scale economies, firms grew more by direct investment abroad (e.g. machinery and transport equipment); where economies of scope were available, growth was through diversification (p. 147). The latter strategy was supported in part by organized research which expanded significantly as firms built R&D facilities in the 1920s first to improve products and processes, and subsequently to develop new ones. The producers of industrial chemicals, along with the electrical equipment manufacturers, used R&D to develop new products. DuPont was an early leader, developing several new products from its core capabilities in the nitrocellulose technology that it used to produce explosives and propellants. The increased complexities of the products and the managerial challenge associated with running multiple businesses increased the role of professional managers at DuPont and elsewhere in the chemical and machinery industries, and further separated management from ownership.

Chandler concludes his review of the American experience (pp. 224–33) with a frontal attack on what he refers to as 'orthodox economics' (p. 227) which views large hierarchies and oligopolistic market structures suspiciously. Chandler points out that at least during the time period studied it was the modern, hierarchical industrial firm that was responsible for America's economic growth. The firms that obtained market power rarely got it through 'artificial barriers' or anticompetitive conduct. Nor did it come in the main from the technical efforts of inventors alone, though Thomas Edison, George Westinghouse, Cyrus McCormick, and George Eastman made important organizational contributions as well. Rather, it came from the ability to develop and commercialize the new technologies through the three pronged strategy of investing in manufacturing, distribution, and management systems and people.[9]

# Personal capitalism in Great Britain

Chandler's thesis is that few large industrial firms appeared in Great Britain – and British economic development during the second industrial revolution suffered as a consequence – because British entrepreneurs frequently failed to make the essential three pronged investment in manufacturing, marketing and distribution, and management. Most importantly, 'the pioneers recruited smaller managerial teams, and the founders and their families continued to dominate the management of the enterprise' (p. 235) until well after World War II, to the considerable detriment of the British economy.[10] Boards of directors were restricted to family and those with family connections or social position, with little place for senior managers.

Thus Cadbury Brothers, Ltd., Britain's leading maker of cocoa and chocolate which began making chocolate in the middle of the 19th century, provides a good example. Cadbury's built a substantial plant in 1879 and had nearly 3,000 workers by 1900. However, its investment in marketing and distribution was limited.[11] The Cadbury family – the sons, daughters, and grandchildren – continued to manage the production, marketing, and sales functions as well as the enterprise as a whole. The senior Cadburys were completely absorbed in day-to-day operational activities. Whether the comparison is German or American, Chandler finds the management structure of Cadbury at the outbreak of World War II to be quite limited (p. 246). [. . .]

Chandler attributes the smaller size, family ownership, and less professional management of British firms to the smaller size of the British economy, the greater importance of foreign trade to the British companies, and the historical fact that Britain had industrialized and urbanized before the coming of the transportation revolution. The smaller geographic size of the island nation and the relative excellence of its pre-rail transportation system, meant that the railroad and telegraph were less watershed factors in Britain. The British railway companies were smaller and did not provide the same organizational challenges as the much larger American ones; accordingly, it is not surprising that they were not pioneers in modern management, accounting, and finance.

While British firms did respond to the opportunities in distribution that appeared, British entrepreneurs too often failed to make an investment in production large enough to utilize fully the economies of scale and scope, to build a product-specific marketing and distribution network, and to recruit a team of salaried managers. So they continued to rely on older forms of industrial enterprise – firms that were personally managed, usually family managed. In many of these new industries substantial tripartite investments were, indeed, made in Britain; but foreign, not British, enterprises made the investment. Foreign firms reaped the profits (pp. 261–62).

However, the British did have some success in branded packaged goods. The new production technologies for refining, distilling, milling, and processing food, drink, tobacco, and consumer chemicals were not complex, and product-specific distribution facilities or specialized marketing services were not required. By the turn of the century many producers of branded consumer goods – names like Cadbury, Huntley & Palmers, and Peek Frean – were among Britain's largest and most successful industrial enterprises (p. 262). Until after World War I, however, the companies producing foods and consumer chemicals rarely operated more than one major factory within Britain (p. 265). Such firms operated much like Cadbury, through functionally departmentalized organization, with department heads who were apt to be family members.[12] [. . .]

[There] were more failures than successes in Great Britain (p. 274). While in oil and meat packing the lack of supplies and natural resources limited opportunities for British firms at home, in light machinery (sewing machines, typewriters, etc.), electrical equipment, chemicals, and metals, the foundations of domestic demand and a domestic supply infrastructure (skills, finance, etc.) were in place. Here

> British entrepreneurs failed to grasp the opportunities the new technologies had opened up, precisely because they failed to make the necessary, interrelated, three-pronged investment in production, marketing, and management. These opportunities within Britain were seized instead by Germans and Americans. (p. 275)[13]

The British failure in organic chemicals ('dyestuffs') is especially striking because in 1870 Britain held a commanding technological lead. In 1856 William Perkin, a Britisher, had invented the first process for making dyes by chemical synthesis. Britain had plenty of the basic raw material (coal) and had domestic demand as well. Indeed, the British textile industry remained the single biggest market for dyes until World War II. But despite these advantages, Britain lost to Germany, as it was the German entrepreneurs who made investments in giant plants, recruited managerial teams, built the worldwide marketing organizations, and educated the users (p. 278).

In steel, the British pioneered in both the invention and early adoption of the Bessemer and open-hearth processes, but quickly fell behind. Here Chandler seems to attribute the failure to the absence of demand. The British rail network was already in place before the great expansion of the American and continental systems, thereby providing less incentive for British entrepreneurs to construct new, integrated facilities. In any case, the British did not do so, and by 1915 American and German steelmakers had taken the lead in all major markets except the British Empire and Britain itself. In aluminum and copper, British firms did adopt the revolutionary electrolytic techniques but failed to utilize them effectively.
[. . .]
Whatever the exact reasons for entrepreneurial failures were, it was the failure to make in a timely fashion the three pronged investment in production,

distribution, and management needed to exploit economies of scale and scope which was the essential failure. The window of opportunity was short; having missed it, continuing innovation by incumbents made it hard for later entrants to catch up. The British bias for small-scale operation and personal management was a significant handicap.[14]

In general, however, Chandler argues that British failures were more often than not a consequence of the basic goals and governance of the enterprise. Whereas in 'American managerial firms the basic goals appear to have been long-term profit and growth . . . in Britain the goal for family firms appears to have been to provide a steady flow of cash to owners – owners who were also managers' (p. 390).[15] For the relatively few British firms run by professional managers – ICI, Unilever, and British Petroleum – success was noteworthy, but the general failure to develop organizational capability weakened British industry and with it the British economy (p. 392).

## Cooperative managerial capitalism in Germany

While in Germany the modern industrial enterprise appeared soon after the completion of the transportation and communication networks, as it did in the United States, German industrial enterprises acquired distinctive features because of differences in markets, sources of supply, methods of finance, the antitrust environment, and the educational system. In particular, the enforceability of contracts in restraint of trade meant that 'German industrials had much less incentive to merge into industry wide holding companies' (p. 298). German universities and institutes were ahead of the United States in providing industrial enterprises with scientific knowledge and skilled technicians and managers and, unlike the United States and Britain, the banks played a major role in providing the finance necessary to facilitate the investment needed to capture the economies of scale and scope inherent in the new technologies. Only in Germany among the three did the bankers play this role; it entitled them to positions on the board of directors of industrial companies, from which they sometimes helped shape critical resource allocation decisions.

A truly distinctive dimension of the German industrial system was the banks. The demand for capital to finance the railroads led in the United States to the centralization and institutionalization of the nation's money and capital market in New York; in Germany, it encouraged the creation of a wholly new financial intermediary – the Kreditbank – which became central to the later financing of large-scale industrial enterprise. 'A handful of the largest Kreditbanken, termed Grossbanken, have dominated German finance ever since' (p. 415), The Grossbanken, like the Credit Mobilier in France, developed as diversified financial institutions simultaneously providing the services of commercial bank, investment bank, development bank, and investment trust. The

Kreditbanken, and particularly the Grossbanken, 'were the instrument[s] that made possible the rapid accumulation of capital on a scale vast enough to finance the building of the new continental transportation and communications infrastructure' (p. 416). As the Grossbanken moved into industrial finance, their extensive staffs developed in-depth knowledge of specific industries and companies. Senior bankers sat on the supervisory boards of the industrial companies the banks financed. The banks provided venture capital as well as the financing needed to exploit the economies of scale and scope so important in the capital intensive industries in which German enterprises clustered.

Besides the role of financial institution, another key differentiating factor was the legal structure. In Germany the common law did not prohibit cartels, nor was there any antitrust legislation. In 1897, one year before the Supreme Court's upholding of the Sherman Act, the German High Court held that cartel agreements were not only enforceable but were also in the public interest (p. 423). As investment in capital-intensive technologies increased, so did the number of cartels, going from four in 1875 to 106 in 1890, then to 385 in 1905 (p. 423). Conventions, consortiums, formal associations, and profit pools were formed in the quest for arrangements with some durability, for even with legal sanction 'contractual arrangements remained difficult to negotiate and even more difficult to enforce' (p. 423). However, because cooperation was legal, there was less incentive for industry-wide mergers to restrict competition. Given Chandler's view that industry-wide mergers were a prerequisite to industry-wide reorganization and rationalization, he concludes that 'far fewer such rationalizations occurred before World War I in Germany than in the U.S.' (p. 424).

The dual board structure that emerged in Germany was another significant difference with the United States and Great Britain. An 1884 law required joint stock companies (AG) to have both a management board for the routine running of the business and a supervisory board for long-term guidance and policy. The functions of the two boards became deeply intertwined . . . Moreover, the supervisory board, by including bankers and officers from other companies, could assist interfirm cooperation.

German institutions of higher education also affected the beginning and the continued growth of the large German industrial enterprise . . . Technical universities were specifically created to train men for industrial appointments . . . Indeed, Chandler suggests that the linkage between the sources of technical knowledge in the universities and institutes and industrial enterprises 'was much closer in Germany that in Britain, where it rarely existed at all, and even in the United States, where at the turn of the century the process was just beginning' (p. 426).

Cooperation was thus a hallmark of the German industrial system, as viewed by Chandler (pp. 498–99).[16] The legal cultural environment fostered cooperation, and the challenge of meeting the needs of a fragmented European market encouraged cooperation at home.[17] The banks preferred cooperation as a way to protect profits and enable debt to be serviced.

The German system was managerial capitalism that involved extensive hierarchies – a concept not at all foreign in Germany with its long tradition of bureaucratic management. In essence, the growth of German industrial power and the weakening of British industrial power resulted from the differential capacities of German and British entrepreneurs and managers. 'German industrial growth and the concomitant British industrial decline emphasize the importance of organizational capabilities in providing the underlying dynamics for modern industrial capitalism' (p. 500). Government played only a minor role – financial and educational institutions (many publicly funded) played a more important role than the government.

# The logic of managerial capitalism

## *The business enterprise (and its management) as the central actor*

Lest the reader not be fully aware of the import of what I believe Chandler has to say, let me reiterate that Chandler sees the historical record as indicating that the business enterprise, through the development of organizational capabilities, played the central role in industrial development in the United States, Britain, and Germany. Organizational capabilities once created had to be maintained for the leading enterprises and nations to stay ahead. Changing technologies and markets constantly make existing facilities and skills obsolete; industrial firms accordingly need to be in a process of constant organizational renewal. While new technologies provided opportunities, it was the business enterprises and their managers that determined whether those opportunities would be converted into sustainable advantages.

Needless to say, this view is not the dominant view reflected in most history books[18] or in the economic literature on growth and development.[19] Certainly those literatures stress the importance of investment, but Chandler's thesis is that the discriminating factor in the advance of the United States and Germany over Britain was not the rate of investment in conventional tangible capital alone. Nor was it government, the personalities of the entrepreneurs, culture, or ideology, though each are of some importance. Rather, it was the development of effective professional management and organizational systems to support the development of vertically integrated business enterprises.

The significance of these conclusions can perhaps be better assessed by what Chandler relegates to subsidiary importance. Already mentioned is the relatively insignificant role of direct government policies and programs. Technology is another factor relegated to a subsidiary role,[20] at least with respect to any particular nation. Chandler is not saying that technology or 'preconditions' or government policy are not important to industrial success. Rather, he seems to be saying that the new technologies in question were in the main open to all; accordingly it is understandable, though perhaps surprising to some, that technological pioneering did not lead inexorably to industrial dominance. Unless supported by the three pronged investments, technological success did not translate through to marketplace or national dominance. It was a necessary but not a sufficient condition for industrial development.

Without Britain, Chandler's thesis would be difficult to advance at the national level, as both American and German firms often did make the critical three pronged investment. But British firms did not, and the consequences are clear. Chandler claims that it is equally clear that the reason was the system of ownership and governance that existed in Britain – what he calls personal capitalism. Needless to say, his thesis here is controversial, as there are numerous competing hypotheses including a failure in entrepreneurship, the preoccupation of British investment banking with overseas investments, and the handicaps that some associate with Britain's early lead.[21] Whatever the cause, the failures of British firms to adequately respond to the opportunities afforded by the new technologies impaired Britain's growth and development.

## Determinants of the scale and scope of the enterprise

*Scale and Scope* ought to do a great deal to combat a rather traditional literature in economics, following Jacob Viner's (1931) classic investigation of cost curves, which posits a rather tight relationship between scale and scope economies, the optimum size of the enterprise, and market structure. As Jean Tirole (1988, p. 18) puts it, 'one of the main determinants of the size of a firm is the extent to which it can exploit economies of scale or scope'. Thus in searching for explanations for optimal firm size and market concentration, many economic theorists still confine their inquiry to the basic technological conditions of production.[22] Chandler's analysis would seem to suggest that explanations for the scale and scope of particular firms and of industry structure lie not so much with the technology-based economies of production or distribution, but with organizational factors, especially the ability of firms to make the investment in plant management and distribution systems necessary to garner competitive advantage. Perhaps this explains why Chandler has not tried all that hard to measure scale and scope economies. His argument seems to be that because the technologies in question are basically available to all, the more interesting question for economists interested in explaining firm size and market structure is how and why different industrial firms respond to and manage the opportunities afforded by new technology.

[. . .]

Yet Chandler seems to suggest that the key inventions quickly become public knowledge, leaving commercial success to depend upon the rapidity and completeness with which the invention is exploited. As W. Arthur Lewis has stated of Britain's lackluster performance:

> it is not necessary to be a pioneer in order to have a large export trade. It is sufficient to be a quick imitator. Britain would have done well enough if she merely imitated

German and American innovations. Japan, Belgium, and Switzerland owe more of their success as exporters of manufactures to imitation than they do to innovation. (Lewis 1957)

Chandler's is a study of entrepreneurship and how different forms of capitalism – competitive, personal, or cooperative – shape the response of firms. It is also a study of the incumbency effects created by the firms movers; and what it suggests is that governance structures, managerial systems, and the institutional-legal contexts are critical to understanding industrial outcomes. If taken seriously, Chandler's thesis requires a rewrite of industrial organization textbooks, both the traditional and the new. [. . .]

## The sustainability and sources of differential competitive advantages

[. . .]
Implicit in Chandler's argument is that just how and when the three pronged investments are made establishes differential organizational capabilities among firms. This would not be remarkable but for what Nelson (1991, p. 61) has referred to as

> the strong tide in economics, particularly in theoretical economics, that downplays or even denies the importance of such differences. The argument in economics is not that firms are all alike . . . rather the position is that the differences are not discretionary, but rather reflect differences in the contexts in which firms operate.

The main thrust of much economic theorizing is that what firms do is determined by the conditions they face, and possibly by certain unique attributes such as possession of a patent or ownership of a choice location. While firms facing different markets will behave and perform differently, if market conditions were reversed, firm behavior would be too. Different firms can produce different products but any firm can choose any niche. As Nelson (1991, p. 65) puts it, 'the theoretical preconceptions shared by most economists lead them to ignore firm differences, unless compelled to attend to them'.

Chandler's histories compel us to attend to firm differences, because they provide numerous illustrations that advantages are created and sustained over long periods.[23] Thus DuPont grew faster and more profitably than its competitors due to first mover advantages as well as far-sighted and insightful strategic and organizational decisions.[24] Firms declined if they were unable to create and maintain key organizational capabilities. However, Chandler's data on rankings of the largest industrial firms (for 1917, 1930, 1948 for Great Britain; 1913, 1928, 1953 for Germany) indicate considerable stability in rankings – at least as compared to what economic theory would predict.[25] The firms that were the leaders (as measured by asset size) in their industrial groupings often remained there over long periods. Indeed, using Chandler's data, across all groupings the probability that a firm ranked 1 or 2 before the outbreak of World War I would still be first or second in the early post World War II period was 0.57 in the United States, 0.56 in Great Britain, and 0.31 in Germany. This would appear to be strong evidence that differential competitive advantages are sustained over long periods of time,[26] and that within industry groupings it is more difficult than economic theory would suggest for challengers to develop superior organizational capabilities to displace first movers.

In Chandler's framework, differential advantages are often path dependent. First movers developed advantages through a variety of mechanisms: (1) *preemption*: in industries with significant scale economies, a large initial investment would entrench the incumbent; (2) *learning*: Chandler frequently notes that first movers gain substantial experience over followers in key functional areas such as sales and marketing as well as in production; (3) *cheaper capital*: Chandler claims that capital is more expensive for challengers than first movers because challengers must confront the behavioral uncertainty stemming from the competitive moves of the incumbent. However, from time to time challengers did succeed due to mistakes by first movers (as with Ford Motor and US Steel), government action (e.g. Britain's support of oil, Germany's support of aluminum, and antitrust action in the United States), and changing technology and markets. Thus oil discoveries in Texas and California gave opportunities to new entrants, and the advent of refrigeration enabled Swift to reconfigure the meat packing industry by using refrigeration cars to distribute dressed meat from central slaughterhouses to East Coast markets.

## Technology strategy

In addition to implications for economic theory, Chandler's work continues to have profound implications for the literature in business strategy. In both *Strategy and Structure* (1962) and now in *Scale and Scope* . . . Chandler has shown how *different* enterprises carried out the *same* activity and how decentralized structures were invented and then implemented in the interwar years by companies including DuPont, General Motors, Standard Oil of New Jersey, and Sears Roebuck. This highlights the topic of differential competitive advantage already discussed. Chandler also crafted one of the most widely accepted definitions of strategy – the determination of the basic long-term goals and objectives of an enterprise, and the adoption of courses of action and the allocation of resources necessary for achieving these goals.[27] [. . .]

The point of possible departure with the recent work in technology strategy is Chandler's emphasis on the need to build managerial hierarchies. At a superficial level, this may seem quite at odds with much of the recent literature on innovation which stresses the advantages of shallow hierarchies and decentralized decision making as a means to ensure the responsiveness needed to compete in today's fast-changing markets (Thomas Peters and Robert Waterman 1982; James Womack, Daniel Jones, and Daniel Roos 1990). However, a deeper reading of the innovation literature would appear to provide considerable support for the key aspect of hierarchy that Chandler recognizes, namely coordinating the internal allocation of resources quickly and efficiently so as to capture economies of scale and scope.[28] Chandler repeatedly argues that the absence of such coordination will lead to fragmented efforts that will prevent these economies from being realized. Interpreted as the recognition by Chandler of the need to coordinate and integrate resource allocation within the firm, there may be much in common between Chandler's historical observation and the thrust of the modern literature on management, which stresses the need to closely couple activities (as with 'concurrent engineering') and integrate functions.

It is important to recognize, however, that the emphasis in Chandler is on how to harness the capital intensive technologies in chemicals, steel, autos, etc. of the second industrial revolution. This was a somewhat different managerial challenge than is confronted by firms today as they deal with what might be called the third industrial revolution, driven by remarkable breakthroughs in microelectronics, biotechnology, and materials. The challenges are somewhat different, and the organizational forms suited to each may vary to some degree, and may also differ from those that were effective in the second revolution. Nevertheless, it is Chandler's thesis that the logic of managerial capitalism is timeless.

## Limits to the logic of managerial capitalism

A key question for all but business historians is whether this logic is now obsolete. In the final chapter of *Scale and Scope*, Chandler suggests that it is not, and in a related publication is quite explicit that 'The passage of time has not made the logic of managerial enterprise obsolete' (1990, p. 136). In the post World War II environment, Xerox is advanced as an example of a company that obtained its early dominance in copiers 'through its massive investment in production, distribution, and management' (p. 610).[29] Similarly for IBM in mainframe computers. It was its massive investment in the IBM System 360 which enabled it to eclipse Sperry Rand, the industry's most successful pioneer.[30] Likewise in personal computers, the first entrepreneurial firms to make substantial investments – Apple, Tandy (Radio Shack), and Commodore – by 1980 accounted for 68 percent of the dollar sales in the United States, a percentage which dropped dramatically lower a decade later.

The historical examples which Chandler advances to support his thesis are indeed compelling. He constantly reminds us that while the Englishman Perkin invented the first man-made dyes in the 1850s, 1860s, and 1870s, and British companies seemed to have all the raw materials at hand, it was German companies like Bayer, BASF, and Hoechst that took the lead because they were willing to invest big. Likewise in electrical equipment where the inventions of Thomas Edison spawned a new industry, one in which British firms like Mather and Platt were active early; it was nonetheless AEG and Siemens in Germany and GE, and Westinghouse in the United States that captured the market. They made large-scale investments that brought them dominance by the end of the century – a dominance that proved durable for at least another half century.

But as Chandler recognizes, from about the 1960s on a new era of managerial capitalism may have been launched – a topic which he hints will be 'the subject of another study' (p. 621). The changes Chandler identifies include proliferation of unrelated diversification strategies,[31] the isolation of top management, the opening up of the market for corporate control, and the expanded roles of pension funds in stock ownership. A key question that affects the utility of Chandler's work for observers of the contemporary scene is whether these and other changes suggest that the strategy Chandler advances – the three pronged investment – is simply a useful generalization about the past or whether it also holds for the present and the future.

In essence, Chandler's thesis is that large integrated enterprises, where free cash flows are carefully invested and coordinated to reduce price and assure quality, are necessary to build and hold market share.[32] Taken literally and projected forward, it would suggest that 'computerless' computer companies like Sun Microsystems and Dell Computer which outsource much of their manufacturing must have uncertain futures, unless they integrate, because their strategy has at most two of the necessary three prongs.[33] Certainly such firms have invested in product design, management control systems, and in limited circumstances distribution; but generally they have only a modicum of manufacturing capabilities, outsourcing many components and subsystems. These companies have undoubtedly been successful, but it is also true that many have been around for barely a decade.

If the Chandler thesis is a little at odds with what seems to work for many US companies today, perhaps it is in part because of the erosion in the relative skill base of the US economy,[34] leaving US firms from Apple (its Notebook computer is made by Sony) to Boeing (the 767 is co-produced with Aeritalia, Shorts, Kawasaki, IHI and Mitsubishi Heavy Industries) to Hewlett Packard (the engine in the Laserjet printer is made by Canon) little choice but to use components manufactured abroad. Perhaps it is because classical economies of scale and the unit price advantages can be accessed contractually in today's markets. Flexible specialization (Michael Piore and Charles Sable 1984) and contracting may today yield greater advantages than economies of scale and scope generated internally.

Indeed, it is arguably the case that firms that do not make the three pronged investment but instead simply build a capacity to manage a customer responsive network (e.g. Nike) can constitute a viable organizational form in today's global economy, with rapid diffusion of know-how and global dispersion of industrial competences. Raymond Miles has called such firms 'network firms' and suggests that they may constitute a new organizational form.[35] If they are, they are distinctly non-Chandleresque. Perhaps Chandler will address this and related phenomena by suggesting that professional managers today need to develop the information technologies and organizational systems to enable companies to achieve responsiveness and efficiency through seamless interaction with peers in different companies.

[. . .]

The logic of managerial capitalism Chandler identifies suggests a theory of firm and markets which is quite different from the standard textbook approaches.

There is one area, the emphasis on scale and scope, where Chandler may appear conventional, but closer investigation indicates that he is definitely not. Chandler clearly recognizes the potential for scale and scope economies afforded by the second industrial revolution. But whereas neoclassical theory presents these economies as immediately available to all (absent intellectual property protection) and attainable by all (absent government interference), Chandler sees the availability and attainability of these economies constrained not by the size of the market (the usual explanation) but by the nature of managerial structures and systems and the investment capabilities represented by the three pronged investment. Put starkly, Chandler appears to view the cost curves suggested by the technology as figments of the economist's mind, as their realization requires a set of supporting infrastructures, organizations, and firm-level strategies. [. . .]

If the conventional production function view of the firm embedded in micro-economic theory is unsatisfactory, what does *Scale and Scope* suggest might be more helpful? As mentioned above, Chandler has no formal theory of the firm to offer as an alternative. However, he has recently suggested the relevance of preliminary work in business strategy, organization theory, and industrial organization which is attempting to grapple with the concept of dynamic capabilities. Bits and pieces of an alternative theory can be found in Penrose (1959), Nelson and Winter (1982), Teece (1980, 1982, 1992), Teece, Gary Amy Pisano, and Shuen, Dosi, Teece, and Winter (1992) and Teece et al. In essence, firms are seen as organizations that are quite distinct from markets, where administrative processes displace market processes, and where both formal and informal organizational structures guide resource allocation and organizational behavior. Firms consist of bundles of generally nontradable firm-specific assets. Firms are heterogeneous with respect to these assets; asset endowments are specific and hence sticky, at least in the short run if not much longer. Firms also lack the organizational capacity to develop new assets quickly; tradability is limited by tacitness. The profitable expansion of firms is both a process of exploiting firm-specific capabilities and developing new ones.

[. . .]

## Notes

*Scale and Scope: The Dynamics of Industrial Capitalism.* By Alfred D. Chandler, Jr. with the assistance of Takashi Hikino. Cambridge, Mass. and London: Harvard U. Press, Belknap Press, 1990. Pp. xviii, 860. $35.00. ISBN 00–674–78994–6.

1   The new processes which emerged in the final quarter of the 19th century were applicable to the refining and distilling of sugar, petroleum, animal and

vegetable oil, whiskey and other liquids; the refining and smelting of iron, copper, aluminum; the mechanical processing and packaging of grains, tobacco, and other agricultural products; the manufacturing of complex, light standardized machinery through the fabrication and assembly of interchangeable parts; the production of technologically advanced industrial machinery and chemicals by a series of interrelated mechanical and chemical processes (p. 23). These technologies. Chandler asserts, were characterized by economies of scale and scope (p. 24).

2    The observation that 19th century technological progress was scale-intensive, requiring large scale to exploit fully its potential, is not original to Chandler. It was the staple of all the great 19th century and early 20th century economists in a line stemming from Smith and stretching to Mill, Bohm Bawerk, Sidgwick, and Allyn Young. In economic history, it is almost a cliché that technological progress has been scale intensive and that one of America's advantages, which helped bring the United States to a position of technological and productivity leadership, was that the US early enjoyed a relatively large, unified, and homogeneous market. Chandler's contribution here is not his perception of the scale-intensity of the dominant path of technological progress, but rather his understanding that to exploit it required managerial structures and systems, and investment in manufacturing and distribution.

3    In Chandler's taxonomy, it is important to recognize that the first movers are not the inventors. 'The first movers were pioneers or other entrepreneurs who made the three interrelated sets of investments in production, distribution, and management required to achieve the competitive advantages of scale, scope, or both'.

4    It probably had something to do with the superior control and incentives that flowed from ownership, coupled with scale and scope opportunities generated by the railroad and telegraph.

5    'It was the investment in the new and improved processes of production – not the innovation – that initially lowered costs and increased productivity. It was the investment, not the innovation, that transformed the structure of industries and affected the performance to national economies' (p. 63).

6    The challenge of managing large, complex hierarchies increased the demand for trained executives, and US colleges and universities responded quickly by expanding the training of engineers and managers. Early providers of business education were the Wharton School at the University of Pennsylvania, founded in 1881, the University of Chicago, and the University of California at Berkeley which set up business schools and colleges in 1898. Harvard followed in 1908 with its Graduate School of Business Administration.

7    Hard driving refers to the practice followed in the US steel industry of driving blast furnaces at pressures of 9 psi, as compared with the British practice of 5 psi. Hard driving required frequent rebricking but permitted higher throughput.

8    'The price of steel rails at Pittsburgh plummeted from $67.50 a ton in 1880 to $29.95 in 1889, to $17.63 a ton in 1898, yet profits soared.

9    Thus it was the integrated capacities, physical capital and human skills of firms (p. 230) that were critical. The 'dynamics came from the organizational capabilities developed after the three pronged investment and enhanced by continuing functional and strategic competition with other first movers and with challengers who made comparable investments' (p. 231). To underscore the importance of organizational capabilities, Chandler points out that it was the new branded, packaged goods with the lowest technology and scale requirements where the large firms had a competitive advantage over small firms (p. 63). Chandler suggests that differential competitive advantage lies not in technology, which is often available to all, but in the firm's capacity to find markets and coordinate production, distribution, and marketing.

10   'In most British enterprises senior executives worked closely in the same office building, located in or near the largest plant, having almost daily personal contact with, and thus directly supervising, middle and often lower-level managers. Such organizations had no need for the detailed organization charts and manuals that had come into common use in large American and German firms before 1914' (p. 242).

11   Cadbury's had its own sales force, and in the 1920s set up depot distribution in major cities and had a small fleet of trucks to supply them.

12   There were a few exceptions, most notably the brewers such as Bass, Worthington, and Watney.

13   Thus while British inventors such as Joseph Swan and Sebastian Ferranti were as able technologically as Thomas Edison and George Westinghouse in the United States, or Werner Siemens in Germany, failures in entrepreneurship prevented the British from building industrial empires around the new developments in electricity.

14   '[In] personally managed firms, growth was not a primary objective . . . profits made by the enterprise went to the owners. Many preferred current income. . . . This view made it easy . . . to hold back on expanding investment in production, distribution, research, and development, and on the recruitment, training, and promotion of salaried managers – all of which were fundamental to the continuing, successful exploitation of new technologies' (p. 292).

15   The implication is that the cash was needed to maintain the expensive lifestyles of the English upper class.

16   However, the weakness in the system of cooperation was, in Chandler's view, that it forestalled the industry-wide rationalization of facilities and personel that merger would have facilitated. In short, in some industries, including chemicals, cooperation 'forestalled the creation of an effective coorporate office comparable to that of Siemens in Germany, ICI in Britain, and the leading chemical and food firms in the U.S.'. Despite these disabilities, German firms still outcompeted British firms because whether a small

cartel office or a large headquarters office ran the business, at least salaried professionals were in charge, as was also the case in the United States (pp. 590–91).

17    Chandler does not explain (p. 427) why the need to serve a fragmented European market fostered cooperation at home. Presumably it was because information about foreign market opportunities could be shared across industries to mutual benefit.

18    David Landes in his monumental work *The Unbound Prometheus* devotes at most only a few pages to the role of firms in industrial development in Western Europe from 1750 to 1950.

19    As Moses Abramovitz (1991, p. 3) points out, the view that still shapes the modern economic approach to the economics of growth was laid out by John Stuart Mill in the *Principles of Political Economy* (1848). Mill's view was the simple production function approach, that sees increases in output as stemming from increases in labor, capital, and land, 'or of their productiveness'. Both Chandler and Abramovitz would undoubtedly argue that the standard approach fails to see organizational innovation as part of 'technological' progress and investments in managerial systems and structures in production, distribution, and marketing as part of aggregate capital formation.

20    However, technological change provided the opportunities and the requirement for organizational responses in the capital intensive industries. If pressed, Chandler would undoubtedly agree that technologies and organizations coevolve, and he would also recognize, along with Nelson and Sidney Winter (1982), Teece (1977), and others, that at minimum there are often significant costs of imitation, technology transfer, and adaptation so that technology was not quite freely transferable among firms.

21    Most persuasive is a thesis, closely aligned with Chandler's, that institutional rigidities were Britain's fundamental problem. As Bernard Elbaum and William Lazonick explain, 'what British industry in general required was the visible hand of coordinated control, not the invisible hand of the self-regulating market' (1986, p. 10). The fragmented industrial structure of many industries like cotton, coupled with reliance on unassisted market adjustment processes, was often the source of the problem, as Lazonick (1983) has shown. This is not the place for a recitation of all the competing hypotheses. Thorstein Veblen's (1915) is an early statement of disadvantages of being the pioneer, while Donald McCloskey (1981) is an excellent treatment of the failure in entrepreneurship thesis. The essential point which Chandler makes is that the system of business organization in Great Britain, whatever its foundation, was the source of the failure. For further discussion, see Roy Church (1990).

22    As one text points out, 'many of the predictions of economic theory, such as those involving price and firm size, revolve around concepts like marginal costs . . . [Moreover] knowing the cost function of a firm and knowing its technology are equivalent' (Dennis Carlton and Jeffrey Perloff 1990, p. 35).

The traditional approach is devoid of any consideration of organization and management (Teece 1980, 1982).

23 As Chandler states, in industries where innovations were particularly revolutionary, first movers had significant competitive advantages that as a general rule allowed them to remain dominant for decades. The first movers in industrial chemicals remained leaders for decades and nearly all of the top firms in 1948 had been long established since 1900 (pp. 171–72).

24 David Hounshell (1992) supports this contention and notes Dupont's abiding 'faith and commitment' to R&D during the eight decades of this century. Its strong R&D orientation distinguished it from its competitors, and was a direct consequence of its strategy.

25 Rankings were by book assets for US and German firms and by market values for British firms. Economic theory predicts a wide range of outcomes, but absent strategic behavior, the predilections of economists are to see entry and exit and changing market shares as occurring with alacrity. This stems from a faith in the workings of adjustment processes and implicit assumptions about the tradability of assets. Certainly, leading firms are viewed as being always vulnerable, and they often are. As one text put it, 'Generally, a dominant firm's share of an industry's sales shrink over time' (Carlton and Perloff 1990, p. 201). In neoclassical theory, as compared to evolutionary theory (Nelson and Winter 1982), the long run is rather short.

26 Wartime dislocation probably helps explain the lower survival rate in Germany.

27 Adhering to these definitions would make for clearer discussion. In the modern literature and in business discussion, choices on practically any decision variable are too frequently referred to as 'strategy'.

28 Cooperation induced and facilitated by administrative processes and formal organization has received less theoretical attention than it deserves. Contributors include Chester Barnard (1938), Herbert Simon (1947), and Williamson (1990b).

29 Further hints as to where he might be going can be found in Chandler (1992a, 1992b).

30 Remington/Sperry Rand failed to make the financial commitment that was necessary and failed to commit the time of senior management to solve the problems that were involved in designing and manufacturing and marketing computer systems at that time. Moreover, Remington Rand's failure to support its computer business did not stem tom a lack of available resources (Franklin Fisher, James McKie, and Richard Mancke 1983, p. 39).

31 In Teece et al. (forthcoming) it is shown, using 1987 data on US business establishments, that as US firms grow more diverse, they maintain a constant level of coherence (relatedness) between neighboring activities. This finding runs counter to the idea that firms with many activities are generally more diversified. It suggests that, in general, as firms grow more diverse, they add activities that relate to some portion of existing activities. This is consistent

with Chandler's notion of how firms generate scope economies. However, variability in the data suggests that at a point in time some firms may stray from the Chandler dicta. We predict that when they do. they are unlikely to be profitable and will eventually abandon unrelated diversification.

32 Chandler's thesis would also appear to be somewhat at odds with his Harvard colleague Michael Jensen (1989) who argues that, at least in mature industries where long-term growth is slow and cash flow outstrips investment opportunities in traditional markets, the public corporation is an anachronism because discretion is capable of being misused by the managerial groups Chandler sees as critical to economic development.

33 This debate has been entered in a series of articles in the *Harvard Business Review*. See Anatol Rappaport and S. Halevi (1991).

34 Certainly relative to other countries; possibly relative to its own recent past.

35 See Miles and Charles Snow (1986). Several other writers have suggested that there may be a 'post modern' successor to the modern corporation, one formulated partly in reaction to the ideal type of integrated Chandleresque corporation (see Thomas Hughes 1990) and partly to adapt it to the realities of today's global marketplace (Gary Pisano and Teece 1988; Teece 1992). That marketplace would appear to require firms to master both information technologies and relationships with supplier networks seamlessly integrated with their customers networks so that the corporation would look almost boundaryless.

# References

Abramovitz, Moses. 'The Elements of Social Capability'. Unpub. mss. Dept. of Economics, Stanford U., 1991.

Barnard, Chester I. *The functions of the executive.* Cambridge: Harvard U. Press, 1938.

Barnard, Chester I. *The functions of the executive.* Cambridge: Harvard U. Press, 1962.

Carlton, Dennis W. and Perloff, Jeffrey M. *Modern industrial organization.* Glenview, IL: Scott, Foresman, 1990.

Chandler, Alfred D. *Strategy and structure: Chapters in the history of the industrial enterprise.* Cambridge, MA: MIT Press, 1962.

Chandler, Alfred D. 'The Enduring Logic of Industrial Success', *Harvard Bus. Rev.,* Mar.–Apr. 1990, 90(2), pp. 130–40.

Chandler, Alfred D. 'Corporate Strategy, Structure and Control Methods in the United States during the 20th Century', *Ind. Corporate Change,* 1992, 1(2), pp. 263–84.

Chandler, Alfred D. 'Organizational Capabilities and the Economic History of the Industrial Enterprise', *J. Econ. Perspectives,* Summer 1992b, 6(3), pp. 79–100.

Church, Roy. 'The Limitations of the Personal Capitalism Paradigm', *Bus. Hist. Rev.*, Winter 1990, 64(4), pp. 703–10.

Elbaum, Bernard and Lazonick, William, eds. *The decline of the British economy.* Oxford: Clarendon Press, 1986.

Fisher, Franklin, M., McKie, James W. and Mancke, Richard B. *IBM and the U.S. data processing industry: An economic history.* NY: Praeger, 1983.

Hounshell, David A. 'Continuity and Change in the Management of Industrial Research: The Dupont Company 1902–1980', in *Technology and enterprise in a historical perspective.* Eds.: Giovanni Dosi, Renato Gianetti, Pier Angelo Toninelli. Oxford: Clarendon Press, 1992.

Hughes, Thomas. 'Managerial Capitalism beyond the Firm', *Bus. Hist. Rev.*, Winter 1990, 64(4), pp. 698–703.

Jensen, Michael C. 'Eclipse of the Public Corporation', *Harvard Bus. Rev.*, Sept.–Oct. 1989, 89(5), pp. 61–74.

Lazonick, William. 'Industrial Organization and Technological Change: The Decline of the British Cotton Industry', *Bus. Hist. Rev.*, Summer 1983, 57(2), pp. 195–236.

Lewis, W. Arthur. 'International Competition in Manufactures', *Amer. Econ. Rev.*, May 1957, 47(2), pp. 578–87.

McCloskey, Donald N. *Enterprise and trade in Victorian Britain: Essays in historical economics.* London: Allen & Unwin, 1981.

Miles, Raymond E. and Snow, Charles C. 'Organizations: New Concepts for New Forms', *Calif. Manage. Rev.*, Spring 1986, 28(3), pp. 62–73.

Mill, John Stuart. *Principles of political economy*, in *The collected works of John Stuart Mill.* Ed.: John M. Robson. Toronto: U. of Toronto Press, 1965, vols. 2 & 3.

Nelson, Richard R. 'Why Do Firms Differ, and How Does It Matter?', *Strategic Management Journal*, Special Issue, 1991, 12, pp. 61–74.

Nelson, Richard R. and Winter, Sidney G. *An evolutionary theory of economic change.* Cambridge: Harvard U. Press, 1982.

Peters, Thomas J. and Waterman, Robert H. *In search of excellence.* NY: Harper & Row, 1982.

Piore, Michael J. and Sable, Charles F. *The second industrial divide.* NY: Basic Books, 1984.

Pisano, Gary and Teece, David J. 'Collaborative Arrangements and Global Technology Transfer'. In *Technology, competition, and organization theory*, eds.: Robert A. Burgelman, Richard S. Rosenbloom. Cambridge, MA: MIT Press, 1988.

Rappaport, Anatol S. and Halevi, S. 'The Computerless Computer Company', *Harvard Bus. Rev.*, July–Aug. 1991. 69, pp. 69–81.

Simon, Herbert. *Administrative behavior.* 2nd edn. NY: Macmillan, [1947] 1961.

Teece, David J. 'Technology Transfer by Multinational Firms: The Resource Cost of Transferring Technological Know-how: *Econ. J.*, June 1977, 87 (346), pp. 242–61.

Teece, David J. 'Economies of Scope and the Scope of an Enterprise', *J. Econ. Behav. Organ.*, Sept. 1980, 1(3), pp. 233–47.

Teece, David J. 'Towards an Economic theory of the Multiproduct Firm', *J. Econ. Behav. Organ.*, Mar. 1982, 3(1), pp. 39–63.

Teece, David J. 'Competition, Cooperation, and Innovation: Organizational Arrangements for Regimes of Rapid Technological Progress,' *J. Econ. Behav. Organ.*, June 1992, 18(1), pp. 1–25.

Teece, David J., Pisano, Gary and Shuen, Amy. 'Dynamic Capabilities and Strategic Management', *Strategic Management Journal*, forthcoming.

Tirole, Jean. *The theory of industrial organization*. Cambridge, MA: MIT Press, 1988.

Veblen, Thorstein. *Imperial Germany and the industrial revolution*. NY: Macmillan, 1915.

Viner, Jacob. 'Cost Curves and Supply Curves', *Z. Nationalökon.*, Sept. 1931, 3, pp. 23–46; in *Readings in price theory*. eds.: George J. Stigler and Kenneth Boulding. Homewood, IL: Irwin, 1952.

Williamson, Oliver E. 'Chester Barnard and the Incipient Science of Organization', in *Organization theory*. ed.: Oliver E. Williamson. NY: Oxford U. Press, 1990b.

Womack, James P., Jones, Daniel T. and Rees, Daniel. *The machine that changed the world*. NY: Macmillan 1990.

# CHAPTER 14

# Absorptive Capacity: a New Perspective on Learning and Innovation

WESLEY M. COHEN AND DANIEL A. LEVINTHAL*

[. . .]

## Introduction

Outside sources of knowledge are often critical to the innovation process, whatever the organizational level at which the innovating unit is defined. [. . .]

The ability to exploit external knowledge is thus a critical component of innovative capabilities. We argue that the ability to evaluate and utilize outside knowledge is largely a function of the level of prior related knowledge. At the most elemental level, this prior knowledge includes basic skills or even a shared language but may also include knowledge of the most recent scientific or technological developments in a given field. Thus, prior related knowledge confers an ability to recognize the value of new information, assimilate it, and apply it to commercial ends. These abilities collectively constitute what we call a firm's 'absorptive capacity'.

At the level of the firm – the innovating unit that is the focus here – absorptive capacity is generated in a variety of ways. Research shows that firms that conduct their own R&D are better able to use externally available information (e.g. Tilton, 1971; Allen, 1977; Mowery, 1983). This implies that absorptive capacity may be created as a byproduct of a firm's R&D investment. Other work suggests that absorptive capacity may also be developed as a byproduct of a firm's

* *Administrative Science Quarterly* for 'Absorptive Capacity: A New Perspective on Learning and Innovation' by Wesley M. Cohen and Daniel A. Levinthal, vol 35, no 1 © *Administrative Science Quarterly*, March 1990.

manufacturing operations. Abernathy (1978) and Rosenberg (1982) have noted that through direct involvement in manufacturing, a firm is better able to recognize and exploit new information relevant to a particular product market. Production experience provides the firm with the background necessary both to recognize the value of and implement methods to reorganize or automate particular manufacturing processes. Firms also invest in absorptive capacity directly, as when they send personnel for advanced technical training. The concept of absorptive capacity can best be developed through an examination of the cognitive structures that underlie learning.

## Cognitive structures

The premise of the notion of absorptive capacity is that the organization needs prior related knowledge to assimilate and use new knowledge. Studies in the area of cognitive and behavioral sciences at the individual level both justify and enrich this observation. Research on memory development suggests that accumulated prior knowledge increases both the ability to put new knowledge into memory, what we would refer to as the acquisition of knowledge, and the ability to recall and use it. With respect to the acquisition of knowledge, Bower and Hilgard (1981: 424) suggested that memory development is self-reinforcing in that the more objects, patterns and concepts that are stored in memory, the more readily is new information about these constructs acquired and the more facile is the individual in using them in new settings.

Some psychologists suggest that prior knowledge enhances learning because memory – or the storage of knowledge – is developed by associative learning in which events are recorded into memory by establishing linkages with pre-existing concepts. Thus, Bower and Hilgard (1981) suggested that the breadth of categories into which prior knowledge is organized, the differentiation of those categories, and the linkages across them permit individuals to make sense of and, in turn, acquire new knowledge. In the context of learning a language, Lindsay and Norman (1977: 517) suggested the problem in learning words is not a result of lack of exposure to them but that 'to understand complex phrases, much more is needed than exposure to the words: a large body of knowledge must first be accumulated. After all, a word is simply a label for a set of structures within the memory system, so the structures must exist before the word can be considered learned'. Lindsay and Norman further suggested that knowledge may be nominally acquired but not well utilized subsequently because the individual did not already possess the appropriate contextual knowledge necessary to make the new knowledge fully intelligible.

The notion that prior knowledge facilitates the learning of new related knowledge can be extended to include the case in which the knowledge in question may itself be a set of learning skills. There may be a transfer of learning skills across bodies of knowledge that are organized and expressed in similar ways.

As a consequence, experience or performance on one learning task may influence and improve performance on some subsequent learning task (Ellis, 1965). This progressive improvement in the performance of learning tasks is a form of knowledge transfer that has been referred to as 'learning to learn' (Ellis, 1965; Estes, 1970). Estes (1916: 16), however, suggested that the term 'learning to learn' is a misnomer in that prior experience with a learning task does not necessarily improve performance because an individual knows how to learn (i.e. form new associations) better, but that an individual may simply have accumulated more prior knowledge so that he or she needs to learn less to attain a given level of performance. Notwithstanding what it is about prior learning experience that may affect subsequent performance, both explanations of the relationship between early learning and subsequent performance emphasize the importance of prior knowledge for learning.

The effect of prior learning experience on subsequent learning tasks can be observed in a variety of tasks. For instance, Ellis (1965: 4) suggested that 'students who have thoroughly mastered the principles of algebra find it easier to grasp advanced work in mathematics such as calculus'. Further illustration is provided by Anderson, Farrell, and Sauers (1984), who compared students learning LISP as a first programming language with students learning LISP after having learned Pascal. The Pascal students learned LISP much more effectively, in part because they better appreciated the semantics of various programming concepts.

The literature also suggests that problem-solving skills develop similarly. In this case, problem-solving methods and heuristics typically constitute the prior knowledge that permits individuals to acquire related problem-solving capabilities. In their work on the development of computer programming skills, Pirolli and Anderson (1985) found that almost all students developed new programs by analogy to example programs and that their success was determined by how well they understood why these examples worked.

We argue that problem-solving and learning capabilities are so similar that there is little reason to differentiate their modes of development, although exactly what is learned may differ: learning capabilities involve the development of the capacity to assimilate existing knowledge, while problem-solving skills represent a capacity to create new knowledge. Supporting the point that there is little difference between the two, Bradshaw, Langley, and Simon (1983) and Simon (1985) suggested that the sort of necessary preconditions for successful learning that we have identified do not differ from the preconditions required for problem solving and, in turn, for the creative process. Moreover, they argued that the processes themselves do not differ much. The prior possession of relevant knowledge and skill is what gives rise to creativity, permitting the sorts of associations and linkages that may have never been considered before. Likewise, Ellis (1965: 35) suggested that Harlow's (1959) findings on the development of learning sets provide a possible explanation for the behavioral phenomenon of 'insight' that typically refers to the rapid solution of a problem. Thus, the psychology literature suggests that creative capacity and what we call absorptive capacity are quite similar.

To develop an effective absorptive capacity, whether it be for general knowledge or problem-solving or learning skills, it is insufficient merely to expose an individual briefly to the relevant prior knowledge. Intensity of effort is critical. With regard to storing knowledge in memory, Lindsay and Norman (1977: 355) noted that the more deeply the material is processed – the more effort used, the more processing makes use of associations between the items to be learned and knowledge already in the memory – the better will be the later retrieval of the item. Similarly, learning-set theory (Harlow, 1949, 1959) implies that important aspects of learning how to solve problems are built up over many practice trials on related problems. Indeed, Harlow (1959) suggested that if practice with a particular type of problem is discontinued before it is reliably learned, then little transfer will occur to the next series of problems. Therefore, he concluded that considerable time and effort should be spent on early problems before moving on to more complex problems.

Two related ideas are implicit in the notion that the ability to assimilate information is a function of the richness of the preexisting knowledge structure: learning is cumulative, and learning performance is greatest when the object of learning is related to what is already known. As a result, learning is more difficult in novel domains, and, more generally, an individual's expertise – what he or she knows well – will change only incrementally. The above discussion also suggests that diversity of knowledge plays an important role. In a setting in which there is uncertainty about the knowledge domains from which potentially useful information may emerge, a diverse background provides a more robust basis for learning because it increases the prospect that incoming information will relate to what is already known. In addition to strengthening assimilative powers, knowledge diversity also facilitates the innovative process by enabling the individual to make novel associations and linkages.

# From individual to organizational absorptive capacity

An organization's absorptive capacity will depend on the absorptive capacities of its individual members. To this extent, the development of an organization's absorptive capacity will build on prior investment in the development of its constituent, individual absorptive capacities, and, like individuals' absorptive capacities, organizational absorptive capacity will tend to develop cumulatively. A firm's absorptive capacity is not, however, simply the sum of the absorptive capacities of its employees, and it is therefore useful to consider what aspects of absorptive capacity are distinctly organizational. Absorptive capacity refers not only to the acquisition or assimilation of information by an organization but also to the organization's ability to exploit it. Therefore, an organization's absorptive capacity does not simply depend on the organization's direct interface with the external environment. It also depends on transfers of knowledge across and within subunits that may be quite removed from the original point of entry. Thus, to understand the sources of a firm's absorptive capacity, we focus on the structure of communication between the external environment and the organization, as well as among the subunits of the organization, and also on the character and distribution of expertise within the organization.

Communication systems may rely on specialized actors to transfer information from the environment or may involve less structured patterns. The problem of designing communication structures cannot be disentangled from the distribution of expertise in the organization. The firm's absorptive capacity depends on the individuals who stand at the interface of the firm and the external environment or at the interface between subunits within the firm. That interface function may be diffused across individuals or be quite centralized. When the expertise of most individuals within the organization differs considerably from that of external actors who can provide useful information, some members of the group are likely to assume relatively centralized 'gatekeeping' or 'boundary-spanning' roles (Allen, 1977; Tushman, 1977). For technical information that is difficult for internal staff to assimilate, a gatekeeper both monitors the environment and translates the technical information into a form understandable to the research group. In contrast, if external information is closely related to ongoing activity, then external information is readily assimilated and gatekeepers or boundary-spanners are not so necessary for translating information. Even in this setting, however, gatekeepers may emerge to the extent that such role specialization relieves others from having to monitor the environment.

A difficulty may emerge under conditions of rapid and uncertain technical change, however, when this interface function is centralized. When information flows are somewhat random and it is not clear where in the firm or subunit a piece of outside knowledge is best applied, a centralized gatekeeper may not provide an effective link to the environment. Under such circumstances, it is best for the organization to expose a fairly broad range of prospective 'receptors' to the environment. Such an organization would exhibit the organic structure of Burns and Stalker (1961: 6), which is more adaptable 'when problems and requirements for action arise which cannot be broken down and distributed among specialist roles within a clearly defined hierarchy'.

Even when a gatekeeper is important, his or her individual absorptive capacity does not constitute the absorptive capacity of his or her unit within the firm. The ease or difficulty of the internal communication process and, in turn, the level of organizational absorptive capacity are a function not only of the gatekeeper's capabilities but also of the expertise of those individuals to whom the gatekeeper is transmitting the information. Therefore, relying on a small set of technological gatekeepers may not be sufficient; the group as a whole must have some level of relevant background knowledge, and when knowledge structures are highly differentiated, the requisite level of background may be rather high.

The background knowledge required by the group as a whole for effective communication with the gatekeeper highlights the more general point that shared knowledge and expertise are essential for communication. At the most basic level, the relevant knowledge that permits effective communication both within and across subunits consists of shared language and symbols (Dearborn and Simon, 1958; Katz and Kahn, 1966; Allen and Cohen, 1969; Tushman, 1978; Zenger and Lawrence, 1989). With regard to the absorptive capacity of the firm as a whole, there may, however, be a trade-off in the efficiency of internal communication against the ability of the subunit to assimilate and exploit information originating from other subunits or the environment. This can be seen as a trade-off between inward-looking versus outward-looking absorptive capacities. While both of these components are necessary for effective organizational learning, excessive dominance by one or the other will be dysfunctional. If all actors in the organization share the same specialized language, they will be effective in communicating with one another, but they may not be able to tap into diverse external knowledge sources. [. . .]

This trade-off between outward- and inward-looking components of absorptive capacity focuses our attention on how the relationship between knowledge sharing and knowledge diversity across individuals affects the development of organizational absorptive capacity. While some overlap of knowledge across individuals is necessary for internal communication, there are benefits to diversity of knowledge structures across individuals that parallel the benefits to diversity of knowledge within individuals. As Simon (1985) pointed out, diverse knowledge structures coexisting in the same mind elicit the sort of learning and problem solving that yields innovation. Assuming a sufficient level of knowledge overlap to ensure effective communication, interactions across individuals who each possess diverse and different knowledge structures will augment the organization's capacity for making novel linkages and associations – innovating – beyond what any one individual can achieve. Utterback (1971). summarizing research on task performance and innovation, noted that diversity in the work setting 'stimulates the generation of new ideas'. Thus, as with Nelson and Winter's (1982) view of organizational capabilities, an organization's absorptive capacity is not resident in any single individual but depends on the links across a mosaic of individual capabilities.

Beyond diverse knowledge structures, the sort of knowledge that individuals should possess to enhance organizational absorptive capacity is also important. Critical knowledge does not simply include substantive, technical knowledge; it also includes awareness of where useful complementary expertise resides within and outside the organization. This sort of knowledge can be knowledge of who knows what, who can help with what problem, or who can exploit new information. With regard to external relationships, von Hippel (1988) has shown the importance for innovation of close relationships with both buyers and suppliers. To the extent that an organization develops a broad and active network of internal and external relationships, individuals' awareness of others' capabilities and knowledge will be strengthened. As a result, individual absorptive capacities are leveraged all the more, and the organization's absorptive capacity is strengthened.

The observation that the ideal knowledge structure for an organizational subunit should reflect only partially overlapping knowledge complemented by nonoverlapping diverse knowledge suggests an organizational trade-off between diversity and commonality of knowledge across individuals. While common knowledge improves communication, commonality should not be carried so far that diversity across individuals is substantially diminished. Likewise, division of labor promoting gains from specialization should not be pushed so far that communication is undermined. The difficulties posed by excessive specialization suggest some liabilities of pursuing production efficiencies via learning by doing under conditions of rapid technical change in which absorptive capacity is important. In learning by doing, the firm becomes more practiced and hence more capable at activities in which it is already engaged. Learning by doing does not contribute to the diversity that is critical to learning about or creating something that is relatively new. Moreover, the notion of 'remembering by doing' (Nelson and Winter, 1982) suggests that the focus on one class of activity entailed by learning by doing may effectively diminish the diversity of background that an individual or organization may have at one time possessed and, consequently, undercut organizational absorptive capacity and innovative performance.

It has become generally accepted that complementary functions within the organization ought to be tightly intermeshed, recognizing that some amount of redundancy in expertise may be desirable to create what can be called cross-function absorptive capacities. Cross-function interfaces that affect organizational absorptive capacity and innovative performance include, for example, the relationships between corporate and divisional R&D labs or, more generally, the relationships among the R&D, design, manufacturing, and marketing functions (e.g. Mansfield, 1968: 86–88). Close linkages between design and manufacturing are often credited for the relative success of Japanese firms in moving products rapidly from the design stage through development and manufacturing (Westney and Sakakibara, 1986). Clark and Fujimoto (1987) argued that overlapping product development cycles facilitate communication and coordination across organizational subunits. They found that the speed of product development is strongly influenced by the links between problem-solving cycles and that successful linking requires 'direct personal contacts across functions, liaison roles at each unit, cross-functional task forces, cross-functional project teams, and a system of "product manager as integrator"' (Clark and Fujimoto, 1987: 24). In contrast, a process in which one unit simply hands off the design to another unit is likely to suffer greater difficulties.

Some management practices also appear to reflect the belief that an excessive degree of overlap in functions may reduce the firm's absorptive capacity and that diversity of backgrounds is useful. The Japanese practice of rotating their R&D personnel through marketing and manufacturing operations, for example, while creating knowledge overlap, also enhances the diversity of background of their personnel. Often involving the assignment of technical personnel to other functions for several years. this practice also suggests that some intensity of experience in each of the complementary knowledge domains is necessary to put an effective absorptive capacity in place; breadth of knowledge cannot be superficial to be effective.

The discussion thus far has focused on internal mechanisms that influence the organization's absorptive capacity. A question remains as to whether absorptive capacity needs to be internally developed or to what extent a firm may simply buy it via, for example, hiring new personnel, contracting for consulting services, or even through corporate acquisitions. We suggest that the effectiveness of such options is somewhat limited when the absorptive capacity in question is to be integrated with the firm's other activities. A critical component of the requisite absorptive capacity for certain types of information, such as those associated with product and process innovation, is often firm-specific and therefore cannot be bought and quickly integrated into the firm. This is reflected in Lee and Allen's (1982) findings that considerable time lags are associated with the integration of new technical staff, particularly those concerned with process and product development. To integrate certain classes of complex and sophisticated technological knowledge successfully into the firm's activities, the firm requires an existing internal staff of technologists and scientists who are both competent in their fields and familiar with the firm's idiosyncratic needs, organizational procedures, routines, complementary capabilities, and extramural relationships. As implied by the discussion above, such diversity of knowledge structures must coexist to some degree in the same minds. Moreover, as Nelson and Winter's (1982) analysis suggests, much of the detailed knowledge of organizational routines and objectives that permit a firm and its R&D labs to function is tacit. As a consequence, such critical complementary knowledge is acquired only through experience within the firm. Illustrating our general argument, Vyssotsky (1977), justifying the placement of Bell Labs within AT&T, argued: 'For research and development to yield effective results for Bell System, it has to be done by . . . creative people who understand as much as they possibly can about the technical state of the art, and about Bell System and what System's problems are. The R&D people must be free to think up new approaches, and they must also be closely coupled to the problems and challenges where innovation is needed. This combination, if one is lucky, will result in insights which help the Bell System. That's why we have Bell Labs in Bell System, instead of having all our R&D done by outside organizations.'

## Path dependence and absorptive capacity

Our discussion of the character of absorptive capacity and its role in assimilating and exploiting knowledge suggests a simple generalization that applies at both the individual and organizational levels: prior knowledge permits the assimilation and exploitation of new knowledge. Some portion of that prior knowledge should be very closely related to the new knowledge to facilitate assimilation, and some fraction of that knowledge must be fairly diverse, although still related, to permit effective, creative utilization of the new knowledge. This simple notion that prior knowledge underlies absorptive capacity has important implications for the development of absorptive capacity over time and, in turn, the innovative performance of organizations. The basic role of prior knowledge suggests two features of absorptive capacity that will affect innovative performance in an evolving, uncertain environment (Cohen and Levinthal, 1989b). Accumulating absorptive capacity in one period will permit its more efficient accumulation in the next. By having already developed some absorptive capacity in a particular area, a firm may more readily accumulate what additional knowledge it needs in the subsequent periods in order to exploit any critical external knowledge that may become available. Second, the possession of related expertise will permit the firm to better understand and therefore evaluate the import of intermediate technological advances that provide signals as to the eventual merit of a new technological development. Thus, in an uncertain environment, absorptive capacity affects expectation formation, permitting the firm to predict more accurately the nature and commercial potential of technological advances. These revised expectations, in turn, condition the incentive to invest in absorptive capacity subsequently. These two features of absorptive capacity – cumulativeness and its effect on expectation formation – imply that its development is domain-specific and is path- or history-dependent.

The cumulativeness of absorptive capacity and its effect on expectation formation suggest an extreme case of path dependence in which once a firm ceases investing in its absorptive capacity in a quickly moving field, it may never assimilate and exploit new information in that field, regardless of the value of that information. There are two reasons for the emergence of this condition which we term 'lockout' (Cohen and Levinthal, 1989b). First, if the firm does not develop its absorptive capacity in some initial period, then its beliefs about the technological opportunities present in a given field will tend not to change over time because the firm may not be aware of the significance of signals that would otherwise revise its expectations. As a result, the firm does not invest in absorptive capacity and, when new opportunities subsequently emerge, the firm may not appreciate them. Compounding this effect, to the extent that prior knowledge facilitates the subsequent development of absorptive capacity, the lack of early investment in absorptive capacity makes it more costly to develop a given level of it in a subsequent period. Consequently, a low initial investment in absorptive capacity diminishes the attractiveness of investing in subsequent periods even if the firm becomes aware of technological opportunities.[1] This possibility of firms being 'locked-out' of subsequent technological developments has recently become a matter of concern with respect to industrial policy. For instance, Reich (1987: 64) declaims Monsanto's exit from 'float-zone' silicon manufacturing because he believes that the decision may be an irreversible exit from a technology, in that 'each new generation of technology builds on that which came before, once off the technological escalator it's difficult to get back on'.

Thus, the cumulative quality of absorptive capacity and its role in conditioning the updating of expectations are forces that tend to confine firms to operating in a particular technological domain. If firms do not invest in developing absorptive capacity in a particular area of expertise early on, it may not be in their interest to develop that capacity subsequently, even after major advances in the field. Thus, the pattern of inertia that Nelson and Winter (1982) highlighted as a central feature of firm behavior may emerge as an implication of rational behavior in a model in which absorptive capacity is cumulative and contributes to expectation formation. The not-invented-here syndrome, in which firms resist accepting innovative ideas from the environment, may also at times reflect what we call lockout. Such ideas may be too distant from the firm's existing knowledge base – its absorptive capacity – to be either appreciated or accessed. In this particular setting, NIH may be pathological behavior only in retrospect. The firm need not have acted irrationally in the development of the capabilities that yields the NIH syndrome as its apparent outcome.

A form of self-reinforcing behavior similar to lockout may also result from the influence of absorptive capacity on organizations' goals or aspiration levels. This argument builds on the behavioral view of organizational innovation that has been molded in large part by the work of March and Simon (1958). In March and Simon's framework, innovative activity is instigated due to a failure to reach some aspiration level. Departing from their model, we suggest that a firm's aspiration level in a technologically progressive environment is not simply determined by past performance or the performance of reference organizations. It also depends on the firm's absorptive capacity. The greater the organization's expertise and associated absorptive capacity, the more sensitive it is likely to be to emerging technological opportunities and the more likely its aspiration level will be defined in terms of the opportunities present in the technical environment rather than strictly in terms of performance measures. Thus, organizations with higher levels of absorptive capacity will tend to be more proactive, exploiting opportunities present in the environment, independent of current performance. Alternatively, organizations that have a modest absorptive capacity will tend to be reactive, searching for new alternatives in response to failure on some performance criterion that is not defined in terms of technical change *per se* (e.g. profitability, market share, etc.).

A systematic and enduring neglect of technical opportunities may result from the effect of absorptive capacity on the organization's aspiration level when innovative activity (e.g. R&D) contributes to absorptive capacity, which is often the case in technologically progressive environments. The reason is that the firm's aspiration level then depends on the very innovative activity that is triggered by a failure to meet the aspiration level itself. If the firm engages in little innovative activity, and is therefore relatively insensitive to the opportunities in the external environment, it will have a low aspiration level with regard to the exploitation of new technology, which in turn implies that it will continue to devote little effort to innovation. This creates a self-reinforcing cycle. Likewise, if an organization has a high aspiration level, influenced by externally generated technical opportunities, it will conduct more innovative activity and thereby increase its awareness of outside opportunities. Consequently, its aspiration level will remain high. This argument implies that reactive and proactive modes of firm behavior should remain rather stable over time. Thus, some organizations (like Hewlett-Packard and Sony) have the requisite technical knowledge to respond proactively to the opportunities present in the environment. These firms do not wait for failure on some performance dimension but aggressively seek out new opportunities to exploit and develop their technological capabilities.[2]

The concept of dynamically self-reinforcing behavior that may lead to the neglect of new technological developments provides some insight into the difficulties firms face when the technological basis of an industry changes – what Schumpeter (1942) called 'the process of creative destruction'. For instance, the change from electromechanical devices to electronic ones in the calculator industry resulted in the exit of a number of firms and a radical change in the market structure (Majumdar, 1982). This is an example of what Tushman and Anderson (1986) termed competence-destroying technical change. A firm without a prior techno-logical base in a particular field may not be able to acquire one readily if absorptive capacity is cumulative. In addition, a firm may be blind to new developments in fields in which it is not investing if its updating capability is low. Accordingly, our argument implies that firms may not realize that they should be developing their absorptive capacity due to an irony associated with its valuation: the firm needs to have some absorptive capacity already to value it appropriately.

[. . .]

## Conclusion

Our empirical analysis of R&D investment suggested that firms are in fact sensitive to the characteristics of the learning environment in which they operate. Thus, absorptive capacity appears to be part of a firm's decision calculus in allocating resources for innovative activity. Despite these findings, because absorptive capacity is intangible and its benefits are indirect, one can have little confidence that the appropriate level, to say nothing of the optimal level, of investment in absorp-tive capacity is reached. Thus, while we have proposed a model to explain R&D investment, in which R&D both generates innovation and facilitates learning, the development of this model may ultimately be as valuable for the prescriptive analysis of organizational policies as its application may be as a positive model of firm behavior.

An important question from a prescriptive perspective is: when is a firm most likely to underinvest in absorptive capacity to its own long-run detriment? Absorptive capacity is more likely to be developed and maintained as a byproduct of routine activity when the knowledge domain that the firm wishes to exploit is closely related to its current knowledge base. When, however, a firm wishes to acquire and use knowledge that is unrelated to its ongoing activity, then the firm must dedicate effort exclusively to creating absorptive capacity (i.e. absorptive capacity is not a byproduct). In this case, absorptive capacity may not even occur to the firm as an investment alternative. Even if it does, due to the intangible nature of absorptive capacity, a firm may be reluctant to sacrifice current output as well as gains from specialization to permit its technical personnel to acquire the requisite breadth of knowledge that would permit absorption of knowledge from new domains. Thus, while the current discussion addresses key features of organizational structure that determine a firm's absorptive capacity and provides evidence that investment is responsive to the need to develop this capability, more research is necessary to understand the decision processes that determine organizations' investments in absorptive capacity.

## Notes

As in Chapter 11, we include here only the theoretical basis of the argument. We exclude the empirical model related on the effect of R&D investment, that the authors build to illustrate the theoretical points on absorptive capacity.

1   A similar result emerges from models of adaptive learning. Levitt and March (1988: 322) noted that 'a competency trap can occur when favorable performance with an inferior procedure leads an organization to accumulate more experience with it, thus keeping experience with a superior procedure inadequate to make it rewarding to use'.

2   This argument that such reactive and proactive behavior may coexist in an industry over the long run assumes that there is slack in the selection environment and that technologically progressive behavior is not essential to survival. One can, alternatively, identify a number of industries, such as semiconductors, in which it appears that only firms that aggressively exploit technical opportunities survive.

## References

Abernathy, William J. 1978 The Productivity Dilemma, Baltimore: Johns Hopkins University Press.

Allen, Thomas J. 1977 Managing the Flow of Technology. Cambridge: MA: MIT Press.

Allen, Thomas J., and Stephen D. Cohen 1969 'Information flows in R&D labs'. Administrative Science Quarterly, 20: 12–19.

Anderson, John R., Robert Farrell, and Ron Sauers 1984 'Learning to program in LISP'. Cognitive Science, 8: 87–129.

Bower, Gordon H., and Ernest R. Hilgard 1981 Theories of Learning. Englewood Cliffs, NJ: Prentice-Hall.

Bradshaw, Gary F., Patrick W. Langley, and Herbert A. Simon 1983 'Studying scientific discovery by computer simulation'. Science, 222: 971–975.

Burns, Tom, and George M. Stalker 1961 The Management of Innovation. London: Tavistock.

Clark, Kim B., and Takahiro Fujimoto 1987 'Overlapping problem solving in product development'. Technical Report, Harvard Business School.

Cohen, Wesley M., and Daniel A. Levinthal 1989b 'Fortune favors the prepared firm'. Technical Report, Dept. of Social and Decision Sciences, Carnegie Melton University.

Dearborn, R., and Herbert A. Simon 1958 'Selective perception in executives'. Sociometry, 21: 140–144.

Ellis, Henry Carlton 1965 The Transfer of Learning. New York: Macmillan.

Estes, William Kay 1970 Learning Theory and Mental Development. New York: Academic Press.

Harlow, H. F. 1949 'The formation of learning sets'. Psychological Review, 56: 51–65.

Harlow, H. F. 1959 'Learning set and error factor theory'. In S. Koch (ed.), Psychology: A Study of Science, 2: 492–537. New York: McGraw-Hill.

Katz, Daniel, and Robert L. Kahn 1966 The Social Psychology of Organizations. New York: Wiley.

Lee, Denis M. S., and Thomas J. Allen 1982 'Integrating new technical staff: Implications for acquiring new technology'. Management Science, 28: 1405–1420.

Levitt, Barbara, and James G. March 1988 'Organizational learning'. Annual Review of Sociology, 14: 319–340.

Lindsay, Peter H., and Donald A. Norman 1977 Human Information Processing. Orlando, FL: Academic Press.

Majumdar, Bodiul Alam 1982 Innovations, Product Developments and Technology Transfers: An Empirical Study of Dynamic Competitive Advantage, The Case of Electronic Calculators. Lanham, MD: University Press of America.

Mansfield, Edwin 1968 Economics of Technological Change. New York: Norton.

Mansfield, Edwin 1988 'The speed and cost of industrial innovation in Japan and the United States: External vs. internal technology.' Management Science, 34(10): 1157–1168.

March, James G., and Herbert A. Simon 1958 Organizations. New York: Wiley.

Mowery, David C. 1983 'The relationship between intrafirm and contractual forms of industrial research in American manufacturing. 1900–1940'. Explorations in Economic History, 20: 351–374.

Nelson, Richard R., and Sidney Winter 1982 An Evolutionary Theory of Economic Change. Cambridge, MA: Harvard University Press.

Pirolli, Peter L., and John R. Anderson 1985 'The role of learning from example in the acquisition of recursive programming skill'. Canadian Journal of Psychology, 39: 240–272.

Reich, Robert B. 1987 'The rise of techno-nationalism'. Atlantic, May: 63–69.

Rosenberg, Nathan 1982 Inside the Black Box: Technology and Economics. New York: Cambridge University Press.

Schumpeter, Joseph A. 1942 Capitalism, Socialism and Democracy. New York: Harper & Row.

Simon, Herbert A. 1985 'What we know about the creative process'. In R. L. Kuhn (ed.), Frontiers in Creative and Innovative Management: 3–20. Cambridge, MA: Ballinger.

Tilton, John E. 1971 International Diffusion of Technology: The Case of Semiconductors. Washington, DC: Brookings Institution.

Tushman, Michael L. 1977 'Special boundary roles in the innovation process'. Administrative Science Quarterly, 22: 587–605.

Tushman, Michael L. 1978 'Technical communication in R&D laboratories: The impact of project work characteristics'. Administrative Science Quarterly, 21: 624–644.

Tushman, Michael L., and Philip Anderson 1986 'Technological discontinuities and organizational environments'. Administrative Science Quarterly, 31: 439–465.

Utterback, James M. 1971 'The process of technological innovation within the firm'. Academy of Management Journal, 12: 75–88.

von Hippel, Eric 1988 The Sources of Innovation. New York: Oxford University Press.

Vyssotsky, V. A. 1977 'The innovation process at Bell Labs'. Technical Report, Bell Laboratories.

Westney, D. Eleanor, and Kiyonori Sakakibara 1986 'The role of Japan-based R&D in global technology strategy'. In M. Hurowitch (ed.), Technology in the Modern Corporation: 217–232, London: Pergamon.

Zenger, Todd R., and Barbara S. Lawrence 1989 'Organizational demography: The differential effects of age and tenure distributions on technical communication'. Academy of Management Journal, 32: 353–376.

# CHAPTER 15

# Strategic Thinking and
# Knowledge Management

YSANNE CARLISLE*

## Introduction

It has long been acknowledged that knowledge is central to wealth creation
and organised competitive performance (e.g. Hayek, 1945; Penrose, 1959;
Teece, 1977). Some authors, like Marshall, writing in 1920, have been explicit
in stating that 'knowledge is our most powerful engine of production; it enables us
to subdue nature and force her to satisfy our wants. Organisation aids knowledge'
(Marshall, 1969: 115). Until recently, however, the full implications of such
observations were still ignored. The terms 'information' and 'knowledge' were
often used synonymously, and knowledge acquisition, creation, exploitation and
transfer in organisations were infrequently researched topics.

From the mid-1980s onwards it became apparent that established understandings of strategy had serious limitations in the increasingly competitive and
changing global environment. These understandings were mostly derived from
organisational economics. Organisational economics underpinned conventional
strategic prescriptions for creating and sustaining a competitive performance, but
during the 1980s these were found to be wanting. A number of well-established
large organisations which had been cited as 'excellent' in accordance with accepted
strategic wisdom actually suffered performance declines. IBM and Microsoft are
examples. Their declines occurred in the face of competition from smaller firms
which conventional theory suggested should not have triumphed. In one sense,
knowledge management is a practical response to this problem. For example,
the efforts of organisations like Skandia and CICB to measure and manage their
knowledge bases are practically oriented towards sustaining and improving
performance. In another sense, the emergence of a new strand of knowledge-based

* Commissioned by the Open University Business School for the course *Managing Knowledge* (B823).
© The Open University 1999.

organisational theory can be viewed as an academic response to the need to provide better theoretical perspectives to inform management practice. This need was highlighted by the declines of companies like IBM and it took on a sense of urgency in the strategy literature of the late 1980s and 1990s. What is emerging is an understanding of organisation focused on the role of knowledge. It underpins a very different approach to strategy from that which was, until recently, accepted as the received wisdom.

Knowledge management is not simply a modern term for information management. It requires the pursuit of different types of objectives and the development of different types of resource strengths, process capabilities and organisational structures. Researching the new knowledge-based understanding requires a focus upon the development of new 'organisational advantages' (Moran and Ghoshal, 1996) to create and sustain a competitive performance in the modern global economy (Gee, 1996). These advantages are derived from superior capabilities in the management of the organisational knowledge process. The development of organisational advantages requires a focus upon issues of internal organisational dynamics. This represents a move away from traditional emphases upon market imperfections and positioning which are to be found in the established literature. This paper contrasts the understandings of organisation found in the conventional and the knowledge-based literatures. Some fundamental differences which affect the role of information and knowledge are summarised in Table 15.1.

The next sections explore these key differences in understanding and outline their implications for strategists. The paper moves on to describe how competitive advantage is created and sustained in both frameworks. Finally, the limitations of the older understandings and approaches are considered along with the contexts in which they came to be questioned. The key questions are: can knowledge

Table 15.1 *Conventional and knowledge-based understandings of organisation*

| Key issues | Conventional understandings | Knowledge-based understandings |
| --- | --- | --- |
| Why do organisations exist? | To process environmental information | To create and exploit knowledge |
| | To deal with problems arising from informational imperfections | |
| | To reduce uncertainty | |
| | To meet shareholder needs | |
| How do we understand human nature? | People are rational, calculating and self-interested individuals | People are creative, visionary and collectively ambitious |
| What is the basis for human relationships in and between organisations? | Explicitly or implicitly contractual | Commitment based upon shared visions, meanings and identities |

management address these limitations and, if so, how radical a shift in strategic thinking is required? Is knowledge management complementary to the older strategic approaches or does it require a more complete paradigm shift?

# The need for organisations

Traditionally, economists have devoted attention to answering the question 'why do organisations exist?' Strategists, building upon their answers, have devised strategies to develop the ways and means by which organisations can fulfil their functions better. Clearly, how we answer this basic question about organisations has implications for the way we conceptualise strategic requirements for performance success. Knowledge may only recently have surfaced as a major focus in the economics and strategy literatures, but several conventional economic theories of the firm have accorded a central place to information in explaining organisation as a means of achieving the effective and efficient deployment of scarce resources. Some of the best-established perspectives are premised, explicitly or otherwise, upon assumptions about information. Information about the competitive environment which organisations process is seen as a major determinant of organisational strategy; imperfect information leads to informational 'asymmetries' and this is why organisations can fail.

For example, Alchian and Demetz (1972) suggest that asymmetries in the information held by people co-operating in a task make it impossible to match their contributions to their remuneration. If efficiency losses are to be avoided, they believe, it is necessary to incur the costs of controlling and monitoring their activities and output. Jensen and Meckling (1976) suggest that informational asymmetries between principals and agents in contractual relationships create the need to incur monitoring costs to ensure that agents act in the interests of principals. Williamson (1975; 1985), whose transaction costs understanding is one of the best-established and most influential economic understandings of the firm, does not accord informational asymmetries a direct role in competitive success, but sees them indirectly as crucial. In Williamson's understanding, informational asymmetries make it possible for individuals to engage in opportunistic behaviour which gives rise to the need for governance structures. For Williamson, market imperfections in the acquisition and utilisation of resources, including informational resources, provide some organisations with opportunities to deploy resources more effectively and efficiently than their rivals.

The 'knowledge-based view of the firm' is a theoretical perspective on organisations which has emerged in the strategy literature to propose an alternative primary reason for organising. From this perspective firms exist to facilitate the acquisition, creation, exploitation and transfer of useful knowledge. This alternative response to the question 'why organise?' is reflected in Kogut and Zander's definition of the firm as 'a social community specialising in the speed and efficiency of the creation and transfer of knowledge' (Kogut and Zander, 1996: 503).

The knowledge-based view explicitly recognises that information and knowledge are distinctly different phenomena. Information can be understood to consist of facts and data pertaining to natural or social states of affairs, natural or social events and the consequences of such events under given circumstances, or states of affairs. The total stock of information available, or potentially available, to organisations is vast but, as Fransman (1988) points out, it is also theoretically finite. At any given point in time there are a finite number of natural and social states of affairs in the world. The events that might occur as a result may be numerous and may not all be anticipated by an organisation. They are nevertheless finite in number, and the number of potential consequences is also finite. In contrast, knowledge is potentially limitless.

Leonard (1995) highlights the fact that knowledge is a potentially limitless 'wellspring' which is 'constantly replenished with streams of new ideas' (Leonard, 1995: 3). Following Nonaka (1991; 1994) and Nonaka and Takeuchi (1995), knowledge is often defined in the knowledge-based literature as 'justified' belief. Information can be an input into the decision-making process, and it can be interpreted to justify belief, but it also depends upon knowledge for that interpretation. Information is seen to be important and relevant in the light of knowledge which may be added to, amended or changed in the light of new information.

Knowledge is a critical resource. Virtually all other resources depend upon some degree of knowledge exploitation for their value – including natural resources. Gas, for example, would have no value if we did not know what to do with it and possess the know-how to extract it and exploit it. At the abstract level of theoretical knowledge, depending upon the nature of the business, organisations may require a wide range of specialist inputs – from business specialisms, such as accountancy and business law, to scientific and technical specialisms, such as chemistry, computer science and engineering. At the concrete level, organisations require practical know-how in a wide range of areas and an ability to exploit these disparate contributions effectively. Some kinds of abstract knowledge can be codified. Such knowledge can be commodified and distributed in the manner of information, but the tacit knowledge embodied in practical know-how cannot.

Within the context of the simple model *input–process–output*, knowledge is a more dynamic resource than many other inputs which may be used up or otherwise deployed time and again in relatively unchanged forms. In the process of exploiting knowledge, knowledge is changed. The input–process–output model can be applied to the process of exploiting knowledge itself. An engineer, for example, may be recruited with a theoretical knowledge gained from a university. As this theoretical knowledge is deployed in the performance of tasks at work the new engineer gains work experience. With work experience practical know-how is acquired to complement the original theoretical knowledge. As a result, the knowledge contribution which the new engineer can make to the firm changes.

The 'knowledge-based view of the firm' is a theoretical perspective which has grown out of the 'resource-based view' in the strategy literature. The inspiration for the development of the resource-based view is generally attributed to

Selznick (1947) and Penrose (1959). Neither of these writers placed the knowledge resource at centre stage, although Penrose pointed to the possibility that knowledge could be a resource with special properties in that the effective utilisation of all other resources depended upon it. She suggested that the need to deploy the underutilised productive services of other resources 'shape(s) the direction of the search for knowledge' (Penrose, 1959: 77). The idea that diversification can bring economies of scope to an organisation if its diversification strategy enables it to use large indivisible assets more efficiently is well established. How can we reconcile this idea with the equally well-known strategic prescription for companies to 'stick to the knitting'? One of the implications of Penrose (1959) is that the acquisition of new knowledge is an essential ingredient in the success of such strategies. It is knowledge that creates a cost advantage in enabling the organisation to deploy its productive resources more efficiently. Resource-based theorists have stressed that over time organisations can develop particular strengths in the form of 'capabilities' and 'competencies'. Capabilities enable organisations to manage particular types of resource-utilising process especially well, for example manufacturing processes. Competencies are strengths in doing particular things especially well, such as manufacture engines. Organisations exploit knowledge by building capabilities and competencies.

## Human nature and the basis of human relationships

Conventional understandings of human nature in organisational economics are based upon a (sometimes jaundiced) view of humanity as inherently rational, calculative and instrumental. For example, we have noted that Alchian and Demetz (1972) see organisation as a means of minimising efficiency loss in the context of co-operative production. Informational asymmetries make it difficult for co-operating team members to assess relative contributions. The presupposition is that human beings are by nature instrumental reasoners who will adopt courses of action from which they can derive maximum benefit for minimum effort. Under such a utilitarian presumption, individuals in co-operative production have an 'incentive to shirk'. Jensen and Meckling (1976) focus upon the nature of the relationship between principals and agents. They see human beings as 'utility maximisers' individually pursuing maximum personal utility. From this perspective agents may not always be motivated to pursue the best possible interests of principals. Hence the need to incur agency costs and to provide agents with appropriate incentives.

Williamson's transaction costs understanding 'characterises human nature as we know it by reference to bounded rationality and opportunism' (Williamson, 1985: 44). Bounded rationality arises to avoid information overload. Information overload leads to selective perception of and attention to information. Information which is attended to is then processed in accordance with accepted 'procedural rationality', which stems from the decision-maker's ideological environment . . .

According to March and Simon, the concept of bounded rationality 'incorporates two fundamental characteristics: (1) choice is always exercised with respect to a limited, approximate simplified model of the real situation. . . . (2) The elements of the definition of the situation are not "given" . . . but are themselves the outcome of psychological and sociological processes, including the chooser's own activities and the activities of those in his environment' (March and Simon, 1958: 12).

The scope for opportunism, defined by Williamson as behaviour which is 'self-interest seeking with guile' (Williamson, 1975; 1985), arises because of informational asymmetries between organisations and between individuals within them. The scope for exercising opportunistic behaviour in organisations may be tempered by the decision maker's ideological environment. Nonetheless, the basic view of human nature which transaction costs theory adopts is one of a rational, instrumentally oriented, self-seeking individual of the type originally characterised by Adam Smith's 1776 *An Inquiry into the Nature and Causes of the Wealth of Nations*.

Organisational economists have adopted a contractual view of human relationships. Jensen and Meckling explicitly define the firm in contractual terms as 'the nexus of a set of contracting relationships between individuals' (Jensen and Meckling, 1976: 315). Relationships between, for example, principals and agents, employers and employees, organisations and customers, organisations and shareholders and other stakeholders can all be analysed from a contractual standpoint. Some contracts are understood to be more implicit than explicit, and the costs of making and monitoring transactions are of central concern in relation to efficiency issues.

Where organisational economics stresses the importance of March and Simon's first characteristic of bounded rationality, knowledge-based theorists stress the second. Writers like Williamson emphasise the rationality in human reasoning and information processing. In contrast the knowledge-based view of the firm emphasises creativity, vision and ambition as essential human traits. Selznick (1947) pointed the way in writing about 'the creative leader' who matches 'aspiration' to the nature of the organisation in guiding it along a path between long-term 'utopianism' and short-term 'opportunism'. For organisational economists, the environment is a source of incomplete information to be processed as rationally as possible in reaching decisions. For Penrose, it is 'an "image" in the entrepreneur's mind of the possibilities and restrictions with which he is confronted, for it is, after all, such an image which in fact determines a man's behaviour' (Penrose, 1959: 5). The 'productive opportunity' of the organisation is therefore shaped as much by subjective judgement and creativity as it is by the rational processing of environmental information.

More modern writings in the knowledge-based mould have adopted a social constructivist approach to the understanding of human relationships. Writers seeking to advance knowledge management as a practical endeavour are therefore crucially concerned with internal organisational dynamics. The social processes which operate in the course of human interaction are central rather than peripheral considerations. Knowledge management attention has been directed towards a diverse range of topics of direct relevance to how people interact with each other in organisational contexts to maintain and change their socially constructed worlds. It would be possible to compile a lengthy list of such topics including, for example, contexts and conditions for information and knowledge sharing, mechanisms for communications and control, organisational structures, language and conservation in organisational and interorganisational contexts, the nature of learning and learning organisations, formal and informal networks, self-managing teams and communities of practice. The point is that human interaction and how it takes place is central to knowledge creation and transfer. It is also formative in shaping organisational routines (Nelson and Winter, 1982) within which useful knowledge can be exploited as an organisational rather than an individual resource.

## Implications for strategists

The conventional and knowledge-based approaches to strategy carry different implications for strategists, as is shown in Table 15.2. Differences in goals and strategic focus are considered in this section and their different implications for creating and sustaining competitive advantage are discussed in the next.

The traditional theoretical underpinnings for strategy derived from organisational economics have encouraged strategy scholars to explore the causes and consequences of market failures. Managers have been encouraged to focus on developing strategies which achieve the best possible fit between the organisation and its environment to secure a favourable and sustainable market position.

Following the conventional understanding of transaction costs and market imperfections identified in the organisation's environment by means of information processing, strategic management must strive to take advantage of the opportunities they present. At the same time it must guard against the adverse effects of the

Table 15.2 *The conventional and knowledge-based approaches to strategy*

| Key differences | Conventional approach | Knowledge-based approach |
| --- | --- | --- |
| Goal for strategists | Achieve a good strategic fit | Achieve an ambitious strategic intent |
| Strategic focus | Value appropriation | Value creation |
| Sources of competitive advantage | Market imperfections providing opportunities for cost and differentiation advantages enabling firms to achieve favourable market positions | Unique competencies and capabilities which cannot be substituted, imitated, replicated or transferred, and are 'causally ambiguous' |
| How competitive advantage is sustained | By maintaining a favourable market position | Through capabilities in knowledge processes which can deliver new competencies for the future |

opportunistic behaviour of those individuals and organisations with which it has business relationships or 'contracts' and those organisations with which it competes.

Andrews (1971) has formulated a classic statement of the approach to strategic analysis that such understandings support. In this statement, strategy formulation and implementation are separated for purposes of analysis, and internal organisational dynamics are considered to be an implementation issue. Strategy formulation is approached as a rational top-down endeavour involving the processing of environmental information to identify opportunities and threats. Alternative courses of action are identified and an assessment of their risks is undertaken. In the light of this analysis and an appraisal of internal organisational strengths and weaknesses, a choice is made. The emphasis is upon rational planning.

The knowledge-based view encourages scholars to explore the structural, social and relational aspects of organisations within which knowledge creation, exploitation and transfer take place. Hamel and Prahalad (1989) argued that many corporations which rise to positions of global market dominance begin with an ambitious vision or 'strategic intent'. Targets are set which demand a great deal of effort and commitment, and involve stretching resources and capabilities beyond their limits. This means that organisations must tap into the creativity and inventiveness of their members to achieve their goals. In the process, unplanned strategies for the exploitation of knowledge created may emerge. Strategy is not viewed as an exclusively top-down process in which formulation and implementation issues are distinct and separate. Good ideas can arise almost anywhere in the organisation and putting them into practice may require an input at the planning stage from almost anywhere. Developing shared meanings and purposes in accordance with an ambitious mission requires more than a directive process, and the importance of emergent strategy is explicitly recognised (Clegg, 1990).

In practical terms, Moran and Ghoshal (1996) and more recently Nahapiet and Ghoshal (1998) have pointed out that transaction costs theory, as an underpinning for strategy, leads strategists to emphasise processes of *value appropriation*. The knowledge-based view leads them to stress processes of *value creation*. This implies a shift in the focus for strategic thinking away from traditional market concerns to issues of internal organisational dynamics. The conventional focus on value appropriation calls for strategies which will ensure the development and maintenance of effective and efficient means of appropriating value from available scarce resources which will add value to organisational outputs. If the organisation can thereby maintain a favourable market position it will sustain its competitive performance. The more recent focus calls for strategies which will create value in knowledge and lead to its effective exploitation to produce outputs based upon unique competencies and capabilities which cannot readily be rivalled. The conventional and knowledge-based approaches therefore seek to create and sustain competitive advantage in different ways: the one by searching out cost efficiencies and differentiation advantages which can lead to unassailable market positions; the other by investing in the creation and exploitation of useful new knowledge which cannot be readily appropriated by competitors irrespective of their market position.

# Creating and sustaining competitive advantage

Porter is one of the most influential strategists to have proposed the type of conventional approach which is described above. For reasons which will be outlined later in this paper, disenchantment with conventional strategic prescriptions from the mid-1980s onwards fuelled a resurrection of the older 'resource-based view' of the firm. The resource-based view is important because it provides the basic theoretical springboard from which knowledge-based theory has taken off. Resource-based theorists argue that capabilities and competencies are intangible assets which provide unique sources of competitive advantage to the firm. Knowledge-based theorists argue that firms which further develop unique capabilities in the management of knowledge processes can build distinctive competencies based upon exploiting the growing knowledge these processes generate.

Selznick (1947) and Penrose (1959) may have provided inspiration for resource- and knowledge-based theory, but it has been left to more modern writers to spell out in greater detail how competitive advantage derived from resources like knowledge can be further created and sustained (e.g. Rumelt, 1984; Wernerfelt, 1984; Dierickx and Cool, 1989; Barney, 1991; Hall, 1993; Peteraf, 1993). These writers have argued that resources can create competitive advantages because each organisation accumulates unique bundles of resources. These unique bundles of resources can potentially sustain a competitive advantage if they are difficult to substitute, replicate, imitate or transfer to other companies. If the precise form of a particular resource is difficult to specify and its precise effect on performance difficult to isolate, it is said to be 'causally ambiguous'. Causal ambiguity is an attribute of some resources which makes it more likely that they can sustain a competitive advantage.

It can be argued that knowledge is a resource which meets these resource-based criteria for sustaining competitive success. Explicit knowledge can be codified, which makes replication and transfer easier to achieve. Indeed, one of the reasons for codifying knowledge is to enable it to be more readily communicated to others, but applications of explicit knowledge may still be causally ambiguous. Tacit knowledge is by definition unarticulated and therefore less amenable to transfer. It is a human resource and only manifest in human use. The resource-based view suggests that organisations exploit their human resources by developing organisational capabilities to deploy them in uniquely advantageous ways. Over time this can lead to the development of core competencies. Core competencies based on knowledge may be sustainable for a time in resource-based terms until or unless they are superseded by developments elsewhere. As Porter (1991) notes, the value of any useful resource can be eroded by innovations elsewhere. All knowledge of course is vulnerable to this process, but tacit knowledge is not so readily appropriated as information.

This means that additional organisational capabilities for managing knowledge processes are required. Grant (1996) suggests that the capability for integrating knowledge from a wide range of disparate sources is an example of a key capability of this type.

Organisational knowledge-based capabilities draw upon tacit knowledge (Polanyi, 1958; 1966) as well as explicit knowledge. They are culturally bounded (Nonaka, 1991; Hall, 1993; Lave, 1993; Blackler, 1995) and context dependent. They develop in organisational cultures which are the unique and path-dependent result of human action, rather than human design (Barney, 1986; Camerer and Vespalainen, 1988; Fiol, 1991). The path-dependency concept is used to refer to the fact that decisions and actions taken in the early days shape the parameters within which future developments can take place. For these reasons, cost and/or differentiation advantages stemming from knowledge-based capabilities cannot normally be installed overnight by would-be competitors. Furthermore, even when knowledge itself can be made fully explicit and transferable, its effective application in one cultural setting does not ensure that it can be exploited to the same effect in another if the capability that enables it to be effectively exploited cannot also be readily transferred.

We have said that, given time, advantages derived from knowledge-based core competencies in doing particular things may be eroded, for example by technological change. Organisations which have developed strong organisational capabilities for managing knowledge creation and exploiting the value in knowledge created are better able to adapt to such change by developing new sustainable core competencies for the future. The importance of both types of capability in managing knowledge for competitive success is illustrated in the biotechnology context in Box 15.1.

## Box 15.1

## Knowledge and knowledge-based capabilities in biotechnology

In biotechnology, scientists bring highly specialised skills and knowledge to research teams. Although they bring specialised explicit knowledge, it is knowledge which could not be acquired overnight by a novice. They also bring tacit knowledge which is by definition difficult to transfer. In the processes of team interaction new knowledge is created and developed as participants pool their knowledge and skills. Developments with commercial potential are patented and are difficult to substitute, replicate or imitate. But with or without patent protection, which does not in any event last indefinitely, most advances are years in the making and could not be repeated independently outside the kinds of scientific culture which are characteristic of many biotechnology firms. These firms may develop a core competency in particular types of process technologies and/or potential new knowledge applications. But if the technologies and/or potential new knowledge applications fail at the development stage, these firms may still survive because of their capability for creating new knowledge with the potential to lead future successful developments.

# Conventional versus knowledge-based strategy

Three key limitations to conventional understandings of and approaches to strategy can at this point be highlighted. The first is an over-reliance upon an information-processing model to understand and explain strategic decision making. The second is a partial and incomplete view of human nature and the basis upon which effective human relationships are built. The third is a neglect of internal organisational dynamics of change.

As we have seen, conventional understandings and approaches to strategy adopt an explicit or implicit information-processing view of the strategy formulation process. It is suggested that this emphasis upon information and information-processing issues neglects other important factors upon which the success of information processing depends. In the mid-1980s, Miller and Porter (1985) pointed out that 'the information revolution' was a key factor affecting relations between organisations and innovation. They suggested that information technologies can affect international organisations in three major ways. First, by changing the industry structure they can alter the rules of competition in some industries. Second, by creating new ways in which companies can out-perform one another to gain competitive advantage, they can create new ways of competing. Third, they can spawn new business, often from within a company's existing operations. Miller and Porter (1985) argued that information technology could transform the linkages between value-creating activities in organisations and the way in which those activities were performed. They argued that every value-creating activity has both a physical and an information-processing component. New information flows enabled companies to exploit the linkages between value-creating activities more effectively, both within the firm and in networks and alliances with other firms. For example, information technologies have made it easier for buyers and suppliers to co-ordinate their activities. Miller and Porter suggested that many industries were moving towards a higher information content in both products and processes and that 'the information revolution' was creating interrelationships between industries that would otherwise have been separate. The fact that information technology had both strategic and structural implications was recognised, and the literature placed a new emphasis upon the strategic significance of information flows.

By stressing the importance of information *flows*, Miller and Porter high-lighted the fact that communications are as important as information-processing capability in explaining the human thinking which underpins decisions. From the mid-1980s onwards, however, it became increasingly apparent that this was only part of the story and that even this refinement to the information processing model of organisations could not on its own explain the changes which were occurring. In some industries, established firms with dominant market positions, many of which had invested heavily in new information and communication technologies, were proving vulnerable to technological challenges from smaller firms, many of which were also industry outsiders. These companies, despite their seeming disadvantages in terms of size, resources, information-processing capabilities, market position and access to industry-specific information, were able to successfully pioneer radical technological changes which transformed the industry. For example in the computer industry, companies like Apple, Compaq and Dell pioneered and promoted the PC which challenged IBM's supremacy in the computer market.

This phenomenon has been dubbed 'the attackers' advantage' (Foster, 1986). It does not appear to be readily explicable in terms of the conventional transaction costs paradigm and contradicts established strategic thinking about the importance of market position. It is possible to argue that there are asymmetries involved in such situations. Market leaders have their positions of dominance to lose by championing radical new technologies, whereas outside attackers have only the opportunity to benefit, but 'the attackers' advantage' does not apply to all cases of radical technological change which transforms an industry. Some established companies have successfully pioneered changes which have eroded their existing technological competencies. Dupont, for example, developed and promoted synthetic fibres, even though synthetics were a challenge to rayon in which Dupont was the market leader (Hounshell and Smith, 1988).

What, therefore, is 'the attackers' advantage'? Did established firms like Dupont also possess it? The point is that information-processing capability is not on its own sufficient to create a competitive advantage in a firm of any size, irrespective of its original market position. The smaller 'attackers' which triumphed in the computer industry with the PC did so in competition with a world-beater in information processing. Some writers (e.g. Remenyi et al., 1995) have commented upon the numerous documented cases in which the large investments in information technology made by comparatively resource-rich firms have failed to deliver expected returns. During the 1980s, recognising the sorts of potential for IT which were highlighted by Miller and Porter above, many organisations invested heavily in IT and in IT training. Some of them later engaged in downsizing exercises in the face of an intensification of competition and subsequently found that, in doing so, they had lost important *knowledge*. Information is only one of the inputs required to create and exploit knowledge.

Knowledge management is about more than the management of hardware and software and solving problems of user friendliness. It is also concerned with making the best possible use of the creativity and expertise of people and the effective management of dynamic social processes which generate and exploit a wide range of differing types of knowledge. It does not matter how sophisticated the information and communication technology is in a firm. If the employees are not inclined and trained to use it to its best advantage it is not the investment that it might be.

The second limitation which was noted earlier was the unrealistic perspective on the nature of human beings and the basis for effective human relationships which has been adopted by some of the conventional approaches to strategy. The rational understanding of human nature and its associated contractual understanding of human relationships in the firm overlooks a range of 'non-rational' behaviours and 'non-contractual' relationships both within and without the organisation that are just as vital to considerations of performance.

Taking transaction costs theory as one of the most important influences on the traditional approach, we may ask a number of questions which are directly relevant to the creation and exploitation of knowledge. For example, if we focus upon the contractual aspect of transaction costs theory, can we arrive at an adequate appreciation of the nature of group knowledge? Is trust in an organisation really part of an implicit contract? If in some ways it is, how far would this implicit contract of trust extend? If knowledge is a source of power in organisational contexts, is sharing knowledge part of an implicit contract of trust? What is contractual about the development of practical know-how based on experience? Does the idea of a contract account for individual differences in personal motivation and development over time?

Human beings clearly are capable of rational instrumental thinking. Rational problem solving is integral to the decision-making process, but human beings have other qualities which are recognised in the knowledge-based literature and these qualities are also important. These are the qualities of vision, ambition, creativity and inventiveness which the knowledge management approach endeavours to tap. Human beings can be 'self-seeking' at times, but to regard them as selfseeking all the time is surely to adopt a jaundiced view. They can also be loyal and altruistic. Human nature is much more complex than the picture of boundedly rational man suggests. Similarly, productive human relationships depend upon more than explicit, implicit or psychological contracts. Common visions, shared ambitions, meanings, and group identities are important in groups and teams. Human beings operate in a world that is socially constructed (Berger and Luckmann, 1967), and organisational worlds are a long way from being rationally planned and constructed.

Most strategies, formally planned or emergent, originate with groups and teams. Group decision making involves rational problem solving and decision making processes of the type Andrews (1971) describes in connection with strategy formulation. It also involves communications and reflective processes of the type described by Schon (1983) as 'reflection in action'. These are the processes stressed in connection with knowledge management. A realistic view of human relationships is one in which *both* types of process are seen to be operative in reaching effective decisions. They are not alternative approaches. They are both integral to effectiveness (Carlisle and Dean, 1999).

Mary Douglas, an anthropologist, had this to say about Williamson's transaction costs theory: 'He believes firms vary, but not individuals. He has the same representative rational individual marching into one kind of contract or refusing to renew it and entering into another kind for the same set of reasons, namely the cost of transactions in a given economic environment' (Douglas, 1990: 102). At this point, it is worth stating that the transaction costs understanding, while adopting the notion of bounded rationality, has tended to stress the rational aspects of decision making at the expense of equally important sociological and psychological ones. These processes are crucial to considerations of internal organisational dynamics and change. We may recall the fact that in March and Simon's original formulation of the bounded rationality concept, these two types of process were seen to be equally important.

The sociological and psychological processes which help to shape 'images' of the competitive environment and through which processes of knowledge creation, exploitation, transfer and change take place are not accorded a high profile in conventional approaches to strategy. Informal networks and communities of practice (Brown and Duguid, 1991), for example, are not discussed in the mainstream literature. It has already been said that conventional strategic approaches regard internal organisational dynamics as a strategy implementation concern. We may also be reminded at this point of Kogut and Zander's (1996) definition of organisation as a 'social community', a definition which directs the attention of knowledge-based theorists towards those very processes as a mainstream strategy concern. In commenting on the charge that the transaction costs understanding neglects the dynamics of organisation development and change, Williamson himself has repeatedly pointed out that his approach to understanding organisations is based on comparative statics. In simple terms this means that one organisation is compared with another and found to have lower transaction costs. Strategists are encouraged to focus upon cost-minimising efficiency at the expense of the dynamic efficiencies of knowledge creation and exploitation, innovation and technological change. Williamson appreciates that his understanding is partial in suggesting that 'much more study of the relations between organisations and innovation is needed' (Williamson, 1985: 144). In the knowledge-based view of the firm these neglected dynamics have a central place.

## Conclusions

This paper has argued that conventional approaches to strategy are based upon a partial understanding of information and knowledge, human nature, human relationships and the dynamics of change. However, partial understandings are not necessarily wrong. Circumstances may arise which highlight their deficiencies, which is what this paper suggests happened in the context of the performance declines of companies like IBM. The tendency which was apparent throughout most of the 1980s to equate knowledge with information can now be seen more clearly to have been a mistake. Knowledge cannot be codified and subsequently commodified in the way that information can, but this is not to say that information and information processing are unimportant. It is simply to say that on their own they are not sufficient to create and sustain a competitive performance. Conventional approaches to strategy highlight rational rather than reflective decision processes, whereas rational *and* reflective communicative processes are equally important. Some aspects of human relationships are contractual, but once again this is only part of the picture and not all change can be understood in directive top-down terms.

This paper has suggested that knowledge-based understandings and approaches to strategy can remedy this kind of shortcoming. Knowledge-based approaches to strategy raise the profile of human interactive processes and the dynamics of organisational change. These are precisely the kinds of process which the conceptualisation of rational people engaging in contractual relationships has a tendency to under-rate.

A knowledge management approach to strategy clearly has the potential to provide a useful antidote. Earlier this paper raised the key question: how radical a shift in strategic thinking is required to move to a knowledge management approach? Does knowledge management require a paradigm shift? Is it incompatible with conventional approaches to strategy? Obviously not, in the opinion of this author. Conventional understandings can still offer useful insights into *what* an organisation needs to achieve in order to sustain a successful performance. Conventional strategy approaches on the other hand might be considered to be somewhat naïve in respect of *how* to do it. The knowledge-based understanding offers a more realistic process perspective. It offers a better understanding of human nature, human relationships and internal organisational dynamics, and it is founded upon a better grasp of the differences between information and knowledge. It may be suggested that the two understandings of strategy are not incompatible and that there are obvious complementarities.

## Referenes

Alchian, A. and Demetz, H. (1972) 'Production information costs and economic organisation', *American Economic Review*, Vol. 62, pp. 777–795.

Andrews, K. (1971) *The Concept of Corporate Strategy*, Homewood, Ill., Dow Jones Irwin.

Barney, J.B. (1986) 'Organizational culture: can it be changed?', *Academy of Management Review*, Vol. 11, pp. 656–665.

Barney, J.B. (1991) 'Firm resources and sustained competitive advantage', *Journal of Management*, Vol. 17, pp. 99–120.

Berger, P. and Luckmann, T. (1967) *The Social Construction of Reality*, Doubleday, New York.

Blackler, F. (1995) 'Knowledge, knowledge work and organisations: an overview and interpretation', *Organisation Studies*, Vol. 16, pp. 1021–1046.

Brown, J.S. and Duguid, P. (1991) 'Organisational learning and communities of practice: towards a unified view of working, learning and innovation', *Organisation Science*, Vol. 2, pp. 40–57.

Camerer, C. and Vespalainen, A. (1988) 'The economic efficiency of corporate culture', *Strategic Management Journal*, Vol. 9, pp. 115–126.

Carlisle, Y.M. and Dean, A. (1999) 'Design as knowledge integration capability', *Creativity and Innovation Management*, Vol. 8, No. 2, pp. 112–121.

Clegg, S.R. (1990) *Modern Organizations: Organization Studies in the Post-Modern World*, London, Sage.

Dierickx, I. and Cool, K. (1989) 'Asset stock accumulation and sustainability of competitive advantage', *Management Science*, Vol. 35, pp. 1504–1511.

Douglas, M. (1990) 'Converging on autonomy: anthropology and institutional economics', in O.E. Williamson (ed.) *Organization Theory: From Chester Barnard to the Present and Beyond*, Oxford, Oxford University Press, pp. 98–115.

Fiol, C.M. (1991) 'Managing culture as a competitive resource: an identity-based view of sustainable competitive advantage', *Journal of Management*, Vol. 17, pp. 191–211.

Foster, R.N. (1986) *Innovation: The Attackers' Advantage*, New York, Summit Books.

Fransman, M. (1998) 'Information, knowledge, vision and theories of the firm', in Dosi, G., Teece, D.J. and Chytry, J. (eds) *Technology, Organization and Competitiveness*, Oxford, Oxford University Press, pp. 147–192.

Gee, P. (1996) 'On mobots and classrooms, the converging languages of the new capitalism and schooling', *Organization*, Vol. 3, pp. 147–192.

Grant, R. (1996) 'Prospecting in dynamically competitive environments: organisational capability as knowledge integration', *Organisation Science*, Vol. 7, pp. 375–387.

Hall, R. (1993) 'A framework linking intangible resources and capabilities to sustainable competitive advantage', *Strategic Management Journal*, Vol. 14, pp. 607–618.

Hamel, G. and Prahalad, C.K. (1989) 'Strategic intent', *Harvard Business Review*, Vol. 67, May/June, pp. 63–76.

Hayek, F. (1945) 'The use of knowledge in society', *American Economic Review*, Vol. 35, No. 4, pp. 519–530.

Hounshell, D.A. and Smith, J.K. (1988) *Science and Corporate Strategy: DuPont R&D, 1902–1980*, Cambridge, Cambridge University Press.

Jensen, M. and Meckling, W. (1976) 'Theory of the firm, managerial behaviour, agency costs and ownership structure', *Journal of Financial Economics*, Vol. 3, pp. 305–360.

Kogut, B. and Zander, U. (1996) 'What do firms do? Coordination, identity and learning', *Organization Science*, Vol. 7, pp. 503–518.

Lave, J. (1993) 'The practice of learning', in Chaiklin, S. and Lave, J. (eds) *Understanding Practice: Perspectives on Activity and Context*, Cambridge, Cambridge University Press, pp. 3–32.

Leonard, D. (1995) *Wellsprings of Knowledge: Building and Sustaining the Sources of Innovation*, Boston, Harvard Business School Press.

March, J.G. and Simon, H.A. (1958) *Organizations*, New York, Wiley.

Marshall, A. (1969) *Principles of Economics*, first published 1920, London, Macmillan.

Miller, V.E. and Porter, M.E. (1985) 'How information gives you competitive advantage', *Harvard Business Review*, Vol. 63, July/August, pp. 149–160.

Moran, P. and Ghoshal, S. (1996) 'Value creation by firms', in Keys, J.P. and Dosier, L.N. (eds) *Academy of Management, Best Paper Proceedings*, Georgia Southern University, pp. 41–45.

Nahapiet, J. and Ghoshal, S. (1998) 'Social capital, intellectual capital and the organizational advantage', *Academy of Management Review*, Vol. 23, pp. 242–266.

Nelson, R.R. and Winter, S.G. (1982) *An Evolutionary Theory of Economic Change*, Cambridge, Mass., Harvard University Press.

Nonaka, I. (1991) 'The knowledge creating company', *Harvard Business Review*, Vol. 69, November/December, pp. 96–104.

Nonaka, I. (1994) 'A dynamic theory of organisational knowledge creation', *Organisation Science*, Vol. 5, No. 1, pp. 14–37.

Nonaka, I. and Takeuchi, H. (1995) *The Knowledge Creating Company*, Oxford, Oxford University Press.

Penrose, E. (1959) *The Theory of the Growth of the Firm*, Oxford, Basil Blackwell.

Peteraf, M.A. (1993) 'The cornerstones of competitive advantage: a resource-based view', *Strategic Management Journal*, Vol. 14, pp. 179–191.

Polanyi, M. (1958) *Personal Knowledge: Towards A Post Critical Philosophy*, London, Routledge & Kegan Paul.

Polanyi, M. (1966) *The Tacit Dimension*, London, Routledge & Kegan Paul.

Porter, M.E. (1991) 'Towards a dynamic theory of strategy', *Strategic Management Journal*, Vol. 12, pp. 95–117.

Remenyi, D., Money, A. and Twite, A. (1995) *Effective Measurement and Management of IT Costs and Benefits*, Oxford, Butterworth-Heinemann.

Rumelt, R.P. (1984) 'Towards a strategic theory of the firm', in Lamb, R.B. (ed.) *Competitive Strategic Management*, Englewood Cliffs, New Jersey, Prentice Hall, pp. 556–570.

Schon, DA. (1983) *The Reflective Practitioner*, New York, Collins.

Selznick, P. (1947) *Leadership in Administration: A Sociological Perspective*, New York, Harper.

Teece, D.J. (1977) 'Technology transfer by multinational firms: the resource cost of transferring technical know-how', *The Economic Journal*, Vol. 87, pp. 242–261.

Wernerfelt, B. (1984) 'A resource-based view of the firm', *Strategic Management Journal*, Vol. 5, pp. 171–180.

Williamson, O.E. (1975) *Markets and Hierarchies: Analysis and Anti-Trust Implications*, New York, Free Press.

Williamson, O.E. (1985) *The Economic Institutions of Capitalism: Firms, Markets, Relational Contracting*, London, Macmillan.

# Changing Contexts: the Global Information Economy

The readings in this section consider the implication of recent changes in the world economy for strategic behaviour. The two main changes considered are the information technology revolution (part of what is often referred to as the New Economy) and the increasingly global nature of competition (sometimes referred to as globalization). The first reading, by Ghoshal, considers how organizations *become* international organizations. They do so by achieving efficiency, managing risks and improving their ability to innovate, learn and adapt. The task is not easy since these different goals sometimes come into conflict. The second reading, by Arthur, emphasizes how information technology has increased the role of positive feedback in the economy where initial advances lead to a 'success breeds success' dynamic. It considers whether information technology has changed the patterns of economic growth. The third reading, by Yip, considers how the rise of information technology has increased the importance of inter-firm networks in allowing firms to generate new knowledge and process information.

## S. Ghoshal: 'Global Strategy: an Organizing Framework'

This reading appeared in the *Strategic Management Journal* in 1987. Ghoshal states that organizations are not born international, they *become* international through specific strategies. That is, the interactions between different national markets arise not from natural characteristics of those markets, but from specific strategies aimed at developing attributes like synergies and economies of scale/scope. Ghoshal claims that the literature on global firms raises many different, sometimes contradictory points. Some focus on the role of scale economies and others on the role of flexibility. To find some order in this literature he constructs a useful mapping between strategic objectives and sources of competitive advantage. He claims that the three main strategic objectives for firms operating in international markets are: achieving efficiency, managing risks and improving their ability to innovate, learn and adapt. He then maps these three objectives against three different sources of competitive advantage: national differences, scale economies, and scope economies. He considers how different firms in the same industry might achieve the same objective (e.g. efficiency) with different sources of competitive advantage (e.g. Fiat via national differences, Toyota via scale economies). It is a particularly useful reading since it draws together many of the points raised in the readings in Sections 2–6.

# W.B. Arthur: 'Increasing Returns and the New World of Business'

This reading appeared in the *Harvard Business Review* in 1996. Arthur looks at how the information technology revolution has changed the dynamics of firm growth. He claims that the static nature of traditional firm growth theory, based on the notion of diminishing returns to scale (negative feedback), is only useful to understand the dynamics of traditional industries that are based on mass production and which yield products that are 'congealed *resources*'. It is, instead, not useful to study the dynamics of new industries that are based on high technology and yield products which are 'congealed *knowledge*'. The existence of up-front costs, 'network effects' and 'customer groove-in' cause these knowledge-intensive industries to be subject to increasing returns to scale (positive feedback). Arthur claims that for managers to be competitive in the world of increasing returns they have to become aware of the positive and negative feedback mechanisms that are at play in their market. They must not only develop their core competencies, but also *hit the market first* so that their early lead will be enhanced by increasing returns to scale. Whereas operations based on diminishing returns require *planning, control and hierarchy*, those based on increasing returns require *observation, positioning, less hierarchy, teamwork*.

# G. Yip: 'Global Strategy in the Twenty-first Century'

This article considers three different models that companies have used to become global in the last fifty years (often co-existing). The *internationalist* model, predominant in Japan in the 70s and 80s and still existent today in some countries like Germany, uses the home market as a basis for overseas expansion. In this model, internationalization is limited to 'extra' activities, not critical to the company's survival. The *federalist* model, common among European multi-nationals from the 1950s to the 1980s, is the classic multinational form in which self-sufficient international subsidiaries operate most of the value chain. This model adapts home country competencies and a globally uniform management system to local national environments. As national environments become less important (e.g. European unification), this model loses relevance. The *global network maximizer* strategy, the only one that Yip calls 'genuine' global strategy and the one most relevant in the 'information age', is one in which multinational companies organize their subsidiaries in independent but interacting activities. The interaction occurs through a network and stimulates creation of new knowledge and more effective processing of information. The author explains why this model is ideal for internet-based 'new economy' companies.

**C**HAPTER 16

# Global Strategy: an Organizing Framework

SUMANTRA GHOSHAL*

Over the past few years the concept of global strategy has taken the world of multinational corporations (MNCs) by storm. Scores of articles in the *Harvard Business Review*, *Fortune*, *The Economist* and other popular journals have urged multinationals to 'go global' in their strategies. The topic has clearly captured the attention of MNC managers. Conferences on global strategy, whether organized by the Conference Board in New York, *The Financial Times* in London, or Nomura Securities in Tokyo, have invariably attracted enthusiastic corporate support and sizeable audiences. Even in the relatively slow-moving world of academe the issue of globalization of industries and companies has emerged as a new bandwagon, as manifest in the large number of papers on the topic presented at recent meetings of the Academy of Management, the Academy of International Business and the Strategic Management Society. 'Manage globally' appears to be the latest battlecry in the world of international business.

## Multiple perspectives, many prescriptions

This enthusiasm notwithstanding, there is a great deal of conceptual ambiguity about what a 'global' strategy really means. As pointed out by Hamel and Prahalad (1985), the distinction among a global industry, a global firm, and a global strategy is somewhat blurred in the literature. According to Hout, Porter and Rudden (1982), a global strategy is appropriate for global industries which are defined as those in which a firm's competitive position in one national market is significantly affected by its competitive position in other national markets. Such interactions between a firm's positions in different markets may arise from scale benefits or from

* John Wiley & Sons Limited for 'Global Strategy: An Organising Framework' by Sumantra Ghoshal © *Strategic Management Journal*, 1987.

the potential of synergies or sharing of costs and resources across markets. However, as argued by Bartlett (1985), Kogut (1984) and many others, those scale and synergy benefits may often be created by strategic actions of individual firms and may not be 'given' in any *a priori* sense. For some industries, such as aeroframes or aeroengines, the economies of scale may be large enough to make the need for global integration of activities obvious. However, in a large number of cases industries may not be born global but may have globalness thrust upon them by the entrepreneurship of a company such as Yoshida Kagyo KK (YKK) or Procter and Gamble. In such cases the global industry–global strategy link may be more useful for ex-post explanation of outcomes than for ex-ante predictions or strategizing.

Further, the concept of a global strategy is not as new as some of the recent authors on the topic have assumed it to be. It was stated quite explicitly about 20 years ago by Perlmutter (1969) when he distinguished between the geocentric, polycentric, and ethnocentric approaches to multinational management. The starting point for Perlmutter's categorization scheme was the world-view of a firm, which was seen as the driving force behind its management processes and the way it structured its world-wide activities (see Robinson, 1978 and Rutenberg, 1982 for detailed reviews and expositions). In much of the current literature, in contrast, the focus has been narrowed and the concept of global strategy has been linked, almost exclusively with how the firm structures the flow of tasks within its world-wide value-adding system. The more integrated and rationalized the flow of tasks appears to be, the more global the firm's strategy is assumed to be (e.g. Leontiades, 1984). On the one hand, this focus has led to improved understanding of the fact that different tasks offer different degrees of advantages from global integration and national differentiation and that, optimally, a firm must configure its value chain to obtain the best possible advantages from both (Porter, 1984). But, on the other hand, it has also led to certain dysfunctional simplifications. The complexities of managing large, world-wide organizations have been obscured by creating polar alternatives between centralization and decentralization, or between global and multidomestic strategies (e.g. Hout *et al.*, 1982). Complex management tasks have been seen as composites of simple global and local components. By emphasizing the importance of rationalizing the flow of components and final products within a multinational system, the importance of internal, flows of people, technology, information, and values has been de-emphasized.

Differences among authors writing on the topic of global strategy are not limited to concepts and perspectives. Their prescriptions on how to manage globally have also been very different, and often contradictory.

1 Levitt (1983) has argued that effective global strategy is not a bag of many tricks but the successful practice of just one: product standardization. According to him, the core of a global strategy lies in developing a standardized product to be produced and sold the same way throughout the world.

2 According to Hout *et al.* (1982), on the other hand, effective global strategy requires the approach not of a hedgehog, who knows only one trick, but that of a fox, who knows many. Exploiting economies of scale through global volume, taking pre-emptive positions through quick and large investments, and managing interdependently to achieve synergies across different activities are, according to these authors, some of the more important moves that a winning global strategist must muster.

3 Hamel and Prahalad's (1985) prescription for a global strategy contradicts that of Levitt (1983) even more sharply. Instead of a single standardized product, they recommend a broad product portfolio, with many product varieties, so that investments on technologies and distribution channels can be shared. Cross-subsidization across products and markets, and the development of a strong world-wide distribution system, are the two moves that find the pride of place in these authors' views on how to succeed in the game of global chess.

4 If Hout *et al.*'s (1982) global strategist is the heavyweight champion who knocks out opponents with scale and pre-emptive investments, Kogut's (1985b) global strategist is the nimble-footed athlete who wins through flexibility and arbitrage. He creates options so as to turn the uncertainties of an increasingly volatile global economy to his own advantage. Multiple sourcing, production shifting to benefit from changing factor costs and exchange rates, and arbitrage to exploit imperfections in financial and information markets are, according to Kogut, some of the hallmarks of a superior global strategy.

These are only a few of the many prescriptions available to MNC managers about how to build a global strategy for their firms. All these suggestions have been derived from rich and insightful analyses of real-life situations. They are all reasonable and intuitively appealing, but their managerial implications are not easy to reconcile.

## The need for an organizing framework

The difficulty for both practitioners and researchers in dealing with the small but rich literature on global strategies is that there is no organizing framework within which the different perspectives and prescriptions can be assimilated. An unfortunate fact of corporate life is that any particular strategic action is rarely an unmixed blessing. Corporate objectives are multidimensional, and often mutually contradictory. Contrary to received wisdom, it is also usually difficult to prioritize them. Actions to achieve a particular objective often impede another equally important objective. Each of these prescriptions is aimed at achieving certain objectives of a global strategy. An overall framework can be particularly useful in identifying the trade-offs between those objectives and therefore in understanding not only the benefits but also the potential costs associated with the different strategic alternatives.

The objective of this paper is to suggest such an organizing framework which may help managers and academics in formulating the various issues that arise in global strategic management. The underlying premise is that simple categorization schemes such as the distinction between global and multidomestic strategies are not very helpful in understanding the complexities of corporate-level strategy in large multinational corporations. Instead, what may be more useful is to understand what the key strategic objectives of an MNC are, and the tools that it possesses for achieving them. An integrated analysis of the different means and the different ends can help both managers and researchers in formulating, describing, classifying and analyzing the content of global strategies. Besides, such a framework can relate academic research, that is often partial, to the totality of real life that managers must deal with.

## The framework: mapping means and ends

The proposed framework is shown in Table 16.1. While the specific construct may be new, the conceptual foundation on which it is built is derived from a synthesis of existing literature.

Table 16.1 *Global strategy: an organizing framework*

| Strategic objectives | Sources of competitive advantage | | |
| --- | --- | --- | --- |
| | National differences | Scale economies | Scope economies |
| Achieving efficiency in current operations | Benefiting from differences in factor costs – wages and cost of capital | Expanding and exploiting potential scale economies in each activity | Sharing of investments and costs across products, markets and businesses |
| Managing risks | Managing different kinds of risks arising from market or policy-induced changes in comparative advantages of different countries | Balancing scale with strategic and operational flexibility | Portfolio diversification of risks and creation of options and side-bets |
| Innovation, learning and adaptation | Learning from societal differences in organizational and managerial processes and systems | Benefiting from experience – cost reduction and innovation | Shared learning across organizational components in different products, markets or businesses |

The basic argument is simple. The goals of a multinational – as indeed of any organization – can be classified into three broad categories. The firm must achieve efficiency in its current activities; it must manage the risks that it assumes in carrying out those activities; and it must develop internal learning capabilities so as to be able to innovate and adapt to future changes. Competitive advantage is developed by taking strategic actions that optimize the firm's achievement of these different and, at times, conflicting goals.

A multinational has three sets of tools for developing such competitive advantage. It can exploit the differences in input and output markets among the many countries in which it operates. It can benefit from scale economies in its different activities. It can also exploit synergies or economies of scope that may be available because of the diversity of its activities and organization.

The strategic task of managing globally is to use all three sources of competitive advantage to optimize efficiency, risk and learning simultaneously in a world-wide business. The key to a successful global strategy is to manage the interactions between these different goals and means. That, in essence, is the organizing framework. Viewing the tasks of global strategy this way can be helpful to both managers and academics in a number of ways. For example, it can help managers in generating a comprehensive checklist of factors and issues that must be considered in reviewing different strategic alternatives. Such a checklist can serve as a basis for mapping the overall strategies of their own companies and those of their competitors so as to understand the comparative strengths and vulnerabilities of both. Table 16.1 shows some illustrative examples of factors that must be considered while carrying out such comprehensive strategic audits. Another practical utility of the framework is that it can highlight the contradictions between the different goals and between the different means, and thereby make salient the strategic dilemmas that may otherwise get resolved through omission.

In the next two sections the framework is explained more fully by describing the two dimensions of its construct, viz the strategic objectives of the firm and the sources of competitive advantage available to a multinational corporation. Subsequent sections show how selected articles contribute to the literature and fit within the overall framework. The paper concludes with a brief discussion of the trade-offs that are implicit in some of the more recent prescriptions on global strategic management.

# The goals: strategic objectives

## *Achieving efficiency*

A general premise in the literature on strategic management is that the concept of strategy is relevant only when the actions of one firm can affect the actions or performance of another. Firms competing in imperfect markets earn different 'efficiency rents' from the use of their resources (Caves, 1980). The objective of strategy, given this perspective, is to enhance such efficiency rents.

Viewing a firm broadly as an input—output system, the overall efficiency of the firm can be defined as the ratio of the value of its outputs to the costs of all its inputs. It is by maximizing this ratio that the firm obtains the surplus resources required to secure its own future. Thus it differentiates its products to enhance the exchange value of its outputs, and seeks low cost factors to minimize the costs of its inputs. It also tries to enhance the efficiency of its throughput processes by achieving higher scale economies or by finding more efficient production processes.

The field of strategic management is currently dominated by this efficiency perspective. The generic strategies of Porter (1980), different versions of the portfolio model, as well as overall strategic management frameworks such as those proposed by Hofer and Schendel (1978) and Haz and Majluf (1984) are all based on the underlying notion of maximizing efficiency rents of the different resources available to the firm.

In the field of global strategy this efficiency perspective has been reflected in the widespread use of the integration—responsiveness framework originally proposed by Prahalad (1975) and subsequently developed and applied by a number of authors including Doz, Bartlett and Prahalad (1981) and Porter (1984). In essence, the framework is a conceptual lens for visualizing the cost advantages of global integration of certain tasks *vis-à-vis* the differentiation benefits of responding to national differences in tastes, industry structures, distribution systems, and government regulations. As suggested by Bartlett (1985), the same framework can be used to understand differences in the benefits of integration and responsiveness at the aggregate level of industries, at the level of individual companies within an industry, or even, at the level of different functions within a company (see Figure 16.1, reproduced from Bartlett, 1985). Thus the consumer electronics industry may be characterized by low differentiation benefits and high integration advantages, while position of the packaged foods industry may be quite the opposite. In the telecommunications switching industry, in contrast, both local and global forces may be strong, while in the automobile industry both may be of moderate and comparable importance.

Within an industry (say, automobile), the strategy of one firm (such as Toyota) may be based on exploiting the advantages of global integration through centralized production and decision-making, while that of another (such as Fiat) may aim at exploiting the benefits of national differentiation by creating integrated and autonomous subsidiaries which can exploit strong links with local stakeholders to defend themselves against more efficient global competitors. Within a firm, research may offer greater efficiency benefits of integration, while sales and service may provide greater differentiation advantages. One can, as illustrated in Figure 16.1, apply the framework to even lower levels of analysis, right down to the level of individual tasks. Based on such analysis, a multinational firm can determine the optimum way to configure its value chain so as to achieve the highest overall efficiency in the use of its resources (Porter, 1984).

However, while efficiency is clearly an important strategic objective, it is not the only one. As argued recently by a number of authors, the broader objective of

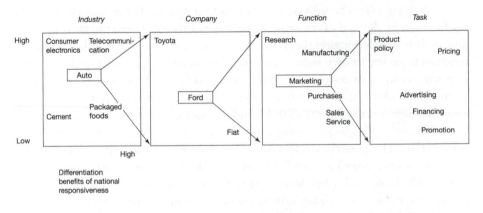

**Figure 16.1** *The integration–responsiveness framework (reproduced from Bartlett, 1985)*

strategic management is to create value which is determined not only by the returns that specific assets are expected to generate, but also by the risks that are assumed in the process (see Woo and Cool, 1985, for a review). This leads to the second strategic objective of firms – that of managing risks.[1]

## Managing risks

A multinational corporation faces many different kinds of risks, some of which are endemic to all firms and some others are unique to organizations operating across national boundaries. For analytical simplicity these different kinds of risks may be collapsed into four broad categories.

First, an MNC faces certain *macroeconomic risks* which are completely outside its control. These include cataclysmic events such as wars and natural calamities, and also equilibrium-seeking or even random movements in wage rates, interest rates, exchange rates, commodity prices, and so on.

Second, the MNC faces what is usually referred to in the literature as political risks but may be more appropriately called *policy risks* to emphasize that they arise from policy actions of national governments and not from either long-term equilibrium-seeking forces of global markets, or short-term random fluctuations in economic variables arising out of stickiness or unpredictability of market mechanisms. The net effect of such policy actions may often be indistinguishable from the effect of macroeconomic forces; for example, both may lead to changes in the exchange rate of a particular currency. But from a management perspective the two must be distinguished, since the former is uncontrollable but the latter is at least partially controllable.

Third, a firm also faces certain *competitive risks* arising from the uncertainties of competitors' responses to its own strategies (including the strategy of doing nothing and trying to maintain the status quo). While all companies face such risks to varying extents (since both monopolies and perfect competition are rare), their implications are particularly complex in the context of global strategies since the responses of competitors may take place in many different forms and in many different markets. Further, technological risk can also be considered as a part of competitive risk since a new technology can adversely affect a firm only when it is adopted by a competitor, and not otherwise.[2]

Finally, a firm also faces what may be called *resource risks*. This is the risk that the adopted strategy will require resources that the firm does not have, cannot acquire, or cannot spare. A key scarce resource for most firms is managerial talent. But resource risks can also arise from lack of appropriate technology, or even capital, (or if managers, for reasons of control, do not want to use capital markets, or if the market is less efficient than finance theorists would have us believe).

One important issue with regard to risks is that they change over time. Vernon (1977) has highlighted this issue in the context of policy risks, but the same is true of the others. Consider resource risks as an example. Often the strategy of a multinational will assume that appropriate resources will be acquired as the strategy unfolds. Yet the initial conditions on which the plans for on-going resource acquisition and development have been based may change over time. Nissan, for instance, based its aggressive internationalization strategy on the expectation of developing technological, financial, and managerial resources out of its home base. Changing competitive positions among local car manufacturers in Japan have affected these resource development plans of the company, and its internationalizing strategy has been threatened significantly. A more careful analysis of alternative competitive scenarios, and of their effects on the resource allocation plans of the company, may have led Nissan either to a slower pace of internationalization, or to a more aggressive process of resource acquisition at an earlier stage of implementing its strategy.

The strategic task, with regard to management of risks, is to consider these different kinds of risks *jointly* in the context of particular strategic. decisions. However, not all forms of risk are strategic since some risks can be easily diversified, shifted, or shared through routine market transactions. It is only those risks which cannot be diversified through a readily available external market that are of concern at the strategic level.

As an example, consider the case of currency risks. These can be classified as contractual, semi-contractual and operating risks (Lessard and Lightstone, 1983). Contractual risks arise when a firm enters into a contract for which costs and revenues are expected to be generated in different currencies: for example a Japanese firm entering into a contract for supplying an item to be made in Japan to an American customer at a price fixed in dollars. Semi-contractual risks are assumed when a firm offers an option denominated in foreign currencies, such as a British company quoting a firm rate in guilders: Operating risks, on the other hand, refer to exchange-rate-related changes in the firm's competitiveness arising out of long-term commitments of revenues or costs in different currencies. For example, to compete with a Korean firm, an American firm may set up production facilities in Singapore for supplying its customers in the United States and Europe. A gradual strengthening of the Singapore dollar, in comparison with the Korean won, can erode the overall competitiveness of the Singapore plant.

Both contractual and semi-contractual currency risks can be easily shifted or diversified, at relatively low cost, through various hedging mechanisms. If a firm does not so hedge these risks, it is essentially operating as a currency speculator and the risks must be associated with the speculation business and not with its product-market operations. Operating risks, on the other hand, cannot be hedged so easily,[3] and must be considered at the strategic rather than the operational level.

Analysis of strategic risks will have significant implications for a firm's decisions regarding the structures and locations of its cost and revenue streams. It will lead to more explicit analysis of the effects of environmental uncertainties on the configuration of its value chain. There may be a shift from ownership to rental of resources: from fixed to variable costs. Output and activity distributions may be broadened to achieve the benefits of diversification. Incrementalism and opportunism may be given greater emphasis in its strategy in comparison to pre-emptive resource commitments and long-term planning. Overall strategies may be formulated in more general and flexible terms, so as to be robust to different environmental scenarios. In addition, side-bets may be laid to cover contingencies and to create strategic options which may or may not be exercised in the future (see Kogut, 1985b; Aaker and Mascarenhas, 1984; and Mascarenhas, 1982).

## Innovation, learning and adaptation

Most existing theories of the multinational corporation view it as an instrument to extract additional rents from capabilities internalized by the firm (see Calvet, 1981, for a review). A firm goes abroad to make more profits by exploiting its technology, or brand name, or management capabilities in different countries around the world. It is assumed that the key competencies of the multinational always reside at the center.

While the search for additional profits or the desire to protect existing revenues may explain why multinationals come to exist, they may not provide an equally complete explanation of why some of them continue to grow and flourish. An alternative view may well be that a key asset of the multinational is the diversity of environments in which it operates. This diversity exposes it to multiple stimuli, allows it to develop diverse capabilities, and provides it with a broader learning opportunity than is available to a purely domestic firm. The enhanced organizational learning that results from the diversity internalized by the multinational may be a key explanator of its ongoing success, while its initial stock of knowledge may well be the strength that allows it to create such organizational diversity in the first place (Bartlett and Ghoshal, 1985).

Internal diversity may lead to strategic advantages for a firm in may different ways. In an unpredictable environment it may not be possible, *ex ante*, to predict the competencies that will be required in the future. Diversity of internal capabilities, following the logic of population ecologists (e.g. Hannan and Freeman, 1977; Aldrich, 1979), will enhance the probability of the firm's survival by enhancing the chances that it will be in possession of the capabilities required to cope with an uncertain future state. Similarly, diversity of resources and competencies may also enhance the firm's ability to create joint innovations, and to exploit them in multiple locations. One example of such benefits of diversity was recently described in the *Wall Street Journal* (April 29, 1985):

> P&G [Procter and Gamble Co.] recently introduced its new Liquid Tide, but the product has a distinctly international heritage. A new ingredient that helps suspend dirt in wash water came from the company's research center near P&G's Cincinnati headquarters. But the formula for Liquid Tide's surfactants, or cleaning agents, was developed by P&G technicians in Japan. The ingredients that fight mineral salts present in hard water came from P&G's scientists in Brussels.

As discussed in the same *WSJ* article, P&G's research center in Brussels has developed a special capability in water softening technology due, in part, to the fact that water in Europe contains more than twice the level of mineral content compared to wash water available in the United States. Similarly, surfactant technology is particularly advanced in Japan because Japanese consumers wash their clothes in colder waters compared to consumers in the US or Europe, and this makes greater demands on the cleaning ability of the surfactants. The advantage of P&G as a multinational is that it is exposed to these different operating environments and has learned, in each environment, the skills and knowledge that coping with that environment specially requires. Liquid Tide is an example of the strategic advantages that accrue from such diverse learning.

The mere existence of diversity, however, does not enhance learning. It only creates the potential for learning. To exploit this potential, the organization must consider learning as an explicit objective, and must create mechanisms and systems for such learning to take place. In the absence of explicit intention and appropriate mechanisms, the learning potential may be lost. In some companies, where all organizational resources are centralized and where the national subsidiaries are seen as mere delivery pipelines to supply the organization's value-added to different countries, diverse learning may not take place either because the subsidiaries may not possess appropriate sensing, analyzing, and responding capabilities to learn from their local environments, or because the centralized decision processes may be insensitive to knowledge accumulated outside the corporate headquarters. Other companies, in which the subsidiaries may enjoy very high levels of local resources and autonomy, may similarly fail to exploit global learning benefits because of their inability to transfer and synthesize knowledge and expertise developed in different organizational components. Local loyalties, turf protection, and the 'not invented here' (NIH) syndrome – the three handmaidens of decentralization – may restrict internal flow of information across national boundaries which is essential for global learning to occur. In other words, both centralization and decentralization may impede learning.

# The means: sources of competitive advantage

Most recent articles on global strategy have been aimed at identifying generic strategies (such as global cost leadership, focus or niche) and advocating particular strategic moves (such as cross-subsidy or pre-emptive investments). Underlying these concepts, however, are three fundamental tools for building global competitive advantage: exploiting differences in input and output markets in different countries, exploiting economies of scale, and exploiting economies of scope (Porter, 1985).

## National differences

The comparative advantage of locations in terms of differences in factor costs is perhaps the most discussed, and also the best understood, source of competitive advantage in international business.

Different nations have different factor endowments, and in the absence of efficient markets this leads to inter-country differences in factor costs. Different activities of the firm, such as R&D, production, marketing, etc., have different factor intensities. A firm can therefore gain cost advantages by configuring its value-chain so that each activity is located in the country which has the least cost for the factor that the activity uses most intensely. This is the core concept of comparative advantage-based competitive advantage — a concept for which highly developed analytical tools are available from the discipline of international economics. Kogut (1985a) provides an excellent managerial overview of this concept.

National differences may also exist in output markets. Customer tastes and preferences may be different in different countries, as may be distribution systems, government regulations applicable to the concerned product-markets, or the effectiveness of different promotion strategies and other marketing techniques. A firm can augment the exchange value of its output by tailoring its offerings to fit the unique requirements in each national market. This, in essence, is the strategy of national differentiation, and it lies at the core of what has come to be referred to as the multidomestic approach in multinational management (Hout et al. 1982).

From a strategic perspective, however, this static and purely economic view of national differences may not be adequate. What may be more useful is to take a dynamic view of comparative advantage and to broaden the concept to include both societal and economic factors.

In the traditional economics view, comparative advantages of countries are determined by their relative factor endowments and they do not change. However, in reality one lesson of the past four decades is that comparative advantages change and a prime objective of the industrial policies of many nations is to effect such changes. Thus, for any nation, the availability and cost of capital change, as do the availability of technical manpower and the wages of skilled and unskilled labor. Such changes take place, in the long run, to accommodate different levels of economic and social performance of nations, and in the short run they occur in response to specific policies and regulations of governments.

This dynamic aspect of comparative advantages adds considerable complexity to the strategic considerations of the firm. There is a first-order effect of such changes – such as possible increases in wage rates, interest rates or currency exchange rates for particular countries – that can affect the future viability of a strategy that has been based on the current levels of these economic variables. There can also be a more intriguing second-order effect. If an activity is located in an economically inefficient environment, and if the firm is able to achieve a higher level of efficiency in its own operations compared to the rest of the local economy, its competitive advantage may actually increase as the local economy slips lower and lower. This is because the macroeconomic variables such as wage or exchange rates may change to reflect the overall performance of the economy relative to the rest of the world and, to the extent that the firm's performance is better than this national aggregate, it may benefit from these macro-level changes (Kiechel, 1981).

Consistent with the discipline that gave birth to the concept, the usual view of comparative advantage is limited to factors that an economist admits into the production function, such as the costs of labor and capital. However, from a managerial perspective it may be more appropriate to take a broader view of societal comparative advantages to include 'all the relative advantages conferred on a society by the quality, quantity and configuration of its material, human and institutional resources, including "soft" resources such as inter-organizational linkages, the nature of its educational system, and organizational and managerial know-how' (Westney, 1985: 4). As argued by Westney, these 'soft' societal factors, if absorbed in the overall organizational system, can provide benefits as real to a multinational as those provided by such economic factors as cheap labor or low-cost capital.

While the concept of comparative advantage is quite clear, available evidence on its actual effect on the overall competitiveness of firms is weak and conflicting. For example, it has often been claimed that one source of competitive advantage for Japanese firms is the lower cost of capital in Japan (Hatsopoulos, 1983). However, more systematic studies have shown that there is practically no difference in the risk-adjusted cost of capital in the United States and Japan, and that capital cost advantages of Japanese firms, if any, arise from complex interactions between government subsidies and corporate ownership structures (Flaherty and Itami, 1984). Similarly, relatively low wage rates in Japan have been suggested by some authors as the primary reason for the success of Japanese companies in the US market (Itami, 1978). However, recently, companies such as Honda and Nissan have commissioned plants in the USA and have been able to retain practically the same levels of cost advantages over US manufacturers as they had for their production in Japan (Allen, 1985). Overall, there is increasing evidence that while comparative advantages of countries can provide competitive advantages to firms, the realization of such benefits is not automatic but depends on complex organizational factors and processes.

## Scale economies

Scale economies, again, is a fairly well established concept, and its implications for competitive advantage are quite well understood. Microeconomic theory provides a strong theoretical and empirical basis for evaluating the effect of scale on cost reduction, and the use of scale as a competitive tool is common in practice. Its primary implication for strategy is that a firm must expand the volume of its output so as to achieve available scale benefits. Otherwise a competitor who can achieve such volume can build cost advantages, and this can lead to a vicious cycle in which the low-volume firm can progressively lose its competitive viability.

While scale, by itself, is a static concept, there may be dynamic benefits of scale through what has been variously described as the experience or learning effect. The higher volume that helps a firm to exploit scale benefits also allows it to accumulate learning, and this leads to progressive cost reduction as the firm moves down its learning curve.

The concept of the value-added chain recently popularized by Porter (1985) adds considerable richness to the analysis of scale as a source of competitive advantage. This conceptual apparatus allows a disaggregated analysis of scale benefits in different value-creating activities of the firm. The efficient scale may vary widely by activity – being higher for component production, say, than for assembly. In contrast to a unitary view of scale, this disaggregated view permits the firm to configure different elements of its value chain to attain optimum scale economies in each.

Traditionally, scale has been seen as an unmixed blessing – something that always helps and never hurts. Recently, however, many researchers have argued otherwise (e.g. Evans, 1982). It has been suggested that scale efficiencies are obtained through increased specialization and through creation of dedicated assets and systems. The same processes cause inflexibilities and limit the firm's ability to cope with change. As environmental turbulence has increased, so has the need for strategic and operational flexibility (Mascarenhas, 1982). At the extreme, this line of argument has led to predictions of a re-emergence of the craft form of production to replace the scale-dominated assembly form (Piore and Sabel, 1984). A more typical argument has been to emphasize the need to balance scale and flexibility, through the use of modern technologies such as CAD/CAM and flexible manufacturing systems (Gold, 1982).

## Scope economies

Relatively speaking, the concept of scope economies is both new and not very well understood. It is based on the notion that certain economies arise from the fact that the cost of the joint production of two or more products can be less than the cost of producing them separately. Such cost reductions can take place due to many reasons – for example resources such as information or technologies, once acquired for use in producing one item, may be available costlessly for production of other items (Baumol, Panzer and Willig, 1982).

Table 16.2 *Scope economies in product and market diversification*

|  | Sources of scope economies | |
|---|---|---|
|  | Product diversification | Market diversification |
| Shared physical assets | Factory automation with flexibility to produce multiple products (Ford) | Global brand name (Coca-Cola) |
| Shared external relations | Using common distribution channel for multiple products (Matsushita) | Servicing multinational customers world-wide (Citibank) |
| Shared learning | Sharing R&D in computer and communications businesses (NEC) | Pooling knowledge developed in different markets (Procter and Gamble) |

The strategic importance of scope economies arises from a diversified firm's ability to share investments and costs across the same or different value chains that competitors, not possessing such internal and external diversity, cannot. Such sharing can take place across segments, products, or markets (Porter, 1985) and may involve joint use of different kinds of assets (see Table 16.2).

A diversified firm may share physical assets such as production equipment, cash, or brand names across different businesses and markets. Flexible manufacturing systems using robots, which can be used for production of different items, is one example of how a firm can exploit such scope benefits. Cross-subsidization of markets and exploitation of a global brand name are other examples of sharing a tangible asset across different components of a firms product and market portfolios.

A second important source of scope economies is shared external relations: with customers, suppliers, distributors, governments, and other institutions. A multinational bank like Citibank can provide relatively more effective service to a multinational customer than can a bank that operates in a single country (see Terpstra, 1982). Similarly, as argued by Hamel and Prahalad (1985), companies such as Matsushita have benefited considerably from their ability to market a diverse range of products through the same distribution channel. In another variation, Japanese trading companies have expanded into new businesses to meet different requirements of their existing customers.

Finally, shared knowledge is the third important component of scope economies. The fundamental thrust of NEC's global strategy is 'C&C' – computers and communication. The company firmly believes that its even strengths in the two technologies and resulting capabilities of merging them in-house to create new products give it a competitive edge over global giants such as IBM and AT&T, who have technological strength in only one of these two areas. Another example of the scope advantages of shared learning is the case of Liquid Tide described earlier in this paper.

Even scope economies, however, may not be costless. Different segments, products or markets of a diversified company face different environmental demands. To succeed, a firm needs to differentiate its management systems and processes so that each of its activities can develop *external consistency* with the requirements of its own environment. The search for scope economies. on the other hand, is a search for *internal consistencies* within the firm and across its different activities. The effort to create such synergies may invariably result in some compromise with the objective of external consistency in each activity.

Further, the search for internal synergies also enhances the complexities in a firm's management processes. In the extreme, such complexities can overwhelm the organization, as it did in the case of EMI, the UK-based music, electronics, and leisure products company which attempted to manage its new CT scanner business within the framework of its existing organizational structure and processes . . . Certain parts of a company's portfolio of businesses or markets may be inherently very different from some others, and it may be best not to look for economies of scope across them. For example, in the soft drinks industry, bottling and distribution are intensely local in scope, while the tasks of creating and maintaining a brand image, or that of designing efficient bottling plants, may offer significant benefits from global integration. Carrying out both these sets of functions in-house would clearly lead to internalizing enormous differences within the company with regard to the organizing, coordinating, and controlling tasks. Instead of trying to cope with these complexities. Coca-Cola has externalized those functions which are purely local in scope (in all but some key strategic markets). In a variation of the same theme. IBM has 'externalized' the PC business by setting up an almost stand-alone organization, instead of trying to exploit scope benefits by integrating this business within the structure of its existing organization (for a more detailed discussion on multinational scope economies and on the conflicts between internal and external consistencies, see Lorange, Scott Morton and Ghoshal, 1986).

## Prescriptions in perspective

Existing literature on global strategy offers analytical insights and helpful prescriptions for almost all the different issues indicated in Table 16.1.
[. . .]

### From parts to the whole

For managers, the advantage of . . . synthesis is that it allows them to combine a set of insightful but often partial analyses to address the totality of a multidimensional and complex phenomenon. Consider, for example, a topic that has been the staple for academics interested in international management: explaining and drawing normative conclusions from the global successes of many Japanese companies. Based on detailed comparisons across a set of matched pairs of US and Japanese firms, Itami concludes that the relative successes of the Japanese firms can be wholly explained as due to the advantages of lower wage rates and higher labor productivity. In the context of a specific industry, on the other hand, Toder (1978) shows that manufacturing scale is the single most important source of the Japanese competitive advantage. In the small car business, for example, the minimum efficient scale requires an annual production level of about 400,000 units. In the late 1970s no US auto manufacturer produced even 200,000 units of any subcompact configuration vehicle, while Toyota produced around 500,000 Corollas and Nissan produced between 300,000 and 400,000 B210s per year. Toder estimates that US manufacturers suffered a cost disadvantage of between 9 and 17 percent on account of inefficient scale alone. Add to it the effects of wage rate differentials and exchange rate movements, and Japanese success in the US auto market may not require any further explanation. Yet process-orientated scholars such as Hamel and Prahalad suggest a much more complex explanation of the Japanese tidal wave. They see it as arising out of a dynamic process of strategic evolution that exploits scope economies as a crucial weapon in the final stages. All these authors provide compelling arguments to support their own explanations, but do not consider or refute each other's hypotheses.

This multiplicity of explanations only shows the complexity of global strategic management. However, though different, these explanations and prescriptions are not always mutually exclusive. The manager's task is to find how these insights can be combined to build a multidimensional and flexible strategy that is robust to the different assumptions and explanations.

## The strategic trade-offs

This, however, is not always possible because there are certain inherent contradictions between the different strategic objectives and between the different sources of competitive advantage. Consider, for instance, the popular distinction between a glob and a multidomestic strategy described by Hout et al. (1982). A global strategy requires that the firm should carefully separate different value elements, and should locate each activity at the most efficient level of scale in the location where the activity can be carried out at the cheapest cost. Each activity should then be integrated and managed interdependently so as to exploit available scope economies. In essence, it is a strategy to maximize efficiency of current operations.

Such a strategy may, however, increase both endogenous and exogenous risks for the firm. Global scale of certain activities such as R&D and manufacturing may result in the firm's costs being concentrated in a few countries, while its revenues accrue globally, from sales in many different countries. This increases the operating exposure of the firm to the vicissitudes of exchange rate movements because of the mismatch between the currencies in which revenues are obtained and those in which costs are incurred. Similarly, the search for efficiency in a global business may lead to greater amounts of intra-company, but inter-country, flows of goods, capital, information and other resources. These flows are visible, salient and tend to attract policy interventions from different host governments. Organizationally, such an integrated system requires a high degree of coordination, which enhances the risks of management failures. These are lessons that many Japanese companies have learned well recently.

Similarly, consideration of the learning objective will again contradict some of the proclaimed benefits of a global strategy. The implementation of a global strategy tends to enhance the forces of centralization and to shift organizational power from the subsidiaries to the headquarters. This may result in demotivation of subsidiary managers and may erode one key asset of the MNC – the potential for learning from its many environments. The experiences of Caterpillar is a case in point. An exemplary practitioner of global strategy. Cat has recently spilled a lot of red ink on its balance sheet and has lost around steadily to its archrival, Komatsu. Many factors contributed to Caterpillar's woes, not the least of which was the inability of its centralized management processes to benefit from the experiences of its foreign subsidiaries.

On the flipside of the coin, strategies aimed at optimizing risk or learning may compromise current efficiency. Poynter (1985) has recommended 'upgrade', i.e. increasing commitment of technology and resources in subsidiaries, as a way to overcome risk of policy interventions by host governments. Kogut (1985b), Mascarenhas (1982) and many others have suggested creating strategic and operational flexibility as a mechanism for coping with macroenvironmental risks. Bartlett and Ghoshal (1985) have proposed the differentiated network model of multinational organizations as a way to operationalize the benefits of global learning. All these recommendations carry certain efficiency penalties. which the authors have ignored.

Similar trade-offs exist between the different sources of competitive advantages. Trying to make the most of factor cost economies may prevent scale efficiency, and may impede benefiting from synergies across products or functions. Trying to benefit from scope through product diversification may affect scale, and so on. In effect these contradictions between the different strategic objectives, and between the different means for achieving them, lead to trade-offs between each cell in the framework and practically all others.

These trade-offs imply that to formulate and implement a global strategy. MNC managers must consider all the issues suggested in Table 16.1, and must evaluate the implications of different strategic alternatives on each of these issues. Under a particular set of circumstances a particular strategic objective may dominate and a particular source of competitive advantage may play a more important role than the others (Fayerweather, 1981). The complexity of global strategic management arises from the need to understand those situational contingencies, and to adopt a strategy after evaluating the trade-offs it implies. Existing prescriptions can sensitize MNC managers to the different factors they must consider, but cannot provide ready-made and standardized solutions for them to adopt.

# Conclusion

This paper has proposed a framework that can help MNC managers in reviewing and analyzing the strategies their firms. It is not a blueprint for formulating strategies; it is a road map for reviewing them. Irrespective of whether strategies are analytically formulated or organizationally formed (Mintzberg, 1978), every firm has a realized strategy. To the extent that the realized strategy may differ from the intended one, managers need to review what the strategies of their firms really are. The paper suggests a scheme for such a review which can be an effective instrument for exercising strategic control.

Three arguments underlie the construct of the framework. First, in the global strategy literature, a kind of industry determinism has come to prevail not unlike the technological determinism that dominated management literature in the 1960s. The structures of industries may often have important influences on the appropriateness of corporate strategy, but they are only one of many such influences. Besides, corporate strategy may influence industry structure just as much as be influenced by it.

Second, simple schemes for categorizing strategies of firms under different labels tend to hide more than they reveal. A map for more detailed comparison of the content of strategies can be more helpful to managers in understanding and improving the competitive positions of their companies.

Third, the issues of risk and learning have not been given adequate importance in the strategy literature in general, and in the area of global strategies in particular. Both these are important strategic objectives and must be explicitly considered while evaluating or reviewing the strategic positions of companies.

The proposed framework is not a replacement of existing analytical tools but an enhancement that incorporates these beliefs. It does not present any new concepts or solutions, but only a synthesis of existing ideas and techniques. The benefit of such synthesis is that it can help managers in integrating an array of strategic moves into an overall strategic thrust by revealing the consistencies and contradictions among those moves.

For academics this brief view of the existing literature on global strategy will clearly reveal the need for more empirically rounded and systematic research to test and validate the hypotheses which currently appear in the literature as prescriptions and research conclusions. For partial analyses to lead to valid conclusions, excluded variables must be controlled for, and rival hypotheses must he considered and eliminated. The existing body of descriptive and normative research is rich enough to allow future researchers to adopt a more rigorous and systematic approach to enhance the reliability and validity of their findings and suggestions. The proposed framework, it is hoped, may be of value to some researchers in thinking about appropriate research issues and designs for furthering the field of global strategic management.

# Acknowledgements

The ideas presented in this paper emerged in the course of discussions with many friends and colleagues. Don Lessard, Eleanor Westney, Bruce Kogut, Chris Bartlett and Nitin Nohria were particularly helpful. I also benefited greatly from the comments and suggestions of the two anonymous referees from the *Strategic Management Journal*.

# Notes

1   In the interest of simplicity the distinction between risk and uncertainty is ignored, as is the distinction between systematic and unsystematic risks.
2   This assumes that the firm has defined its business correctly and has identified as competitors all the firms whose offerings are aimed at meeting the same set of market needs that the firm meets.
3   Some market mechanisms such as long-term currency swaps are now available which can allow at least partial hedging of moderating risks.

# References

Aaker, D. A. and B. Mascarenhas. 'The need for strategic flexibility', *Journal of Business Strategy*, 5(2), Fall 1984, pp. 74–82.

Aldrich, H. E. *Organizations and Environments*, Prentice-Hall, Englewood Cliffs, NJ, 1979.

Allen, M. K. 'Japanese companies in the United States: the success of Nissan and Honda', unpublished manuscript, Sloan School of Management, MIT. November 1985.

Bartlett, C. A. 'Global competition and MNC managers', ICCH Note No. 0–385–287, Harvard Business School, Boston, 1985.

Bartlett, C. A. and S. Ghoshal. 'The new global organization: differentiated roles and dispersed responsibilities', Working Paper No. 9–786–013, Harvard Business School, Boston, October 1985.

Baumol, W. J., J. C. Panzer and R. D. Willig. *Contestable Markets and the Theory of Industry Structure*, Harcourt Brace, Jovanovich. New York, 1982.

Calvet, A. L. 'A synthesis of foreign direct investment theories and theories of the multinational firm', *Journal of International Business Studies*, Spring–Summer 1981, pp. 43–60.

Caves, R. E. 'Industrial organization, corporate strategy and structure', *Journal of Economic Literature*, XVIII, March 1980, pp. 64–92.

Doz, Y. L., C. A. Bartlett and C. K. Prahalad. 'Global competitive pressures and host country demands: managing tensions in MNCs', *California Management Review*, Spring 1981, pp. 63–74.

Evans, J. S. *Strategic Flexibility in Business*, Report No. 678. SRI International, December 1982.

Fayerweather, J. 'Four winning strategies for the international corporation', *Journal of Business Strategy*, Fall 1981, pp. 25–36.

Flaherty, M. T. and H. Itami. 'Finance', in Okimoto, D. I., T. Sugano and F. B. Weinstein (Eds), *Competitive Edge*, Stanford University Press, Stanford, CA, 1984.

Gold, B. 'Robotics, programmable automation, and international competitiveness', *IEEE Transactions on Engineering Management*, November 1982.

Hamel, G. and C. K. Prahalad. 'Do you really have a global strategy?', *Harvard Business Review*, July–August 1985, pp. 139–148.

Hannan, M. T. and J. Freeman. 'The population ecology of organizations'. *American Journal of Sociology*, 82, 1977, pp. 929–964.

Hatsopoulos, G. N. 'High cost of capital: handicap of American industry'. Report sponsored by the American Business Conference and Thermo-Electron Corporation, April 1983.

Hax, A. C. and N. S. Majluf. *Strategic Management: An Integrative Perspective*, Prentice-Hall, Englewood Cliffs, NJ, 1984.

Hofer, C. W. and D. Schendel. *Strategy Formulation: Analytical Concepts*, West Publishing Co., St Paul, MN, 1978.

Hout, T., M. E. Porter and E. Rudden. 'How global companies win out'. *Harvard Business Review*, September–October 1982, pp. 98–108.

Itami, H. 'Japanese–U.S. comparison of managerial productivity', *Japanese Economic Studies*, Fall 1978.

Kiechel, W. 'Playing the global game', *Fortune*, November 16, 1981, pp. 111–126.

Kogut, B. 'Normative observations on the international value-added chain and strategic groups', *Journal of International Business Studies*, Fall 1984, pp. 151–167.

Kogut, B. 'Designing global strategies: comparative and competitive value added chains', *Sloan Management Review*, **26**(4), Summer 1985a, pp. 15–28.

Kogut, B. 'Designing global strategies: profiting from operational flexibility', *Sloan Management Review*, Fall 1985b, pp. 27–38.

Leontiades, J. 'Market share and corporate strategy in international industries', *Journal of Business Strategy*, **5**(1), Summer 1984, pp. 30–37.

Lessard, D. and J. Lightstone. 'The impact of exchange rates on operating profits: new business and financial responses', mimeo, Lightstone-Lessard Associates, 1983.

Levitt, T. 'The globalization of markets', *Harvard Business Review*, May–June 1983, pp. 92–102.

Lorange, P., M. S. Scott Morton and S. Ghoshal. *Strategic Control*, West Publishing Co., St Paul, MN, 1986.

Mascarenhas, B. 'Coping with uncertainty in international business', *Journal of International Business Studies*, Fall 1982, pp. 87–98.

Mintzberg, H. 'Patterns in strategic formation', *Management Science*, **24**, 1978, pp. 934–948.

Perlmutter, H. V. 'The tortuous evolution of the multinational corporation', *Columbia Journal of World Business*, January–February 1969, pp. 9–18.

Piore, M. J. and C. Sabel. *The Second Industrial Divide: Possibilities and Prospects*. Basic Books, New York, 1984.

Porter, M. E. *Competitive Strategy*, Basic Books, New York, 1980.

Porter, M. E. 'Competition in global industries: a conceptual framework', paper presented to the Colloquium on Competition in Global Industries, Harvard Business School, 1984.

Porter, M. E. *Competitive Advantage*, Free Press, New York, 1985.

Poynter, T. A. *International Enterprises and Government Intervention*, Croom Helm, London, 1985.

Prahalad, C. K. 'The strategic process in a multinational corporation', unpublished doctoral dissertation, Graduate School of Business Administration, Harvard University, 1975.

Robinson, R. D. *International Business Management: A Guide to Decision Making*, Dryden Press, Illinois, 1978.

Rutenberg, D. P. *Multinational Management*, Little, Brown, Boston, MA, 1982.

Terpstra, V. *International Dimensions of Marketing*, Kent, Boston, MA, 1982.

Toder, E. J. *Trade Policy and the U.S. Automobile Industry*, Praeger Special Studies, New York, 1978.

Vernon, R. *Storm Over the Multinationals*, Harvard University Press, Cambridge, MA, 1977.

*The Wall Street Journal*, April 29, 1985, p. 1.

Westney, D. E. 'International dimensions of information and communications technology', unpublished manuscript, Sloan School of Management, MIT, 1985.

Woo, C. Y. and K. O. Cool, 'The impact of strategic management of systematic risk', mimeo, Krannert Graduate School of Management, Purdue University, 1985.

# C HAPTER 17

# Increasing Returns and the New World of Business

W. BRIAN ARTHUR*

O ur understanding of how markets and businesses operate was passed down to us more than a century ago by a handful of European economists – Alfred Marshall in England and a few of his contemporaries on the continent. It is an understanding based squarely upon the assumption of diminishing returns: products or companies that get ahead in a market eventually run into limitations, so that a predictable equilibrium of prices and market shares is reached. The theory was roughly valid for the bulk-processing, smokestack economy of Marshall's day. And it still thrives in today's economics textbooks. But steadily and continuously in this century, Western economies have undergone a transformation from bulk-material manufacturing to design and use of technology – from processing of resources to processing of information, from application of raw energy to application of ideas. As this shift has occurred, the underlying mechanisms that determine economic behavior have shifted from ones of diminishing to ones of *increasing* returns.

Increasing returns are the tendency for that which is ahead to get further ahead, for that which loses advantage to lose further advantage. They are mechanisms of positive feedback that operate – within markets, businesses, and industries – to reinforce that which gains success or aggravate that which suffers loss. Increasing returns generate not equilibrium but instability: if a product or a company or a technology – one of many competing in a market – gets ahead by chance or clever strategy, increasing returns can magnify this advantage, and the product or company or technology can go on to lock in the market. More than causing products to become standards, increasing returns cause businesses to work differently, and they stand many of our notions of how business operates on their head.

Mechanisms of increasing returns exist alongside those of diminishing returns in all industries. But roughly speaking, diminishing returns hold sway in the traditional part of the economy – the processing industries. Increasing returns reign in the newer part – the knowledge-based industries. Modern economies have therefore bifurcated into two interrelated worlds of business corresponding to the two types of returns. The two worlds have different economics. They differ in behavior, style, and culture. They call for different management techniques, strategies, and codes of government regulation.

They call for different understandings.

## Alfred Marshall's world

Let's go back to beginnings – to the diminishing-returns view of Alfred Marshall and his contemporaries. Marshall's world of the 1880s and 1890s was one of bulk production: of metal ores, aniline dyes, pig iron, coal, lumber, heavy chemicals, soybeans, coffee – commodities heavy on resources, light on know-how. In that world it was reasonable to suppose, for example, that if a coffee plantation expanded production it would ultimately be driven to use land less suitable for coffee. In other words, it would run into diminishing returns. So if coffee plantations competed, each one would expand until it ran into limitations in the form of rising costs or diminishing profits. The market would be shared by many plantations, and a market price would be established at a predictable level – depending on tastes for coffee and the availability of suitable farmland. Planters would produce coffee so long as doing so was profitable, but because the price would be squeezed down to the average cost of production, no one would be able to make a killing. Marshall said such a market was in perfect competition, and the economic world he envisaged fitted beautifully with the Victorian values of his time. It was at equilibrium and therefore orderly, predictable and therefore amenable to scientific analysis, stable and therefore safe, slow to change and therefore continuous. Not too rushed, not too profitable. In a word, mannerly. In a word, genteel.

With a few changes, Marshall's world lives on a century later within that part of the modern economy still devoted to bulk processing: of grains, livestock, heavy chemicals, metals and ores, foodstuffs, retail goods – the part where operations are largely repetitive day to day or week to week. Product differentiation and brand names now mean that a few companies rather than many compete in a given market. But typically, if these companies try to expand, they run into some limitation: in numbers of consumers who prefer their brand, in regional demand, in access to raw materials. So no company can corner the market. And because such products are normally substitutable for one another, something like a standard price emerges. Margins are thin and nobody makes a killing. This isn't exactly Marshall's perfect competition, but it approximates it.

# The increasing-returns world

What would happen if Marshall's diminishing returns were reversed so that there were *increasing* returns? If products that got ahead thereby got further ahead, how would markets work?

Let's look at the market for operating systems for personal computers in the early 1980s when CP/M, DOS, and Apple's Macintosh systems were competing. Operating systems show increasing returns: if one system gets ahead, it attracts further software developers and hardware manufacturers to adopt it, which helps it get further ahead. CP/M was first in the market and by 1979 was well established. The Mac arrived later, but it was wonderfully easy to use. DOS was born when Microsoft locked up a deal in 1980 to supply an operating system for the IBM PC. For a year or two, it was by no means clear which system would prevail. The new IBM PC – DOS's platform – was a kludge. But the growing base of DOS/IBM users encouraged software developers such as Lotus to write for DOS. DOS's prevalence – and the IBM PC's – bred further prevalence, and eventually the DOS/IBM combination came to dominate a considerable portion of the market. That history is now well known. But notice several things. It was not predictable in advance (before the IBM deal) which system would come to dominate. Once DOS/IBM got ahead, it locked in the market because it did not pay for users to switch. The dominant system was not the best: DOS was derided by computer professionals. And once DOS locked in the market, its sponsor, Microsoft, was able to spread its costs over a large base of users. The company enjoyed killer margins.

These properties, then, have become the hallmarks of increasing returns: market instability (the market tilts to favor a product that gets ahead), multiple potential outcomes (under different events in history, different operating systems could have won), unpredictability, the ability to lock in a market, the possible predominance of an inferior product, and fat profits for the winner. They surprised me when I first perceived them in the late 1970s. They were also repulsive to economists brought up on the order, predictability, and optimality of Marshall's world. Glimpsing some of these properties in 1939, English economist John Hicks warned that admitting increasing returns would lead to 'the wreckage of the greater part of economic theory'. But Hicks had it wrong: the theory of increasing returns does not destroy the standard theory – it complements it. Hicks felt repugnance not just because of unsavory properties but also because in his, day no mathematical apparatus existed to analyze increasing-returns markets. That situation has now changed. Using sophisticated techniques from qualitative dynamics and probability theory, I and others have developed methods to analyze increasing-returns markets. The theory of increasing returns is new, but it already is well established. And it renders such markets amenable to economic understanding.

In the early days of my work on increasing returns, I was told they were an anomaly. Like some exotic particle in physics, they might exist in theory but would be rare in practice. And if they did exist, they would last for only a few seconds before being arbitraged away. But by the mid-1980s, I realized increasing returns were neither rare nor ephemeral. In fact, a major part of the economy was subject to increasing returns – high technology.

Why should this be so? There are several reasons:

*Up-front costs*   High-tech products – pharmaceuticals, computer hardware and software, aircraft and missiles, telecommunications equipment, bio-engineered drugs, and suchlike – are by definition complicated to design and to deliver to the marketplace. They are heavy on know-how and light on resources. Hence they typically have R&D costs that are large relative to their unit production costs. The first disk of Windows to go out the door cost Microsoft $50 million; the second and subsequent disks cost $3. Unit costs fall as sales increase.

*Network effects*   Many high-tech products need to be compatible with a network of users. So if much downloadable software on the Internet will soon appear as programs written in Sun Microsystems' Java language, users will need Java on their computers to run them. Java has competitors. But the more it gains prevalence, the more likely it will emerge as a standard.

*Customer groove-in*   High-tech products are typically difficult to use. They require training. Once users invest in this training – say, the maintenance and piloting of Airbus passenger aircraft – they merely need to update these skills for subsequent versions of the product. As more market is captured, it becomes easier to capture future markets.

In high-tech markets, such mechanisms ensure that products that gain market advantage stand to gain further advantage, making these markets unstable and subject to lock-in. Of course, lock-in is not forever. Technology comes in waves, and a lock-in such as DOS's can last only as long as a particular wave lasts.

So we can usefully think of two economic regimes or worlds: a bulk-production world yielding products that essentially are congealed resources with a little knowledge and operating according to Marshall's principles of diminishing returns, and a knowledge-based part of the economy yielding products that essentially are congealed knowledge with a little resources and operating under increasing returns. The two worlds are not neatly split. Hewlett-Packard, for example, designs knowledge-based devices in Palo Alto, California, and manufactures them in bulk in places like Corvallis, Oregon, or Greeley, Colorado. Most high-tech companies have both knowledge-based operations and bulk-processing operations. But because the rules of the game differ for each, companies often separate them – as Hewlett-Packard does. Conversely, manufacturing companies have operations such as logistics, branding, marketing, and distribution, which belong largely to the knowledge world. And some products – like the IBM PC – start in the increasing-returns world but later in their life cycle become virtual commodities that belong to Marshall's processing world.

# The halls of production and the casino of technology

Because the two worlds of business – processing bulk goods and crafting knowledge into products – differ in their underlying economics, it follows that they differ in their character of competition and their culture of management. It is a mistake to think that what works in one world is appropriate for the other.

There is much talk these days about a new management style that involves flat hierarchies, mission orientation, flexibility in strategy, market positioning, reinvention, restructuring, reengineering, repositioning, reorganization, and re-everything else. Are these new insights or are they fads? Are they appropriate for all organizations? Why are we seeing this new management style?

Let us look at the two cultures of competition. In bulk processing, a set of standard prices typically emerges. Production tends to be repetitive – much the same from day to day or even from year to year. Competing therefore means keeping product flowing, trying to improve quality, getting costs down. There is an art to this sort of management, one widely discussed in the literature. It favors an environment free of surprises or glitches – an environment characterized by control and planning. Such an environment requires not just people to carry out production but also people to plan and control it. So it favors a hierarchy of bosses and workers. Because bulk processing is repetitive, it allows constant improvement, constant optimization. And so, Marshall's world tends to be one that favors hierarchy, planning, and controls. Above all, it is a world of optimization.

Competition is different in knowledge-based industries because the economics are different. If knowledge-based companies are competing in winner-take-most markets, then managing becomes redefined as a series of quests for the next technological winner – the next cash cow. The goal becomes the search for the Next Big Thing. In this milieu, management becomes not production oriented but mission oriented. Hierarchies flatten not because democracy is suddenly bestowed on the workforce or because computers can cut out much of middle management. They flatten because, to be effective, the deliverers of the next-thing-for-the-company need to be organized like commando units in small teams that report directly to the CEO or to the board. Such people need free rein. The company's future survival depends upon them. So they – and the commando teams that report to them in turn – will be treated not as employees but as equals in the business of the company's success. Hierarchy dissipates and dissolves.

Does this mean that hierarchy should disappear in meatpacking, steel production, or the navy? Contrary to recent management evangelizing, a style that is called for in Silicon Valley will not necessarily be appropriate in the processing world. An aircraft's safe arrival depends on the captain, not on the flight attendants. The cabin crew can usefully be 'empowered' and treated as human beings. This approach is wise and proper. But forever there will be a distinction – a hierarchy – between cockpit and cabin crews.

In fact, the style in the diminishing-returns Halls of Production is much like that of a sophisticated modern factory: the goal is to keep high-quality product flowing at low cost. There is little need to watch the market every day, and when things are going smoothly the tempo can be leisurely. By contrast, the style of competition in the increasing-returns arena is more like gambling. Not poker, where the game is static and the players vie for a succession of pots. It is casino gambling, where part of the game is to choose which games to play, as well as playing them with skill. We can imagine the top figures in high tech – the Gateses and Gerstners and Groves of their industries – as milling in a large casino. Over at this table, a game is starting called multimedia. Over at that one, a game called Web services. In the corner is electronic banking. There are many such tables. You sit at one. How much to play? you ask. Three billion, the croupier replies. Who'll be playing? We won't know until they show up. What are the rules? Those'll emerge as the game unfolds. What are my odds of winning? We can't say. Do you still want to play?

High technology, pursued at this level, is not for the timid.

In fact, the art of playing the tables in the Casino of Technology is primarily a psychological one. What counts to some degree – but only to some degree – is technical expertise, deep pockets, will, and courage. Above all, the rewards go to the players who are first to make sense of the new games looming out of the technological fog, to see their shape, to cognize them. Bill Gates is not so much a wizard of technology as a wizard of precognition, of discerning the shape of the next game.

We can now begin to see that the new style of management is not a fad. The knowledge-based part of the economy demands flat hierarchies, mission orientation, above all a sense of direction. Not five-year plans. We can also fathom the mystery of what I've alluded to as *re-everything*. Much of this 're-everything' predilection – in the bulk-processing world – is a fancy label for streamlining, computerizing, downsizing. However, in the increasing-returns world, especially in high tech, re-everything has become necessary because every time the quest changes, the company needs to change. It needs to reinvent its purpose, its goals, its way of doing things. In short, it needs to adapt. And adaptation never stops. In fact, in the increasing-returns environment I've just sketched, standard optimization makes little sense. You cannot optimize in the casino of increasing-returns games. You can be smart. You can be cunning. You can position. You can observe. But when the games themselves are not even fully defined, you cannot optimize. What you *can* do is adapt. Adaptation, in the proactive sense, means watching for the next wave that is coming, figuring out what shape it will take, and positioning the company to take advantage of it. Adaptation is what drives increasing-returns businesses, not optimization.

# Playing the high-tech tables

Suppose you are a player in the knowledge-industry casino, in this increasing-returns world. What can you do to capitalize on the increasing returns at your disposal? How can you use them to capture markets? What strategic issues do you need to think about? In the processing world, strategy typically hinges upon capitalizing on core competencies, pricing competitively, getting costs down, bringing quality up. These are important also in the knowledge-based world, but so, too, are other strategies that make use of the special economics of positive feedbacks.

Two maxims are widely accepted in knowledge-based markets: it pays to hit the market first, and it pays to have superb technology. These maxims are true but do not guarantee success. Prodigy was first into the on-line services market but was passive in building its subscriber base to take advantage of increasing returns. As a result, it has fallen from its leading position and currently lags the other services. As for technology, Steve Jobs's NeXT workstation was superb. But it was launched into a market already dominated by Sun Microsystems and Hewlett-Packard. It failed. A new product often has to be two or three times better in some dimension – price, speed, convenience – to dislodge a locked-in rival. So in know-ledge-based markets, entering first with a fine product can yield advantage. But as strategy, this is still too passive. What is needed is *active* management of increasing returns.

One active strategy is to discount heavily initially to build up an installed base. Netscape handed out its Internet browser for free and won 70% of its market. Now it can profit from spin-off software and applications. Although such discounting is effective – and widely understood – it is not always implemented. Companies often err by pricing high initially to recoup expensive R&D costs. Yet even smart discounting to seed the market is ineffective unless the resulting installed base is exploited later. America Online built up a lead of more than 4.5 million subscribers by giving away free services. But because of the Internet's dominance, it is not yet clear whether it can transform this huge base into later profits.

Let's get a bit more sophisticated. Technological products do not stand alone. They depend on the existence of other products and other technologies. The Internet's World Wide Web operates within a grouping of businesses that include browsers, on-line news, E-mail, network retailing, and financial services. Pharmaceuticals exist within a network of physicians, testing labs, hospitals, and HMOs. Laser printers are part of a grouping of products that include computers, publishing software, scanners, and photo-input devices. Unlike products of the processing world, such as soybeans or rolled steel, technological products exist within local groupings of products that support and enhance them. They exist in mini-ecologies.

This interdependence has deep implications for strategy. When, in the mid-1980s, Novell introduced its network-operating system, NetWare, as a way of connecting personal computers in local networks, Novell made sure that NetWare was technically superior to its rivals. It also heavily discounted NetWare to build an installed base. But these tactics were not enough. Novell recognized that NetWare's success depended on attracting software applications to run on NetWare – which was a part of the ecology outside the company's control. So it set up incentives for software developers to write for NetWare rather than for its rivals. The software writers did just that. And by building NetWare's success, they ensured their own. Novell managed these cross-product positive feedbacks actively to lock in its market. It went on to profit hugely from upgrades, spin-offs, and applications of its own.

Another strategy that uses ecologies is linking and leveraging. This means transferring a user base built up upon one node of the ecology (one product) to neighboring nodes, or products. The strategy is very much like that in the game Go: you surround neighboring markets one by one, lever your user base onto them, and take them over – all the time enhancing your position in the industry. Microsoft levered its 60-million-person user base in DOS onto Windows, then onto Windows 95, and then onto Microsoft Network by offering inexpensive up-grades and by bundling applications. The strategy has been challenged legally. But it recognizes that positive feedbacks apply across markets as well as within markets (Box 17.1).

---

**Box 17.1**

# In the case of Microsoft . . .

What should be legal in this powerful and as yet unregulated world of increasing returns? What constitutes fair play? Should technology markets be regulated, and if so in what way? These questions have come to a head with the enormous amount of publicity generated by the US Justice Department's current antitrust case against Microsoft.

In Marshall's world, antitrust regulation is well understood. Allowing a single player to control, say, more than 35% of the silver market is tantamount to allowing monopoly pricing, and the government rightly steps in. In the increasing-returns world, things are more complicated. There are arguments in favor of allowing a product or company in the web of technology to dominate a market, as well as arguments against. Consider these pros and cons:

*Convenience*   A locked-in product may provide a single standard of convenience. If a software company such as Microsoft allows us to double-click all the way from our computer screen straight to our bank account (by controlling all the technologies in between), this avoids a tedious Balkanizing of standards, where we have to spend useless time getting into a succession of on-line connection products.

*Fairness*  If a product locks in because it is superior, this is fair, and it would be foolish to penalize such success. If it locks in merely because the user base was levered over from a neighboring lock-in, this is unfair.

*Technology development*  A locked-in product may obstruct technological advancement. If a clunker such as DOS locks up the PC market for ten years, there is little incentive for other companies to develop alternatives. The result is impeded technological progress.

*Pricing*  To lock in, a product usually has been discounted, and this established low price is often hard to raise. So monopoly pricing – of great concern in bulk-processing markets – is therefore rarely a major worry.

Added to these considerations, high tech is not a commodity industry. Dominance may consist not so much in cornering a single product as in successively taking over more and more threads of the web of technology, thereby preventing other players from getting access to new, breaking markets. It would be difficult to separate out each thread and to regulate it. And of course it may be impracticable to regulate a market before it forms – before it is even fully defined. There are no simple answers to antitrust regulation in the increasing-returns world. On balance, I would favor a high degree of regulatory restraint, with the addition of two key principles:

*Do not penalize success*  Short-term monopolization of an increasing-returns market is correctly perceived as a reward or prize for innovation and risk taking. There is a temptation to single out dominant players and hit them with an antitrust suit. This reduces regulation to something like a brawl in an Old West saloon – if you see a head, hit it. Not a policy that preserves an incentive to innovate in the first place.

*Don't allow head starts for the privileged*  This means that as a new market opens up – such as electronic consumer banking – companies that already dominate standards, operating systems, and neighboring technologies should not be allowed a ten-mile head start in the land rush that follows. All competitors should have fair and open access to the applicable technologies and standards.

In practice, these principles would mean allowing the possibility of winner-take-all jackpots in each new subindustry, in each new wave of technology. But each contender should have access to whatever degree possible to the same technologies, the same open standards, so that all are lined up behind the same starting line. If industry does not make such provisions voluntarily, government regulation will impose them.

In fact, if technological ecologies are now the basic units for strategy in the knowledge-based world, players compete not by locking in a product on their own but by building *webs* – loose alliances of companies organized around a mini-ecology – that amplify positive feedbacks to the base technology. Apple, in closing its Macintosh system to outsiders in the 1980s, opted not to create such a web. It believed that with its superior technology, it could hold its increasing-returns market to itself. Apple indeed dominates its Mac-based ecology. But this ecology is now only 8% of the personal computer business. IBM erred in the other direction. By passively allowing other companies to join its PC web as clones, IBM achieved a huge user base and locked in the market. But the company itself wound up with a small share of the spoils. The key in web building is active management of the cross-company mutual feedbacks. This means making a careful choice of partners to build upon. It also means that, rather than attempting to take over all products in the ecology, dominant players in a web should allow dependent players to lock in their dependent products by piggybacking on the web's success. By thus ceding some of the profits, the dominant players ensure that all participants remain committed to the alliance.

Important also to strategy in knowledge-based markets is psychological positioning. Under increasing returns, rivals will back off in a market not only if it is locked in but if they *believe* it will be locked in by someone else. Hence we see psychological jockeying in the form of preannouncements, feints, threatened alliances, technological preening, touted future partnerships, parades of vaporware (announced products that don't yet exist). This posturing and puffing acts much the way similar behavior does in a primate colony: it discourages competitors from taking on a potentially dominant rival. No moves need be made in this strategy of premarket facedown. It is purely a matter of psychology.

What if you hold a losing hand? Sometimes it pays to hold on for residual revenue. Sometimes a fix can be provided by updated technology, fresh alliances, or product changes. But usually under heavy lock-in, these tactics do not work. The alternatives are then slow death or graceful exit – relinquishing the field to concentrate on positioning for the next technology wave. Exit may not mean quitting the business entirely. America Online, Compuserve, Prodigy, and Microsoft Network have all ceded dominance of the on-line computer networking market to the Internet. But instead of exiting, they are steadily becoming adjuncts of the Net, supplying content services such as financial quotations or games and entertainment. They have lost the main game. But they will likely continue in a side game with its own competition for dominance within the Net's ecology.

Above all, strategy in the knowledge world requires CEOs to recognize that a different kind of economics is at work. CEOs need to understand which positive and negative feedback mechanisms are at play in the market ecologies in which they compete. Often there are several such mechanisms? – interbraided, operating over different time frames, each needing to be understood, observed, and actively managed.

## What about service industries?

So far, I've talked mainly about high tech. Where do service industries such as insurance, restaurants, and banking fit in? Which world do they belong to? The question is tricky. It would appear that such industries belong to the diminishing-returns, processing part of the economy because often there are regional limits to the demand for a given service, most services do consist of 'processing' clients, and services are low-tech.

The truth is that network or user-base effects often operate in services. Certainly, retail franchises exist because of increasing returns. The more McDonald's restaurants or Motel 6 franchises are out there geographically, the better they are known. Such businesses are patronized not just for their quality but also because people want to know exactly what to expect. So the more prevalent they are, the more prevalent they can become. Similarly, the larger a bank's or insurance company's customer base, the more it can spread its fixed costs of headquarters staff, real estate, and computer operations. These industries, too, are subject to mild increasing returns.

So we can say more accurately that service industries are a hybrid. From day to day, they act like bulk-processing industries. But over the long term, increasing returns will dominate – even though their destabilizing effects are not as pronounced as in high tech. The US airline business, for example, processes passengers day to day. So it seemed in 1981 that deregulation should enhance competition, as it normally does under diminishing returns. But over the long term, airlines in fact experience a positive feedback: under the hub-and-spoke system, once an airline gets into trouble, it cannot work the feeder system for its routes properly, its fleet ages, it starts a downward spiral, and it loses further routes. The result of deregulation over the long term has been a steady decline in large carriers, from 15 airlines in 1981 to approximately 6 at present. Some routes have become virtual monopolies, with resulting higher fares. None of this was intended. But it should have been predicted – given increasing returns.

In fact, the increasing-returns character of service industries is steadily strengthening. One of the marks of our time is that in services everything is going software – everything that is information based. So operations that were once handled by people – designing fancy financial instruments or automobiles or fashion goods, processing insurance claims, supplying and inventorying in retail, conducting paralegal searches for case precedents – are increasingly being handled by software. As this reengineering of services plays out, centralized software facilities come to the fore. Service providers become hitched into software networks, regional limitations weaken, and user-base network effects kick in.

This phenomenon can have two consequences. First, where the local character of service remains important, it can preserve a large number of service companies but clustered round a dominant software provider – like the large numbers of small, independent law firms tied in to the dominant computer-search network, Lexis-Nexis. Or physicians tied in to an HMO. Second, where locality is unimportant, network effects can transform competition toward the winner-take-most character we see in high tech. For example, when Internet-based retail banking arrives, regional demand limitations will vanish. Each virtual bank will gain in advantage as its network increases. Barring regulation, consumer banking will then become a contest among a few large banking networks. It will become an increasing-returns business.

Services belong to both the processing and the increasing-returns world. But their center of gravity is crossing over to the latter.

# Thoughts for managers

Where does all this leave us? At the beginning of this century, industrial economies were based largely on the bulk processing of resources. At the close of the century, they are based on the processing of resources *and* on the processing of knowledge. Economies have bifurcated into two worlds – intertwined, overlapping, and different. These two worlds operate under different economic principles. Marshall's world is characterized by planning, control, and hierarchy. It is a world of materials, of processing, of optimization. The increasing-returns world is characterized by observation, positioning, flattened organizations, missions, teams, and cunning. It is a world of psychology, of cognition, of adaptation.

Many managers have some intuitive grasp of this new increasing-returns world. Few understand it thoroughly. Here are some questions managers need to ask themselves when they operate in knowledge-based markets:

*Do I understand the feedbacks in my market?* In the processing world, understanding markets means understanding consumers' needs, distribution channels, and rivals' products. In the knowledge world, success requires a thorough understanding of the self-negating and self-reinforcing feedbacks in the market – the diminishing- and increasing-returns mechanisms. These feedbacks are interwoven and operate at different levels in the market and over different time frames.

*Which ecologies am I in?* Technologies exist not alone but in an interlinked web, or ecology. It is important to understand the ecologies a company's products belong to. Success or failure is often decided not just by the company but also by the success or failure of the web it belongs to. Active management of such a web can be an important magnifier of increasing returns.

*Do I have the resources to play?* Playing one of the increasing-returns games in the Casino of Technology requires several things: excellent technology, the ability to hit the market at the right time, deep pockets, strategic pricing, and a willingness to sacrifice current profits for future advantage. All this is a matter not just of resources but also of courage, resolution, will. And part of that resolution, that courage, is also the decisiveness to leave the market when increasing returns are moving against one. Hanging on to a losing position that is being further eroded by positive feedbacks requires throwing reinforcements into a battle already lost. Better to exit with financial dignity.

*What games are coming next?* Technology comes in successive waves. Those who have lost out on this wave can position for the next. Conversely, those who have made a killing on this cycle should not become complacent. The ability to profit under increasing returns is only as good as the ability to see what's coming in the next cycle and to position oneself for it – technologically, psychologically, and cooperatively. In high tech, it is as if we are moving slowly on a ship, with new technologies looming, taking shape, through a fog of unknowingness. Success goes to those who have the vision to foresee, to imagine, what shapes these next games will take.

These considerations appear daunting. But increasing-returns games provide large payoffs for those brave enough to play them and win. And they are exciting. Processing, in the service or manufacturing industries, has its own risks. Precisely because processing is low-margin, operations must struggle to stay afloat. Neither world of business is for the fainthearted.

In his book *Microcosm*, technology thinker George Gilder remarked, 'The central event of the twentieth century is the overthrow of matter. In technology, economics, and the politics of nations, wealth in the form of physical resources is steadily declining in value and significance. The powers of mind are everywhere ascendant over the brute force of things.' As the economy shifts steadily away from the brute force of things into the powers of mind, from resource-based bulk processing into knowledge-based design and reproduction, so it is shifting from a base of diminishing returns to one of increasing returns. A new economics – one very different from that in the textbooks – now applies, and nowhere is this more true than in high technology. Success will strongly favor those who understand this new way of thinking.

# Global Strategy in the Twenty-first Century

GEORGE S. YIP*

I n the 1980s and the mid-1990s, many companies were still debating whether they should globalize. In the twenty-first century this debate has ended. Companies now assume that they should globalize unless they can find very good reasons not to.

The spread of the web provides one compelling reason. Any company that mounts a website has instant global reach and overseas customers follow very quickly, with corresponding demands for delivery and service. [. . .]

The world has seen great convergence in customer needs and tastes, the drastic reduction of many government barriers to free trade and investment, an acceleration of globalization enablers in communications, and a surge in globally applicable new technological products and services. All this does not mean that every industry has become entirely global. But today, nearly every industry has a significant global segment in which customers prefer products or services that are much more global than they are local. Around the global segment are still regional, national, or sub-national niches. The size of the global segment varies, from very large in the personal computer industry to relatively small in many parts of the food industry. But the global segment is increasing in size in nearly all cases.

Increasingly, global strategy is also converging with global excellence. Global strategy requires a company to manage effectively on an integrated basis, but the company needs to be excellent to be able to do that. Global strategy also means being able to deploy a company's best achievements in any country to the rest of the world. But what does it mean for a company to be excellent at global strategy?

* Prentice Hall for an extract from *Financial Times Handbook of Management* by Stuart Crainer and Des Dearlove
© George S. Yip, 2001.

# Overall global strategy and organizational forms

In globalization, strategy and organization are inextricably intertwined. The organizational form facilitates some types of international strategy and not others. Individual companies typically evolve over time from one form to another as their international activities and strategies evolve. Today, multinational companies can take one of three main forms, internationalist, federalist, or global maximizer.[1]

## The internationalist

Most companies start with what might be termed an 'internationalist' strategy and organization (Figure 18.1). In this posture, home market activities dominate and foreign activities are often opportunistic, without too much investment or adaptation. A simple test is whether the company could survive without its international activities.

Many American companies took this approach as they focused first on their enormous home market. Some, like Chrysler, never got beyond this stage. Many quite large and most *Mittelstand* (mid-sized) German companies are still in this mode. Most Japanese exporters started in this fashion and the cornerstone of their success in the 1970s and 1980s was the exploitation of their home market as a base for overseas expansion.

As the extent of international revenues increases most companies move on to other forms. For example, the US brewing giant Anheuser-Busch is now trying to break out of this mode as it increases its international activities. Companies that cannot grow organically beyond this stage typically have to acquire internationally or be acquired (or, as Wall Street bankers put it, to 'eat lunch or be lunch'). The latter has been the fate of Chrysler and Mazda in the automotive industry and in 2000 of Ben and Jerry's, the socially responsible US ice-cream maker, whose new owner, Unilever, will leverage its worldwide distribution capabilities to take Cherry Garcia and Peace Pops global.

Some companies are stuck in this form, typically because they compete in regulated industries that allow only limited internationalization; because of being in sensitive industries such as defence, where home governments discourage the overseas relocation of critical activities; or in industries where the minimum efficient scale of operations, particularly production, is so great that concentration is best. Typical companies and industries are British Aerospace and Northrop Grumman in their defence-related businesses; British Telecom and other national telecom service operators; most airline companies; most utility operators; most law firms; and many media companies.

For internationally blocked industries, there are three main paths for globalization. First, they can make acquisitions of foreign participants in the same industry, if allowed. But there are severe restrictions in many industries on foreign

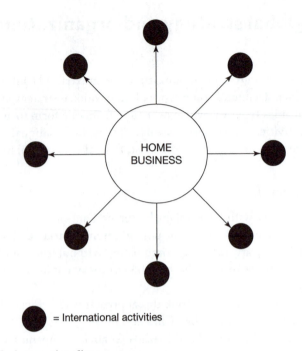

**Figure 18.1** *The internationalist*

ownership, including in airlines, defence, and media. Rupert Murdoch had to become a US citizen in order to be able to buy US radio and television companies.

Second, they can form international strategic alliances. British Airways continues to seek to build a transatlantic alliance that can operate as seamlessly as will be allowed by national regulators. Its global One World alliance (co-led with American Airlines), the Star Alliance (spearheaded by the United States' United Airlines) and the pan-European Qualiflyer alliance[2] all seek to achieve in alliance mode what their members are not allowed to do as national air carriers.

Third, companies in blocked industries can hire out their expertise to foreign partners or customers, or globalize in unrestricted activities. For example, Singapore Airlines has many training and support contracts with other carriers and also operates globally some specialized airline-related businesses, such as catering. Thames Water, one of the UK's largest utility companies, is using both acquisition and technology-transfer modes in its globalization efforts. In summary, internationalists face a hard challenge of achieving and maintaining global excellence when most of the world is blocked for many of their most critical activities.

## The federalist

The classic multinational form has been that of the federalist (Figure 18.2). In this mode each international subsidiary operates most, if not all, of the value chain, and has considerable autonomy. The home market becomes just another country and the head office primarily a holding company.

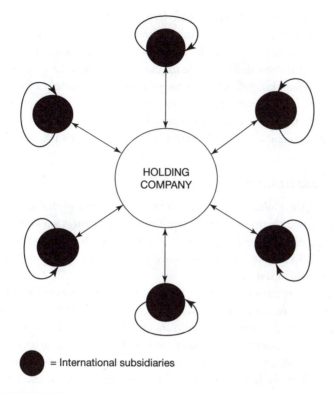

**Figure 18.2** *The federalist*

This mode was particularly common among European multinationals from the 1950s to the 1980s. With relatively small home markets, such as Switzerland or the Netherlands, and in an earlier era of high transportation costs, poor communications and large differences in country tastes, companies like Nestlé, Unilever, and Philips created a far-flung chain of subsidiaries where the country manager was king. The success formula for these companies was the transfer of home country competencies (such as products, technology, or marketing know-how), a globally uniform management system and set of standards (extensive and common procedures), use of local managers leavened by expatriates, and significant independence in local business decisions. So the product had to meet Unilever's worldwide standards and had to be developed and marketed 'by the book', but it could be called by different names in different countries or be a different product even though under a globally common name such as 'Omo', perhaps the world's least consistent global brand.

The federalist model has great advantages where adaptation to the local environment, including customer tastes and government rules, is critical. With global convergence, most industries no longer favour this approach. So companies like Philips struggled in the 1980s to convert to a global mode, and Procter & Gamble reorganized in the late 1990s from a regionally based organization into just seven global strategic business units.

Some remaining industries still have mostly federalist companies and constitute the current frontier in global change. These include accounting and engineering consulting services. In all these industries knowledge of national environments is still critical. So most firms continue to operate as loose multilocals, although most are making efforts to achieve more global integration. Advertising agencies have moved somewhat faster, spurred by the advent of global advertising in the 1980s and by the pre-emptive claims of Britain's Saatchi and Saatchi to be the world's first advertising agency able to deliver global advertising.

## The global maximizer

The third mode, the global maximizer, constitutes genuine global strategy. Japanese companies provided the most extreme application of the first version of this model: pure global strategy. In the 1970s and 1980s, firms such as Toyota and Matsushita swept world markets with globally standardized products made in a small number of factories, mostly based In Japan.

By the 1990s, a more complex form of the global maximizer had emerged, the global network maximizer (GNM) (Figure 18.3).[3] In this form, multinational companies break up the value chain and locate individual activities in as few locations as possible. No part of the organization, whether headquarters or subsidiary, is self-sufficient. Instead, all work together in a network. Perhaps the prime current example is ABB Asea Brown Boveri. Most leading American, European and Japanese companies are now converging on this model, albeit from different starting points.

The internet and the web have consolidated the dominance of the GNM as the key model for multinational companies for the foreseeable future. The GNM model seeks to reduce duplication of activities. As an electronic network, the web, through both intranets and extranets, offers the potential to complete this process of deduplication. This model is, therefore, also ideal for internet-based 'new economy' companies, many of which are 'born global'. The rest of this chapter focuses on how to operate the GNM model.

# Globalization of individual activities[4]

I am often asked, 'What is the world's most global company or the most globally effective?' My answer is that different companies excel in globalization of different activities but none excels in all – not surprising given the complexity of global management of even a single activity. In addition, global excellence does not always mean the most global standardized solution. For each activity, global excellence means being able to develop and implement the most appropriate combination of global, regional and national solutions.

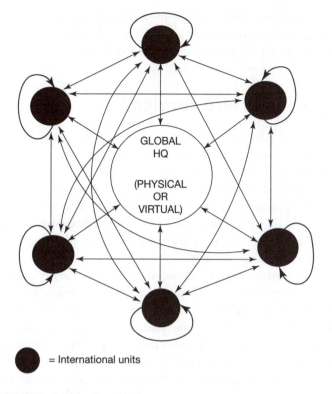

**Figure 18.3** *The global network maximizer*

## *Global research and development*

Global excellence in R&D means being able to access new knowledge and capabilities anywhere in the world and develop globally appealing products and services that can be produced on a globally competitive basis.

In terms of accessing knowledge, multinational companies have historically concentrated their R&D activities in their home countries, thereby greatly reducing their ability to access overseas knowledge and innovation. This mattered less when the creation of new knowledge was the near-monopoly of North America, Western Europe and Japan (Kenichi Ohmae's Triad economies),[5] also the home bases of most multinationals. However, the exponential rise in technology and knowledge creation has created a global diaspora of expertise. Global companies now need to access knowledge and development capabilities not just in Triad nations but in emerging economies such as China, India, and Russia.

Several routes exist: physically setting up R&D overseas but keeping these units plugged into the global network, by electronic means constantly and in-person sometimes; hiring scientists and technologists from overseas; or frequent visits to and other contacts with countries that are sources of innovation. For example, Canon conducts R&D activities in eight facilities in five countries, Motorola has 14 facilities in seven countries and Bristol-Myers Squibb has 12 facilities in six countries.[6] Microsoft has invested in an R&D centre in Cambridge, UK, in order to tap into the expertise of Cambridge University, Cambridge's Science Park, and the area's phenomenon of 'Silicon Fen'.

# Global products and services

The output of global R&D should be global products and services, but these are seldom totally standardized worldwide. Instead, such products are designed with global markets in mind, and they have as large a common core as possible. Some industries and categories, such as ethical pharmaceuticals and express package delivery allow the potential for a very large common core, while others, such as furniture and legal services, allow for less commonality. Most companies now actively seek to maximize this global core, even if, for marketing reasons, they do not talk about global products as such.

Honda's Accord passenger automobile illustrates the new kind of thinking in designing global products. Developing a new automobile platform costs over US$1 billion. But a major challenge is that US drivers prefer wider cars, and hence platforms, than do drivers in Europe and Asia. Thus many companies operate with at least two platforms or even completely different product lines between the US (and Canada) and the rest of the world. Honda's solution in the late 1990s was to develop the world's first adjustable-width automobile platform. its development cost was about halfway between that for one platform and that for two. Such global products cannot be developed on a country-by-country basis but only on a globally integrated basis. In the service sector, American Express leads the word in offering a range of credit cards with a very high degree of global commonality. An American Express Gold Card provides the same core functionality whatever the home country of the card holder.

## Global sourcing and production

Global sourcing and production have to reconcile several conflicting objectives: cost, productivity, quality, reliability, protection of expertise, and trade barriers. So there is seldom a single sourcing and production configuration that can maximize all of these objectives, merely optimize them. Hourly labour costs now range from US$30 an hour in Germany to under 25 cents in Indonesia, or a ratio of more than 100:1. With such large differences, even companies in non-labour-intensive industries need to think seriously about where to locate activities. Furthermore, companies should not be put off by the low *average* productivity in low-cost economies. These figures include all the unmodernized, often state-owned companies. The whole point is to achieve higher levels of productivity by making investments and transferring technology and expertise. Motorola, the proselytiser of 'six-sigma' quality, excels at operating world-class manufacturing in developing countries.

As described, for the global network maximizer, the global solution typically means a network of sourcing and production nodes in different countries, specializing by product or sub-activity. For example, Nippon Denso, a Japanese producer of air conditioners and other automobile parts, operates an Asia-Pacific network in which starters, alternators, and wiper-motors are made in Thailand, engine ECUs, alternating current amplifiers, and relay arms in Malaysia; compressors and spark plugs in Indonesia; meters in the Philippines; and evaporators and condensers in Australia.[7]

## Global logistics

Global logistics embody the challenge for global companies to deliver their intermediate and final products anywhere in the world in a cost-effective and timely manner. The solution can seldom be one single distribution hub, but a network of hubs, exemplified by the systems of the global delivery companies, such as FedEx, DHL, and UPS. Another issue is whether to use a globally common distribution system or a differentiated one. Coca-Cola has achieved great success by replacing local distribution systems with its effective and efficient standardized distribution methods.[8]

## Global marketing and selling

Global marketing and selling strive for the appropriate balance of global uniformity and local adaptation in all elements of the marketing mix, but with a probable bias in favour of uniformity, unless a good case can be made for local exceptions. This means casting aside the previous conventional wisdom that companies should globally standardize the marketing process but not the marketing content. Global excellence in marketing now means looking for uniformity. For example, Unilever recognized that it was hampered by marketing too many different brands around the world. In 1999 it began an initiative to reduce the number of brands from over 1,600 to about 400. And Diageo's United Distillers Vintners unit focuses on nine 'global power brands'.

Research on global marketing shows that different elements of the mix need to have different degrees of global uniformity, with brand names and packaging the most uniformity; pricing, advertising, and distribution moderate uniformity; and selling and promotion the least.[9] Germany's Beiersdorf, the marketer of the Nivea brand, provides an excellent example of global marketing that maintains tight and effective worldwide consistency.

However, companies can go too far. In the late 1990s British Airways made an attempt to reposition itself as a global rather than just a British airline by replacing the national flag on the tails of its planes with art designs from around the world. Domestic opposition mounted and the designs were dubbed; 'global graffiti'. British Airways ended this experiment after just a few years.

## Global customer service

Customers today require service anytime, anywhere. As the world's leading global retail bank, Citibank goes even further. Its global motto is that customers can do business with it 'anytime, anywhere, anyway'. Citibank invested hugely in the 1990s in both physical infrastructure, such as branches and ATMs, and computer and communication systems to make real its boast.

Hewlett-Packard is a global leader in computer-based customer support services for its customers. It maintains a globally standardized set of services that range from site design to systems integration to remote diagnostics. This global standardization includes seamless service at any hour of the day or night from anywhere in the world.[10] To do so, H-P maintains a global chain of 30 customer response centres, integrated into a global network.

## Global capital and financial management

Global companies now seek to diversify their shareholder bases geographically by listing on multiple exchanges and doing other things to encourage foreign shareholders. Broadening the shareholder base increases demand for the company's shares and also provides exposure and insight into the needs of foreign capital markets. Recent transatlantically merged companies, such as Daimler-Chrysler and BP-Amoco, actively manage their multiple shareholder bases.

Today, the globally excellent company should keep track of the global mix of its shareholders. In general, excellent approaches to global capital and financial management include improving access to company information, reducing the real after-tax cost of capital, minimizing currency risk, and improving global treasury management.[11]

## Global human resource management

In the internationalist model companies tend to rely on expatriates, while in the federalist or multilocal model they aim to have as many local managers as possible. Global excellence now requires a balance of global, regional, and national managers. A global network can be operated only if many members have had international experience and also have many interpersonal connections and shared experiences.

Furthermore, individuals can take different roles at different stages of their career or family lifecycle. Global companies need to invest in building a portfolio of the necessary capabilities, not just in technical or business terms, but in terms of language and cultural capabilities and types of international experience.

Japanese and Korean companies may find it difficult to incorporate foreign nationals into their management systems, but they also invest heavily in preparing their own nationals for foreign assignments. Samsung puts executives through a one-year programme before they are sent abroad, and also spends two months debriefing them on return at its Global Management Institute. AMP, a US producer of electrical connectors, began an extensive programme in 1992 to develop what it calls 'globe-able leaders'.[12] Statoil, the Norwegian oil company, finds that many of its international opportunities lie in Central Asia. Few Norwegians speak the languages of Kazakhstan or Uzbekistan! Perhaps it should fund students in Norwegian schools to learn those languages.

## Global governance and leadership

Lastly, excellence in global governance and leadership means getting the best top executives and board members from anywhere in the world. Few of even the largest multinational companies have representation from all continents on their boards, even though non-executive directors provide an easy source of such expertise. Some companies, such as Portugal's innovative Sonae group, now have global advisory boards as a way to tap this global expertise without having to change their legal boards. And for top management, companies are beginning to follow the example of top football (soccer) teams, such as Real Madrid and Chelsea, by searching for the best talent worldwide.

# The global challenge

Global strategy sets very tough challenges for companies. They need to be globally excellent in nearly every activity, and find the right balance of global, regional, and national solutions. This concept is best summed up in the philosophy at Beiersdorf: 'As global as possible, as local as necessary.'

The global company does not have to be everywhere, but it has the capability to go anywhere, deploy any assets, and access any resources, and it maximizes profits on a global basis. Now global companies also need to do it all very fast – at Internet speed. And if they do not do all this, their competitors will. Globalization means there is no place to hide.

# Notes

1  I thank José de la Torre of the Anderson School at UCLA for sharing with me these three models and their conceptualizations.

2  Qualiflyer includes Swissair, Austrian Airlines, Sabena, Air Portugal, Turkish Airlines, AOM, Crossair, Lauda-air, and Tyrolean.

3  See Bartlett, Christopher A. and Ghoshal, Sumantra, *Managing Across Borders: The Transnational Solution*, Boston, Harvard Business School Press, 1989; and Nohria, Nitin and Ghoshal, Sumantra (contributor), *The Differentiated Network: Organizing the Multinational Corporation for Value Creation*, San Francisco, The Jossey-Bass Business & Management Series, Jossey-Bass Publishers, 1997.

4    This section has benefited from my association with the Deloitte & Touche programme on 'Innovative Leaders in Globalization'.

5    Ohmae, Kenichi, *Triad Power: The Coming Shape of Global Competition*, Free Press, New York, 1985.

6    Kuemmerle, Walter, 'Building Effective R&D Capabilities Abroad', *Harvard Business Review*, March–April 1997.

7    See Kondo, Mari and Yip, George S., Chapter 16 'Regional Groupings– ASEAN, APFTA, APEC, Etc', in George S. Yip, *Asian Advantage*, Reading, MA, Addison-Wesley, 1998; and *Asian Advantage: Updated – After the Crisis*, Cambridge, MA, Perseus Books, 2000.

8    Ohmae, Kenichi, *The Evolving Global Economy: Making Sense of the New World Order*, Boston, MA, Harvard Business School Press, 1995.

9    Yip, George S., 'Patterns and Determinants of Global Marketing', *Journal of Marketing Management*, 13, pp. 153–164, 1997.

10   Lovelock, Christopher H. and Yip, George S., 'Developing Global Strategies for Service Businesses', *California Management Review*, vol. 38, no. 2, Winter 1996, pp. 65–86.

11   *Innovative Leaders in Globalization – Program Discussion Document*, New York, Deloitte Touche and World Economic Forum, 1998. See also *Innovative Leaders in Globalization*, Deloitte Touche Tohatsu, New York, 1999.

12   Marquardt, M. and Reynolds, A., *The Global Learning Organisation: Gaining Competitive Advantage through Continuous Learning*, Homewood, Illinois, Irwin, 1994.

# Bibliography

Bartlett, Christopher A. and Ghoshal, Sumantra, *Managing Across Borders: The Transnational Solutions*, Harvard Business School Press, Boston, 1989.

Marquardt, M. and Reynolds, A., *The Global Learning Organisation: Gaining Competitive Advantage through Continuous Learning*, Irwin, Homewood, Illinois, 1994.

Nohria, Nitin and Ghoshal, Sumantra (contributor), *The Differentiated Network: Organizing the Multinational Cooperation for Value Creation*, Jossey Bass, San Francisco, 1997.

Ohmae, Kenichi, *Triad Power: The Coming Shape of Global Competition*, Free Press, New York, 1985.

Ohmae, Kenichi, *The Evolving Global Economy: Making Sense of the New World Order*, Harvard Business School Press, Boston, 1995.

Yip, George S., *Total Global Strategy: Managing for Worldwide Competitive Advantage*, Prentice Hall, Englewood Cliffs, NJ, 1992.